YEAR A ▪ 2008

workbook
FOR LECTORS AND GOSPEL READERS

James L. Weaver

LTP
LITURGY
TRAINING
PUBLICATIONS

New American Bible readings are taken from *Lectionary for Mass for Use in the Dioceses of the United States of America, second typical edition* © 1998, 1997, 1970 by the Confraternity of Christian Doctrine, Washington, D.C., and are reproduced herein by license of the copyright owner. All rights reserved. No part of *Lectionary for Mass* may be reproduced in any form without permission in writing from the Confraternity of Christian Doctrine, Washington, D.C.

WORKBOOK FOR LECTORS AND GOSPEL READERS 2008, UNITED STATES EDITION © 2007 Archdiocese of Chicago. All rights reserved.

Liturgy Training Publications, 1800 North Hermitage Avenue, Chicago IL 60622; 1-800-933-1800, fax 1-800-933-7094, orders@ltp.org, www.LTP.org

Editor: Kris Fankhouser
Typesetter: Jim Mellody-Pizzato
Original book design: Jill Smith
Revised design: Anna Manhart and Jim Mellody-Pizzato
Cover art: Barbara Simcoe
Interior art: Anna Manhart

Printed in the United States of America.

ISBN 978-1-56854-618-6
WL08

The paper used to print this year's *Workbook for Lectors and Gospel Readers* was carefully chosen with our customers in mind and with a commitment to the environment. After extensive searching, we found a highly opaque paper that fits both of those needs. The 40# Remarque Offset paper that this book is printed on is 100% recycled and contains a minimum of 40% postconsumer waste. The non-postconsumer portion consists of pre-consumer recycled fiber. Although many de-inking processes use highly toxic bleach, this paper was processed using PCF (Processed Chlorine Free) technologies. This paper is also acid-free to reduce yellowing as it ages.

CONTENTS

ORDINARY TIME

The Author

James L. Weaver was received into the Roman Catholic Church at the age of 26. He received the sacraments of Baptism, Eucharist, and Confirmation during the Easter Vigil Mass at St. Thomas More Chapel of New Haven, Connecticut, in 1995. Jay holds degrees from Yale and the University of Chicago in History, Divinity, and New Testament and Early Christian Literature. He is currently at work on a doctorate in the Department of New Testament and Early Christian Literature at the University of Chicago.

Dedication

This edition of *Workbook* is gratefully, respectfully, and lovingly dedicated to the following people: to my parents, Larry and Anne, my first church; to everyone—students, parents, teachers, administrators, laypeople, staff, ministers, and clergy—at St. Thomas the Apostle parish in the Hyde Park neighborhood of Chicago, Illinois; to Carol Steele, Diedre Brewster, and R. J. of the Cabrini Rowhouse Tenants Association, and to James Pfluecke of the Coalition to Protect Public Housing, whose hard and patient work on behalf of public housing residents in the city of Chicago brings the Gospel to life; to the Leonard family; and to Nicole Erin Urbach.

Nihil Obstat

Reverend Louis J. Cameli, STD
Censor Deputatus
October 25, 2006

Imprimatur

Reverend John F. Canary, STL, DMin
Vicar General
Archdiocese of Chicago
October 26, 2006

The Purpose of *Workbook*

The intention of *Workbook for Lectors and Gospel Readers* is to offer assistance to all who proclaim scripture in Catholic worship. In the spirit of the Dogmatic Constitution on Divine Revelation *(Dei verbum)* issued by the Second Vatican Council on November 18, 1965, this edition *Workbook* has been made available so that "ministers of the divine Word may be able to distribute fruitfully the nourishment of the Scriptures of the People of God" (*Dei verbum*, #6.23). Laypeople, as well as the ordained, who are charged with catechesis, direction of liturgy and music, religious education, preaching, and other pastoral ministries, may find *Workbook* a useful tool in their attempts to proclaim scripture and to understand the readings of the Lectionary in the literary, historical, cultural, and theological contexts of the authors who produced them.

The Church, according to the edition of the *Catechism of the Catholic Church* (CCC) published by the United States Catholic Conference and quoting the text of *Dei verbum*, concludes that "access to Sacred Scripture ought to be open wide to the Christian faithful" and encourages the "frequent reading of the Divine Scriptures" by all Christians (CCC, #131, 133). If the study of scripture is therefore a duty, one should hasten to add that the performance of this duty could be a profound joy. It is the hope of this author that this edition of *Workbook* will help kindle this joy.

The Catholic Bible: Unity amid Difference

The Catholic Bible contains writings composed over more than a thousand years of human history. The early Hebrew poetry of Exodus 15, for example, was composed well before Alexander's conquests spread the Greek language throughout the Mediterranean, before a little village on the Italian peninsula called Rome even existed. By contrast, the Greek of 2 Peter, perhaps the latest of our texts, was composed when Rome was no longer a village, but a metropolis, and not merely a metropolis, but an empire ruling the entirety of the author's known world. The Bible contains the vast difference one expects among authors writing in different places, social and cultural settings, languages, and historical circumstances. But the variety within the Bible is even greater than this. It includes in its pages histories, letters, love poetry, war poetry, novellas, oracles, apocalypses, and gospels. Its contents run from Psalm 118, a liturgical text of the Jerusalem temple in celebration of the monarchy of Judah, to Paul's letter to a well-heeled friend called Philemon asking that mercy be shown to his runaway slave. They span the philosophical speculations of Ecclesiastes and the book of Wisdom to the prophetic oracles of Jeremiah, from the practical theological wisdom of Paul's letter to the Philippians to the vision of heaven and of the end time disclosed to John of Patmos in the book of Revelation.

To this fact of the Bible's variety, one may add the fact that the Catholic Bible, in part or in whole, is authoritative for a variety of peoples, denominations, and religions. This is true not only for other Christian

In the beginning was the Word, and the Word was with God, and the Word was God.

denominations, such as the Orthodox and Protestant Churches, but also for the religions of Judaism and Islam. People of uncertain or no religious commitment also make beneficial use of it. Scripture, therefore, is a shared "inheritance."

A third fact stands beside these two. In addition to the varied contents of the Bible and the authority it has for other denominations and religions, the teaching authority of the Catholic Church, the magisterium, interprets the Bible in the theological context of its traditional use within the Catholic Church. It declares the Bible's two Testaments, Old and New, to be a single unity revealing and testifying to Jesus Christ. The *Catechism of the Catholic Church*, borrowing the words of Hugh of St. Victor, describes this unity quite plainly: "All Sacred Scripture is but one book, and that one book is Christ, because all divine Scripture speaks of Christ, and all divine Scripture is fulfilled in Christ" (CCC, #134).

For ministers of the word to "be attentive to what the human authors truly wanted to affirm and to what God wanted to reveal to us by their words" means difficulty in some cases, particularly where the Old Testament is concerned (CCC, #109). If "all divine Scripture speaks of Christ," then ministers must grapple with how to be faithful to the unity of scripture while at the same time respecting its many human authors writing well before the advent of Christ and the institutional development of the Catholic Church. The commentaries, it is hoped, will help in this capacity.

Exile and Return

Due to the sheer number of Old Testament readings in the Lectionary dealing with events surrounding the captivity of Israel in Babylon, it makes sense to sketch briefly the historical circumstances that led to it. The creation of the Israelite monarchy, for the most part, was probably a response to frictions among the various peoples and kingdoms in the region. Names such as Moab, Philistia, and Edom, which may be familiar to some readers, belonged to neighboring kingdoms and peoples with whom Israel's clans and tribes alternately warred and made alliances. Unity under a single king meant that the people's military resources could be allocated more efficiently. Beginning in the eleventh century BC, the united monarchy, first under Saul, then under David and Solomon, made Israel an important regional power. With the death of Solomon around the middle of the tenth century BC, Israel split into two kingdoms, each ruled by a son of Solomon. The kingdom of Judah, with its capital at Jerusalem, incorporated the territory assigned by tradition to the tribes of Judah and Benjamin. The northern kingdom of Israel, with its capital in the city of Samaria, incorporated the territory of the remaining tribes.

It was the lot of Judah and Israel to occupy the Levant, a name for the geographical region adjacent to the Mediterranean Sea connecting the continents of Asia and Africa. The Levant had strategic importance to the ancient kingdom of Egypt to the southwest and to a series of Mesopotamian, Asian, and European powers with which Egypt contended. Another way to put it is that Israel and Judah, along with the Levant's other kingdoms, stood right in the way of the great powers of the ancient world whenever they marched against another.

When the kingdom of Assyria rose in the mid-eighth century BC, it began to put steady pressure on both Israel and Judah. For a time Israel aligned itself with Assyria. But this temporary alliance faltered, and Assyria laid waste to Israel and its capital at Samaria in 721 BC. Many of Israel's people were slain or taken by the Assyrians as prizes of war, while new people arrived to settle on the land. At this time the northern kingdom ceased to exist.

Judah was spared Israel's fate, although in the year 701 BC the Assyrians came very close to annihilating Judah as well. Judah's good fortune, however, was only temporary.

In the middle of the seventh century, the kingdom of Babylon began to challenge the Assyrians for regional dominance. In 612 BC, the Babylonians defeated the Assyrians decisively and set their sights on Egypt. The kingdom of Judah, as always, sat in the way. In 598 BC, Babylon's army arrived at Jerusalem. The king of Judah, Jehoiakim, died at this time and was succeeded by his son, Jehoiachin. A year later in 597 BC, Jehoiachin surrendered to the Babylonians. Along with his officials and many of Jerusalem's skilled laborers, Jehoiachin was led away captive to Babylon. In 587 BC, Babylon stormed Jerusalem. The Babylonians killed many people and looted and burned the city, including the temple. More captives were taken away. The prophet Jeremiah, who left Jerusalem for Egypt, performed his duties during Judah's final decades.

Some of the captives from Jerusalem were taken to Babylon itself, while some others, like the prophet Ezekiel, were settled in other regions. Babylon's heyday lasted until the middle of the sixth century BC, when the Persian empire began to challenge it. The early success of Cyrus of Persia against Babylon was taken as good news by some of the exiles, notably the authors of Isaiah 40—55. In 536 BC, two years after he conquered Babylon, Cyrus granted the people of Judah the right to return home. A very few of the captives returned immediately. More flowed back over the next century, helping to rebuild the temple. Some chose to remain where they were. The early post-exilic period is the likely historical context of Isaiah 56—66.

The historical books of Joshua, Judges, 1 and 2 Samuel, 1 and 2 Kings, and 1 and 2 Chronicles are important witnesses to the history of Israel from the time the Israelites began to settle in Canaan after the events of the Exodus to the destruction of Jerusalem by Babylon.

The Gospel of Matthew, Year A

For the Catholic Church, the canon of scripture was essentially settled by the widespread acceptance in the West of the Latin version of the Bible translated by Saint Jerome known as the Vulgate. The *Catechism of the Catholic Church* acknowledges four canonical Gospels, those according to Matthew, Mark, Luke, and John. The formation of this quartet of scriptural voices from among the chorus of the great literary output of the early Church was likely due to its perceived apostolic authorship and/or character, as well as the relative antiquity of each of its four members. The cycle of the Catholic Lectionary in the United States is three years in length, with the three so-called synoptic Gospels comprising the bulk of the readings during each three-year cycle: Matthew in Year A, Mark in Year B, and Luke in Year C. During all three years, we find the Gospel of John on specified feast days and solemnities. In the commentaries and the introduction, the custom of referring to evangelists and Gospels by their traditional names is observed.

God so loved the world that he gave his only Son, so that everyone who believes in him might not perish but might have eternal life.

The Gospel for 2008, Year A, is the Gospel of Matthew. Because this Gospel will be proclaimed all year, it makes sense to offer a little general information about it in the introduction to this issue of *Workbook*. All proclaimers of the Gospel of Matthew will do well to read the whole Gospel in the course of one or several sittings.

By tradition, Matthew the evangelist has usually been identified with Matthew the tax collector, whose call to discipleship we find in Matthew 9:9: "As Jesus passed on from there, he saw a man named Matthew sitting at the customs post. He said to him, 'Follow me.' And he got up and followed him." Matthew later lists one "Matthew the tax collector" among the 12 apostles (Matthew 10:3). Mark and Luke also include a Matthew among the original 12, but offer no other details (Mark 3:18; Luke 6:15; see also Acts 1:13). It is also true, however, that the author of Matthew never identifies himself within the text of the Gospel. Additionally, the Gospel was probably written in the latter decades of the first century AD when Jesus' disciples would have been, at best, very old men. Whatever the case, it is a fact that whoever wrote this Gospel held Matthew and his fellow apostles in quite high esteem.

Up until the modern period, most Christian interpreters have believed that Matthew was the first of the four Gospels written. This was the position, for example, of Irenaeus of Lyons at the close of the second century AD. Augustine, writing some 200 years later, thought Mark was actually an abridged version of Matthew. Most modern interpreters, however, have come to the conclusion that Mark was written before both Matthew and Luke, and that Matthew and Luke had at least Mark and one other written source (modern interpreters call it "Q" from the German word *Quelle*, which means "source") in common when they composed their own Gospels. While Matthew and Mark agree to the point where it is clear that one depends on the other, Matthew's Greek grammar and style are often of a better quality than Mark's. It is most probable that Matthew knew and used Mark's Gospel when he composed his own, but took care to smooth out many of the grammatical and stylistic kinks of his predecessor.

Eusebius of Caesarea, who composed his great *Ecclesiastical History* near the turn of the fourth century AD, records a tradition that the "sayings" or "oracles" (in Greek, *logia*) of Matthew were originally composed in Hebrew (*Ecclesiastical History*, III.39.16; see also VI.25.3–6). Perhaps this means that pieces of what would later become the Greek text of Matthew were believed to have been composed in Hebrew or Aramaic. In any case, the tradition of Matthew's Hebrew origin was widely accepted by early Christian interpreters, most of whom also thought it was written for Jews. None of these supposed Hebrew or Aramaic originals have ever been found, however. And at many points Matthew's Greek agrees word for word with the Greek text of Mark and Luke, both of which were undoubtedly composed in Greek. Most modern interpreters have therefore come to agree that Matthew was, like the rest of the New Testament, originally composed in Greek. There can be little doubt, however, that the community or communities out of which this author's work emerged contained many Jews.

Jesus' fulfillment of Jewish scripture is a persistent theme in all four Gospels, although it has a special prominence in Matthew. Repeatedly, we read that something Jesus does, or something happening to him, fulfills scripture. Matthew typically alerts his readers to Jesus' fulfillment of scripture with a statement such as we find in Jesus' triumphal entry to Jerusalem mounted on two beasts at the same time: "This happened so that what had been spoken through the prophet might be fulfilled: 'Say to daughter Zion, "Behold, your king comes to you, meek and riding on an ass, and on a colt, the foal of a beast of burden"'" (Matthew 21:1–5).

Another signature feature of Matthew is its author's careful attention to the order, structure, and organization of the Gospel's contents. We see this attention to order right from the beginning, in the record of male descent from Abraham to Jesus arranged into three neat groups of 14 generations each (Matthew 1:1–17). Matthew's concern for order extends beyond the text of his Gospel, for in the line from Abraham to Jesus, Matthew shows that Israel's history itself has a precise structure. Matthew's orderly presentation of his Gospel seeks to mirror and reveal the order he perceives in Israel's history. And he additionally wants to show that one can understand Israel's history *only* when one also understands that Jesus of Nazareth completes that history.

The opening genealogy is but one example of the theological meaning of Matthew's attention to order. At the conclusion of the Sermon on the Mount (Matthew 5:1—7:28), we read the following: "When Jesus finished these words, the crowds were astonished at his teaching" (Matthew 7:28). This passage

This is my commandment: love one another as I love you.

Magnify the LORD with me; let us exalt his name together.

resembles several more in Matthew describing the conclusion of various phases of Jesus' ministry and serving as important transitions from one part of the Gospel to the next (11:1; 13:53; 19:1; 26:1). According to Matthew, Jesus conducts his entire ministry in as orderly a fashion as Israel's history has unfolded.

Another of the unique features of Matthew's Jesus is his keen interest in Jewish law. "Do not think that I have come to abolish the law or the prophets. I have come not to abolish but to fulfill," proclaims Jesus near the beginning of the Sermon on the Mount (Matthew 5:17). What Jesus means by the law's fulfillment becomes clearer in the coming verses where Jesus repeatedly quotes a commandment or custom and then interprets it: "You have heard that it was said, 'An eye for an eye and a tooth for a tooth.' But I say to you, offer no resistance to one who is evil. When someone strikes you on [your] right cheek, turn the other one to him as well" (Matthew 5:38–39). This basic formula ("You have heard that it was said . . . . But I say to you") occurs throughout the fifth chapter of Matthew (5:21–22, 27–28, 33–34, 38–39, 43–44). Like Moses, on whose early childhood Matthew bases his depiction of Jesus' infancy (Matthew 2:1–18; see Exodus 1—2), Matthew's Jesus is a lawgiver.

It is also true that Jesus almost always either interprets the law more strictly than the rule he quotes, or, as in the example directly above, so radically changes its meaning as to create a totally new teaching. The reason Jesus gives his disciples for his strict rendering of the law is that the kingdom of heaven has drawn near: "I tell you, unless your righteousness surpasses that of the scribes and Pharisees, you will not enter into the kingdom of heaven" (Matthew 5:20). Matthew's Jesus thus bears witness to the need to *practice* discipleship. According to

Matthew, how his disciples behave has much to do with whether or not their ultimate destiny is with him in heaven. This active discipleship, Jesus teaches, must also translate into an active compassion. Feeding the hungry, welcoming the stranger, clothing the naked, and visiting those in prison are not suggestions, but rather conditions for entering the kingdom of heaven (Matthew 25:31–46; CCC, #1033; 2831).

Discipleship in Matthew is not only a matter of practice, but of faith. In Matthew, faith in Jesus is a kind of saving power. In the ninth chapter of Matthew, Jesus performs a number of healings. To one person, Jesus says, "Courage, daughter! Your faith has saved you" (Matthew 9:22). In another instance, Jesus and two blind men have a conversation about their faith before Jesus heals them: " 'Do you believe that I can do this?' 'Yes, Lord,' they said to him. Then he touched their eyes and said, "Let it be done for you according to your faith' " Matthew's Jesus praises some people for their faith (8:10; 15:28), but rebukes others for having too little of it (Matthew 6:30; 14:31; 16:8; 17:20; 21:25, 32).

Although the Church as we know it was not yet in existence during Jesus' ministry, Matthew records that Jesus himself spoke of "the Church" (in Greek, *ekklēsia*; see Matthew 16:18; 18:17). Much of chapter 18 concerns how the Church should govern itself. And in Matthew 16:17–19, Jesus blesses Simon Peter in the following way: "Blessed are you, Simon son of Jonah. For flesh and blood has not revealed this to you, but my heavenly Father. And so I say to you, you are Peter, and upon this rock I will build my church." Here, Jesus plays on the meaning of the name "Peter," which comes from a Greek word for "rock" or "stone" *(petra)*. This blessing has been extremely important to Catholic belief in the primacy of Peter among the apostles, as well as the primacy of Rome, the Petrine See, among the dioceses of the world.

Jesus is many things in Matthew. He is infant, preacher, teacher, debater, healer, prophet, miracle worker, prisoner, victim of execution, and resurrected Lord. We could expand this list considerably. But perhaps, above all, Matthew's Jesus is "God with us." We read in Matthew 1:23 that Jesus' birth fulfills Isaiah 7:14: "Therefore the Lord himself will give you this sign: the virgin shall be with child, and bear a son, and shall name him Immanuel." The Hebrew word

Immanuel (or *Emmanuel*), which Matthew translates in 1:23 for his Greek-speaking readers, literally means "God with us" (im/em = with; anu = us; el = God). When the resurrected Christ commissions his disciples in Galilee "to make disciples of all nations," he also gives them this word of reassurance: "And behold, I am *with you* always, until the end of the age" (Matthew 28:20).

In Matthew's understanding, Jesus is not "God with" his disciples individually, but rather in the context of the community of the Church. In Matthew 18, Jesus explains why decisions of the Church, when made properly, are binding decisions: "For where two or three are gathered together in my name, there am I in the midst of them" (Matthew 18:20). For Matthew, Jesus remains present and incarnate in the Church that he has called into existence.

Blessed are the poor in spirit, for theirs is the kingdom of heaven.

Scripture and Prayer

The nourishment that scripture's proclamation provides both lector and community is enhanced if the lector makes a regular practice of prayer and meditation on the pages of scripture.

Scripture, although divinely inspired, is not itself divine; rather, it reveals the divine. As a matter of tradition, Catholics have not worshipped the pages of scripture, but rather the one to whom they point. The Church indeed reveres scripture, which one may witness in the treatment of the Book of the Gospels in the celebration of the Mass. The book is carried in procession at the beginning of the Eucharistic celebration, enthroned on the altar, incensed, and kissed after the proclamation of the Gospel. The *Catechism of the Catholic Church* cites Luke 24:45 in connection with scripture's vital importance to the right understanding and worship of God through scripture. Here, in his depiction of the risen Jesus' second appearance, Luke reports that the risen Jesus joined his disciples in a village outside of Jerusalem and there "opened their minds to understand the Scriptures" (CCC, #108). One must also note that in Luke's depiction of the first appearance of the risen Jesus, the disciples only recognize their Lord "in the breaking of the bread" (Luke 24:35). Scripture and Eucharist thus join to disclose Jesus' powerful presence among his people.

Pronunciation Guides, Margin Notes, and General Suggestions

Proclaiming a reading of scripture requires a bit of practice and preparation. If it is at all possible, a lector or Gospel reader should go over the reading several times, silently and out loud, before getting up to proclaim it in worship. Strive to know your text well enough to be confident when you deliver it.

The pronunciation guides are meant to help with the clear proclamation of scripture. Some biblical words and names, such as "David" or "Jerusalem," are so common as to require no guide. Other words and names, while commonly known, may still not be known by all. They have been listed in the guides according to their standard pronunciation and accenting. Words and names that are relatively unknown and have no standard English pronunciation have been accented as they are found in either Hebrew or Greek as the case may be.

The margin notes are suggestions that will likely help with the effective proclamation of scripture. Perhaps the most consistent directions are "slow down," "emphasize," "make eye contact," and "pause." (The reason for "slow down" perhaps has more to do with the author's personal experience as a lector than anything else.) It is difficult for some people to avoid rushing through a reading, particularly in a public setting when one feels the weight of many pairs of eyes and ears. In such a situation it is a relief to recall a simple truth: *the message, not the messenger, is what people have come to hear.* It is the lector's task to read in such a way that God's people, gathered together for worship, may best take the words of scripture to heart, mind, and spirit.

It is almost always the case that electing to read more slowly than one is originally inclined is a good choice. A number of the Lectionary's selections are pieces excerpted from fairly complicated theological arguments. To speed through anything from Hebrews or Galatians, for example, is almost always to leave many people behind in a cloud of "therefores," "hences," and "howevers." Aim for slow, patient, clear delivery—loud enough for people to hear, but without shouting. In the event that one has a habit of reading too quickly, make it a practice to take a moment of brief silence before beginning. Use it to ask for any help God might care to give.

The LORD's word is true; all his works are trustworthy.

The modulation of one's reading speed and the volume of one's voice is an effective means of emphasizing particular words in relation to those going before and coming after. The word "emphasize" in the margin notes usually refers to particular words or lines. The direction to pause in the middle of a reading also has to do with emphasis. The margin notes, for example, often direct lectors to pause after "brothers and sisters" and to make eye contact with the assembly. The pause is here intended to emphasize the content of what has just been proclaimed and to encourage the assembly to understand themselves as family united by God.

From time to time, the margin notes urge a reader to take note of a reading's multiple speaking parts. *Please do not take this as encouragement to perform an overly dramatic reading.* Rather, simply proclaim the multiple speaking parts in such a way that the difference among the chorus of voices is clear. Take Luke 15:11–32, the return of the prodigal son, as an example. The mood of the first son, the one who claims his inheritance and promptly squanders it, changes over the course of the reading. He goes from haughtily demanding his inheritance to miserably scheming to throw himself on his father's mercy. His Father, it is safe to say, is happy beyond description when his son, whom he feared dead, comes walking home. The second son, the one who stayed behind and slaved away for his father, is understandably angry. It is quite possible to communicate all of this without unseemly and overwrought delivery.

Eye contact in normal speech is very important for effective communication. This is no less the case in the proclamation of scripture. Know your text well enough that you need only look down at it from time to time. Sometimes, of course, one gets the call to fill in for someone and there is not enough time to learn the reading well. In this case, make sure that you read slowly enough that you at least have a shot at looking up once or twice.

One should also dress in a manner appropriate for your community. Naturally, this will vary from place to place. Dressing in a flashy or showy way on the one hand, or in a sloppy manner on the other, are the two poles to avoid. Once again, the message, not the messenger, is the focus. Modest, clean dress almost always fits the bill.

Proclaiming a reading you have practiced, prepared, and learned something about can be immensely enjoyable and gratifying. Public reading is among the most ancient forms of Christian ministry. Consider for a moment that when someone calling himself Paul, an apostle, wrote letters to Churches, it fell to lectors to stand up and read them aloud (see 1 Thessalonians 5:27).

1ST SUNDAY OF ADVENT

Lectionary #1

READING I   Isaiah 2:1–5

A reading from the Book of the Prophet Isaiah

Note the parallel structure of the clauses, how they occur in pairs with the second clause restating or completing the idea of the first. Bring out this feature of the poetry in your delivery.

Amoz = AY-muhz

Judah = JOO-duh

This is what Isaiah, son of Amoz,
   saw concerning Judah and Jerusalem.
In days to come,
the mountain of the LORD's house
   shall be established as the **highest mountain**
   and raised above the **hills**.
All nations shall stream toward it;
   many peoples shall come and say:
"Come, let us climb the **LORD'S** mountain,
   to the house of the **God** of **Jacob**,
that he may **instruct** us in his ways,
   and we may **walk** in his paths."

Zion = ZI-yon

For from Zion shall go forth **instruction**,
   and the **word** of the LORD from Jerusalem.

Be sure to slow down and clearly enunciate this verse.

He shall **judge** between the **nations**,
   and impose **terms** on many **peoples**.
They shall beat their **swords** into **plowshares**
   and their **spears** into **pruning hooks**;
one nation shall **not** raise the **sword** against another,
   nor shall they train for **war** again.
O house of Jacob, **come**,
   let us **walk** in the **light** of the LORD!

READING I Throughout the book of Isaiah runs the persistent theme that Israel's selection by God for a uniquely intimate relationship is important not only to Israel, but also to other nations and peoples. In Isaiah's final chapter, for example, God declares, "I come to gather nations of every language." "Fugitives" proclaiming God's glory "shall bring all your brethren from all the nations as an offering to the Lord" (Isaiah 66:18–20). (Much hinges, of course, on whether one thinks "your brethren" refers strictly to other Jews or signifies a group including Gentiles.)

In today's reading, Jerusalem's temple mount ("the mountain of the Lord's house") is the goal toward which the nations "stream." Isaiah gives no specific date when this is to take place. "In days to come" is as precise as the text gets. A reign of peace is the predicted result of the nations' reception of God's instruction, walking in God's ways, and submission to God's judgment. Tools of war beaten into tools of farming depict a future, difficult to imagine, in which the cultivation of the earth replaces violence and the threat of violence as the chief occupation of nations.

In this reading, the condition of universal peace is universal submission to God. There is no hint, however, that this submission can occur by force. In Hebrew, the phrase "Come, let us climb the Lord's mountain" is an invitation, not an order.

READING II Romans 13:11–14 urges the letter's addressees to "throw off the works of darkness, and put on the armor of light." What might this mean?

In verses 8–10, Paul contends that love is the sole duty of the addressees toward

READING II   Romans 13:11–14

A reading from the Letter of Saint Paul to the Romans

Brothers and sisters:
You **know** the time;
   it is the hour now for you to **awake** from sleep.
For our **salvation** is nearer now than when we first **believed**;
   the **night** is **advanced**, the **day** is at **hand**.
Let us then **throw off** the works of **darkness**
   and **put on** the armor of **light**;
   let us conduct ourselves **properly** as in the day,
   not in **orgies** and **drunkenness**,
   not in **promiscuity** and **lust**,
   not in **rivalry** and **jealousy**.
But **put on** the Lord Jesus Christ,
   and make **no** provision for the **desires** of the **flesh**.

Slow down to emphasize this verse.

one another. He then specifically refers to commandments 6, 5, 7, and 10 of the Ten Commandments (see Exodus 20:2–17; compare Deuteronomy 5:6–21) "and whatever other commandment there may be" before saying that all of them are summed up by these words: "You shall love your neighbor as yourself."

Paul's argument here likely depends on the words of Jesus reported in Matthew 22:39 (see also Mark 12:31 and Luke 10:27). The words do not originate with Jesus, however. They are also found in Leviticus 19:18.

How can Paul claim that the Romans have one command only, which is love, but then follow this statement up with warnings not to do the things he lists in 13:13? Aren't these additional commands?

Paul makes a similar move in Galatians 5:13–26, where he is trying to show that faith in Christ, not observance of Jewish law, is what justifies a person in God's sight. For Paul, the vices of Galatians 5:19–21, like those of Romans 13:13, oppose love. Love for Paul is not only, or even mainly, an emotion. It is a social adhesive. It is mortar supporting the structure of the Roman community.

Contained within Paul's love command is encouragement of whatever deeds or behaviors strengthen and prepare the Christians of Rome for Christ's return, a second advent that Paul hopes will be every bit as dramatic and welcome for them as rays of dawn after long night.

GOSPEL   There is more to the new day rising in the previous reading than the fact that it is a vivid and perhaps pleasing image of how Paul believes the Church will experience the

GOSPEL   Matthew 24:37–44

A reading from the holy Gospel according to Matthew

Jesus said to his disciples:
"As it was in the days of **Noah**,
   so it will be at the coming of the **Son** of **Man**.
In those days before the flood,
   they were **eating** and **drinking**,
    marrying and giving in **marriage**,
   up to the day that Noah entered the ark.
They did **not** know until the flood came
    and carried them all away.
So will it be also at the coming of the **Son** of **Man**.
Two **men** will be out in the field;
   one will be **taken**, and **one** will be **left**.
Two **women** will be grinding at the mill;
   one will be **taken**, and **one** will be **left**.
Therefore, **stay awake**!
For you do not know on which day your Lord will come.
Be sure of this: if the master of the house
   had known the hour of night when the **thief** was coming,
   he would have stayed awake
   and **not** let his house be broken into.
So too, **you also** must be **prepared**,
   for at an hour you do **not** expect, the Son of Man will **come**."

This is Jesus' description of what the end of days will be like.

Make sure you slow down to emphasize these verses.

return of Jesus Christ. Many Jews of Paul's and Jesus' time believed that on a particular day in their not-too-distant future, God would quite suddenly and dramatically establish divine rule and authority over human affairs. One encounters a variety of ideas in the Old and New Testaments, as well as in other ancient Jewish and Christian literature, about what this day might involve. Some sources give no hint that this Day of the Lord would concern any nation other than Israel, while others assumed the whole world would be included. Most writers conceived of the Day of the Lord as a day of

judgment when God would reward the righteous and either ignore or punish sinners. Some believed that God would undo the very structure of the world, while others conceived of the day as one on which social, economic, and political wrong would be set right.

In today's Gospel, which will make more sense if you read all of chapter 24, Jesus speaks of this Day of the Lord. He compares it to the cataclysm of the Flood in the days of Noah (see Genesis 6:5—9:17). He predicts that some will be taken and some left behind. Moreover, he urges his hearers

to be watchful, always watchful, for there is no way to divine when it will all happen.

The word Advent ultimately derives from the Latin *adveniō*, which means "to arrive." In this season the liturgy of the Catholic Church focuses both on the Christmas remembrance of the birth of Jesus and his second arrival at the end of time.

IMMACULATE CONCEPTION

Lectionary #689

READING I   Genesis 3:9–15, 20

A reading from the Book of Genesis

If you back up to Genesis 3:8, you will see that Adam and Eve do not want to have this conversation at all. Try to project the couple's fear as the awareness of what they have done dawns on them. God's shock and anger should be clearly distinguished from the speaking parts of the two frightened people.

After the man, **Adam**, had eaten of the tree,
    the LORD God called to the man and asked him,
        "**Where are you**?"
He answered, "I **heard** you in the garden;
    but I was **afraid**, because I was **naked**,
        so I hid myself."
Then he asked, "**Who** told you that you were naked?
You have eaten, then,
    from the tree of which I had **forbidden** you to eat!"
The man replied, "The **woman** whom you put here with me—
    she gave me fruit from the tree, and so I ate it."
The LORD God then asked the woman,
    "**Why** did you do such a thing?"
The woman answered, "The **serpent** tricked me into it,
    so I ate it."

Then the LORD God said to the serpent:
"Because you have done this, you shall be **banned**
        from **all** the animals
        and from **all** the wild creatures;
    on your **belly** shall you **crawl**,
        and **dirt** shall you **eat**
        all the days of your life.

READING I   The decision by Adam and Eve to do what God forbade them, together with the deed itself, is what we commonly call the Fall or Original Sin.

But Adam and Eve did not disobey God on their own. They were encouraged to disobey by the serpent, which by Jesus' day some Jews had begun to associate with the devil (see Wisdom 2:23–24). For Christians the identification of Satan with the serpent has long been standard.

Adam, Eve, and Satan excited the imagination of the American humorist Mark Twain, who composed a short work about what Eve and Satan might have written in their diaries. The excerpt from Satan's diary reveals a clever creature persuading by confusion. Adam and Eve are new to life and therefore ignorant of a great deal. Satan knows it and he uses their ignorance to his advantage, dazzling them with words and ideas they cannot as yet possibly understand. Still uncomprehending, they disobey and eat.

Living right and well does not necessarily require much intelligence. But it is probably the case that each one of us has the responsibility to make vigorous use of whatever mental gifts we have been given. The responsible use of conscience requires that one be willing to accept responsibility for outcomes, intended and unintended, of what one chooses to do. See how Adam and Eve do not take responsibility for their

I will put **enmity** between **you** and the **woman**,
   and between **your** offspring and **hers**;
he will **strike** at your head,
   while you **strike** at his heel."

The man called his wife **Eve**,
   because she became the **mother** of all the **living**.

READING II   Ephesians 1:3–6, 11–12

A reading from the Letter of Saint Paul to the Ephesians

Brothers and sisters:
Blessed be the **God** and **Father** of our Lord **Jesus Christ**,
   who has **blessed** us in Christ
   with **every** spiritual blessing in the heavens,
   as he chose us in him, **before** the **foundation** of the world,
   to be **holy** and **without blemish** before him.
In **love** he destined us for adoption to himself
      through Jesus Christ,
   in accord with the favor of his **will**,
   for the praise of the glory of his **grace**
   that he granted us in the **beloved**.
In him we were also **chosen**,
   destined in accord with the **purpose** of the **One**
   who accomplishes **all** things according to the intention
      of his **will**,
   so that we might exist for the **praise** of his **glory**,
   we who first **hoped** in **Christ**.

This reading deals with the special place of Christians in God's plan for the world, their selection as God's children due to God's love and grace, and their divine destiny. This is a complicated set of ideas. The sentences are no less complicated grammatically and will be difficult to follow if proclaimed too quickly. Break the reading down into clauses, pausing briefly after each comma, and for slightly longer duration between sentences.

actions, but instead point the finger at others: Adam at Eve, Eve at the serpent. In Adam's explanation one can even hear the hint of a reproach to God for even putting Eve in the garden: "the woman whom *you* put here with me" (3:12).

READING II   Although most biblical scholars do not believe that Paul actually wrote the letter to the Ephesians, it is quite likely that someone personally familiar with Paul or his reputation composed it.

One thing quite clear in this passage is that Jesus Christ has come, and the Church has grown, according to a plan God made before Creation. The Crucifixion was not a tragic wrong set right when God raised Jesus from the dead—God planned the cross from the beginning. Neither is the Church made up of people who chose to join it—*God* chose *them*. Everything has happened because God in ages past wanted it that way. This is quite clear from the Greek text of 1:3–12, in which five words are prefixed with the Greek preposition *pro,* which means "before."

This reading declares that God has selected Christians for "adoption to himself through Jesus Christ, in accord with the favor of his will" (1:5). You will probably want to especially emphasize this verse in your delivery. The idea is an important one, perhaps for Catholics in particular among the major North American Christian denominations. Although many of us call ourselves "cradle Catholics," no one is born a Christian. As today's reading shows (along with texts such as John 1:12 and Galatians 3:19-4:7), for early Christians, moving from their former

Gabriel's name in Hebrew means something like "God is my might" or "God is my strong one." Therefore, proclaim his name and words strongly and with conviction.

As the text says, Mary is "greatly troubled" by Gabriel's greeting. Let her shock and surprise come through as she asks her question.

Pause briefly before you deliver Mary's speaking parts as this will highlight them and draw the assembly's attention to them.

GOSPEL   Luke 1:26–38

A reading from the holy Gospel according to Luke

The angel **Gabriel** was sent from God
　　to a town of **Galilee** called **Nazareth**,
　　to a **virgin** betrothed to a man named **Joseph**,
　　of the house of **David**,
　　and the virgin's name was **Mary**.
And coming to her, he said,
　　"**Hail**, full of **grace**! The **Lord** is **with you**."
But she was greatly **troubled** at what was said
　　and **pondered** what sort of greeting this might be.
Then the angel said to her,
　　"Do **not** be afraid, Mary,
　　for you have found **favor** with God.
Behold, you will **conceive** in your womb and bear a son,
　　and you shall **name** him **Jesus**.
He will be **great** and will be called **Son** of the **Most High**,
　　and the Lord God will **give** him the **throne** of David his father,
　　and he will **rule** over the house of Jacob **forever**,
　　and of his Kingdom there will be **no** end."
But Mary said to the angel,
　　"**How** can this **be**,
　　since I have no relations with a man?"

---

identities to thinking of themselves as God's children was a very important subject.

GOSPEL On most feasts we read passages from scripture that clearly and obviously relate to the feast. On the feast of the Annunciation we read today's Gospel because it describes the annunciation of the archangel Gabriel to Mary. On the feast of the Ascension, we read the first 11 verses of the Acts of the Apostles because those verses narrate Jesus' Ascension into

heaven. This is not the case with the feast of the Immaculate Conception.

Before we ask why today's scripture selections do not specifically concern the Immaculate Conception, it is important to first point out a common misunderstanding about this doctrine. Many people, Catholics included, think that the doctrine of the Immaculate Conception refers to Mary's conception of Jesus by the Holy Spirit. In fact, the doctrine refers not to Jesus' conception, but to Mary's.

So why are there no passages of scripture in the Lectionary about the Immaculate Conception? The reason is that, unlike the Annunciation, the Ascension, and pretty much every other major feast on the liturgical calendar, canonical scripture never mentions Mary's conception. There is an early Christian text called the *Infancy Gospel of James* that contains an account of Mary's quite unusual conception. But this text is not a part of the Catholic canon of scripture. The doctrine of the Immaculate Conception is a consequence of the doctrine

And the angel said to her in reply,
    "The **Holy Spirit** will **come upon** you,
    and the **power** of the Most High will **overshadow** you.
Therefore the child to be born
    will be called **holy**, the Son of God.
And behold, Elizabeth, your relative,
    has **also** conceived a son in her old age,
    and this is the sixth month for her who was called barren;
    for **nothing** will be impossible for **God**."
Mary said, "Behold, **I** am the handmaid of the **Lord**.
May it be done to me according to your word."
Then the angel departed from her.

But also let Mary's resolution, despite her fears, come through.

that Jesus was human in all respects except for sin. If Jesus was without sin, some reasoned, then he must have been conceived by a woman who was herself conceived without sin. The doctrine is therefore not so much scriptural as the product of considerable theological ingenuity. As a result of this longstanding belief in Mary's Immaculate Conception, in the Constitution *Ineffabilis Deus*, issued on December 8, 1854, Blessed Pope Pius IX pronounced and defined that the Blessed Virgin Mary "in the first instance of her conception, by a singular privilege and grace granted by God, in view of the merits of Jesus Christ, the Saviour of the human race, was preserved exempt from all stain of original sin."

2ND SUNDAY OF ADVENT

Lectionary #4

READING I   Isaiah 11:1–10

A reading from the Book of the Prophet Isaiah

Pay attention to the parallel structure of this passage. Emphasize what you consider to be the most significant words in the pairs.

On that day, a **shoot** shall **sprout** from the stump of Jesse,
 and from his **roots** a **bud** shall **blossom**.
The **spirit** of the LORD shall **rest** upon him:
 a spirit of **wisdom** and of **understanding**,
a spirit of **counsel** and of **strength**,
 a spirit of **knowledge** and of **fear** of the LORD,
 and his **delight** shall be the **fear** of the LORD.
Not by **appearance** shall he **judge**,
 nor by **hearsay** shall he **decide**,
but he shall **judge** the **poor** with **justice**,
 and decide **aright** for the land's **afflicted**.
He shall **strike** the **ruthless** with the **rod** of his **mouth**,
 and with the **breath** of his **lips** he shall **slay** the **wicked**.
Justice shall be the band around his waist,
 and **faithfulness** a belt upon his hips.
Then the **wolf** shall be a guest of the **lamb**,
 and the **leopard** shall lie down with the **kid**;
the **calf** and the young **lion** shall browse together,
 with a **little child** to guide them.

READING I The prophet Isaiah lived in Jerusalem during the latter part of the eighth century BC. These were years of crisis, not only for the kingdoms of Judah and Israel, but also for many small kingdoms in the Middle East. The reason for the crisis was the expansion of the Assyrian Empire. Against such force, the little kingdoms hardly stood a chance. One of the kingdoms to fall before Assyria was the northern kingdom of Israel, which was destroyed in 721 BC.

The attitude toward Israel's destruction in the early chapters of Isaiah is complicated. Having watched Assyria blaze a trail of destruction southward, the prophet reports that God has named Assyria "My rod in anger, my staff in wrath." The northern kingdom, according to the prophet, suffers Assyria's violence because God wills it to suffer: "Against an impious nation I send him, and against a people under my wrath I order him to seize plunder, carry off loot, and tread them down like the mud of the streets" (Isaiah 10:6). It must be said that the prophet records all of this from the relative safety of Jerusalem, well south of the Assyrians' northern rapine.

Despite the disaster of the north, the prophet predicts that God will not permit the southern kingdom of Judah to suffer the same fate. The prophet envisions a future time when Judah *and* Israel, kingdoms north and south, will be reunited and its dispersed and captive people returned (Isaiah 11:10–16). In today's reading, the shoot sprouting from the "stump of Jesse," by which the prophet means a king of David's line (see 1 Samuel 16:1–13), is predicted to reign with strength and justice, even as he becomes the object of Gentile fascination. This king is not named, although the author may have meant Hezekiah, king of Judah, who ruled during

The **cow** and the **bear** shall be neighbors,
    together their young shall **rest**;
    the **lion** shall eat hay like the **ox**.
The **baby** shall play by the **cobra's** den,
    and the **child** lay his hand on the **adder's** lair.
There shall be **no harm** or **ruin** on **all** my holy mountain;
    for the **earth** shall be **filled** with **knowledge** of the LORD,
    as **water** covers the **sea**.
On that day, the root of **Jesse**,
    set up as a signal for the nations,
the **Gentiles** shall seek out,
    for his **dwelling** shall be **glorious**.

READING II   Romans 15:4–9

A reading from the Letter of Saint Paul to the Romans

Brothers and sisters:
Whatever was written **previously** was written for **our** instruction,
    that by **endurance** and by the **encouragement** of the Scriptures
    we might have **hope**.
May the God of **endurance** and **encouragement**
    grant you to think in **harmony** with one another,
    in keeping with **Christ Jesus**,
    that with **one accord** you may with one voice
    glorify the God and Father of our Lord Jesus Christ.

The unity of Gentiles and Jews in God's plan of salvation as it is revealed in Christ, proclaimed by apostles, and eagerly awaited by the Church is the dominant theme of this letter. Stress those portions of this reading having to do with this theme.

the period of Assyria's closest encroachment upon Jerusalem and Judah.

The shoot sprouting from Jesse's stump has often been taken by Christians to refer to Jesus. This interpretation removes the king and his reign from a particular historical time and place and projects both forward to the return of Christ in glory at some future time. One can see in the pastoral image of carnivorous animals relaxing with their prey, and children playing with venomous snakes without fear, a depiction of the kingdom of God as a reign of reconciliation— reconciliation among the members of God's creation, and creation's reconciliation with its Creator.

READING II   What could it mean to imitate Christ? Some Christians will say it is impossible, reasoning that Christ's divinity makes him impossible for ordinary people to imitate. Imitate Christ? Imitate "The Only Son, God, who is at the Father's side" (John 1:18)? Imitate the one who bears "the name that is above every name" (Philippians 2:9)? Imitate "the image of the invisible God, the firstborn of all creation" (Colossians 1:15)? A dog would have better luck at imitating a man.

And yet discipleship is, in large part, a matter of imitation. Although Paul describes Jesus in especially exalted terms in Philippians 2:6–11, this Christ who willingly emptied himself, who took the form of a slave and accepted even death on a cross, is also a self-sacrificial example to which Paul believes he himself conforms (Philippians 1:12–26) and to which he urges the Philippians to conform themselves (2:1–5; 4:2–3). Christ's thoughtful concern for others, expressed above all in his acceptance of the cross,

Welcome one another, then, as **Christ** welcomed **you**,
for the **glory** of God.
For I say that **Christ** became a **minister** of the **circumcised**
to show God's **truthfulness**,
to confirm the **promises** to the patriarchs,
but so that the **Gentiles** might **glorify** God for his **mercy**.
As it is written:
*Therefore, I will **praise** you among the **Gentiles***
*and sing **praises** to your **name**.*

GOSPEL   Matthew 3:1–12

A reading from the holy Gospel according to Matthew

John the **Baptist** appeared, preaching in the **desert** of **Judea**
and saying, "**Repent**, for the **kingdom** of **heaven** is **at hand**!"
It was of **him** that the prophet Isaiah had spoken when he said:
A voice of one crying out in the desert,
***Prepare** the way of the Lord,*
*   **make straight** his paths.*
John wore clothing made of **camel's** hair
and had a leather belt around his waist.
His food was **locusts** and **wild honey**.
At that time **Jerusalem**, **all** Judea,
and the **whole** region around the **Jordan**
were going **out** to him
and were being **baptized** by him in the Jordan River
as they **acknowledged** their sins.

Make sure you emphasize and project the passage quoted from Isaiah as well as John's responses to the Pharisees' and Sadducees' questions. These are strong words.

provides the theological basis for a topic Paul returns to again and again in his letters: the need for social unity in the Churches.

For Paul, the sign of the successful imitation of Christ, as in today's reading, is community agreement. In 1 Corinthians 1:10, Paul urges "that all of you agree in what you say, and that there be no divisions among you, but that you be united in the same mind and in the same purpose." Noting that significant divisions exist in the community at Corinth, Paul asks, "Is Christ divided?" The answer demands a negative answer, of course, but in Paul's view the Corinthians' disagreements

show that they are acting as though he is. To the Philippians, with whom Paul was enjoying quite warm relations when he wrote to them, Paul says, "complete my joy by being of the same mind, with the same love, united in heart, thinking one thing" (Philippians 2:2).

In this reading from Romans, we see a similar appeal: "May the God of endurance and encouragement grant you to think in harmony with one another, in keeping with Christ Jesus" (Romans 15:5). For Paul, concord in mind and heart reveal a community composed of true disciples, and therefore imitators, of Jesus Christ.

GOSPEL   If you go to an art gallery with a nice collection of medieval and renaissance religious art, you will probably find many depictions of John the Baptist. He's very easy to spot. He's the one wearing the camel hair.

Before you proclaim this passage, you might meditate awhile on Matthew's physical description of John, his speech, and his manner of life. What sort of man, one might ask, leaves civilization behind to make his home in the wild, chooses to live on locusts and honey, and, when religious big shots start showing up, does not defer to them, but

When he saw many of the **Pharisees** and **Sadducees**
    coming to his **baptism**, he said to them, "You **brood** of **vipers**!
Who warned you to **flee** from the coming **wrath**?
Produce good fruit as evidence of your **repentance**.
And do **not** presume to say to yourselves,
    '**We** have Abraham as our father.'
For I tell you,
    God can raise up children to Abraham from these stones.
Even now the **ax** lies at the **root** of the **trees**.
Therefore **every** tree that does not bear good fruit
    will be **cut** down and **thrown** into the fire.
I am baptizing you with **water**, for **repentance**,
    but the one who is coming **after** me is **mightier** than I.
I am not **worthy** to carry his **sandals**.
He will baptize you with the **Holy Spirit** and **fire**."
His **winnowing** fan is in his **hand**.
He will **clear** his threshing floor
    and **gather** his wheat into his **barn**,
    but the **chaff** he will burn with unquenchable **fire**."

instead shouts insults: "You brood of vipers!" What kind of man is he? Do we know someone, anyone, like him? If so, what kind of attention, if any, would we give such a person?

John the Baptist was famous in his time. In the course of his second missionary journey as recorded in Acts 19:1–7, Paul encounters people in Ephesus, a city of Asia minor (present-day Turkey), who know of John's baptism. Judging by what the Jewish historian Flavius Josephus wrote about both him and Jesus near the turn of the second century, it appears that John was the better

known of the two in Palestine during the first century. Matthew mentions that Herod feared harming John because of the great esteem in which people held him (Matthew 14:5). One of the firmest pieces of historical information we have about Jesus is that he was first associated with John the Baptist before setting off on his own.

Matthew sums up the content of John's preaching in a single sentence: "Repent, for the kingdom of heaven is at hand." Matthew immediately thereafter says that John is the specific person whom Isaiah meant in Isaiah 40:3. Neither Mark nor Luke is as

exclusive in his application of this passage to John (Mark 1:2–3; Luke 3:4–6). According to Matthew, John the Baptist, and presumably no one else, is whom Isaiah meant. In the Gospel of John (*not* named for John the Baptist), John the Baptist himself proclaims the line from Isaiah 40:3 (1:23).

As will become increasingly clear in the course of this liturgical year, Matthew understands the birth, ministry, Passion, and death of Jesus to be the direct fulfillment of scripture. So do the other three evange-lists, but none so plainly states the case as Matthew.

3RD SUNDAY OF ADVENT

Lectionary #7

READING I   Isaiah 35:1–6a, 10

A reading from the Book of the Prophet Isaiah

This is a joyful reading about the natural world's celebration of God's ransom of captives from slavery. Stress those words especially communicating this joy.

Carmel = CAR-mel

Sharon = Shar-RON

The desert and the parched land will **exult**;
　the steppe will **rejoice** and **bloom**.
They will **bloom** with **abundant** flowers,
　and **rejoice** with **joyful** song.
The **glory** of **Lebanon** will be given to them,
　the **splendor** of **Carmel** and **Sharon**;
they will **see** the **glory** of the LORD,
　the **splendor** of our **God**.
Strengthen the hands that are **feeble**,
　make **firm** the knees that are **weak**,
say to those whose hearts are frightened:
　Be **strong**, fear **not**!
Here is your God,
　he comes with **vindication**;
with **divine** recompense
　he comes to **save** you.
Then will the eyes of the **blind** be **opened**,
　the **ears** of the **deaf** be **cleared**;
then will the **lame leap** like a **stag**,
　then the **tongue** of the **mute** will **sing**.

READING I | On the sixth day of Creation according to the account of Genesis 1:1—2:3, God speaks to human beings for the first time. In Genesis 1:28–30, God gives human beings dominion over the earth, telling them to "subdue it" (Genesis 1:28). In the ancient Mediterranean, as in pre-modern peasant societies generally, subduing the earth was a life or death proposition. The laborious protection of crops against wild animals, choking weeds, and inclement weather was what it took to

wrest another year's survival from the earth.

It may not surprise us, therefore, that the provision of water in the wilderness is a common and joyous expression of praise in the books of the prophets. Israel's God even has some traditional attributes of a Mediterranean storm God, as we see in Psalm 68:5 ("exalt the rider of the clouds"), 68:33–34 ("the Lord who rides the heights of the ancient heavens, whose voice is thunder, mighty thunder"), Psalm 29:3 ("the voice of the Lord is over the waters; the God of glory thunders"), and many other places.

Note especially in this reading how the blooming of parched land in Isaiah 35:1 heralds the ransom of people from captivity in 35:10. In 35:6b–8, which the Lectionary omits, streams, rivers, springs, pools, and marshes appear in what was formerly arid land. The coming of water to dry places, no less than the ransom of captives, promises renewed prospects for human survival in a dangerous world and invites humanity's praise and awe.

Zion = ZI-yon

Those whom the LORD has **ransomed** will return
  and enter Zion **singing**,
    crowned with everlasting **joy**;
they will meet with **joy** and **gladness**,
  sorrow and mourning will **flee**.

READING II   James 5:7–10

A reading from the Letter of Saint James

Be **patient**, brothers and sisters,
  until the **coming** of the **Lord**.
See how the farmer **waits** for the precious **fruit** of the **earth**,
  being **patient** with it
  until it receives the **early** and the **late** rains.
You too must be **patient**.
Make your hearts **firm**,
  because the **coming** of the Lord is **at hand**.
Do not **complain**, brothers and sisters, about one another,
  that you may not be **judged**.
Behold, the Judge is **standing** before the **gates**.
Take as an example of **hardship** and **patience**, brothers
    and sisters,
  the **prophets** who spoke in the name of the **Lord**.

Pause briefly after "rains," and then emphasize the words "You too." This will communicate the author's intention, that his audience apply the farmer's patient example to themselves.

Pause after "at hand" and before beginning the next section, since there is a slight shift in subject here.

Boldly proclaim the line of 5:9 beginning "Behold."

READING II "Let us know," proclaims the prophet Hosea, "let us strive to know the Lord; as certain as the dawn is his coming, and his judgment shines forth like the light of day! He will come to us like the rain, like spring rain that waters the earth" (Hosea 6:3). The spring rain to which Hosea refers is equivalent to the "late rains" in the letter of James. Historically, there have been two main rainy seasons in Israel. The heavier of the two comes in winter ("the early rains" mentioned

by James) while the lighter one arrives in spring. According to Hosea, the Lord's coming is like the spring rains—gentle.

James does not liken the "coming of the Lord" to the rains, but rather compares the patience of believers to that of the farmer who must wait for both early and late rains. The rains will not arrive any sooner simply because the farmer wishes it. Neither will the rains delay because she is not prepared. The rains will come when they come. Their schedule is not subject to her review. It is like that with Jesus, James says. The only additional information James

has is that "the coming of the Lord is at hand" and "Behold, the judge is standing before the gates." "Soon" is James's answer to the question of "When?"

It is probably fair to say that most people do not expect Jesus to return any time soon. But our earliest ancestors in faith, like James, provide evidence that they expected it in the not-too-distant future. In Paul's first letter to the Thessalonians, we read of the anxiety of these early converts in dealing with the deaths of Church members (1 Thessalonians 4:13). They had not expected

GOSPEL Matthew 11:2–11

A reading from the holy Gospel according to Matthew

When John the Baptist heard in **prison** of the works of the **Christ**,
  he sent his disciples to **Jesus** with this **question**,
  "Are **you** the one who is to come,
  or should we look for **another**?"
Jesus said to them in reply,
  "**Go** and **tell** John what you **hear** and **see**:
  the **blind** regain their **sight**,
  the **lame walk**,
  lepers are **cleansed**,
  the **deaf hear**,
  the **dead** are **raised**,
  and the **poor** have the good news **proclaimed** to them.
And **blessed** is the one who takes **no offense** at me."

Pause between each clause describing those Jesus has healed and stress both their former infirmity and what they now are able to do. This is Jesus' answer to John.

Jesus to delay so long that some of them would die while they waited!

As we prepare for the future, consider that Christian time is borrowed time. The Church is a community in both constant and conscious preparation for the end of all we have known and the beginning of a new order of life we can scarcely imagine.

GOSPEL In Matthew, the report of John the Baptist's imprisonment reaches Jesus immediately after his temptation by the devil in the wilderness

(4:12). Only after John's imprisonment does Jesus strike out on his own, settle in the Galilean village of Capernaum, and proclaim his Gospel: "Repent, for the kingdom of heaven is at hand" (4:17). If these words sound familiar, they should. Matthew uses exactly the same ones to summarize the proclamation of John the Baptist in 3:2. Matthew is here directing our attention to the close relationship between Jesus and the man who baptized him and was perhaps also his teacher.

This is an appropriate occasion to talk a little about the word "Gospel." The word translates a Greek word, *euaggelion,* which means "good news." We use "Gospel" in different ways. First, we can speak of Jesus' Gospel, by which we mean the content of Jesus' own preaching. Matthew probably sums this up well in 4:17 and 11:4–5. Second, we can speak of the Gospel about Jesus, such as Paul outlines in 1 Corinthians 15:1–11. In Paul's Gospel *about* Jesus, the death and Resurrection of Jesus has become the Good News. Third, we can also speak of

Emphasize Jesus' closing testimony to John's greatness as well as the surprising information that the least in the kingdom of heaven is still greater than he.

As they were going off,
  Jesus began to speak to the crowds about John,
  "**What** did you go out to the desert to **see**?
A reed **swayed** by the **wind**?
Then **what** did you go out to **see**?
Someone **dressed** in **fine clothing**?
Those who wear fine clothing are in royal palaces.
Then **why** did you go out? To see a **prophet**?
Yes, I tell you, and **more** than a prophet.
This is the one about whom it is written:
  *Behold, I am sending my messenger **ahead** of you;*
    *he will **prepare** your way before you.*
Amen, I say to you,
  among those born of **women**
  there has been **none** greater than **John** the **Baptist**;
  yet the **least** in the kingdom of heaven is **greater** than he."

Gospels, as in the Gospel of Matthew, by which we mean written accounts of Jesus' deeds and/or words. In this reading, we are concerned with the first of these three, for Jesus' proclamation of the Good News is not only rendered in speech, but in merciful acts of power.

When the disciples of John the Baptist come to Jesus, they ask him John's question: "Are you the one who is to come?" Note that Jesus does not chide them for a lack of faith, or simply reply, "Yes, I am." Instead, he refers John's disciples to evidence that will allow them and their teacher to draw their own conclusions.

4TH SUNDAY OF ADVENT

Lectionary #10

READING I   Isaiah 7:10–14

A reading from the Book of the Prophet Isaiah

The LORD spoke to **Ahaz**, saying:
Ask for a sign from the LORD, your **God**;
   let it be **deep** as the **netherworld**, or **high** as the **sky**!
But Ahaz answered,
   "I will **not** ask! I will **not** tempt the LORD!"
Then **Isaiah** said:
   Listen, O house of David!
Is it not enough for you to weary **people**,
   must you **also** weary my **God**?
Therefore the LORD himself will give you **this sign**:
   the **virgin** shall **conceive**, and **bear** a son,
   and shall name him **Emmanuel**.

Ahaz = Ah-HAZ

Proclaim the words of Ahaz, the obstinate king, with a commanding tone. Emphasize both occurrences of the word "not." But proclaim Isaiah's words even more boldly, for he is not only speaking an oracle of God, but also rebuking his king.

Emmanuel = Em-man-u-EL

READING I   The situation of the southern kingdom of Judah in the 730s BC was very grave. The combined strength of Assyria and its allies well exceeded Judah's. The very future of the southern kingdom seems to have been in doubt (see Isaiah 7:1–9). According to 2 Kings 16, King Ahaz of Judah at one time sought to join in an alliance with Assyria in order to protect his land and throne. The immediate historical context of today's reading, however, is Assyria's and its allies' encroachment on Judah.

In today's reading, King Ahaz neglects to seek a sign from God even though God has asked him to do so. Ahaz justifies his refusal in language strongly reminiscent of Deuteronomy 6:16. The basis of his refusal is therefore pious. But pious or not, Isaiah's prophetic word to the king rebukes him for not seeking the sign he was instructed to seek.

The "virgin" with child appears to be a woman both Isaiah and Ahaz know, perhaps someone from Judah's royal family. We cannot say for certain who she was any more than we can determine with any precision the identity of the Immanuel child she will bear. But some scholars, often identifying the Immanuel child with the child celebrated in Isaiah 9:1–6, think the woman was Ahaz's wife and the child Hezekiah, Ahaz's successor. The point of the oracle is that the suffering of Judah will be relieved within the time it takes the Immanuel child to grow from infancy into a toddler.

Note also that this reading describes the search of God for human beings. God does not accept the king's "no" and directs Ahaz through Isaiah to the sign he would not seek himself.

A reading from the Letter of Saint Paul to the Romans

Paul, a **slave** of Christ Jesus,
  called to be an **apostle** and **set apart** for the **gospel** of **God**,
  which he **promised** previously through his **prophets**
    in the holy **Scriptures**,
the **gospel** about his **Son**, descended from **David**
    according to the **flesh**,
  but **established** as **Son** of **God** in **power**
  according to the **Spirit** of **holiness**
  through **resurrection** from the **dead**, Jesus Christ **our** Lord.
Through him we have received the **grace** of **apostleship**,
  to bring about the **obedience** of **faith**,
  for the **sake** of his **name**, among **all** the Gentiles,
  among whom are **you also**, who are **called** to **belong**
    to **Jesus Christ**;
  to **all** the beloved of **God** in **Rome**, called to be **holy**.
Grace to you and **peace** from **God** our **Father**
  and the **Lord Jesus Christ**.

This is a fairly complicated reading from a grammatical standpoint. It will be easy for the assembly to get lost if you proclaim it too fast. So read the whole thing clearly and slowly.

READING II By introducing himself as a "slave," Paul seeks to communicate that he has the moral authority to urge the Philippians to submit themselves to one another for the benefit of the whole community (see also Philippians 2:7). The longest introduction in any of Paul's letters is today's reading from Romans. Why is this one so long in comparison with the other letters?

For one thing, Romans is quite a long letter. The majority of it is a sustained argument in favor of Gentile and Jewish unity in not only the common predicament of sin and

death, but also the common solution of Jesus Christ as predicted in scripture. There is much terrain to cover, and thus Paul crafts a roadmap equal to the challenge.

For another thing, Paul had never visited the Roman Churches. Unlike Philippi, Corinth, and some towns of Galatia, Paul did not found the Christian community of Rome. Although Paul knew a great many members of the Roman community personally and by reputation, he had never formally met the community as a whole in Rome. Romans is, in some sense, Paul's introduction of himself and his Gospel to the community at Rome.

Rome's Christian community likely had a significant percentage that was of Jewish extraction. Thus it is not surprising that Romans so extensively deals with the relation between Jews and Christians, and therefore also refers to Jesus' Jewish royal lineage and the scriptures' prediction of his advent.

GOSPEL In this selection from Matthew's Gospel, we read of Joseph's dream and the revelation that

GOSPEL   Matthew 1:18–24

A reading from the holy Gospel according to Matthew

This is how the **birth** of Jesus Christ came about.
When his **mother Mary** was betrothed to **Joseph**,
    but **before** they lived together,
    she was found with **child** through the **Holy Spirit**.
Joseph her **husband**, since he was a **righteous** man,
    yet unwilling to expose her to **shame**,
    decided to **divorce** her quietly.
Such was his **intention** when, **behold**,
    the **angel** of the **Lord** appeared to him in a **dream** and said,
    "**Joseph**, son of **David**,
    do **not** be afraid to take **Mary** your wife into your home.
For it is **through** the **Holy Spirit**
    that this child has been **conceived** in her.
She will bear **a son** and you are to name him **Jesus**,
    because he will **save** his people from their **sins**."
All this took place to **fulfill** what the Lord had said
        through the **prophet**:
    Behold, *the virgin shall* **conceive** *and bear a* **son**,
    and they shall **name** *him* **Emmanuel**,
    which means "**God** is **with** us."
When Joseph **awoke**,
    he **did** as the **angel** of the **Lord** had **commanded** him
    and took his **wife** into his **home**.

Boldly proclaim the angel's words
to Joseph.

Pause briefly before and after the first
word of the prophecy quoted from Isaiah:
"Behold."
Emmanuel = Em-man-u-EL

Jesus' birth will fulfill the words of the prophet Isaiah (see Isaiah 7:14).

In the first two chapters of Matthew, there are reports of five dreams providing important information. We read of the first dream in today's reading. Matthew's dreams show God's guidance of Jesus' birth and protection of him and his family from harm.

The angel offers Joseph a reason why he should name his son Jesus. "You are to name him Jesus," the angel says, "because he will save his people from their sins" (Matthew 1:21). The relationship between

the name "Jesus" and salvation is not obvious in English. Neither would it have been obvious in the Greek of Matthew's Gospel. But in both biblical Hebrew and the related language of Aramaic, the connection is clear. Jesus' name, *Yeshua*, is an Aramaic version of the Hebrew name Joshua *(Yoshua)*. Both names derive from a verb meaning "help," "deliver," "rescue," or "save."

Because of this and other hints in Matthew, some ancients and a few modern scholars believe Matthew was originally written in Aramaic or Hebrew. This is not at all likely. Matthew, like the rest of the

New Testament, was written in Greek. But Matthew likely understood some Aramaic and Hebrew and may have written for people who would have understood that Jesus is not only a savior in deed, but in name as well.

Lectionary #4

READING I   Isaiah 62:1–5

A reading from the Book of the Prophet Isaiah

Zion = ZI-yon

For Zion's sake I will **not** be silent,
    for Jerusalem's sake I will **not** be quiet,
until her **vindication** shines forth like the **dawn**
    and her **victory** like a burning **torch**.

Note the way the second clause or sentence of each pair completes or mirrors the first clause or sentence. This is typical of Hebrew poetic structure.

Nations shall **behold** your **vindication**,
    and all the **kings** your **glory**;
you shall be called by a **new** name
    pronounced by the **mouth** of the LORD.
You shall be a **glorious crown** in the hand of the LORD,
    a royal **diadem** held by your **God**.
No more shall people call you "**Forsaken**,"
    or your land "**Desolate**,"
but you shall be called "**My Delight**,"
    and your land "**Espoused**."
For the LORD delights in you
    and makes your land his **spouse**.
As a young **man** marries a **virgin**,
    your **Builder** shall **marry you**;
and as a **bridegroom** rejoices in his **bride**
    so shall your **God rejoice** in **you**.

READING I   "Whoever is without love does not know God, for God is love." So says the first letter of John (1 John 4:8). With this statement the writer makes an extraordinary claim about human knowledge of God based on an even more extraordinary claim about God's own nature. People know God by loving, and God loves because love is what God is.

The great love of God for Zion and Jerusalem is the subject of today's reading from Isaiah. But this topic presents some difficulties for us. The composition of this passage likely came near the end of an especially traumatic and brutal period in the history of Israel. In 721 BC the empire of Assyria wiped the northern kingdom of Israel off the map forever. In 587 BC, after years of harassment, waves of kidnapping, theft, and

violence, the empire of Babylon finally conquered Judah, destroyed Jerusalem, plundered its temple, slaughtered its residents, and led many survivors away into captivity. While the prophet writes decades later in response to Judah's and Jerusalem's improved circumstances, one can easily see the difficulties. What sort of bridegroom treats his bride this way? What sort of bride would consent to marry someone like that?

READING II   Acts 13:16–17, 22–25

A reading from the Acts of the Apostles

Antioch = AN-ti-ock
Pisidiah = Pi-SIH-di-ah

Paul is preaching. Proclaim his words
boldly and exuberantly. Stress in
particular the opening line.

Saul = SAWL

John the Baptist spoke these words that
Paul here quotes in the course of rebuking,
commanding, and challenging his
audiences (see Luke 3:7–18). Slow down
and adopt a stronger tone when you
deliver John's words.

When Paul reached **Antioch** in Pisidia and entered
 the **synagogue**,
 he stood up, motioned with his hand, and said,
  "**Fellow Israelites** and you others who are **God-fearing**, **listen**.
The **God** of this people **Israel** chose our ancestors
 and **exalted** the people during their sojourn
  in the land of **Egypt**.
With uplifted arm he led them out of it.
Then he **removed Saul** and **raised up David** as king;
 of him he **testified**,
  'I have found David, son of Jesse, a man after **my own** heart;
  he will carry out my every wish.'
From **this** man's descendants God, according to his **promise**,
 has brought to Israel a **savior**, Jesus.
John heralded his coming by **proclaiming** a **baptism** of **repentance**
 to **all** the people of Israel;
 and as John was **completing** his course, he would say,
  '**What** do you suppose that **I** am? I am **not** he.
Behold, one is coming **after** me;
 I am not **worthy** to **unfasten** the **sandals** of his **feet**.'"

" 'For my thoughts are not your thoughts,
nor are your ways my ways,' says the LORD."
So says Isaiah 55:8. The passage is sometimes cited to explain the seemingly mysterious behavior of a God at once loving and
all-powerful. God, the argument goes, cannot be held to human standards of love,
mercy, justice, and so on. To say the least,
this may not be a very comforting answer.

If God's expression of love remains a
mystery, the expression of human love does
not. We usually know, if we are honest,
when we are acting out of love and when
we aren't. We can usually distinguish kindness from cruelty, peace from war, love from
hate. Although one may not understand how
God can love, and also be love, in the face
of so many human tragedies both global and
personal, there may lie within human power
some measure of vindication through lives
lived in loving care for one another.

READING II   The Acts of the Apostles
reports that Paul proclaimed
these words on the Sabbath in a synagogue

in the city of Perga, which was located
slightly inland on the southern coast of Asia
Minor (Acts 13:13–15). Paul and his companions, we read, were invited to speak (13:13)
and the response from both the assembled
Jews and Gentile converts to Judaism was
quite favorable (13:42–43). The speech is
quite long, stretching over 26 verses.

One of the features of Paul's preaching
in Acts is that he preaches differently to different audiences. In Athens, where Paul
addresses people who know a little philosophy, he makes his case for the Gospel

GOSPEL Matthew 1:1–25

A reading from the holy Gospel according to Matthew

The book of the genealogy of **Jesus Christ**,
  the son of **David**, the son of **Abraham**.

Abraham became the father of **Isaac**,
  Isaac the father of **Jacob**,
  Jacob the father of **Judah** and his **brothers**.
Judah became the father of **Perez** and **Zerah**,
  whose **mother** was **Tamar**.
Perez became the father of **Hezron**,
  Hezron the father of **Ram**,
  Ram the father of **Amminadab**.
Amminadab became the **father** of **Nahshon**,
  Nahshon the father of **Salmon**,
  Salmon the father of **Boaz**,
  whose **mother** was **Rahab**.
Boaz became the father of **Obed**,
  whose **mother** was **Ruth**.
Obed became the father of **Jesse**,
  Jesse the father of **David** the **king**.

David became the father of **Solomon**,
  whose **mother** had been the wife of **Uriah**.
Solomon became the father of **Rehoboam**,
  Rehoboam the father of **Abijah**,
  Abijah the father of **Asaph**.
Asaph became the father of **Jehoshaphat**,
  Jehoshaphat the father of **Joram**,
  Joram the father of **Uzziah**.

Matthew 1:2–17 contains the genealogy of Jesus. Readings like this one, which have a repetitive structure or rhythm, require special attention for good delivery. When reading this passage, make sure that you do not let it become a drone. Take care to emphasize every departure, no matter how slight, from the basic format of Jesus' genealogy.

Abraham = AY-bra-ham
Perez = PER-rez

Hezron = Hez-RONE
Ram = RAHM
Amminadab = Ah-min-ah-DAB

Nahshon = Nah-SHONE
Salmon = Sal-MONE
Boaz = BO-az
Rahad = Rah-HAB
Obed = O-BAYD

Uriah = U-RI-yah
Rehoboam = Reh-ho-bo-AM
Abijah = Ah-bi-JAH
Asaph = Ah-SAF
Jehoshaphat = Jeh-ho-shah-FAT
Joram = Jo-RAM
Uzziah = U-ZI-yah

---

using philosophical language and concepts (Acts 17:22–31). In today's reading, Paul begins to make his case for the Gospel by highlighting Jesus' Jewish heritage and royal lineage. In both Athens and the synagogue at Perga, Paul preaches to people, as the saying goes, "where they are."

Acts is a historical work. It does not look like a modern work of history in many respects, but it fits the ancient definition of a historical work in a number of respects. Like the ancient Greek historians Herodotus and Thucydides, the author of Acts "invents" speeches for the characters about whom he wrote. The author of Acts invents speeches in an attempt to provide his readers with writing more interesting than a dry recitation of facts and events, but which is also appropriate to the speaker and the events described. Lest we forget it, the Acts of the Apostles was meant to entertain in addition to telling its readership of the growth of the Church under God's direction.

In 1 Corinthians 9:20–23, we read Paul's own description of his missionary strategy that squares with the portrait of Paul in Acts as someone willing to preach differently to different people. In 1 Corinthians, Paul says that he has come as a Jew to Jews, as one under Jewish law to those under Jewish law, and as one not under Jewish law to those not under Jewish law—all in an effort to save a few of each group. In today's reading we see the author of Acts attempting to portray Paul practicing his documented missionary strategy.

GOSPEL The first verse of Mark's Gospel is this: "The beginning of the Gospel of Jesus Christ (the Son

Jotham = Jo-THAM
Ahaz = Ah-HAZ
Hezekiah = Heh-zeh-KI-yah
Manasseh = Mah-nah-SHE

Jechoniah = Jeh-cho-NI-yah

Shealtiel = She-al-ti-EL
Zerubbabel = Zeh-rub-bah-BEL
Abiud = Ah-bi-UD
Eliakim = El-i-yah-KEEM
Azor = Ah-ZOR
Zadok = Zah-DOK
Achim = Ah-CHEEM
Eliud = El-i-YUD
Eleazar = El-i-ah-ZAR
Matthan = Mat-TAN

Uzziah became the father of **Jotham**,
    Jotham the father of **Ahaz**,
    Ahaz the father of **Hezekiah**.
Hezekiah became the father of **Manasseh**,
    Manasseh the father of **Amos**,
    Amos the father of **Josiah**.
Josiah became the father of **Jechoniah** and his **brothers**
    at the time of the Babylonian **exile**.

After the Babylonian exile,
    Jechoniah became the father of **Shealtiel**,
    Shealtiel the father of **Zerubbabel**,
    Zerubbabel the father of **Abiud**.
Abiud became the father of **Eliakim**,
    Eliakim the father of **Azor**,
    Azor the father of **Zadok**.
Zadok became the father of **Achim**,
    Achim the father of **Eliud**,
    Eliud the father of **Eleazar**.
Eleazar became the father of **Matthan**,
    Matthan the father of **Jacob**,
    Jacob the father of **Joseph**, the **husband** of **Mary**.
Of **her** was born **Jesus** who is called the **Christ**.

Thus the **total** number of generations
    from **Abraham** to **David**
    is **fourteen** generations;
    from **David** to the Babylonian **exile**,
    fourteen generations;
    from the Babylonian **exile** to the **Christ**,
    fourteen generations.

of God).″ Compare these words to the first verse of Matthew′s Gospel: ″The book of the genealogy of Jesus Christ, the son of David, the son of Abraham.″ Now look at Luke 3:23–38. Luke′s genealogy begins with Jesus and moves backward and extends beyond Abraham, culminating in ″the son of Adam, the son of God.″

As a result of this ″synoptic″ reading (synoptic means ″seeing together″), one can see that Matthew at the outset of his Gospel puts Jesus′ ″Jewishness″ front and center. Jesus is both the son of Abraham, the first patriarch of Israel, and of David, the first king of the royal lines that ruled Israel and Judah until the Babylonian captivity. The first information that Matthew provides his readers, therefore, is that Jesus has a Jewish and royal pedigree.

We find several women in this list. There is Tamar (1:3), Ruth (1:5), ″the wife of Uriah″ (1:6), and Mary (1:16). Tamar and ″the wife of Uriah,″ also known as Bathsheba, have little in common except for some dubious sexual behavior (for Tamar, see Genesis 38:1–30; for Bathsheba, see 2 Samuel 11:1–27). Ruth has no such association. But she was not an Israelite but a Gentile from Moab, a people with whom Israel often warred (see Ruth 1:4). Why is Mary in their company? Why in the company of Bathsheba and Tamar in particular?

Now **this** is how the **birth** of Jesus Christ came about.
When his **mother Mary** was betrothed to **Joseph**,
    but **before** they lived together,
    she was found with **child** through the **Holy Spirit**.
Joseph her **husband**, since he was a **righteous** man,
    yet unwilling to expose her to **shame**,
    decided to **divorce** her quietly.
Such was his **intention** when, **behold**,
    the **angel** of the **Lord** appeared to him in a **dream** and said,
    "**Joseph**, son of **David**,
    do **not** be afraid to take **Mary** your wife into your home.
For it is **through** the **Holy Spirit**
    that this child has been **conceived** in her.
She will bear a **son** and you are to name him **Jesus**,
    because he will **save** his people from their **sins**."
All this took place to **fulfill**
    what the Lord had said through the **prophet**:
    Behold, *the virgin shall* **conceive** *and bear a* **son**,
      and they shall **name** *him* **Emmanuel**,
    which means "**God** is **with** us."
When Joseph **awoke**,
    he **did** as the **angel** of the **Lord** had **commanded** him
    and took his **wife** into his **home**.
He had **no** relations with her until she bore a **son**,
    and he **named** him Jesus.

[Shorter: Matthew 1:18–25]

Emmanuel = Em-man-u-EL

Perhaps Matthew places Mary in the company of Bathsheba and Tamar in order to show that he is aware of a common charge leveled against Christians in antiquity: that Jesus was not conceived by the Holy Spirit, but was rather the product of an illicit union between his mother and a stranger. While Matthew does not acknowledge this charge head-on, he effectively takes the wind out of the sails of those who would make it by calling attention to women whose sexual exploits were not impediments—and in Tamar's case necessary—to God's establishment of Israel and its monarchy. Israel's illustrious patriarchal and royal line, Matthew is saying, has an august history of unusual pregnancies. Why shouldn't Mary's pregnancy be unusual too?

Lectionary #14

READING I   Isaiah 9:1–6

A reading from the Book of the Prophet Isaiah

Notice how the prophet says very similar things, nearly repeating himself, in several of the adjacent clauses. Be sure to stress these pairings.

Midian = MIH-di-yan

The people who walked in **darkness**
    have seen a great **light**;
upon those who dwelt in the **land** of **gloom**
    a **light** has shone.
You have brought them **abundant joy**
    and **great rejoicing**,
as they rejoice before you as at the **harvest**,
    as people make **merry** when **dividing spoils**.
For the **yoke** that **burdened** them,
    the **pole** on their **shoulder**,
and the **rod** of their **taskmaster**
    you have **smashed**, as on the day of Midian.
For every **boot** that tramped in **battle**,
    every **cloak** rolled in **blood**,
    will be **burned** as **fuel** for **flames**.
For a **child** is born to **us**, a **son** is given **us**;
    upon his shoulder **dominion** rests.
They name him **Wonder-Counselor**, **God-Hero**,
    Father-Forever, **Prince** of **Peace**.
His dominion is **vast**
    and forever **peaceful**,

READING I   In the commentary for the first reading of the Fourth Sunday of Advent, December 23, it was noted that the likely original context of Isaiah 7:14 was the prediction of the birth of a son to the royal house of Judah, perhaps Hezekiah, who was the son of Ahaz and ruled during the last quarter of the eighth century BC when Assyria was encroaching ever closer on the small kingdom of Judah. Today's reading from Isaiah probably celebrates this birth.

Births, deaths, and other significant events in the lives of ancient royalty were often closely watched, interpreted, and celebrated by religious figures. The fate of a people was often popularly believed to be closely associated with the fate of its royal house. In Judah at the time of Isaiah, prophets were some of those who heralded the important events in the lives of its monarchs. The birth of a prince, an heir to the throne, would have been quite sufficient reason for a prophet like Isaiah, who lived in Jerusalem in close relation to its kings, to craft a passage such as today's reading.

The *Catechism of the Catholic Church* (CCC) gives a Christological interpretation of Isaiah 9:6, identifying Jesus as "the messianic 'Prince of Peace'" (CCC, #2305). We also find evidence of a Christ-centered tradition of the reading's interpretation in the New Testament. In Matthew 4:15, Isaiah 8:23—9:1 is fulfilled when Jesus settles in the Galilean fishing village of Capernaum and shortly thereafter begins his ministry.

It is fitting at Christmas, when we celebrate the mystery of the Incarnation to consider how Christ is present in our midst today. Consider not only when we have recognized Christ among us, but also when we could have and did not.

from David's **throne**, and over his **kingdom**,
   which he **confirms** and **sustains**
by **judgment** and **justice**,
   both **now** and **forever**.
The **zeal** of the LORD of hosts will do this!

READING II Titus 2:11–14

A reading from the Letter of Saint Paul to Titus

Beloved:
The **grace** of God has **appeared**, saving **all**
   and **training** us to **reject** godless ways and worldly desires
   and to live **temperately**, **justly**, and **devoutly** in this age,
as we await the **blessed** hope,
   the **appearance** of the **glory** of **our** great **God**
   and **savior** Jesus Christ,
who **gave** himself for **us** to **deliver** us from **all** lawlessness
   and to **cleanse** for himself a **people** as his **own**,
eager to do what is **good**.

GOSPEL Luke 2:1–14

A reading from the holy Gospel according to Luke

In those days a decree went out from **Caesar Augustus**
   that the **whole world** should be **enrolled**.
This was the **first** enrollment,
   when **Quirinius** was governor of **Syria**.

Because it is a single sentence, this reading can be difficult for people to follow. Read it slowly, pausing between the clauses.

Caesar = SEE-zer
Augustus = Aw-GUS-tus

Quirinius = Queer-IN-i-us
Syria = SEER-i-ya

READING II **Although Titus 1:1 claims Paul as the author of this letter, most modern biblical scholars think the letter was composed by someone other than Paul. As is the case with five other New Testament letters written in Paul's name (Ephesians, Colossians, 2 Thessalonians, 1 Timothy, and 2 Timothy), it is most probable that Titus was written after Paul's death. The author of the letter to Titus uses Paul's august and famous name to say what its author thinks, and subsequent generations of Christians have agreed, are some very important things.**

Some of these important things concern the personal conduct of Christians, in 2:2–10. Men and women, old and young, must be encouraged to live virtuous lives. Titus 2:11 provides the reason for this behavior: "For the grace of God has appeared, saving all." For the author of Titus the advent of saving grace is the basis for the virtuous behavior he also encourages.

This is a significant point. Most Catholic Christians no doubt agree with the members of other religions and schools of thought on many points of ethics and morals. There is nothing distinctively Christian, for example,

about holding your tongue instead of telling someone off when you really want to. The author of Titus, despite his harsh words for some in 1:10–16, would almost certainly agree, for he certainly knew that much of the exhortation in this letter squares with common Greco-Roman moral and ethical ideals. What is distinctively Christian is to hold one's tongue when one would rather speak, not only because it's decent and prudent to do so, but also *because* the grace of God has appeared on earth, and *because* Christians await the return of Christ (Titus 2:13 calls this an "epiphany"; in Greek, *epiphaneia*).

Galilee = GAL-li-lee
Nazareth = NAH-zah-reth
Bethlehem = BETH-leh-hem

So **all** went to be enrolled, **each** to his own town.
And Joseph too went up from **Galilee** from the town of **Nazareth**
   to **Judea**, to the city of **David** that is called **Bethlehem**,
     because he was of the **house** and **family** of **David**,
   to be enrolled with **Mary**, his betrothed, who was with **child**.
While they were there,
   the **time** came for her to have her child,
   and she gave **birth** to her firstborn **son**.
She **wrapped** him in swaddling clothes and **laid** him in a manger,
   because there was no room for them in the inn.

Now there were **shepherds** in that region living in the fields
   and keeping the night watch over their **flock**.
The **angel** of the **Lord appeared** to them
   and the **glory** of the Lord shone around them,
   and they were **struck** with great **fear**.
The **angel** said to them,
   "Do **not** be afraid;
   for behold, I proclaim to you **good news** of great **joy**
   that will be for **all** the people.
For **today** in the city of David
   a **savior** has been born for you who is **Christ** and **Lord**.
And this will be a **sign** for you:
   you will **find** an **infant** wrapped in swaddling clothes
   and lying in a manger."
And suddenly there was a **multitude** of the heavenly host
    with the **angel**,
   praising God and saying:
    "**Glory** to **God** in the **highest**
     and on earth **peace** to those on whom his **favor** rests."

Proclaim the words of the angels in a clear, strong way.

| GOSPEL | The author of Luke's Gospel and the Acts of the Apostles were undoubtedly the same person. You can read the opening verses of each work in order to begin to get a sense for why modern biblical scholars, along with many ancient interpreters, have believed this.

In the commentary for the second reading of the Christmas Vigil, December 24, it was observed that "invented" speeches, such as we find in Acts, were commonly composed by ancient historians. Most modern historians, however, would not accept this as a valid practice for a writer of history.

But modern historians are also quite concerned with providing their readers with reliable dates. And this is what Luke attempts to offer his readers in today's reading. The "enrollment" was what we call a census, and was taken for purposes of taxation. Luke tells us which Roman emperor (Augustus) issued the decree, which Roman official was then ruling Syria (Quirinius), and that this was the first census taken. Whether or not Luke got all of his facts straight, Luke's desire to fix the birth of Jesus to a particular date in the history of his readers' world is clear.

Luke cared very much about when, where, how, and why Jesus came to us, enough so that he researched the question for us and wrote up his findings. Interest in the history of Christian origins is no modern invention, but has been handed down to us by those who first wrote about Jesus and his Church.

NATIVITY OF THE LORD: DAWN

Lectionary #15

Zion = ZI-yon

READING I   Isaiah 62:11–12

A reading from the Book of the Prophet Isaiah

See, the LORD **proclaims**
   to the ends of the **earth**:
say to daughter **Zion**,
   your **savior comes**!
Here is his **reward** with him,
   his **recompense** before him.
They shall be called the **holy people**,
   the **redeemed** of the LORD,
and you shall be called "**Frequented**,"
   a city that is **not** forsaken.

READING I This reading rejoices in Jerusalem's reestablishment and the return of its citizens, many of whom had been held captive for decades in Babylon. While the first captives to come home would have found the city in much the same ruined condition as the Babylonians had left it, this reading celebrates their arrival in Jerusalem as a joyful occasion. As the books of Ezra and Nehemiah make clear, the rebuilding of Jerusalem was a slow business.

In the Hebrew and Greek of Isaiah 62:11–12, we find the language of buying and selling used metaphorically to describe what God has done for Jerusalem and its residents. The text describes the release of the captives from Babylon as having been purchased by God. God has paid the ransom price, has bought the slaves their freedom, and allowed them to return home. This holy people, the text says, shall be called "the redeemed of the LORD." There is little question in the Hebrew, and none in the Greek, that the people are not just the redeemed the Lord, but people redeemed *by* the Lord.

Isaiah's interpretation of the end of Babylon's captivity as God's ransom of Israel from slavery was important to the development of Christian ideas about redemption. The Christian tradition quite early picked up on similar language and metaphors to describe what God accomplished by the cross. Twice Paul reminds the Corinthians that "you have been purchased at a price" by way of warning them about particular behaviors and decisions (1 Corinthians 6:20; see also 7:23). The letter to the Galatians is filled with fervent exhortation against submission to Jewish law. To do so, Paul reasons, is to accept a kind of slavery from which Christians have been freed in Christ.

This reading is a single sentence. Read it slowly enough so that the assembly doesn't get lost.

A reading from the Letter of Saint Paul to Titus

Beloved:
When the **kindness** and **generous love**
    of God our savior **appeared**,
not because of any righteous deeds **we** had done
    but because of his **mercy**,
he **saved** us through the **bath** of **rebirth**
    and **renewal** by the Holy Spirit,
whom he **richly** poured out on us
    through **Jesus Christ** our **savior**,
so that we might be **justified** by his **grace**
    and become **heirs** in **hope** of **eternal life**.

READING II | **First Timothy, 2 Timothy, and Titus make up what are commonly called the Pastoral Epistles. These three letters are commonly grouped together because of similar vocabulary, style, and topics treated. The letters are called "pastoral" due to their keen interest in ordering Church leadership, discipline, and practice.**

There is a possibility that this reading is a prayer, or contains many elements of a prayer, that originated in baptismal liturgy. The phrase "This saying is trustworthy," which we find in Titus 3:8, probably means that the preceding text is in some way authoritative. We find the phrase multple times in the Pastoral Epistles either introducing or concluding important bits of instruction or tradition (1 Timothy 1:15; 3:1; 4:9; 2 Timothy 2:11).

The author understands Baptism as a rite of regeneration, a "bath of rebirth and renewal by the holy Spirit" (Titus 3:4–7). There is no mention of Baptism as a kind of death as we find, for example, in Romans 6:1–11 or Colossians 2:12. In those passages, Baptism is a ritual means by which the Christian is conformed to Christ in death (Colossians 2:12 even speaks of burial) followed by the reception of new life. Ephesians 5:14, which is a fragment of a prayer or song originating in a baptismal setting, speaks of an awakening from the sleep of death into the light of Christ. In today's reading, Baptism is conceived as a kind of spiritual rejuvenation or healing by the power of the Spirit. We do not see Baptism understood as death.

The text also makes clear that the "rebirth and renewal" granted in Baptism is not offered due to any human merit, but because it is God's wish to do so.

GOSPEL   Luke 2:15–20

A reading from the holy Gospel according to Luke

When the **angels** went away from them to **heaven**,
   the shepherds said to one another,
   "Let us **go**, then, to **Bethlehem**
   to **see** this thing that has taken place,
   which the **Lord** has made known to **us**."
So they went in haste and found **Mary** and **Joseph**,
   and the **infant** lying in the manger.
When they **saw** this,
   they made known the **message**
   that had been told them about **this child**.
All who heard it were **amazed**
   by what had been **told** them by the shepherds.
And **Mary** kept **all** these things,
   reflecting on them in her **heart**.
Then the shepherds returned,
   glorifying and **praising** God
   for **all** they had **heard** and **seen**,
   just as it had been **told** to them.

Pay special attention to the passage about Mary's reaction to the shepherds. Set it off somewhat from the surrounding text by pausing before and after it. Pause before "And Mary kept all these things, reflecting on them in her heart." Read this verse a little more slowly than the rest of the passage.

GOSPEL The specific vocabulary of divine epiphany found in the previous reading is not present in Luke's account of what the shepherds witness in 2:8–14. But the vocabulary of epiphany is nevertheless present. Luke reports that a divine being, an angel, "appeared to them" (from the Greek verb *ephistēmi*), told the shepherds not to be afraid, and gave them a message before the heavenly host of angels revealed themselves in splendor. All of these elements fit well with a standard Greek epiphany of a god or divine being, although we encounter similar meetings between mortals and angels in the Old Testament where little Greek cultural or religious influence can be seen.

In this Gospel selection, the shepherds tell Mary what they have just seen and heard. Imagine you have just given birth in a strange place and all of a sudden some shepherds turn up. They tell you that they have just seen some angels and that they have something to do with you and your baby. We can only wonder what Mary's response would have been had she herself not previously witnessed an epiphany (Luke 1:26–38).

In addition to the shepherds and Mary, we can add Zechariah, the father of John the Baptist, to our list of people in the first two chapters of Luke to witness epiphanies of angels (1:11–20). Luke's angels, like Matthew's dreams (see Gospel commentary, December 23), propel the story of Jesus' birth forward, reflecting its author's conviction that the advent of Jesus was guided by divine power and that he is under God's protection.

NATIVITY OF THE LORD: DAY

Lectionary #16

READING I   Isaiah 52:7–10

A reading from the Book of the Prophet Isaiah

How **beautiful** upon the mountains
    are the **feet** of him who brings **glad tidings**,
announcing **peace**, bearing **good news**,
    announcing **salvation**, and saying to Zion,
    "Your **God** is **King**!"

Hark! Your sentinels raise a **cry**,
    together they **shout** for **joy**,
for they see **directly**, before their **eyes**,
    the LORD restoring **Zion**.
Break out together in **song**,
    O **ruins** of Jerusalem!
For the LORD **comforts** his people,
    he **redeems** Jerusalem.
The LORD has **bared** his holy arm
    in the **sight** of **all** the **nations**;
all the **ends** of the **earth** will **behold**
    the **salvation** of **our** God.

This is a joyful reading. Proclaim it boldly and in a cheerful tone. Emphasize those words in particular that communicate the joyful message.

Zion = ZI-yon

READING I In the Greek translation of the Hebrew text of Isaiah 52:7, we find several words of special importance to the New Testament. The first word is *euaggelizesthai*, which means "to announce good news." We can even break the word apart a little to see why it means what it does. The first two letters, *eu*, are often found as prefix on the front of several English words, such as "euphony," which means "a good sound" or "sounding good." *Eu* means "good" or "well" And *aggeliz* means to announce, from which the word

"angel" comes. Angels are God's messengers, announcing to mortals what God has ordered them to say. In Christianity, the activity *euaggelizesthai* signifies the proclamation of the Gospel: "The law and the prophets lasted until John; but from then on the kingdom of God is proclaimed" *(euaggelizesthai)* (Luke 16:16).

Another word with a particular New Testament meaning and significance is *sōtēria*. The word means "salvation" in the New Testament, but also means "rescue," "deliverance," or even simply "help." A Greek-speaking king or ruler in the ancient

world would often apply a related noun to himself, *sōtēr* ("savior"), in official proclamations, in public inscriptions, and on coins. By this title he meant to identify himself as a people's deliverer, protector, or benefactor. The original Hebrew word translated by the Greek *sōtēria* is *yeshua*, which is closely related to the name "Jesus" (see the Gospel commentary for the Fourth Sunday of Advent, December 23).

In Isaiah, the good news being proclaimed is the restoration of Jerusalem after the Babylonian captivity. The salvation announced is the release of the captives

Let the commas mark brief pauses for you in this rather long and complicated reading.

This reading commences a comparison between Jesus and the angels. Emphasize this comparison by stressing the words "far superior" and making sure your vocal intonation communicates the author's questions. (The expected answer to them, of course, is "to none of the angels did God ever say such a thing.")

READING II   Hebrews 1:1–6

A reading from the Letter to the Hebrews

Brothers and **sisters**:
In times **past**, God **spoke** in partial and various ways
    to **our** ancestors through the **prophets**;
    in **these** last days, he has spoken to **us** through the **Son**,
    whom he made **heir** of **all** things
    and **through** whom he **created** the universe,
        who is the refulgence of his **glory**, the very **imprint**
            of his **being**,
        and who sustains **all** things by his mighty **word**.
        When he had accomplished **purification** from **sins**,
        he took his seat at the **right hand** of the Majesty on high,
        as far **superior** to the **angels**
        as the **name** he has **inherited** is more **excellent** than **theirs**.

For to which of the **angels** did God ever say:
    You are my **son**; *this day I have* **begotten** *you?*
Or again:
    I will be a **father** *to him, and he shall be a* **son** *to me?*
And again, when he leads the firstborn into the world, he says:
    Let **all** *the angels of God* **worship** *him.*

and their eventual return from Babylon to Jerusalem. But the reason we find this reading in our Catholic Lectionary heading up the readings for Christmas Day is that it has traditionally been taken to prophesy the advent of Jesus Christ. Most probably, the compilers of the Lectionary would like us to hear these words and think of Jesus Christ, whose coming among us as an infant human child we celebrate today.

| READING II | The Gospel accounts of Jesus' birth in Matthew and

Luke, both of which turn up in Advent, feature angels at every turn. The "angel of the Lord" three times appears to Joseph in dreams in Matthew's first two chapters (1:20–23; 2:13, 19-20). In Luke's Gospel, the "angel of the Lord" appears to the shepherds in the company of the angelic host of heaven (2:9–14), while the angel Gabriel appears to both the father of John the Baptist (1:11–20) and the mother of Jesus (1:26–38). In these accounts, "the angel of the Lord," Gabriel, and the host of heaven appear and act as angels typically do in Old Testament and Jewish apocryphal writings: they act as

God's messengers and in great numbers praise the God they serve.

The Hebrew word for angel also means messenger. Sometimes the only way to distinguish a human messenger from an angel in the Old Testament is to take note of whom the angel or messenger represents (God or a human being), as well as the behavior, appearance, and message given by the angel or messenger.

In this reading from Hebrews, the author compares Jesus with angels in an effort to show that, despite some basic similarities, Jesus is far greater than any angel. Like an

This reading lays out a great many of the most important ideas and subjects that the rest of the Gospel will cover. Read it slowly!

See how many clauses have two main subjects. Most clauses take the second subject of the previous clause and put it first, then adding another subject. The next clause often does the same. Thus, we have "him" and "life," "life" and "light," "light" and "darkness." As you carefully prepare this reading (and you will do yourself and the assembly a favor if you spend some time with it), pay attention to this structure and stress the pairs when you see them.

GOSPEL John 1:1–18

A reading from the holy Gospel according to John

In the **beginning** was the **Word**,
   and the **Word** was with **God**,
   and the **Word was** God.
He was in the **beginning** with God.
All things came to be **through** him,
   and **without** him **nothing** came to be.
What came to be through him was **life**,
   and this **life** was the **light** of the human race;
   the **light** shines in the **darkness**,
   and the **darkness** has **not** overcome it.
A man named **John** was sent from **God**.
He came for **testimony**, to testify to the **light**,
   so that **all** might **believe** through him.
He was **not** the light,
   but came to **testify** to the **light**.
The **true** light, which enlightens **everyone**,
   was **coming** into the **world**.
He was **in** the world,
   and the world came to be **through** him,
   but the world did **not** know him.
He came to what was his **own**,
   but his own people did **not** accept him.

angel, the author says, Jesus sits in close proximity to God. But the author also points out that God has called Jesus "son," which God has not declared of any angel (1:5), and that the angels have even been commanded to worship Jesus (1:6). Though Jesus and the angels reside with God in heaven, Jesus' greatness exceeds that of the angels.

Each Christmas, without fail, the image of Clarence, the wingless angel of Frank Capra's *It's a Wonderful Life,* grins wryly from millions of television sets throughout North America. Perhaps Clarence, with his

modern clothes and all-knowing compassion, permits viewers to toy with the idea of the connection of the natural world to the supernatural. But our author wants his readers to do much more than that. To him, Jesus Christ is a far more fitting object of human interest than any angel.

GOSPEL   In John's Gospel, Jesus travels in secret to the celebration of the festival of Sukkoth in Jerusalem (7:10). By this point in the story, Jesus has become quite famous for perform-

ing signs. In Jerusalem, the question of the day is "Where is he?" While Jesus teaches in the temple area, members of his audience, marveling at his erudition (7:15), begin to wonder: "Could the authorities have realized that he is the Messiah?" Their trouble with calling Jesus the Messiah, however, is that they believe they know way too much about Jesus for him to be a credible candidate: "But we know where he is from. When the Messiah comes, no one will know where he is from" (John 7:26–27). Jesus is from Nazareth of Galilee, right? How could he be the Messiah (see John 7:52)?

But to those who **did** accept him
 he gave **power** to become **children** of **God**,
 to those who **believe** in his name,
 who were born **not** by natural generation
 nor by human choice **nor** by a man's decision
 but of **God**.
 And the **Word** became **flesh**
  and made his **dwelling among us**,
  and **we** saw his **glory**,
  the **glory** as of the Father's **only** Son,
  full of **grace** and **truth**.
John **testified** to him and **cried out**, saying,
 "This was he of whom I said,
 'The one who is coming **after** me ranks **ahead** of me
 because he existed **before** me.'"
From his **fullness** we have **all** received,
 grace in place of **grace**,
 because while the **law** was given **through Moses**,
 grace and **truth** came **through Jesus Christ**.
No one has ever seen God.
The **only Son**, **God**, who is at the Father's **side**,
 has **revealed** him.

[Shorter: John 1:1–5, 9–14]

Where is Jesus from? This question comes up repeatedly in John's Gospel. In the controversy of John 9 over the man born blind, the people and the Pharisees react angrily to the man's claim that Jesus healed his blindness: "You are that man's disciple," they declare, "we are disciples of Moses! We know that God spoke to Moses, but we do not know where this one is from" (John 9:28–29). When in John 8 Pharisees question Jesus about his testimony, Jesus replies this way: "Even if I do testify on my own behalf, my testimony can be verified, because I know where I came from and where I am going. But you do not know where I come from or where I am going" (John 8:14). And during Jesus' trial, Pilate asks Jesus "Where are you from?" Jesus does not reply.

Where is Jesus from? We find the answer to this question that is debated throughout the Gospel present in its first verse. The word, Jesus, "was with God" and "was God." John's answer is that Jesus is from heaven.

But why can't everyone see this? Is it because people can't or won't? John has no clearly defined position on this question. But it seems true that over time the view grows from dimness to brilliance among Jesus' disciples that who Jesus is, and what he does, are bound up with where he comes from. Thus, the man born blind, in the first flush of faith, answers his accusers: "This is what is so amazing, that you do not know where he is from, yet he opened my eyes." "You've seen what he did," the man is saying, "what more do you require to believe that this man comes from God?"

HOLY FAMILY OF JESUS, MARY, AND JOSEPH

Lectionary #17

READING I   Sirach 3:2–6, 12–14

A reading from the Book of Sirach

God sets a **father** in **honor** over his **children**;
    a **mother's authority** he confirms over her **sons**.
Whoever **honors** his **father atones** for **sins**,
    and **preserves** himself from them.
When he **prays**, he is **heard**;
    he stores up **riches** who reveres his **mother**.
Whoever **honors** his **father** is gladdened by children,
    and, when he **prays**, is **heard**.
Whoever **reveres** his **father** will live a long life;
    he who **obeys** his **father** brings **comfort** to his **mother**.

My son, take **care** of your father when he is **old**;
    grieve him **not** as long as he **lives**.
Even if his mind **fail**, be **considerate** of him;
    revile him **not** all the days of **his life**;
kindness to a father will **not** be forgotten,
    firmly **planted** against the **debt** of your sins
    —a house **raised** in **justice** to you.

The rhythm provided by the repeated refrain "whoever" can easily become a drone if you do not vary your delivery. So take care to emphasize the verbs in particular.

READING I In chapter 15 of Matthew's Gospel, Pharisees and scribes travel from Jerusalem to Gennesaret after Jesus has healed many people there (Matthew 14:34–36). They come in order to ask, "Why do your disciples break the tradition of the elders? They do not wash [their] hands when they eat a meal" (Matthew 15:2). What the Pharisees are really trying to gauge is the position of Jesus and his disciples on Jewish dietary law.

Jesus replies with a question of his own: "And why do you break the commandment of God for the sake of your tradition? For God said, 'Honor your father and your mother,' and 'Whoever curses father or mother shall die.' But you say, 'Whoever says to father or mother, "Any support you might have had from me is dedicated to God," need not honor his father.' You have nullified the word of God for the sake of your tradition." What Jesus wants to show is that the Pharisees' reliance upon tradition does

not always have the support of scripture, and in at least one instance even stands in clear opposition.

Both Jesus and Sirach in today's reading offer interpretations of the fourth of the Ten Commandments (Exodus 20:12; Deuteronomy 5:16). Both Sirach and Jesus agree that honoring one's parents is more than having an attitude of respect and gratitude toward them. Honoring parents means caring for the

A reading from the Letter of Saint Paul to the Colossians

Brothers and **sisters**:
Put on, as God's chosen ones, **holy** and **beloved**,
   heartfelt **compassion**, **kindness**, **humility**, **gentleness**,
     and **patience**,
   bearing with one another and **forgiving** one another,
   if one has a **grievance** against another;
   as the **Lord** has forgiven **you**, so must **you** also do.
And over **all** these put on **love**,
   that is, the **bond** of **perfection**.
And let the **peace** of **Christ** control your **hearts**,
   the **peace** into which you were **also** called in one body.
And be **thankful**.
Let the **word** of **Christ** dwell in you **richly**,
   as in all **wisdom** you **teach** and **admonish** one another,
   singing **psalms**, **hymns**, and **spiritual songs**
   with **gratitude** in your hearts to **God**.
And **whatever** you do, in **word** or in **deed**,
   do **everything** in the name of the Lord **Jesus**,
   giving **thanks** to God the Father **through** him.

Wives, be subordinate to your **husbands**,
   as is **proper** in the Lord.
Husbands, love your **wives**,
   and **avoid** any bitterness toward them.

Slow down when you read the list of virtues so that each one can register with the assembly. Pronounce the name of each virtue clearly and distinctly, and then pause for a brief moment before announcing the name of the second virtue.

---

needs of the people who raised you, supporting them financially if need be, restraining one's criticism of them—in short, to love them in deed as well as in word.

READING II In today's reading from Colossians, particularly 3:18–21, we find what was already a well-worn literary theme by the time of its composition: the proper governance and hierarchy of the household. The author's advice does

not stop at 3:21, but continues on until 4:1. In 3:22—4:1 he advises slaves to be obedient to their masters and masters to be decent and fair to their slaves. Parents, children, and slaves were all considered members of the ancient household. Our author is interested in all of them.

The subject of the household assumes a special importance in early Christianity not only because the household was the most basic social unit of the Church, but also because Christian worship typically

happened in houses. Atheism was a common early charge aimed at Christians by their far more numerous non-Christian neighbors. Why? Because the Christians usually had no public religious architecture: no temples, no altars, no statues of gods, and no sacred groves. In short, early Christianity had few, if any, of the public signs of a religion to first-century Mediterranean eyes. Christian gatherings happened in homes. Therefore, order within homes was very important to the health of the Christian religion.

Children, obey your **parents** in **everything**,
　　for this is **pleasing** to the Lord.
Fathers, do **not** provoke your **children**,
　　so they may not become **discouraged**.

[Shorter: Colossians 3:12–17]

GOSPEL　Matthew 2:13–15, 19–23

A reading from the holy Gospel according to Matthew

When the magi had departed, **behold**,
　　the **angel** of the **Lord** appeared to Joseph in a **dream** and said,
　　"Rise, take the **child** and his **mother**; flee to **Egypt**,
　　and **stay** there until I tell you.
Herod is going to **search** for the child to **destroy** him."
Joseph **rose** and **took** the child and his mother by night
　　and departed for **Egypt**.
He **stayed** there until the **death** of Herod,
　　that what the **Lord** had said through the **prophet**
　　　might be **fulfilled**,
　　Out of **Egypt** *I called my* **son***.*

When Herod had died, **behold**,
　　the **angel** of the **Lord** appeared in a **dream**
　　to **Joseph** in Egypt and said,
　　"**Rise**, take the child and his mother and
　　　go to the land of **Israel**,
　　for those who **sought** the child's life are **dead**."
He rose, took the child and his mother,
　　and went to the land of **Israel**.

Boldly proclaim the angel's words here.

Emphasize the word "fulfilled." It is very important to Matthew's Christology that Jesus' birth, life, ministry, Passion, death, and Resurrection fulfill scripture.

Christian worship and fellowship in urban settings first happened in private homes. If we continue reading in Colossians, we will meet a woman from Laodicea named Nympha. Paul greets her and "the Church in her house" (Colossians 4:15). In Romans, Paul sends greetings to the Roman Christians from Gaius, a Corinthian man, whom Paul calls "host to me and to the whole church" (Romans 16:23). In addition to Philemon, to whom Paul wrote a letter about a runaway slave, Paul greets "the church at your house" (Philemon 2). Among the earliest Christian

Churches excavated by archaeologists is a simple house of the Syrian city of Dura that Christians had specifically modified for sacramental worship. In Rome today one can visit churches, called *tituli,* standing on the sites once occupied by the first houses in which Roman Christians gathered in petition and praise of Jesus Christ.

GOSPEL　There are reports of five dreams in Matthew's first two chapters (see the Gospel commentary for the Fourth Sunday of Advent, December

23). Joseph has four of them. In three of these dreams (1:20; 2:13, 19), Matthew makes clear that it is "the angel of the Lord" who appears to Joseph. Some angels have proper names in the New Testament, such as Gabriel (Luke 1:19, 26) and Michael (Jude 9; Revelation 12:7). We often meet individual angels in Revelation who are not named. And sometimes we meet figures acting like angels, and whom we suspect may be angels, but are not identified as such (see Mark 16:5–7, Luke 24:4–7).

Archelaus = ar-keh-LAY-us

Nazorean = naz-oh-REE-un

But when he heard that **Archelaus** was ruling over **Judea**
in place of his father Herod,
he was **afraid** to go back there.
And because he had been warned in a **dream**,
he departed for the region of **Galilee**.
He went and **dwelt** in a town called **Nazareth**,
so that what had been **spoken** through the **prophets**
might be **fulfilled**,
*He shall be called a **Nazorean***.

Aren't all angels, by definition, "of the Lord"? Why specify, as Matthew does, that it is "the angel of the Lord" who speaks to Joseph in dreams?

The angel of the Lord is the title of a divine messenger from God given a special commission to deliver certain information to mortals. It is "the angel of the Lord" who speaks to Moses from the burning bush (Exodus 3:2). We encounter the angel of the Lord in the episode of Balaam and the ass (Numbers 22). The angel of the Lord gives Israel some bad news in Judges 2:1–5, appears to Gideon in Judges 6, helps Elijah in 1 Kings 19:5–7, attacks the Assyrian army on behalf of Jerusalem in 2 Kings 19:35, and pops up repeatedly in the books of the prophets Daniel and Zechariah.

In specifying that the angel who appears to Joseph is "the angel of the Lord," Matthew tells his readers that God's own divine ambassador, the messenger who gave oracles to Moses from the burning bush and encouraged the prophet Elijah in the wilderness, is the same angel who now helps Joseph protect Jesus from those who want to harm him. The angel of the Lord thus connects the story of Joseph and his family to the sacred history of Israel.

MARY, THE MOTHER OF GOD

Aaron = AIR-ron

Make eye contact with the congregation
as you read the blessing.

Lectionary #18

READING I   Numbers 6:22–27

A reading from the Book of Numbers

The LORD said to Moses:
"Speak to **Aaron** and his **sons** and tell them:
   This is how you shall bless the Israelites.
Say to them:
   The LORD **bless** you and **keep** you!
   The LORD let his face **shine** upon you, and be **gracious** to you!
   The LORD look upon you **kindly** and give you **peace**!
So shall they invoke **my name** upon the Israelites,
   and I will **bless** them."

READING I   This blessing found in this reading may be familiar to many in the assembly. One hears it from time to time as a final blessing.

The priests of Israel and Judah did not live celibate lives. The priestly office in Israel and Judah was handed down from father to son. Priestly lineage, as one can see from Numbers 3, mattered a great deal. The introductory verses to the book of the prophet Jeremiah mention not only Jeremiah's ancestry and his family's hometown of Anathoth, but his priestly lineage as well.

To the various compilers and editors of the five books of Moses (Genesis, Exodus, Leviticus, Numbers, and Deuteronomy), information about liturgical celebrations from the days of Moses and Aaron were clearly of great interest. Some of them were undoubtedly priests themselves. While the extensive genealogical information of the book of Numbers may strike many modern readers as tedious, one imagines that these seemingly tedious parts were of keen interest to priests of Israel and Judah, who, as members of priestly lineages, likely viewed Numbers as family history.

Like Aaron, Moses was considered the patriarch of several priestly lines. But Moses' function during the exodus is more prophetic than priestly. Indeed, little information comes to Aaron's priestly line except through Moses' mediation.

In both the original Hebrew and its Greek translation, this blessing is composed of several statements expressed in the verbal moods used for commands or the expression of urgent hopes and desires. This is the typical language of prayer and petition in the Hebrew Bible and its Greek translations.

READING II   Galatians 4:4–7

A reading from the Letter of Saint Paul to the Galatians

Brothers and **sisters**:
When the **fullness** of time had come, **God** sent his **Son**,
   born of a **woman**, **born** under the **law**,
   to **ransom** those under the law,
   so that we might receive **adoption** as sons.
As **proof** that you are **sons**,
   God sent the **Spirit** of his **Son** into our **hearts**,
   crying out, "**Abba**, **Father**!"
So you are no longer a **slave** but a **son**,
   and if a **son** then also an **heir**, through God.

Let the commas mark brief pauses in your delivery.

Abba = AH-bah

With a fair degree of accuracy, one may understand this blessing as a set of strongly stated requests of God.

READING II Paul's letter to the Galatians is a single, multipronged argument spanning six chapters. The word "argument" describes Galatians not because the letter records both sides of an angry dispute, but because Paul builds and defends a case much as an ancient lawyer might have prepared a case to present before a judge.

It seems that the Galatian men, who are predominately Gentile by birth, have been told by visiting Christian missionaries that they need to be circumcised in order to be genuine Christians. Paul not only disagrees, but also argues that for the Galatians to accept circumcision, or to observe any rule, with such a belief undermines not only his own apostolate but also the Gospel itself. One gets a proper relationship with God, Paul claims, by faith in Jesus Christ, not by observing any religious laws.

Prior to today's selection, Paul has been describing the law as something fitting for spiritual childhood. The law, he says, has been a "disciplinarian for Christ" (3:24). The Greek word our Bible translates as "disciplinarian" *(paidagōgos)* is the title of a slave whose job it was to walk a child to and from school. But now that Christ has come, the Galatians are God's mature sons and daughters. Why would mature adults need someone to walk them to school? They're done with school!

In today's reading, Paul contends that the Crucifixion, death, and Resurrection of Jesus Christ are God's way of removing the Galatians out from under anyone's power but God's. The Galatians, once orphaned children, are now God's own adopted heirs.

Bethlehem = BETH-leh-hem

Pause before and after Mary's reaction to the shepherds.

GOSPEL   Luke 2:16–21

A reading from the holy Gospel according to Luke

The **shepherds** went in **haste** to **Bethlehem**
     and found **Mary** and **Joseph**,
   and the **infant** lying in the manger.
When they **saw** this,
   they made known the **message**
     that had been told them about **this child**.
All who heard it were **amazed**
     by what had been **told** them by the shepherds.
And **Mary** kept **all** these things,
   reflecting on them in her **heart**.
Then the shepherds returned,
   glorifying and **praising** God
     for **all** they had **heard** and **seen**,
   just as it had been **told** to them.

When eight days were **completed** for his circumcision,
   he was named **Jesus**, the name given him by the **angel**
     before he was conceived in the **womb**.

GOSPEL   "Mother of God" is a title of Mary with an interesting history. This phrase is a translation of the Greek word *Theotokos*. It does not occur in today's Gospel selection or in the New Testament. Subsequent generations of Christians gave her this title after reaching decisions about Jesus' divine and human natures.

This title assumed a special importance in the fifth century AD. A hundred years earlier in 325, the Council of Nicea had sought to settle some doctrinal questions regarding divine nature and the relationship among the members of the Holy Trinity.

People came to Nicea to debate some questions. Did the God the Father create God the Son? Was there ever a time when the Father existed but the Son did not? In answer to both of these questions, just two of many addressed, the Council said, "No." Jesus was "eternally begotten" and "one in being with the Father." But as is often the case with getting firm answers to a question, some Christians found themselves with new questions.

If Jesus' divinity was equal to the Father's, how did his human nature relate to

his divine nature? How could it? In particular, did Mary give birth to both Jesus' divine and human natures, or just to his human nature? A bishop called Nestorius said that while Mary clearly bore Jesus, it was improper on the basis of scripture to call her the Mother of God. Against Nestorius, bishop Cyril of Alexandria argued before the Council of Ephesus in 431 AD that Mary bore Jesus in both his natures. Like Nestorius, he too appealed to scripture. Cyril eventually carried the day and the Council condemned Nestorius' opinions.

EPIPHANY OF THE LORD

Lectionary #20

READING I   Isaiah 60:1–6

A reading from the Book of the Prophet Isaiah

> **Rise up** in splendor, Jerusalem! Your **light** has **come**,
>   the **glory** of the LORD shines upon you.
> See, **darkness** covers the **earth**,
>   and thick **clouds** cover the **peoples**;
> but upon **you** the LORD **shines**,
>   and over **you** appears his **glory**.
> **Nations** shall walk by your **light**,
>   and **kings** by your shining **radiance**.
> **Raise** your eyes and **look** about;
>   they all **gather** and **come** to you:
> your **sons** come from **afar**,
>   and your **daughters** in the **arms** of their **nurses**.
>
> Then you shall be **radiant** at what you see,
>   your heart shall **throb** and **overflow**,
> for the **riches** of the **sea** shall be **emptied** out before you,
>   the **wealth** of **nations** shall be **brought** to you.
> Caravans of **camels** shall fill you,
>   dromedaries from **Midian** and **Ephah**;
> all from **Sheba** shall **come**
>   bearing gold and **frankincense**,
>   and proclaiming the **praises** of the LORD.

When you read the line "Raise your eyes and look about," look up and make eye contact with the assembly.

Midian = MID-ee-un
Ephah = EE-fah
Sheba = SHEE-buh

READING I If you look back and scan the readings for Advent and Christmas, you will find several Old Testament selections from the latter chapters of the book of Isaiah. This is no accident. From New Testament times on, Christians have seen in Isaiah 40—66 prophesy not only of the advent of Christ, but the mission and growth of the Church.

While Isaiah is not separated into several distinct books (one does not open Isaiah and find 1 Isaiah, 2 Isaiah, and 3 Isaiah), it has nevertheless been the opinion of many modern scholars wanting to understand how the book was composed, that Isaiah 40—66 almost exclusively comes from a period at the close of the exile in Babylon. The fall of the kingdom of Judah and the destruction of the city of Jerusalem, the period of Babylonian exile and captivity, and the promise and beginning of the exiles' return is the main set of events Isaiah 40—66 interprets.

In its original context, today's selection predicted the grandeur of Jerusalem restored and rebuilt. The prophet imagined a total reversal of fortune for the once ruined city. Not only will its former residents return, but Gentiles will come, not in war as the Assyrians and Babylonians did, but with great wealth while "proclaiming the praises of the Lord" (Isaiah 60:6).

But this reading heads up today's readings for the feast of the Epiphany for a different reason. Most probably, the compilers of our Lectionary encourage us to see in "the wealth of nations" flowing into Israel from Gentile lands a prophecy of the three eastern magi who came from the east with lavish gifts for the infant Jesus and the inclusion of the Gentiles in God's covenantal relationship with Israel.

READING II — Ephesians 3:2–3a, 5–6

A reading from the Letter of Saint Paul to the Ephesians

Brothers and **sisters**:
You have **heard** of the stewardship of God's **grace**
　　that was given to me for your **benefit**,
　　　　namely, that the **mystery** was made known to me
　　　　　　by **revelation**.
It was **not** made known to people in **other** generations
　　as it has **now** been revealed
　　to his holy **apostles** and **prophets** by the **Spirit**:
　　that the **Gentiles** are **coheirs**, members of the **same** body,
　　and **copartners** in the **promise** in **Christ Jesus**
　　　　through the **gospel**.

Emphasize in particular the words "coheirs," "same," and "copartners."

GOSPEL — Matthew 2:1–12

A reading from the holy Gospel according to Matthew

When **Jesus** was born in **Bethlehem** of **Judea**,
　　in the days of King **Herod**,
　　behold, **magi** from the **east** arrived in **Jerusalem**, saying,
　　"**Where** is the newborn king of the Jews?
We saw his **star** at its **rising**
　　and have come to do him **homage**."

Bethlehem = BETH-leh-hem
Judea = Ju-DEE-yah

READING II Today's selection from the letter to the Christians of Ephesus, though probably not written by Paul (see commentary for Reading II, Immaculate Conception, December 8), includes what was perhaps the best-known bit of biographical information about him, namely that he encountered Jesus Christ through some kind of revelation. This revelation of Jesus to Paul was something about which Paul wrote himself and which sufficiently interested others, including our present author, to write about it as well. In the letter to the Churches of Galatia, which Paul certainly wrote, Paul describes himself as a persecutor of the Church, but that when God "was pleased to reveal his Son to me," he reports that his ministry began straightaway. In 1 Corinthians 9:1, Paul mentions that he has seen the Lord, and later in 15:8 places himself as the last among those to whom Jesus appeared. Perhaps most well-known of all is the account of Acts 9, in which the author depicts Paul's reception of a revelation of Jesus on the road to Damascus that leaves him temporarily blinded.

This reading from Ephesians refers to this personal revelation to Paul (3:3) and another revelation, which was "revealed to his holy apostles and prophets by the Spirit" (3:5). What this revelation contains is the information that the Gentiles are "coheirs, members of the same body, and copartners in the promise in Christ Jesus through the gospel" (3:6).

This was not obvious information. We read that Jesus himself had the idea that he had come on behalf of Israel alone (Matthew 15:24; see also 10:6). Some Christians were convinced that Gentiles who wanted to

Harod = HAIR-rud

When King Herod heard this,
  he was **greatly troubled**,
  and **all** Jerusalem with him.
Assembling all the chief **priests** and the **scribes** of the **people**,
  he **inquired** of them where the **Christ** was to be **born**.
They said to him, "In **Bethlehem** of **Judea**,
  for thus it has been **written** through the **prophet**:
    *And you, **Bethlehem**, land of **Judah**,*
      *are by **no** means **least** among the **rulers** of Judah;*
      *since from **you** shall come a **ruler**,*
      *who is to **shepherd** my people **Israel**."*
Then **Herod** called the **magi** secretly
  and ascertained from them the **time** of the star's appearance.
He sent them to **Bethlehem** and said,
  "Go and search **diligently** for the **child**.

When you proclaim Herod's lines, let your delivery reflect the fact that he is scheming and lying to the Magi.

When you have **found** him, bring me **word**,
  that I too may **go** and do him **homage**."
After their **audience** with the **king** they set out.
And **behold**, the star that they had **seen** at its **rising**
    preceded them,
  until it **came** and **stopped** over the place where the child was.
They were **overjoyed** at seeing the star,
  and on **entering** the house
  they saw the **child** with **Mary** his **mother**.
They prostrated themselves and did him **homage**.
Then they **opened** their **treasures**

myrrh = mur

  and offered him gifts of **gold**, **frankincense**, and **myrrh**.
And having been **warned** in a **dream** not to return to Herod,
  they departed for their country by another way.

become Christians had first to take some steps toward observance of Jewish religious law. The degree of Jewish practice, if any, that Gentiles had to adopt was a controversy that occupied the Christian movement for much of the first century. It emerged quite naturally and understandably from the kind of belief expressed in Ephesians 3:6.

GOSPEL   Matthew and Luke are the only evangelists who tell of Jesus' birth, and one of the most interesting features of these two Gospels is how they account for Jesus' birth in Bethlehem. As

we know, all four Gospels record that Jesus was from Galilee and that much of his ministry took place there. But Bethlehem is not in Galilee; in fact, it is many miles to the south. Luke records that Jesus was born in Bethlehem during his family's visit there (Luke 2:1–7), while in today's selection from Matthew it appears that Jesus is born at home (Matthew 2:11). While the evangelists differ on how Jesus and his family found themselves in Bethlehem, the little town remains their common feature. Why?

Among first-century Jews who hoped for a "messiah," many speculated that a

royal figure, perhaps someone descended from King David, truly fit the bill. David's family was originally from Bethlehem (1 Samuel 16), which gave rise to the messianic tradition Matthew places in the mouths of the high priests and scribes of Herod's court (2:4–6; see also John 7:42). Joseph, according to Matthew's and Luke's genealogies, was of David's line and so Bethlehem was his ancestral village (Matthew 1:1–17; Luke 3:23–38).

BAPTISM OF THE LORD

Lectionary #21

READING I Isaiah 42:1–4, 6–7

A reading from the Book of the Prophet Isaiah

Let the rhythm of your proclamation reflect the parallel structure of the poetry. There are often two, sometimes three, words or ideas describing similar things.

Thus says the LORD:
Here is my servant whom I **uphold**,
  my **chosen** one with whom I am **pleased**,
upon whom I have put my **spirit**;
  he shall bring forth **justice** to the **nations**,
not crying out, **not** shouting,
  not making his voice heard in the street.
A **bruised reed** he shall **not** break,
  and a **smoldering wick** he shall **not** quench,
until he establishes **justice** on the **earth**;
  the coastlands will wait for his **teaching**.

I, the LORD, have called **you** for the victory of **justice**,
  I have **grasped** you by the hand;
I **formed you**, and set **you**
  as a **covenant** of the **people**,
  a **light** for the **nations**,
to open the **eyes** of the **blind**,
  to bring out **prisoners** from **confinement**,
  and from the **dungeon**, those who live in **darkness**.

READING I Biblical scholars have traditionally divided the book of the prophet Isaiah into three major sections based on the judgment that these three major sections were likely composed at different times, by different people, and in response to different circumstances. According to this traditional division, Isaiah 1—39 contains the oldest material, 40—55 the next oldest, and 56—66 the most recent. In recent decades, scholars agree less about these divisions. Some have shown that one can find significant themes in all three of the book's sections (see commentary I, First Sunday of Advent, December 2).

Today's reading is one of the pieces of evidence scholars have long used to distinguish Isaiah 40—55 from what comes before and after it. This reading comes from the first of four so-called "servant songs" found in Isaiah (42:1–9; 49:1–7; 50:4–11; 52:13—53:12) and which, some have maintained, reflect the interest in redemptive suffering characterizing Isaiah 40—55.

In their original historical context, these songs may have referred to a particular but unnamed individual. Many candidates have been put forward: Jeremiah, one of the kings of Judah, Isaiah and his students, the Persian king Cyrus (see Isaiah 44:28; 45:1). In the second of these songs, it seems as though the servant is Israel itself (49:3).

To Matthew the evangelist, there can be no confusion about the identity of the servant in today's reading. It is Jesus.

READING II Previous commentaries contain the opinion that Luke and Acts are two parts of a single historical

READING II   Acts 10:34–38

A reading from the Acts of the Apostles

Peter proceeded to speak to those gathered
  in the house of Cornelius, saying:
"In truth, I see that God shows **no** partiality.
Rather, in **every** nation whoever fears him and acts uprightly
  is **acceptable** to him.
You know the **word** that he sent to the **Israelites**
  as he proclaimed **peace** through **Jesus Christ**, who is **Lord** of **all**,
  what has **happened** all over Judea,
  beginning in **Galilee** after the **baptism**
  that **John** preached,
  how God **anointed** Jesus of Nazareth
  with the **Holy Spirit** and **power**.
He went about doing **good**
  and **healing** all those oppressed by the **devil**,
  for **God** was **with** him."

Cornelius = Cor-NEE-li-us

Galilee = GAL-li-lee

Nazareth = NAH-zah-reth

Pause and look up at the assembly when you proclaim the final words of this reading.

---

work. A few of the problems with understanding these books as a history have been discussed (commentary II, Christmas Vigil, December 24; Gospel commentary, Christmas Midnight, December 25). Today we encounter some other unusual features of viewing Luke and Acts as a history.

Today's reading takes place in Cesaraea, a city on Palestine's Mediterranean coast. There, Peter confesses to the centurion Cornelius that he has learned something quite new. "In truth," Peter says, "I see that God shows no partiality. Rather, in every nation whoever fears him and acts uprightly

is acceptable to him." This unlikely pair, the Galilean fisherman and the Roman army officer, have been brought together by equally unlikely means. Cornelius has been instructed by an angel to fetch someone called Peter from Joppa (Acts 10:1–8), and a day later Peter has experienced his own perplexing vision bringing into question everything he thinks he knows about the ritual cleanliness of food (10:9–16).

According to the description offered us in Acts, the early Church was not an institution built by enterprising men and women. *God* created it, perhaps more in spite of its

early members than because of them. But by remaining open and obedient to God, Peter is blessed with the opportunity to change his mind and bear witness to the growth of the Church to include people he would never have imagined.

GOSPEL   All four Gospels place Jesus with John at the Jordan River before the beginning of Jesus' own ministry. This fact has led some interpreters to speculate that Jesus was himself first a disciple of John before beginning his own

Galilee = GAL-li-lee
Jordan = JOR-dan

Try to communicate the strength of John's objection. He can scarcely believe what he's hearing. Use your voice to communicate his shock and surprise.

Pause before you proclaim the words "This is my beloved son." Read them slowly and clearly.

GOSPEL   Matthew 3:13–17

A reading from the holy Gospel according to Matthew

Jesus came from **Galilee** to **John** at the **Jordan**
    to be baptized by him.
John tried to **prevent** him, saying,
    "I need to be baptized by **you**,
    and yet **you** are coming to **me**?"
Jesus said to him in reply,
    "Allow it now, for thus it is **fitting** for us
    to **fulfill** all righteousness."
Then he allowed him.
After Jesus was **baptized**,
    he came up from the water and **behold**,
    the **heavens** were **opened** for him,
    and he saw the **Spirit** of **God** descending like a **dove**
    and coming upon him.
And a **voice** came from the **heavens**, saying,
    "**This** is my beloved **Son**, with whom I am **well pleased**."

ministry. The testimony of Acts 1:15–26 and John 1:35–42 suggests that Jesus and his first disciples met one another through their association with John the Baptist's ministry.

It helps to compare the four different accounts of Jesus' Baptism by John (Matthew 3:13–17; Mark 1:9–11; Luke 3:21–22; and John 1:29–34). Mark says simply that Jesus came, and John baptized him. Matthew provides the same information, but includes a minor argument between John and Jesus on whether it is more fitting for John or Jesus to be baptized by the other.

Luke says only that Jesus was baptized, but never says who did it. If we want to assume that it was John, then we must account for the immediately preceding verses (3:19–20) in which Luke writes of John's incarceration. John (the evangelist) does not narrate Jesus' Baptism at all. But like the other three evangelists, John (the evangelist) puts Jesus with John (the Baptist) before Jesus begins his own ministry.

Why do we have such different accounts of Jesus' Baptism and time spent with John? Acts records that Christian missionaries met people in far-flung locales

who knew of John's baptism (Acts 18:25; 19:3–4). To admit that John baptized Jesus might have meant to some that John was Jesus' superior. In the Gospels we have echoes of possible rivalry between the disciples of John and Jesus (in Matthew see 9:14 and 11:11). If this is so, then Matthew does not blink, but acknowledges the issue head-on with his description of the argument between Jesus and John (3:14–15).

2ND SUNDAY IN ORDINARY TIME

Lectionary #64

Emphasize the first line of this reading in particular.

READING I   Isaiah 49:3, 5−6

A reading from the Book of the Prophet Isaiah

The LORD said to me: **You** are my **servant**,
   Israel, through whom I show my **glory**.
Now the LORD has **spoken**
   who **formed** me as his **servant** from the **womb**,
that **Jacob** may be **brought back** to him
   and **Israel** gathered to him;
and I am made **glorious** in the sight of the LORD,
   and my God is now my **strength**!
It is too little, the LORD says, for you to be my **servant**,
   to raise up the **tribes** of Jacob,
      and restore the **survivors** of Israel;
I will make you a **light** to the **nations**,
   that my **salvation** may reach to the ends of the earth.

READING I   In a previous commentary, it was noted that some scholars have identified certain "servant songs" in the book of Isaiah (commentary I, Baptism of the Lord, January 13). This reading comes from the second of these four songs (Isaiah 49:1–7).

   While the identity of the servant is not certain in the other songs (52:13—53:12, for example), in this passage the servant is plainly identified as Israel (49:3). And if we interpret the passage against recent historical events to which Isaiah 40—66 in part responds, then we see a brief, nutshell interpretation of the history and destiny of the people of Israel.

   From the time of its infancy, Israel has been God's chosen servant, selected as a means for God to be glorified before all people (49:1–3). While the servant confesses his own past doubts about his success (49:4), he explains how God put those doubts to rest by making him "a light to the nations, that my salvation may reach to the ends of the earth" (Isaiah 49:5–7).

   Times come in many, perhaps most, human lives when a person feels utterly destroyed. These times are probably hardest if you can look at your situation squarely and see that you actually contributed to things being the way they are. In the pit of those times it is often impossible to imagine future happiness, passion for work or family, or that there is any value at all to be found in life. Isaiah 49:4 recalls such a time, when the servant believed the mission he was born to complete had failed completely. The song's final verses inform us of what is now clear to the servant, but back then was impossible to understand—that even in the midst of all that failure, misery, and even despair, God was quietly at work for good.

Read the address slowly enough that the assembly can follow the relation of the clauses to one another. Let the commas mark your pauses.

Sosthenes = Sos-THEN-eez

Corinth-COR-inth

Make a point of slowing down and pronouncing with great clarity the phrase "with all those everywhere who call upon the name of our Lord Jesus Christ, their Lord and ours." These words set up the theme of unity that will dominate the letter.

READING II   1 Corinthians 1:1–3

A reading from the first Letter of Saint Paul to the Corinthians

Paul, called to be an **apostle** of Christ **Jesus** by the will of **God**,
    and **Sosthenes** our **brother**,
    to the church of **God** that is in **Corinth**,
    to you who have been **sanctified** in Christ Jesus,
    called to be **holy**,
    with all those **everywhere** who call upon the name of our **Lord**
        Jesus Christ, **their** Lord and **ours**.
Grace to you and **peace** from **God** our Father
    and the Lord **Jesus Christ**.

READING II | Paul usually tips his hand in the opening addresses of his letters to let the careful reader know something about the words to come. These normally brief, introductory passages tell us the identities of senders and recipients, but they also tell us something about the letter we are getting ready to read.

But before peeking into Paul's tipped hand, note that Paul is not the letter's only sender. In the first verse we meet someone named Sosthenes. Who is he? Is he the same Sosthenes of Acts 18:17, the synagogue official who is beaten by a mob? We

cannot even reliably speculate about this, because the name was so common. But we know, for example, that Paul worked with an extensive network of fellow missionaries. In sixteenth chapter of Romans, for example, we meet many people who supported Paul. Some of these Paul also supported. Paul was not a lone apostle, but rather a member, albeit an important one, of a team.

We also learn from this first verse that Paul is an "apostle" and Sosthenes a "brother." In light of Paul's understanding of his apostolate (see Galatians 1:1–5), this

is likely a significant distinction. Paul is the superior, apparently, for "brother" and "sister" are terms used of all Christians. "Apostle," to Paul, is an exclusive term.

And now for the tipped hand. In verse two, we learn that Paul is writing "to the church of God that is in Corinth." But what else do we learn about this Church? This is not a Church in isolation, but a Church standing "with all those everywhere who call upon the name of our Lord Jesus Christ, their Lord and ours." Why does Paul link the Corinthians to Christians everywhere?

GOSPEL   John 1:29–34

A reading from the holy Gospel according to John

John the **Baptist** saw **Jesus** coming toward him and said,
  "**Behold**, the **Lamb** of **God**, who takes away the **sin**
    of the **world**.
He is the one of whom I said,
  'A man is coming **after** me who ranks **ahead** of me
  because he existed **before** me.'
I did **not know** him,
  but the reason why I came **baptizing** with water
  was that he might be made **known** to **Israel**."
John testified **further**, saying,
  "I saw the **Spirit** come down like a **dove** from **heaven**
  and **remain** upon him.
I did **not know** him,
  but the one who **sent** me to **baptize** with **water** told me,
  'On **whomever** you see the Spirit come down and remain,
  he is the one who will **baptize** with the **Holy Spirit**.'
Now I have **seen** and **testified** that he is the **Son** of **God**."

John the evangelist wants to make absolutely clear that the sole purpose of the ministry of John the Baptist, as John the Baptist acknowledges in this reading, is to testify to Jesus.

In later chapters, particularly chapters 1 through 4, Paul will admonish the Corinthians for their factions and disunity at the same time that they suppose themselves more spiritual than even Paul and his missionary network. By the second verse of his letter, Paul has already given a first hint that the theme of Christian unity will occupy him in the pages yet to come.

GOSPEL   "Behold, the Lamb of God, who takes away the sin of the world." In John 1:29 and 1:36, John the Baptist calls Jesus "the lamb of God." We know these words from the Mass. But what is the significance of this title?

The sacrifice of animals to remove guilt for wrongs committed was part of the religious landscape of Israel (see, for example, Leviticus 9). The sacrifice of the Passover lamb originally belonged to liturgy celebrated in the home (see Exodus 12). In time, the Passover liturgy and the sacrifice of the lamb formed a part of the annual Passover liturgy of the temple. Part of the significance attached to this liturgy was the removal of the people's sin and guilt accumulated during the preceding year.

Matthew, Mark, and Luke place Jesus' Crucifixion on the day of Passover itself. But John places it one day earlier, on the Day of Preparation (19:31). It was on this day that the Passover lamb would have been sacrificed in the temple. John probably wants his readers to think of Jesus as the *true* Passover sacrifice. He would like his readers to understand Jesus, and not the lamb slaughtered in the temple precincts, as the lamb that takes away the sins of the world. We also see the identification of Jesus with the Passover lamb in 1 Corinthians 5:7 and 1 Peter 1:19.

3RD SUNDAY IN ORDINARY TIME

Lectionary #67

READING I   Isaiah 8:23 — 9:3

Zebulun = ZEB-bu-lun
Naphtali = Naf-TAH-lee

Jordan = JOR-dan

Note how the prophet says very similar things, nearly repeating himself, in several of the adjacent clauses. Be sure to stress these pairings.

Midian = MID-ee-un

A reading from the Book of the Prophet Isaiah

First the Lord **degraded** the land of **Zebulun**
　　and the land of **Naphtali**;
　　but in the end he has **glorified** the seaward road,
　　the land west of the **Jordan**,
　　the District of the **Gentiles**.

Anguish has taken **wing, dispelled** is **darkness**:
　　for there is **no gloom** where but now there was **distress**.
The people who walked in **darkness**
　　have seen a great **light**;
　　upon those who **dwelt** in the **land** of **gloom**
　　a **light** has **shone**.
You have brought them **abundant joy**
　　and **great rejoicing**,
as they **rejoice** before you as at the **harvest**,
　　as people make **merry** when dividing **spoils**.
For the **yoke** that **burdened** them,
　　the **pole** on their **shoulder**,
and the **rod** of their **taskmaster**
　　you have **smashed**, as on the day of Midian.

READING I The land of Israel lies on the most direct route between North Africa and the Middle East. Sometimes this has meant that Israel enjoyed the many benefits of lying on a major trade route. Other times it's meant that Israel stood in the way of one or another empire intent on controlling its territory. At various times, Egypt, Assyria, Babylon, Persia, Greece, and Rome all decided this land was vital to their governance of the eastern Mediterranean.

The view of the world from the Jerusalem temple, where the prophet Isaiah received his call to prophesy (Isaiah 6), was quite different from the view of the world from Nineveh, Babylon, or Rome. These cities and their rulers often had little understanding of the lands they invaded and subdued. In Isaiah's day, it was Assyria's turn to gobble up people, families, villages, towns, cities, and kingdoms. In Jerusalem, hearing reports of atrocities from wild-eyed refugees, Isaiah and his contemporaries may have feared for the survival of their city and people.

"The people who walked in darkness have seen a great light; upon those who dwelt in the land of gloom a light has shone." If indeed this oracle in its original historical context celebrated the birth of a prince to the royal family of Judah (see commentary I, Christmas Midnight, December 25), how are we to understand it in the context of Assyria's encroachment on Judah and Jerusalem? To the prophet, the birth of the child probably meant that God had favored the royal line of Judah to continue. The powers arrayed against Jerusalem were undeniable. But hard to deny was the joy of encountering new life in the midst of such great uncertainty. In similar fashion is

READING II   1 Corinthians 1:10–13, 17

A reading from the first Letter of Saint Paul to the Corinthians

I **urge** you, brothers and sisters, in the **name** of our **Lord**
    Jesus Christ,
    that **all** of you agree in what you say,
    and that there be **no** divisions among you,
    but that you be **united** in the **same** mind
        and in the **same** purpose.
For it has been reported to me about you, my brothers and sisters,
    by Chloe's people, that there are **rivalries** among you.
I mean that each of you is saying,
    "**I** belong to Paul," or "**I** belong to Apollos,"
    or "**I** belong to Cephas," or "**I** belong to Christ."
Is Christ **divided**?
Was **Paul** crucified for you?
Or were you **baptized** in the name of **Paul**?
For Christ did **not** send me to **baptize** but to **preach** the **gospel**,
    and **not** with the wisdom of **human eloquence**,
        so that the cross of Christ might not be emptied
            of its meaning.

Chloe's = KLOH-eez

Appollos = Ah-PAUL-lus

Cephas = KAY-phas
Let your proclamation of Paul's questions reflect his strong disapproval. These questions are not open-ended. They demand negative answers. The trouble is that Paul thinks the Corinthians are acting as though someone could actually answer "yes."

Christ with us, tearing down present anxieties by reminding us that our true destiny lies with him.

READING II It was suggested in the commentary on the second reading for last Sunday that Paul, in the first verses of 1 Corinthians, is already hinting at the letter's main theme of unity among "all those everywhere who call upon the name of our Lord Jesus Christ" (1 Corinthians 1:2). In 1 Corinthians 1:10, we get a much clearer indication that unity will be his theme. Here, Paul urges "that all of you agree in what you

say, and that there be no divisions among you, but that you be united in the same mind and in the same purpose."

But why does unity matter so much to Paul here? Apparently, Paul has learned from "Chloe's people" (probably Christian slaves or freedmen sent to Paul by their Christian mistress) that there are "rivalries" in the Corinthian Church. The "rivalries" have to do with the Corinthians' alignment of themselves with various Church leaders and, one assumes, their refusal to acknowledge the full authority of other leaders. Some claim Paul as their leader, some

Apollos (see Acts 18:24; 19:1; Titus 3:13), some Kephas (another name for Peter; see John 1:42), and some Jesus himself.

Of this divided people, Paul asks, "Is Christ divided?" The Corinthians know the right answer. And Paul knows they know it. Contained within his question is an accusation, that even if the Corinthians do not think that Christ "is divided," they are certainly acting like it.

Paul urged unity not only at Corinth, but also in the Church at Philippi, a city of northern Greece. Like the Church at Corinth, Paul founded the Church at Philippi. See how

Galilee = GAL-li-lee

Nazareth = NAH-zah-reth

Capernaum = Cah-PER-nah-um

Zebulun = ZEB-bu-lun

Naphtali = Naf-TAH-lee

Jordan = JOR-dan

GOSPEL   Matthew 4:12–23

A reading from the holy Gospel according to Matthew

When Jesus heard that John had been **arrested**,
    he withdrew to Galilee.
He left **Nazareth** and went to live in **Capernaum** by the sea,
    in the region of **Zebulun** and **Naphtali**,
    that what had been said through Isaiah the prophet
    might be **fulfilled**:
       Land of Zebulun and land of Naphtali,
          *the way to the **sea**, beyond the **Jordan**,*
          Galilee of the Gentiles,
       *the people who sit in **darkness** have seen a great **light**,*
       *on those **dwelling** in a land overshadowed by **death***
          light has arisen.
From **that time** on, Jesus began to **preach** and **say**,
    "**Repent**, for the **kingdom** of **heaven** is at **hand**."

As he was **walking** by the Sea of Galilee, he saw two brothers,
    Simon who is called **Peter**, and his brother **Andrew**,
    casting a net into the sea; they were **fishermen**.

---

similar is the instruction of 1 Corinthians 1:10 to Philippians 2:2: "complete my joy by being of the same mind, with the same love, united in heart, thinking one thing." As in the Corinthian Church, there has been division in Philippi. How serious it is we cannot tell, but what seems certain is that two women, Euodia and Syntyche, who are perhaps quite powerful women in the Philippian Church, have been having some kind of feud (Philippians 4:2–3). Paul urges them to reconcile in language strongly reminiscent of both 1 Corinthians 1:10 and Philippians 2:2: "I urge Euodia and I urge Syntyche to come to a mutual understanding in the Lord" (Philippians 4:2). From these examples we begin see that one of Paul's literary prescriptions for division in "his" Churches was the language of loving unity.

GOSPEL   Jesus did not choose a famous or well-known place to begin his work. Had he wanted his ministry to have the most cosmopolitan character possible, he would have had to travel to some place like Alexandria or Athens. Had he decided to settle for what sophistication his own region had to offer, he could have tried Jerusalem or, closer to home, Cesarea or even the Galilean city of Sepphoris. But Jesus stayed out of these places; rather, he settled himself in the little fishing village of Capernaum amid the green hills of the Galilee. Then one day he woke up, went for a walk along the beach, called four fishermen away from their work, and changed their lives forever.

Unlike Paul, who worked in exclusively urban settings, Jesus conducted his ministry on the road and on the move in the countryside and villages of Galilee. His parables are

When you proclaim Jesus' words to Peter and Andrew, call them out in a clear, confident, and above all cheerful voice— the sort of voice a person might drop everything to hear more of.
Zebedee = ZEH-beh-dee

He said to them,
   "**Come** after **me**, and **I** will make you **fishers** of **men**."
At once they left their nets and **followed** him.
He walked along from there and saw two other brothers,
   James, the son of **Zebedee**, and his brother **John**.
They were in a **boat**, with their father **Zebedee**,
      mending their nets.
He **called** them, and **immediately** they left their **boat**
      and their **father**
   and **followed** him.

He went around **all** of Galilee,
   teaching in their synagogues, **proclaiming** the gospel
      of the kingdom,
   and **curing every** disease and illness among the people.

[Shorter: Matthew 4:12–17]

laden with the rustic images of Palestine's villages and farms. While the first-century Church would flourish in the cities, Jesus' followers were people like the first four disciples we meet today, men who toiled with their hands to pull another year's survival from earth and water.

In Matthew 3:2, the evangelist provides a summary statement of the preaching of John the Baptist: "Repent, for the kingdom of heaven is at hand!" In 4:17, Matthew gives the message that Jesus began to proclaim after John's ministry ended with his incarceration and he himself had relocated to the Galilean fishing village of Capernaum: "Repent, for the kingdom of heaven is at hand." Despite the rivalry that probably existed between the disciples of Jesus and John the Baptist, Matthew is giving us a clear sign that Jesus was taking up John's mantle and continuing the work he had begun.

4TH SUNDAY IN ORDINARY TIME

Lectionary #70

Zephaniah = Zeh-fan-I-yah

READING I   Zephaniah 2:3; 3:12–13

A reading from the Book of the Prophet Zephaniah

Seek the LORD, all you **humble** of the earth,
  who have **observed** his law;
seek **justice**, seek **humility**;
  perhaps you may be **sheltered**
  on the **day** of the LORD's **anger**.

But I will **leave** as a **remnant** in your **midst**
  a people **humble** and **lowly**,
who shall take **refuge** in the name of the LORD:
  the **remnant** of Israel.
They shall do no **wrong**
  and speak no **lies**;
nor shall there be **found** in their mouths
  a deceitful **tongue**;
they shall **pasture** and **couch** their flocks
  with **none** to disturb them.

READING I The introduction to the book of the prophet Zephaniah places the prophet's career during the reign of Josiah, who reigned in Judah in the last decades of the seventh century BC. Nothing else beside the information contained in Zephaniah 1:1 is known about this prophet. The book is a collection of oracles, some of which concern Jerusalem (1:2—2:3), some foreign kingdoms (2:4–15). The last section prophesies God's purifying judgment of Jerusalem and the salvation of its righteous citizens (3:1–20).

The first verse from today's reading is the final verse of an oracle excoriating Jerusalem's tolerance and patronage of multiple gods. 2 Kings 23 relates that Josiah undertook major religious reforms during his reign designed to end Jerusalem's tolerance and patronage of religions other than the worship of Yahweh. The situation the prophet describes in this section fits well enough with what little historical knowledge we have of the religious behavior of Jerusalemites and the reform of Josiah. Josiah, presumably because of his reforms, is one of a small number of kings of Israel and Judah positively described in 1 and 2 Kings (see 2 Kings 22:2).

In today's reading, the prophet declares to the "humble of the earth" that they should seek "justice" and "humility" in order to be spared the destruction wrought by God's "anger" (Zephaniah 2:3). The presence of religions the prophet deems invalid in the land brings everyone into danger. The remnant described in the second two verses of today's reading is composed of those who have chosen to live rightly despite the sin of their neighbors.

READING II   1 Corinthians 1:26–31

A reading from the first Letter of Saint Paul to the Corinthians

Consider your **own** calling, brothers and sisters.
Not many of **you** were **wise** by human standards,
 not many were **powerful**,
 not many were of **noble birth**.
Rather, God chose the **foolish** of the world to shame the **wise**,
 and God chose the **weak** of the world to shame the **strong**,
 and God chose the **lowly** and **despised** of the world,
 those who count for **nothing**,
 to **reduce** to nothing those who are **something**,
 so that **no** human being might **boast** before **God**.
It is due to him that you are in **Christ Jesus**,
 who became for us **wisdom** from God,
 as well as **righteousness**, **sanctification**, and **redemption**,
 so that, as it is written,
 "**Whoever** boasts, should boast in the **Lord**."

Paul is addressing people who, he believes, have a somewhat inflated opinion of themselves. Therefore, use a tone you might use with a slightly disobedient child, for this is how Paul portrays the Corinthians in the first four chapters of this letter.

READING II Through the grapevine, or perhaps spilling from the rumor mill, reports have reached Paul's ears that the Corinthian Church is divided within itself (1:11). In 1 Corinthians 1:10, he plainly states this letter's theme: unity in the Corinthian Church. And he also discloses the purpose of his letter: encouragement of the Corinthians to renew the bonds of unity and concord that should tie together the members of the Church. If Christ is not divided, then the Church must not tolerate internal divisions either.

Between 1:10–17 and today's reading, one finds the theological basis for the ethical instruction of this letter. "The message of the cross," Paul says, "is foolishness to those who are perishing, but to us who are being saved it is the power of God." This message of foolishness is an incredible story about Jesus, a nobody from a land of nobodies, who was executed in pain and humiliation, but who was raised from the dead by God. And the wild tale of the cross doesn't end there. For through this Resurrection God has declared that anyone who believes in

this story about Jesus has access to the same fate after death.

Paul stands by this story. And in today's reading, Paul suggests that the Corinthians have missed its point. If the Corinthians would simply take stock of themselves, Paul is saying, then they would see that they are people well suited to this story of foolishness. For despite the put-on airs that have led to their divisions, not many of them are wise, powerful, or wellborn. And that's good news, because God, in raising this crucified Jesus from death, has shown that it is the

There are two main pitfalls to avoid here. First, don't let the beatitudes run together. So take care to pause between them. Second, if you repeatedly put your main stress on "Blessed are," the reading will be hard on the assembly's ears and difficult to comprehend. So put your main stress both on the description of the blessed and what they will enjoy in the future.

GOSPEL   Matthew 5:1–12a

A reading from the holy Gospel according to Matthew

When **Jesus** saw the crowds, he went up the mountain,
　　and after he had sat down, his disciples came to him.
He began to teach them, saying:
　　"**Blessed** are the **poor** in **spirit**,
　　　　for **theirs** is the **kingdom** of **heaven**.
　　Blessed are they who **mourn**,
　　　　for they will be **comforted**.
　　Blessed are the **meek**,
　　　　for they will **inherit** the land.
　　Blessed are they who **hunger** and **thirst** for **righteousness**,
　　　　for they will be **satisfied**.
　　Blessed are the **merciful**,
　　　　for they will be shown **mercy**.
　　Blessed are the **clean** of **heart**,
　　　　for they will **see God**.
　　Blessed are the **peacemakers**,
　　　　for they will be called **children** of **God**.
　　Blessed are they who are **persecuted**
　　　　for the sake of **righteousness**,
　　　　for **theirs** is the **kingdom** of **heaven**.
　　Blessed are you when they **insult** you and **persecute** you
　　　　and utter **every** kind of **evil** against you **falsely** because of **me**.
　　Rejoice and be **glad**,
　　　　for your reward will be **great** in heaven."

lowly, the despised, and the nobodies, not the high and the mighty, who will be exalted.

GOSPEL Matthew 5:1—7:29 is the record of a single homily preached on a mountaintop by Jesus to his disciples. What we have been told about Jesus' preaching thus far has been summed up for us in a single verse: "Repent, for the kingdom of heaven is at hand" (Matthew 4:17). In Matthew 5:1—7:29, we meet Jesus the thinker and teacher.

Today's reading is the homily's introduction, traditionally referred to as "the beatitudes" from the Latin word for "blessed" *(beatus).* You can find much of the same text in Luke's Gospel (6:17–26), although there Jesus balances his blessings with sayings of woe (Luke 6:17–26). And it is interesting that Matthew says that Jesus preached this homily on a mountain (Matthew 5:1), while Luke is equally clear that Jesus preached it standing "on a stretch of level ground" (Luke 6:17).

If we look at Matthew 5:3–6, we see that what is promised to the poor in spirit, mourners, the meek, and those hungering and thirsting after righteousness is the complete reversal of their present circumstances.

Such reversal characterizes the coming kingdom of heaven as proclaimed by Jesus in Matthew's Gospel. And notice how those suffering, who seem more cursed than blessed, are the ones promised circumstances changed for the better.

ASH WEDNESDAY

Lectionary #219

READING I   Joel 2:12–18

A reading from the Book of the Prophet Joel

Even now, says the LORD,
    return to me with your whole heart,
    with **fasting**, and **weeping**, and **mourning**;
Rend your **hearts**, not your **garments**,
    and **return** to the LORD, your God.
For **gracious** and **merciful** is he,
    slow to anger, **rich** in kindness,
    and **relenting** in punishment.
Perhaps he will **again** relent
    and leave behind him a **blessing**,
Offerings and **libations**
    for the **LORD**, your **God**.

Blow the **trumpet** in Zion!
    proclaim a **fast**,
    call an **assembly**;
Gather the **people**,
    notify the **congregation**;
Assemble the **elders**,
    gather the **children**
    and the **infants** at the breast;
Let the **bridegroom** quit his room,
    and the **bride** her chamber.

Zion = ZI-yon

READING I It is practically impossible to date the book of Joel. The introduction contains neither any reference to the king (see Zephaniah 1:1) or kings (see Isaiah 1:1) who reigned during his career, nor any other additional and potentially dateable information (see Amos 1:1; Jeremiah 1:1–3). The fact that the monarchy is absent not only from the introduction, but also from the book itself, has led some scholars to suppose that the book was written after the Babylonian captivity, perhaps around 500 BC, when the monarchy was essentially defunct. This is a speculative and not terribly persuasive argument, but scholars have little more than conjecture to offer on this point.

One of the most fascinating aspects of Joel is the way in which he blends images of swarming locusts gobbling the produce of the land with those of hosts of marauding armies. Again, it is impossible to tell if Joel has a particular famine or enemy in mind. Sometimes the events described seem to lie in the future (2:1–11), sometimes in the recent past (1:2–12).

What the people are trying to avoid by this public rite of repentance appears to be the onset of the fearsome calamity mentioned in 2:1–11. This calamity is the "day of the Lord," which is a major theme of Joel (1:15; 2:1; 2:11; 2:31; 3:4). In ancient Israel and Judah, the day of the Lord was conceived as a day of judgment when God would punish the people for their sins and transgressions. It is a common prophetic subject. "Woe to those who yearn for the day of the Lord!" declared the prophet Amos. "What will this

Between the **porch** and the **altar**
   let the **priests**, the **ministers** of the LORD, **weep**,
And say, "**Spare**, O LORD, **your people**,
   and make **not** your heritage a **reproach**,
   with the **nations** ruling **over** them!
Why should they say among the peoples,
   '**Where** is their **God**?'"

Then the Lord was **stirred** to concern for his **land**
   and took **pity** on his people.

READING II   2 Corinthians 5:20—6:2

A reading from the second Letter of Paul to the Corinthians

Brothers and **sisters**:
We are **ambassadors** for **Christ**,
   as if **God** were appealing through **us**.
We **implore** you on behalf of Christ,
   be **reconciled** to God.
For our sake he made him to **be** sin who did **not know** sin,
   so that **we** might become the **righteousness** of God **in him**.

Working together, then,
   we **appeal** to you not to **receive** the grace of God **in vain**.
For he says:
   *In an **acceptable** time I **heard** you;*
      *and on a day of **salvation** I **helped** you.*
Behold, **now** is a **very** acceptable time;
   behold, **now** is the day of **salvation**.

Emphasize in particular the words "reconcile" and "reconciliation" in this reading. Paul is encouraging the Corinthians in this section of 2 Corinthians to reconcile themselves with himself, the validity of his apostolate, and the Gospel he proclaims. The theme of reconciliation dominates this portion of the letter.

---

day of the Lord mean for you? Darkness and not light! As if a man went to flee from a lion, and a bear should meet him; or as if on entering his house he were to rest his hand against the wall, and a snake should bite him" (Amos 5:18–19).

READING II   Paul probably founded the Church at Corinth in 50–51 AD. As missionaries often do, he soon moved on. After that, there began a vigorous written correspondence between the apostle and the Church he founded; 1 and 2 Corinthians

are what remain of it. We know that before he wrote 1 Corinthians, Paul had already sent another letter to Corinth (see 1 Corinthians 5:9–10). The Corinthians had responded to this letter with a letter of their own in which they seem to have asked for guidance on some issues (1 Corinthians 7:1). To this Paul responded with 1 Corinthians.

At this point in the correspondence things get a little complicated. The letter we call 2 Corinthians is actually a combination of several of Paul's letters, perhaps as

many as five, which the early Church wanted to preserve. Today's reading comes from the earliest of these letter fragments. In other words, it comes from the next letter Paul wrote to Corinth after he wrote 1 Corinthians. What is left of this letter spans 2:14—6:13, 7:2–4.

The Corinthians have asked Paul some questions apparently under the influence some new Christian missionaries who showed up in Corinth after Paul left. These missionaries provided the Corinthians with letters of recommendation, perhaps from the

GOSPEL   Matthew 6:1–6, 16–18

A reading from the holy Gospel according to Matthew

Jesus said to his disciples:
  "Take care **not** to perform righteous deeds
  in order that **people** may **see** them;
  otherwise, you will have **no** recompense
    from your heavenly Father.
When you give alms,
  do **not** blow a **trumpet** before you,
  as the **hypocrites** do in the synagogues
    and in the **streets**
  to win the **praise** of others.
Amen, **I** say to **you**,
  they have **received** their reward.
But **when you** give alms,
  do **not** let your **left** hand know what your **right** is doing,
  so that your **almsgiving** may be **secret**.
And your **Father** who **sees** in secret will **repay** you.

Proclaim in a strong and resolute tone the phrase "Amen, I say to you, they have received their reward." Then, as you read the following line, look out at the assembly and stress the word "you."

Jerusalem Church itself. The Corinthians suddenly had a host of questions. Where were Paul's letters? Who sent him? Whom does he represent? Does he have the right to call himself an apostle?

    In today's reading, Paul identifies himself as an ambassador of Christ. Paul contends that it is a sign of his legitimacy that he has *not* been sent out by the Jerusalem Church (or anyone else) and therefore carries no letter of recommendation. He is

Christ's apostle, Christ's ambassador, and needs no letter. His "letter" is what he has already accomplished among the Corinthians (2 Corinthians 3:1–3).

GOSPEL   As Catholic Christians, we are probably familiar with the idea that sacraments do not work because of the goodness of the person celebrating them. Christ instituted the sacraments so that they would work regardless of the merits or deficits of the person celebrating them.

    In today's Gospel, however, we are reminded that motives mattered a great deal to Jesus. He is not here talking about sacraments, but the activities of prayer, giving money and help to the poor, and fasting. Jesus more than disapproves of the practice of prayer, almsgiving, and fasting done for show. He calls this hypocrisy. Prayer, almsgiving, and fasting are to be done in secret or not at all. What can this mean?

"When you **pray**,
   do **not** be like the hypocrites,
   who **love** to stand and **pray** in the **synagogues** and on
      street corners
   so that **others** may **see** them.
Amen, **I** say to **you**,
   they have **received** their reward.
But **when you** pray, **go** to your inner room,
   close the door, and **pray** to your Father in **secret**.
And your **Father** who **sees** in secret will **repay** you.

"**When** you fast,
   do **not** look gloomy like the **hypocrites**.
They **neglect** their appearance,
   so that they may **appear** to others to be **fasting**.
Amen, I say to you, they have **received** their reward.
But **when you** fast,
   anoint your head and **wash** your face,
   so that you may **not** appear to be fasting,
   except to your Father who is **hidden**.
And your **Father** who **sees** what is hidden will **repay** you."

Matthew, more than the other evangelists, places Jesus in stark opposition to other pious Jews, particularly the scribes and Pharisees, who are the most likely candidates for the "hypocrites" named in today's Gospel selection. But notice that Jesus does not attack their religious observances in principle. He approves of fasting and almsgiving. He approves of prayer, even telling his disciples how to do it properly (Matthew 6:9–15). Matthew's Jesus affirms and scribes adhere, but thinks that genuine observance of Jewish law requires a much higher standard of practice than what the scribes and Pharisees submit themselves to (see 5:17–20, 43–8; 18:15–18; 23:5–7, 23–26).

1ST SUNDAY OF LENT

Lectionary #22

READING I Genesis 2:7–9; 3:1–7

A reading from the Book of Genesis

The LORD God **formed** man out of the **clay** of the **ground**
  and blew into his nostrils the **breath** of **life**,
  and so man became a **living being**.

Then the LORD God planted a garden in **Eden**, in the east,
  and placed there the **man** whom he had **formed**.
Out of the **ground** the LORD God made various **trees** grow
  that were **delightful** to look at and **good** for food,
  with the **tree** of **life** in the middle of the garden
  and the **tree** of the **knowledge** of **good** and **evil**.

Now the **serpent** was the most **cunning** of **all** the animals
  that the LORD God had made.
The **serpent** asked the **woman**,
  "Did God **really** tell you not to eat
  from **any** of the trees in the **garden**?"
The woman answered the serpent:
  "We **may** eat of the **fruit** of the **trees** in the **garden**;
  it is **only** about the **fruit** of the **tree**
  in the **middle** of the garden that God said,
  'You shall **not** eat it or even **touch** it, lest you **die**.'"
But the serpent said to the woman:
  "You **certainly** will not **die**!

Eden = EE-den

The serpent, as the text says, was "the most cunning of all the animals." Deliver its words in a sly-sounding tone of voice. But deliver Eve's words in a clear, straightforward manner. She is still an innocent.

| READING I | "For God formed man to be imperishable; the image of his own nature he made him. But by the envy of the devil, death entered the world, and they who are in his possession experience it" (Wisdom 2:23–24). The author of the book of Wisdom, most likely a Jew from Alexandria in Egypt, is among the first writers we know of to associate the serpent of today's reading with the devil. Early

Christians seem to have found this a congenial interpretation. In any case, the association has remained a part of Christian interpretive tradition for centuries.

The serpent tells neither the whole truth nor a complete lie. It is right, for instance, that if the human pair eats of the fruit from the tree in the middle of the garden, they will see things quite differently. Indeed, upon eating the fruit, Adam and Eve notice their nakedness for the first time.

Whether they shall "be like gods" and "not die" after eating the fruit turned out to be another matter entirely.

Half-truths are among the most perverse sorts of deception, for they rely on a partial truth, or the ring of truth, to establish a lie. The alleged half-truths told by some visiting apostles to Corinth led Paul to excoriate the Corinthian Church in these terms: "But I am afraid that, as the serpent deceived Eve by his cunning, your thoughts may be

No, God **knows well** that the **moment** you eat of it
    your eyes will be **opened** and you will be like **gods**
    who **know** what is **good** and what is **evil**."
The woman saw that the tree was good for food,
    pleasing to the eyes, and **desirable** for gaining wisdom.
So she took some of its fruit and ate it;
    and she also gave some to her **husband**, who was with her,
    and **he** ate it.

Pause briefly here.

Then the eyes of **both** of them were **opened**,
    and they realized that they were **naked**;
    so they sewed fig leaves together
    and made loincloths for themselves.

READING II   Romans 5:12–19

A reading from the Letter of Saint Paul to the Romans

Let the commas mark brief pauses for you.

Brothers and **sisters**:
Through **one** man **sin** entered the world,
    and **through** sin, **death**,
    and thus **death** came to **all** men, inasmuch as **all sinned**—
    for up to the time of the **law**, sin was in the **world**,
    though sin is **not** accounted when there is **no law**.
But death **reigned** from Adam to Moses,
    even over those who did not **sin**
    after the **pattern** of the trespass of **Adam**,
    who is the **type** of the one who was to **come**.

But the gift is **not** like the transgression.
For if by the **transgression** of the one, the many **died**,
    how much more did the **grace** of God

In this reading Paul repeatedly compares the persons and attributes of Adam and Christ in order to show how far superior Christ is. Emphasize these comparisons.

corrupted from a sincere [and pure] commitment to Christ" (2 Corinthians 11:3). Paul concedes that some of what these apostles say about themselves is true. But this basis in truth, Paul contends, is simply a platform for an edifice of lies about himself and his apostolate. We do well to examine our own consciences this Lent and ask forgiveness for those half-truths we have too willingly believed, as well as those we ourselves may have told.

READING II Today's reading from Paul's letter to the Romans is a comparison between Adam and Jesus. This is not the only place in Paul's letters where we encounter such a comparison. We also find it in 1 Corinthians where it is stated much more succinctly. In 1 Corinthians 15, Paul is arguing in favor of the idea of the bodily Resurrection. He does not mean, however, the Resurrection of believers' flesh-and-blood bodies, but of their spiritual bodies. Paul describes Adam as "the first

man, Adam," "a living being," and "from the earth." Paul describes Jesus as "the last Adam," "life-giving spirit," "spiritual," and "from heaven" (1 Corinthians 15:45–47). As believers carry the image of the earthly man, so also do they carry the image of the heavenly man through their incorporation into Christ's body, the Church.

In Romans 5:12–19, Paul compares Adam and Christ in a similar way, but for a different purpose. Here, he wants to argue

and the gracious **gift** of the one man Jesus Christ
  overflow for the **many**.
And the gift is **not** like the result of the one who sinned.
For after **one** sin there was the **judgment**
    that brought **condemnation**;
  but the **gift**, after **many** transgressions, brought **acquittal**.
For **if**, by the **transgression** of the **one**,
  death came to **reign** through that one,
  how much more will those who receive the **abundance** of **grace**
  and of the **gift** of **justification**
  come to **reign** in life through the **one Jesus Christ**.
In conclusion, just as through **one** transgression
  condemnation came upon **all**,
  so, through **one** righteous act,
  acquittal and **life** came to **all**.
For just as through the **disobedience** of the **one** man
  the **many** were made **sinners**,
  so, through the **obedience** of the **one**,
  the **many** will be made **righteous**.

[Shorter: Romans 5:12, 17–19]

Slow down and enunciate each occurrence of the phrase "how much more." Paul means to show that grace is more than sufficient to overcome sin.

GOSPEL Matthew 4:1–11

A reading from the holy Gospel according to Matthew

At that time Jesus was **led** by the Spirit into the **desert**
  to be **tempted** by the **devil**.
He fasted for forty **days** and forty **nights**,
  and afterwards he was **hungry**.

---

that God's grace is more than sufficient to deal with human sin. As in 1 Corinthians, Adam and Christ share some fundamental similarities. In 1 Corinthians 15:45, Christ is "the last Adam," while in Romans 5:14, Adam is "the type of the one who was to come." In Romans 5:15–16, "the gift" (grace) and all its effects are far greater than Adam's sin and all its effects.

In these two passages from 1 Corinthians 15 and Romans 5, Paul is trying to say something about the human condition

as he sees it. Paul's grim reality is that the hostile powers of sin and death rule human life. But through the work of Jesus Christ, God offers a way out from under the thumbs of these powers. The sin enslaving people to these powers has been overthrown by the free gift of grace.

GOSPEL The Greek word translated by "tempted" in this reading *(peirazō)* not only means "tempt" but also "test." There are a number of places in the

New Testament referring to tests or temptations Jesus faced. Luke 4:1–13 depicts the same events as today's reading (also see Mark 1:12–13). The theme recurs in John 6:15, where Jesus flees a crowd about to make him a king after he has multiplied the loaves and fishes. In John 7:1–4, Jesus' brothers, who do not believe in him, challenge him to do his works in public. "No one," they say, "works in secret if he wants to be known publicly. If you do these things, manifest yourself to the world." Like the

While the serpent in the first reading is merely "cunning," the devil seeks mastery of Jesus. Use a sinister tone when you deliver his words. Proclaim Jesus' replies in a strong, confident voice.

The **tempter** approached and said to him,
    "If you are the **Son** of **God**,
    command that these **stones** become loaves of **bread**."
He said in **reply**,
    "It is **written**:
    *One does **not** live on **bread** alone,*
        *but on **every** word that comes **forth***
        *from the mouth of **God**.*"

Then the **devil** took him to the holy city,
    and made him stand on the parapet of the temple,
    and said to him, "**If** you are the Son of God,
        throw yourself **down**.
For it is **written**:
    *He will **command** his angels concerning you*
        *and with their **hands** they will **support** you,*
    *lest you dash your **foot** against a **stone**.*"
Jesus answered him,
    "**Again** it is **written**,
    *You shall **not** put the **Lord**, your **God**, to the **test**.*"

Then the **devil** took him up to a **very** high mountain,
    and showed him **all** the kingdoms of the world
        in their **magnificence**,
    and he said to him, "**All** these I shall give to you,
    if you will **prostrate** yourself and **worship** me."
At this, Jesus said to him,
    "**Get away, Satan!**
It is **written**:
    *The **Lord**, your **God**, shall you **worship***
        *and him **alone** shall you **serve**.*"

Then the devil left him and, **behold**,
    angels came and **ministered** to him.

---

devil's challenges to Jesus, telling him to turn stones into bread and throw himself from the pinnacle of the Jerusalem temple, Jesus refuses acclaim in exchange for deeds he could easily perform.

In the letter to Hebrews, the author observes that Jesus can help people who are being tested *(peirazō)* because he himself has been tested "through what he suffered" (Hebrews 2:17–18). Later, the author returns to this subject, saying that Christians

"do not have a high priest who is unable to sympathize with our weaknesses, but one who has similarly been tested in every way, yet without sin" (Hebrews 4:15).

The tests and temptations facing most of us are not, it is safe to say, of the extraordinary sort Satan presented Jesus. But the daily lures of money, power, popularity, and sex—to name a few—are no less threatening because they are so ordinary, common, and perhaps even boring. In the moment of temptation we have a choice. We can ignore

the standing offer of help from Christ who knows our problem from personal experience. Or we can request help and thus step closer toward the full life that our Creator desires for us.

2ND SUNDAY OF LENT

Lectionary #25

READING I   Genesis 12:1–4a

A reading from the Book of Genesis

The LORD said to **Abram**:
"**Go forth** from the land of your **kinsfolk**
 and from your **father**'s house to a **land** that **I** will show you.

"I will make of you a **great** nation,
  and I will **bless** you;
I will make your name **great**,
  so that you will be a **blessing**.
I will **bless** those who **bless** you
  and **curse** those who **curse** you.
All the communities of the earth
  shall find **blessing** in **you**."

Abram went as the LORD directed him.

Abram = AY-bram

Emphasize God's promises to Abram.

Pause before the narration of Abram's response to God.

READING I Based on popular Middle Eastern folk legends and tribal history, the first 11 chapters of Genesis were fashioned by nimble writers to recount the history of the world until the beginning of the nation of Israel. The disobedience of Adam and Eve (Genesis 3:1–7) and Cain's murder of his brother Abel (Genesis 4:1–16) are preludes to such a sorry state of affairs on the earth that God finally regrets ever having created human beings in the first place and decides to wipe them out and start all over with Noah, who is the one decent person God can find (Genesis 6:5–7,

11–13). So when human beings start building a tower to heaven, God does not attempt to talk or reason with them, but simply confuses their speech.

God's relationship with Abram is the first relationship between God and human beings to function fairly well over time and successive generations. God puts it to Abram in the form of a deal. If Abram will leave his father's house and city for an unknown land, he will have God as his ally. God keeps trying to know his creatures and succeeds to some degree with Abram (later

called Abraham; see Genesis 17:5) and his descendants.

Whether we seek God or not, God is seeking us. Despite repeated human efforts to ignore, challenge, or flee God, God does not give up trying to know us. It is in awareness of this that Isaiah 51:2–3 refers to Abram's call in relation to God's plans for ruined Jerusalem. Despite seeming evidence to the contrary, God is no more finished with Jerusalem after its people's captivity than God was finished with humanity before the call of Abram. God isn't finished with any of us.

READING II   2 Timothy 1:8b–10

A reading from the second Letter of Saint Paul to Timothy

Beloved:
Bear your share of **hardship** for the gospel
   with the **strength** that comes from God.

He **saved** us and **called** us to a holy life,
   not according to our works
   but according to his **own** design
   and the **grace** bestowed on us in **Christ Jesus**
     before time began,
   but **now** made manifest
   through the **appearance** of our savior Christ Jesus,
   who destroyed **death** and brought **life** and **immortality**
   to **light** through the **gospel**.

GOSPEL   Matthew 17:1–9

A reading from the holy Gospel according to Matthew

Jesus took **Peter**, **James**, and **John** his brother,
   and led them up a high mountain by themselves.
And he was **transfigured** before them;
   his **face shone** like the **sun**
   and his **clothes** became **white** as **light**.
And **behold**, **Moses** and **Elijah** appeared to them,
   conversing with him.

READING II   There are two personal letters addressed to Timothy in the New Testament. Their purported author is Paul, although there are good reasons to think these letters to Timothy were written by someone else decades after Paul died, but who knew Paul's work and legacy well. Writing under an assumed name was a fairly common literary convention in the ancient world. Perhaps the actual author felt that a letter from Paul to one of his closest associates would add some authority to its content.

One idea that comes through loud and clear in today's selection from 2 Timothy is that God did not select the members of the Church due to any special virtue on their part. Church members did not impress God with their holiness, or wow God with myriad good deeds. Instead, it was due to God's "own design and the grace bestowed on us in Christ Jesus before time began" (2 Timothy 1:9).

Only through "the appearance of our savior Christ Jesus" was the gift of grace discovered. The author's description of Christ and his work does not focus on his earthly ministry, but rather concentrates on his destruction of death and offer of new life. But this is not all: Christ destroys death and brings life "through the gospel." The work of Christ may have been completed, but its life-giving effects are ongoing in the proclamation of the Good News.

GOSPEL   Jesus' Transfiguration is not a public revelation of his divinity. Peter, James, and John are the only three to witness it. In Matthew 17:1, it seems clear that Jesus has intentionally selected these three for a private revelation.

Do your best to express the awe and amazement that Peter would have experienced.

Then Peter said to Jesus in reply,
  "Lord, it is **good** that we are here.
If you **wish**, I will make three tents here,
  one for **you**, one for **Moses**, and one for **Elijah**."
While he was still speaking, **behold**,
  a **bright** cloud cast a **shadow** over them,
  then from the **cloud** came a **voice** that said,
  "**This** is my beloved **Son**, with whom I am well **pleased**;
  listen to him."
When the disciples heard this, they fell **prostrate**
  and were **very** much afraid.
But **Jesus** came and touched them, saying,
  "**Rise**, and do **not** be afraid."
And when the disciples **raised** their eyes,
  they saw no one else but Jesus **alone**.

As they were coming down from the mountain,
  Jesus charged them,
  "Do **not** tell the **vision** to **anyone**
  until the **Son** of **Man** has been **raised** from the **dead**."

In the Gospels, we find several places when Jesus informs his disciples of his divine identity and that his earthly journey ends on a cross. At best, the disciples understand this only partially. Peter appears to understand better than any of them, as his confession that Jesus is the Christ (Matthew 16:13–20; Mark 8:27–30; Luke 9:18–21). But Matthew, despite his high view of the foundational role played by Peter in the Church, records Jesus' stinging attack on Peter, whom he actually calls "Satan," after Peter's rebuke of Jesus' prediction of his Passion (Matthew 16:21–28). It seems that

Peter, although he has just confessed that Jesus is "the Messiah, the Son of the living God," does not understand what it means for Jesus to be the Messiah (Matthew 16:16; see also Mark 8:29 and Luke 9:20). With his Transfiguration, Jesus provides yet another clue of his divine identity. But even this is not enough for his uncomprehending disciples.

It is important for us to take note of those with whom we identify in the Gospel. Do we identify with Jesus? From a literary point of view it makes sense that we might. He is, after all, the main character of the story. And by repeatedly predicting his

Passion, Jesus demonstrates that he knows, as we to whom the story is familiar also do, how his earthly journey will conclude. But in daily life we are probably much more like the disciples, for many of us are daily presented with hints and signs of God's presence among us and cannot find the willing faith to accept them fully.

3RD SUNDAY OF LENT

Lectionary #28

READING I   Exodus 17:3–7

A reading from the Book of Exodus

In those days, in their **thirst** for **water**,
    the people **grumbled** against Moses,
    saying, "**Why** did you **ever** make us leave **Egypt**?
Was it just to have us **die** here of **thirst**
    with our **children** and our **livestock**?"
So **Moses cried out** to the LORD,
    "**What** shall I do with this **people**?
A little more and they will **stone** me!"
The LORD answered **Moses**,
    "Go over there in front of the **people**,
    along with some of the **elders** of **Israel**,
    holding in your **hand**, as you go,
    the **staff** with which you **struck** the river.
I will be standing there in front of you on the **rock** in **Horeb**.
Strike the rock, and the water will **flow** from it
    for the people to **drink**."
This Moses did, in the presence of the **elders** of **Israel**.
The place was called **Massah** and **Meribah**,
    because the Israelites **quarreled** there
    and **tested** the LORD, saying,
    "Is the LORD in our **midst** or **not**?"

Horeb = HOH-reb

Massah = Mah-SAH

Meribah = Mer-ri-BAH

READING I   In its first verse, Psalm 95 refers to God as the "rock of our salvation!" Much of the psalm praises God as Creator and controller of everything that exists. But in its eighth verse, praise shifts to stern warning. It refers to the events described in today's reading from Exodus, saying, "Do not harden your hearts as at Meribah, as on the day of Massah in the desert." For the author of this psalm, Israel in the wilderness provides an example of how *not* to behave toward God.

There is something comic about this reading. Here are the Israelites, saved from slavery and Pharaoh's wrath, asking Moses what is easily the second-most irritating question in the Bible: "Why did you ever make us leave Egypt? Was it just to have us die here of thirst with our children and our livestock?" (For the most irritating question, see Exodus 14:11.) And imagine Moses' exasperation: one day he was tending his father-in-law's livestock when an angel suddenly appeared and gave him a job he didn't want (Exodus 3) and tried over and

over to turn down (Exodus 4), and now he finds himself in the middle of the desert with a horde of ungrateful people who want to know if he's trying to kill them.

For Paul, what happened in the wilderness both foreshadows the sacramental and moral life of the Church (1 Corinthians 10:1–13). In the rock from which the water sprang, Paul sees Christ. Baptism was foreshadowed in the Israelites' safe passage through the parted sea and the pillar of cloud leading them in the desert. The Eucharist was

READING II   Romans 5:1–2, 5–8

A reading from the Letter of Saint Paul to the Romans

Brothers and sisters:
Since we have been **justified** by **faith**,
    we have **peace** with God through our Lord **Jesus Christ**,
    through whom we have gained **access** by **faith**
    to this **grace** in which we **stand**,
    and we boast in **hope** of the **glory** of God.

And **hope** does not **disappoint**,
    because the **love** of **God** has been **poured out** into our **hearts**
    through the **Holy Spirit** who has been given to us.
For **Christ**, while we were still **helpless**,
    died at the appointed time for the **ungodly**.
Indeed, only with **difficulty** does one die for a **just** person,
    though perhaps for a **good** person one might even
        find **courage** to **die**.
But **God** proves his **love** for **us**
    in that while **we** were still **sinners Christ** died for **us**.

Emphasize in particular the word "not" in the phrase "hope does not disappoint."

foreshadowed in the manna from heaven. But above all, the fate of the desert generation of Israel serves as an example for the Church. Like the author of Psalm 95, for Paul in 1 Corinthians the story of Israel in the wilderness was a cautionary tale.

READING II In the first four chapters of Romans, Paul explains the human condition as he sees it: people are fundamentally rebellious toward God. It is not simply that most people probably would not honor God properly if given the chance.

It is that human beings are incapable of self-justification by any means. Justification, Paul contends, is not something people can accomplish by themselves on their own strength, dedication, or willpower. Justification is something *God* has made available to all humanity through the Gospel.

As we see from this reading, faith in Christ is the means to God's saving grace. By faith in Christ, Paul means a precise kind of belief about Jesus. Later in Romans he will offer a simple expression of what this belief

is and how it relates to both justification and salvation: "if you confess with your mouth that Jesus is Lord and believe in your heart that God raised him from the dead, you will be saved. For one believes with the heart and so is justified, and one confesses with the mouth and so is saved" (Romans 10:9–10).

Boasting is a common topic in Paul's letters. The most influential moral philosophies of the ancient world contained much the same opinion about boasting that well-mannered people do today: don't do it, unless you boast of someone or something for which you do not take the credit yourself.

Samaria = Sah-MAR-i-ya

Sychar = Suh-CHAR

Samaritan = Sah-MAR-i-tan

Note that Jesus and the Samaritan woman are talking on different levels. She thinks she is talking about a convenient access to water. Jesus is talking about Baptism.

GOSPEL   John 4:5–42

A reading from the holy Gospel according to John

Jesus came to a town of **Samaria** called **Sychar**,
    near the plot of land that **Jacob** had given to his son **Joseph**.
Jacob's well was there.
Jesus, **tired** from his journey, sat down there at the **well**.
It was about **noon**.

A **woman** of **Samaria** came to draw **water**.
Jesus **said** to her,
    "**Give** me a **drink**."
His disciples had gone into the town to buy food.
The **Samaritan woman** said to him,
    "**How** can **you**, a **Jew**, ask **me**, a **Samaritan woman**,
        for a **drink**?"
—For Jews use **nothing** in common with **Samaritans**.—
Jesus **answered** and **said** to her,
    "If you **knew** the gift of **God**
    and **who** is saying to you, '**Give** me a **drink**,'
    you would have **asked** him
    and he would have **given** you **living water**."
The woman **said** to him,
    "Sir, you do not even have a **bucket** and the **cistern** is **deep**;
    where then can you get this **living water**?
Are you **greater** than our father **Jacob**,
    who gave us this **cistern** and drank from it **himself**
    with his **children** and his **flocks**?"

This is the same principle underlying the boast of the justified Christian in Romans 5:2: boast not that you are justified, but that God justified you together with the rest of the Church. In 1 Corinthians, Paul calls the Corinthians on what he thinks is spiritual pretension on their parts. Reminding them of their humble origins, he concludes the first chapter with a citation of Jeremiah 9:23–24: "Whoever boasts, should boast in the Lord" (1 Corinthians 1:31). The Corinthians, as will become much clearer later in this letter,

have less to boast about than some of them may think (see, for example, 1 Corinthians 4:7). Similarly, Paul removes the possibility of personal boasting for the Romans as well, reminding them that "while we were still sinners Christ died for us" (Romans 5:8).

GOSPEL The geography of Palestine matters a great deal, although in a unique way, to each of the four evangelists. Mark, for example, contains two miraculous feedings in which Jesus multiplies a meager amount of food into an

amount sufficient to feed thousands. The first of these occurs in the Galilee (Mark 6:35–44). The second occurs in the area southeast of the Sea of Galilee in the region of the Decapolis, so named for the ten Gentile cities there (7:31; 8:1–9). In other words, Mark records two near identical feedings in his Gospel, one in Jewish territory, one in Gentile. The geographical details of Mark's information provide the careful reader with clues that Jesus' ministry extended not only to Israel, but into Gentile territory as well.

Jesus **answered** and **said** to her,
  "**Everyone** who drinks this **water** will be thirsty **again**;
  but **whoever** drinks the water I shall give will **never** thirst;
  the water I shall give will become in him
  a spring of water welling up to **eternal life**."
The woman **said** to him,
  "Sir, give me this **water**, so that I may not be **thirsty**
  or have to keep **coming** here to draw **water**."

Jesus said to her,
  "**Go call** your **husband** and come back."
The woman **answered** and **said** to him,
  "I do **not** have a husband."
Jesus **answered** her,
  "You are **right** in saying, 'I do **not** have a **husband**.'
For you have had **five** husbands,
  and the one you have **now** is **not** your **husband**.
What you have said is **true**."
The woman **said** to him,
  "Sir, I can see that you are a **prophet**.
Our **ancestors** worshiped on this **mountain**;
  but **you** people say that the place to worship is in **Jerusalem**."
Jesus **said** to her,
  "**Believe** me, woman, the **hour** is **coming**
  when you will **worship** the Father
  neither on this mountain **nor** in Jerusalem.
You people worship what you do **not understand**;
  we worship what we **understand**,
  because **salvation** is from the **Jews**.

Samaritan worship on Mount Gerizim instead of the temple mount in Jerusalem was one of the religious points of contention between the Samaritans and the Jews.

In the Gospel of John, northern Palestine is favored space. Unlike in Judea, where Jesus causes division and acrimony, in Samaria and the Galilee, which are located respectively north and farther north of Judea, Jesus wins a good reception (John 4:43–45). Unlike in Judea, Jesus is safe from Jews who would harm him (John 7:1). In the other three Gospels, there is no depiction of Samaritans so positive as what we find in John 4:39–42. The next most positive depiction of a Samaritan is found in Luke's Gospel in the parable of the Good Samaritan (Luke 10:30–37), although Luke earlier depicts a Samaritan village rejecting Jesus (9:52–56).

In today's Gospel, we encounter much of Jesus' humanity. He is tired and thirsty after his long journey (4:6–7). And his riddling conversation with the Samaritan woman is joking and playful. She quite reasonably thinks this stranger's offer of living water has to do with removing her daily hassle of getting water from the well to her home. But in fact Jesus is speaking of eternal life conferred by the waters of Baptism. See how Jesus does not dispel her ignorance, but rather permits a conversation to develop that is full of misunderstandings and laced with double meanings (4:7–15). And when Jesus tells the woman to fetch her husband, but then reveals his full knowledge of some embarrassing details of her complicated marital history, one can easily imagine him grinning ear to ear.

But the **hour** is **coming**, and is now **here**,
   when **true** worshipers will worship the **Father**
      in **Spirit** and **truth**;
   and indeed the **Father** seeks such people to **worship** him.
God is **Spirit**, and those who **worship** him
   must **worship** in **Spirit** and **truth**."
The woman **said** to him,
   "**I know** that the **Messiah** is **coming**, the one called **the Christ**;
   when he comes, he will tell us **everything**."
Jesus **said** to her,
   "**I am he**, the one **speaking** with you."

At that moment his disciples returned,
   and were **amazed** that he was talking with a **woman**,
   but still **no one** said, "**What** are you **looking** for?"
   or "**Why** are you **talking** with her?"
The woman **left** her water jar
   and went into the town and said to the people,
   "**Come see** a man who told me **everything** I have **done**.
Could he **possibly** be the **Christ**?"
They went out of the town and came to him.
Meanwhile, the disciples urged him, "**Rabbi, eat**."
But he **said** to them,
   "**I** have **food** to **eat** of which you do **not** know."
So the disciples said to one another,
   "Could **someone** have brought him something to **eat**?"
Jesus **said** to them,
   "**My** food is to do the **will** of the one who **sent** me
   and to **finish** his work.
Do **you** not say, 'In four months the **harvest** will be here'?
I tell you, **look up** and **see** the fields **ripe** for the **harvest**.

The reaper is **already** receiving payment
    and gathering **crops** for **eternal life**,
    so that the **sower** and **reaper** can **rejoice** together.
For **here** the saying is **verified** that '**One sows** and **another reaps**.'
I sent you to **reap** what you have **not** worked for;
    others have done the work,
    and you are **sharing** the **fruits** of their **work**."

Many of the **Samaritans** of that town began to **believe** in him
    because of the **word** of the woman who **testified**,
    "He told me **everything** I have done."
When the **Samaritans** came to him,
    they **invited** him to stay with them;
    and he stayed there two days.
Many more began to **believe** in him because of his **word**,
    and they **said** to the woman,
    "We **no longer** believe because of **your** word;
    for **we** have **heard** for **ourselves**,
    and we **know** that this is **truly** the **savior** of the **world**."

[Shorter: John 4:5–15, 19b–26, 39a, 40–42]

4TH SUNDAY OF LENT

Lectionary #31

READING I   1 Samuel 16:1b, 6–7, 10–13a

Bethlehem = BETH-leh-hem

Eliab = El-ee-AB

Samuel is certain that one of the sons Jesse presents for his review must be the king God wants. Emphasize the word "Surely" in order to express Samuel's certainty, and pause before you deliver God's reply.

Pause before you deliver God's reply, looking out at the assembly when you proclaim the phrase "for the LORD does not see as mortals see."

A reading from the first Book of Samuel

The LORD said to Samuel:
    "Fill your horn with **oil**, and be on your **way**.
I am sending you to **Jesse** of **Bethlehem**,
    for I have chosen my **king** from among his **sons**."

As **Jesse** and his **sons** came to the **sacrifice**,
    Samuel looked at **Eliab** and thought,
    "**Surely** the LORD's **anointed** is here before him."
But the LORD said to **Samuel**:
    "Do not **judge** from his **appearance** or from his **lofty stature**,
    because I have **rejected** him.
Not as **man** sees does **God** see,
    because **man** sees the **appearance**
    but the LORD looks into the **heart**."
In the same way **Jesse** presented **seven sons** before **Samuel**,
    but **Samuel** said to **Jesse**,
    "The LORD has **not** chosen **any one** of these."
Then **Samuel** asked **Jesse**,
    "Are these **all** the sons you have?"
Jesse replied,
    "There is still the **youngest**, who is **tending** the **sheep**."
Samuel said to **Jesse**,
    "**Send** for him;
    we will **not** begin the sacrificial **banquet** until he **arrives** here."

READING I   **Monarchy probably arose in Israel partly because it was a fairly efficient institution when it came to meeting military threats. But 1 Samuel reflects a great deal of ambivalence about monarchy in Israel, with some of the book's ancient authors and editors clearly regarding it as alien to Israelite tradition and a sign of the people's abandonment of God.**

    According to 1 Samuel, Saul became Israel's first king over the judge Samuel's strong objections. Samuel initially had no

personal problem with Saul, but rather objected to the very idea of monarchy. A king, Samuel warns, will send Israel's sons to war, put its daughters to work, and take the people's property for himself, his family, his servants, and his friends (1 Samuel 8:1–22). "You yourselves," Samuel predicts in 1 Samuel 8:17, "will become his slaves." Israel, however, demands a king anyway. Both Samuel and God eventually relent; Saul is anointed king in secret by Samuel (1 Samuel 10:1) and later proclaimed king before a public gathering of Israel's tribes (Samuel 10:17–27).

    But Saul loses the favor of both God and Samuel after he makes sacrifices before a battle in Samuel's absence and against his instructions. When Samuel finally arrives, he informs Saul that, because he disobeyed, he and his descendants will lose the throne (1 Samuel 13:13–14). God later expresses regret at having made Saul king (1 Samuel 15:11) and, in today's reading, sends Samuel out to anoint a new one.

Jesse sent and had the young man brought to them.
He was **ruddy**, a youth **handsome** to behold
    and making a **splendid** appearance.
The LORD said,
    "There—**anoint** him, for **this** is the **one!**"
Then **Samuel**, with the horn of **oil** in hand,
    anointed **David** in the presence of his **brothers**;
    and from **that day on**, the **spirit** of the LORD
        rushed upon **David**.

Emphasize in particular the word "rushed."

READING II   Ephesians 5:8–14

A reading from the Letter of Saint Paul to the Ephesians

Brothers and **sisters**:
You were **once darkness**,
    but **now** you are **light** in the **Lord**.
Live as **children** of **light**,
    for **light** produces every kind of **goodness**
    and **righteousness** and **truth**.
Try to learn what is **pleasing** to the Lord.
Take **no part** in the **fruitless** works of **darkness**;
    rather **expose** them, for it is **shameful** even to **mention**
    the things done by them in **secret**;
    but **everything** exposed by the **light** becomes **visible**,
    for **everything** that becomes **visible** is **light**.
Therefore, it says:
"**Awake**, O sleeper,
    and **arise** from the **dead**,
    and **Christ** will give you **light**."

Look out at the assembly and proclaim this quotation in a clear, exuberant, and cheerful tone.

This king is David, the youngest son of Jesse of the tribe of Judah. He did not seem much like a king to his father, who did not even offer him for Samuel's inspection. And Samuel appears to have found acceptable more than one of the candidates presented to him before David was called away from his labor. Although neither Samuel's nor his own father's first choice, David was God's sole chosen one, and from the day of his anointing "the spirit of the LORD rushed upon David" (1 Samuel 16:13).

READING II | The majority of Christians of the first century were not born into their religion. They became Christians in adulthood. Thus, the author of Ephesians can meaningfully compare his audience to their pre-Christian selves: "For you were once darkness, but now you are light in the Lord" (5:8).

What might it mean not simply to walk *in* darkness (see 1 Thessalonians 5:4) but to *be* darkness? The probable answer is what the author says in the immediately preceding passage of 5:1–7. In 5:3–4, the author

mentions seven vices, some of which, like the words our Bible translates as "immorality" *(porneia)* and "impurity" *(akatharsia)*, probably have to do with unspecified illicit sexual behavior. Some of the vices have to do principally with speech: "obscenity" *(aischrotēs)*, "silly talk" *(mōrologia)*, and "suggestive talk" *(eutrapelia)*. The last is "greed" *(pleonexia)*. According to our author, the common root of at least three of these vices is idolatry: "Be sure of this, that no immoral or impure or greedy person, that is,

Rabbi = RA-bye

Proclaim Jesus' words in a clear, strong tone.

GOSPEL   John 9:1–41

A reading from the holy Gospel according to John

As **Jesus** passed by he saw a man **blind** from birth.
His disciples asked him,
      "Rabbi, **who sinned**, this **man** or his **parents**,
      that he was born **blind**?"
Jesus answered,
      "**Neither** he **nor** his parents **sinned**;
      it is so that the **works** of **God** might be made **visible**
            through him.
We have to do the **works** of the **one** who sent me while it is **day**.
Night is coming when **no one** can work.
While **I** am in the **world**, I am the **light** of the world."
When he had **said** this, he **spat** on the **ground**
      and made **clay** with the **saliva**,
      and **smeared** the clay on his **eyes**, and said to him,
      "Go **wash** in the Pool of **Siloam**"—which means **Sent**—.
So he went and washed, and came back able to **see**.

Siloam = Sil-LOAM

His neighbors and those who had seen him earlier
      as a beggar said,
      "Isn't **this** the one who used to **sit** and **beg**?"
Some said, "**It is**,"
      but others said, "**No**, he just **looks** like him."
He said, "**I am**."
So they **said** to him, "**How** were your eyes opened?"
He replied,
      "The man called **Jesus** made **clay** and **anointed** my eyes
      and told me, 'Go to Siloam and **wash**.'
So I went there and **washed** and was able to **see**."
And they **said** to him, "**Where** is he?"

Use a tone similar to the one you use for Jesus' lines when you read the replies of the man born blind to those questioning and challenging him.

an idolater, has any inheritance in the kingdom of Christ and of God" (Ephesians 5:5; see Romans 1:23–24).

What might "silly talk" mean? Is our author talking about unnecessary speech? Does he mean gossip? Jokes? And what is his definition of greed? Lending money at interest, perhaps? The general character of these vices requires his audience to make carefully reasoned decisions about the specific behaviors that make them either darkness or light.

This author advises in favor of a firm boundary between Church and world, which is symbolized by the opposition of light to darkness. But our author's Church was not free of vice any more than his world was free of virtue. He does not disapprove of the vices simply because they are wrong in and of themselves.

Our author disapproves of the vices he mentions because they hinder their practitioners' inheritance of the kingdom (5:5). And he approves of "thanksgiving" "goodness," righteousness," and "truth" because he finds them in Jesus Christ, into whose death

Christians are baptized and awakened to brilliant new life (5:4, 9).

GOSPEL   In 9:1–5, Jesus' disciples assume a common ancient belief that sickness, like other misfortunes, was a punishment or a sign of divine displeasure: someone must have sinned, they reason, either the blind man or his parents, or else he would not be blind. Jesus rejects their question. No one, he says, sinned and made the man blind. He is blind rather "so that the works of God might be made visible

He said, "I don't know."

They brought the **one** who was once **blind** to the Pharisees.
Now Jesus had made **clay** and opened his **eyes** on a sabbath.
So then the **Pharisees** also asked him how he was able to see.
He **said** to them,
 "He put **clay** on my **eyes**, and I **washed**, and now I can **see**."
So **some** of the Pharisees said,
 "This man is **not** from God,
 because he does not keep the **sabbath**."
But **others** said,
 "**How** can a **sinful** man do such **signs**?"
And there was a **division** among them.
So they **said** to the blind man **again**,
 "**What** do you have to **say** about him,
 since he opened your **eyes**?"
He said, "He is a **prophet**."

Now the **Jews** did not **believe**
 that he had been **blind** and gained his **sight**
 until they summoned the parents of the one
 who had gained his **sight**.
They **asked** them,
 "Is **this** your son, who you say was born **blind**?
How does he now **see**?"
His parents **answered** and **said**,
 "We **know** that this is our **son** and that he was born **blind**.
We do **not** know **how** he sees now,
 nor do we know **who** opened his eyes.
Ask him, he is of age;
 he can speak for **himself**."

through him" (John 9:3). Then Jesus makes some cryptic statements: "We have to do the works of the one who sent me while it is day. Night is coming when no one can work. While I am in the world, I am the light of the world" (John 9:4–5).

What is the significance of "night" in these verses? From them we learn that Jesus defines night as a time when no one, presumably including himself, can work. Night is also when Nicodemus, meaning well but

completely uncomprehending, comes to speak with Jesus and is confounded by him (3:2; 19:39). Immediately after Judas leaves to betray Jesus we read, "And it was night" (13:30). Quite interesting in light of 9:6 ("I am the light of the world") is John 11:9–10: "If one walks during the day, he does not stumble, because he sees *the light of this world.* But if one walks at night, he stumbles, because the light is not in him." One finds the description of Jesus as "the light" in the first chapter of John (1:4–5, 7–9), in one of

the narrator's asides (3:19–21), at the beginning of one of the bitterest disputes of the Gospel (8:12), and in 12:35–36 and 12:46 summing up Jesus' public ministry as light in the midst of people who either prefer or cannot escape darkness.

We have perhaps begun to suspect that John uses words like "light," "darkness," "night," and "blind" in a symbolic way. To John, "darkness," "night," and "blindness" describe the mental and spiritual condition

His parents said this because they were **afraid**
    of the Jews, for the Jews had **already** agreed
    that if **anyone** acknowledged him as the **Christ**,
    he would be **expelled** from the synagogue.
For this reason his parents said,
    "He is of age; **question** him."

So a **second** time they called the man who had been **blind**
    and said to him, "**Give God** the **praise**!
We **know** that this man is a **sinner**."
He replied,
    "**If** he is a **sinner**, **I** do not **know**.
One thing I **do** know is that I was **blind** and now I **see**."
So they **said** to him,
    "**What** did he do to you?
    How did he open your eyes?"
He answered them,
    "I **told** you **already** and you did **not** listen.
Why do you want to hear it **again**?
Do **you** want to become his disciples, **too**?"
They **ridiculed** him and said,
    "**You** are that man's **disciple**;
    we are **disciples** of **Moses**!
We know that God spoke to **Moses**,
    but we do **not** know where **this one** is from."
The man **answered** and **said** to them,
    "**This** is what is so **amazing**,
    that you do **not** know where he is **from**,
        yet he **opened** my eyes.
We know that God does not **listen** to sinners,
    but if one is **devout** and does his **will**, he **listens** to him.

of a person who either cannot or will not believe in what Jesus says about himself and in the signs he performs. The symbolic use of "darkness" and "light" is apparent from the Gospel's very beginning (John 1:1–10).

The foundation of this reading is a healing story, which John probably knew from common Christian tradition but which he may also have known from Mark (see Mark 8:22–26). The healing takes up all of two verses. The remainder of the reading is a controversy about what spiritual sight and blindness means. Observe how the neighbors, like people who cannot see clearly, argue over the identity of a blind man whom they see every day (9:8–9). See how Jesus himself disappears from view, much to the consternation of the man's antagonists (9:12). And take note of how the Pharisees suspect that all this talk of blindness actually refers to them after all (9:39–41).

It is **unheard** of that **anyone** ever opened the eyes
of a person born **blind**.
If this man were not from God,
he would **not** be able to do **anything**."
They **answered** and **said** to him,
"You were born **totally** in sin,
and are **you** trying to teach **us**?"
Then they threw him out.

When Jesus heard that they had thrown him **out**,
he **found** him and said, "Do you **believe** in the **Son** of **Man**?"
He **answered** and **said**,
"**Who** is he, sir, that I may **believe** in him?"
Jesus **said** to him,
"You have **seen** him,
the one **speaking** with you is he."
He said,
"I **do** believe, Lord," and he **worshiped** him.
Then Jesus said,
"I came into this world for **judgment**,
so that those who do **not** see **might see**,
and those who **do** see might become **blind**."

Some of the **Pharisees** who were with him **heard** this
and **said** to him, "**Surely** we are not **also** blind, are we?"
Jesus said to them,
"**If** you were blind, you would have **no** sin;
but **now** you are saying, '**We see**,' so your sin **remains**."

[Shorter: John 9:1, 6–9, 13–17, 34–38]

When the man born blind meets Jesus, switch to a quieter and more humble tone than you use in his debate with the crowds and Pharisees.

5TH SUNDAY OF LENT

Lectionary #34

READING I   Ezekiel 37:12–14

A reading from the Book of the prophet Ezekiel

Thus says the Lord GOD:
O my **people**, I will **open** your graves
   and have you **rise** from them,
   and **bring** you back to the **land** of Israel.
Then **you** shall **know** that I am the LORD,
   when I **open** your **graves** and have you **rise** from them,
   O my **people**!
I will put my **spirit** in you that you may **live**,
   and I will **settle** you upon your **land**;
   thus you shall **know** that I am the LORD.
I have **promised**, and I will **do** it, says the LORD.

Look out at the assembly as you proclaim the words "O my people."

Slow down and emphasize each word in both occurrences of the phrase "I am the Lord."

READING I   The Lectionary gives us a mere three verses of Ezekiel 37. Some additional context is in order. Ezekiel prophesied in the first decades of the sixth century BC. He did not do so from Jerusalem, or even from Judah, but from exile in or near Mesopotamia, where he, like many other Jews, had been led to as captives. He had been a priest of the Jerusalem temple and was among the first of those taken away by Babylon. He did not personally witness the breaching of Jerusalem's

walls, the slaughter in its streets, the ruin of the temple. He heard about it from refugees of the carnage (33:21).

In the religious thought of many Jews in Ezekiel's day, the temple was much more than a holy place. It was not just a site where priests offered praise, petition, and sacrifice to God. It was believed to be the one, unique place on earth where God had chosen to remain. One can only imagine what it was like for Ezekiel, for whom the

temple and its service defined life itself, to have heard of the temple's destruction while captive. What could it mean for Israel that the only earthly place its God had chosen to dwell lay in ruins?

In the first of many visions Ezekiel records, the prophet sees God's throne borne aloft on four "living creatures" and wheels, all having an extraordinary appearance (Ezekiel 1). The "living creatures" are probably angelic guardian spirits of the temple (see Isaiah 6). The wheels, however, are

READING II   Romans 8:8–11

A reading from the Letter of Saint Paul to the Romans

Brothers and **sisters**:
Those who are in the flesh **cannot** please God.
But **you** are **not** in the flesh;
   on the **contrary**, you are in the **spirit**,
   if only the **Spirit** of **God** dwells in **you**.
Whoever does **not** have the **Spirit** of **Christ**
   does **not** belong to him.
But if **Christ** is in you,
   although the **body** is **dead** because of **sin**,
   the **spirit** is **alive** because of **righteousness**.
If the **Spirit** of the one who raised Jesus from the **dead**
   dwells in you,
   the one who raised **Christ** from the **dead**
   will give **life** to your **mortal** bodies **also**,
   through his **Spirit** dwelling in **you**.

Emphasize in particular the word "cannot" and all of the occurrences of the word "not."

Paul is contrasting "flesh" and "spirit" in this passage. To help him bring out this contrast, emphasize each member of the opposing pairs.

GOSPEL   John 11:1–45

A reading from the holy Gospel according to John

Now a man was ill, **Lazarus** from **Bethany**,
   the village of **Mary** and her sister **Martha**.
Mary was the one who had anointed the Lord with perfumed oil
   and dried his **feet** with her **hair**;
   it was **her** brother Lazarus who was ill.

Lazarus = LAH-zar-rus
Bethany = BETH-ah-nee

new. They signify what will later become clearer (see, for example, Ezekiel 10): that God has left the temple and followed Israel into captivity.

Today's reading comes from Ezekiel 37, which contains another of the prophet's visions. "The hand of the Lord" sets the prophet down in a valley, where all around dry bones lie strewn. God instructs Ezekiel to prophesy to the bones. He does, and soon sees the bones arrange themselves before

his eyes, grow flesh, and receive the breath of life. God then says to Ezekiel in 37:11: "Son of man, these bones are the whole house of Israel. They have been saying, 'Our bones are dried up, our hope is lost, and we are cut off.' "

Today's reading dispels this despair. It is a prophecy of resurrection to "the whole house of Israel." It portends more than the raising of the bodies of dead people at some

future time. It promises the raising of a beaten people from the grave of defeat, slavery, humiliation, and despair. It promises to restore all they imagine they have lost and more.

READING II Spirituality, like religion, means different things to different people. One of the ways some people use the word in contemporary North America is in opposition to religion. "I'm spiritual, but not religious," someone may say.

Judea = joo-DEE-uh

Rabbi = RAH-bye

So the sisters sent word to Jesus saying,
"**Master**, the one you **love** is ill."
When Jesus heard this he said,
"This illness is **not** to end in death,
but is for the **glory** of **God**,
that the **Son** of **God** may be **glorified** through it."
Now Jesus **loved** Martha and her sister and Lazarus.
So when he heard that he was ill,
he remained for **two days** in the place where he was.
Then after this he said to his **disciples**,
"Let us go **back** to Judea."
The disciples said to him,
"**Rabbi**, the Jews were just trying to **stone** you,
and you want to go **back** there?"
Jesus answered,
"Are there not **twelve** hours in a day?
If one **walks** during the **day**, he does not **stumble**,
because he sees the **light** of this **world**.
But if one walks at **night**, he **stumbles**,
because the **light** is **not** in him."
He said this, and then told them,
"Our friend **Lazarus** is **asleep**,
but I am going to **awaken** him."
So the disciples said to him,
"Master, if he is **asleep**, he will be **saved**."
But Jesus was talking about his **death**,
while they thought that he meant **ordinary** sleep.
So then Jesus said to them **clearly**,
"**Lazarus** has **died**.
And I am glad for you that I was not there,
that **you** may **believe**.
Let us go to him."

In today's reading, we do not read of an opposition between spirituality and religion. Religion never arises. Instead, we see Paul oppose flesh, death, and sin to spirit, life, and righteousness. For Paul, to be "in the spirit" cannot be reconciled with being "in the flesh" (Romans 5:8–9). The two states are utterly contrary and cannot inhabit the same mortal body.

Flesh *(sarx)*, in today's reading, does not mean the physical human body. Sometimes Paul uses the word in this ordinary way (1 Corinthians 15:39; 2 Corinthians 7:5). But he does not do so here. Here flesh describes something very difficult to put simply into words. It is something like a supernatural realm of authority, or a sphere of influence, that is opposed to Christ and outwardly characterized by wrongdoing, sin, and vice. "Now the works of the flesh," Paul says in

Galatians 5:19–21, "are obvious: immorality, impurity, licentiousness, idolatry, sorcery, hatreds, rivalry, jealousy, outbursts of fury, acts of selfishness, dissensions, factions, occasions of envy, drinking bouts, orgies, and the like."

In Paul's view, the Spirit is conferred in the rite of Baptism. We encounter Paul's most expansive discussion of his theology of Baptism in Romans 6. There, we see

So **Thomas**, called **Didymus**, said to his fellow disciples,
  "Let us **also** go to **die** with him."

When **Jesus** arrived, he found that **Lazarus**
  had already been in the tomb for **four days**.
Now **Bethany** was near **Jerusalem**, only about **two** miles away.
And **many** of the Jews had come to **Martha** and **Mary**
  to **comfort** them about their **brother**.
When **Martha** heard that **Jesus** was coming,
  she went to **meet** him;
  but **Mary** sat at home.
Martha said to **Jesus**,
  "Lord, if you had **been** here,
  my brother would **not** have died.
But **even now** I know that **whatever** you ask of God,
  God will **give** you."
Jesus **said** to her,
  "Your **brother** will **rise**."
Martha **said** to him,
  "I **know** he will rise,
  in the **resurrection** on the **last** day."
Jesus **told** her,
  "**I** am the **resurrection** and the **life**;
  whoever believes in me, **even** if he dies, will **live**,
  and **everyone** who **lives** and **believes** in me will **never** die.
Do you **believe** this?"
She said to him, "**Yes**, Lord.
I have **come** to **believe** that **you** are the **Christ**, the **Son** of **God**,
  the one who is **coming** into the **world**."

Deliver Mary's and Martha's words as tired and grieving women might by using a sad or flat tone of voice. Let their sadness and exhaustion come through in their conversations with Jesus.

that Baptism is a rebirth into a new life of freedom—but freedom from what? If one imagines that sin, law, and death are wardens over the prison of "the flesh" (indeed, to be "in the flesh" is, to Paul, a kind of incarceration), then Baptism is the means by which one becomes free.

A useful text to read together with Paul's writings on spirit and flesh is Galatians 5:19–22, which details the "works of the flesh" and where Paul names "the fruit of the spirit" as "love, joy, peace, patience, kindness, generosity, faithfulness, gentleness, self-control."

GOSPEL   Lazarus is not the only person Jesus raises in the Gospels. He also raises the daughter of Jairus, a synagogue leader, in both Mark 5:22–24, 35–43 and Luke 8:41–42, 49–56. (In 9:18–19, 23–26 of his Gospel, Matthew includes the same incident but does not name the man.) Luke 7:11–17 recounts the raising of a widow's son. Acts 20:9-10 also describes the raising of a boy called Eutychus by Paul. Having gone to sleep while sitting in a window, Eutychus falls three stories. The boy appears dead by the time his friends get to him. But when Paul takes hold of him, signs of life return. (It is fitting that this boy's Greek name, Eutychus, can be translated as "good luck.")

When she had **said** this,
    she went and called her sister **Mary** secretly, saying,
    "The **teacher** is here and is **asking** for you."
As soon as she **heard** this,
    she rose **quickly** and went to him.
For Jesus had **not yet** come into the **village**,
    but was still where **Martha** had met him.
So when the **Jews** who were **with** her in the **house** comforting her
    saw **Mary** get up quickly and go out,
    they **followed** her,
    presuming that she was going to the **tomb** to weep there.
When **Mary** came to where **Jesus** was and **saw** him,
    she **fell** at his **feet** and **said** to him,
    "Lord, if you had **been** here,
    my brother would **not** have died."
When Jesus saw her **weeping** and the Jews who had come
      with her **weeping**,
    he became **perturbed** and **deeply** troubled, and said,
    "**Where** have you **laid** him?"
They said to him, "Sir, come and see."
And Jesus **wept**.
So the Jews said, "**See** how he **loved** him."
But **some** of them said,
    "Could not the **one** who opened the **eyes** of the **blind** man
    have done **something** so that this man would not have **died**?"

So Jesus, **perturbed** again, came to the **tomb**.
It was a **cave**, and a **stone** lay across it.
Jesus said, "Take **away** the stone."
Martha, the dead man's sister, said to him,
    "Lord, by now there will be a **stench**;
    he has been dead for **four days**."

As in the case of the man born blind in John 9:3, the death of Lazarus has a greater purpose than the disciples at first realize. Jesus spells out this purpose in 11:4: "This illness is not to end in death, but is for the glory of God, that the Son of God may be glorified through it." The disciples, however, do not understand this; as 11:11–15 makes clear, sometimes Jesus has to make things incredibly plain to these men.

The disciples are frightened that Jesus wants to go back to the village of Bethany, which is in the region of Judea. For the Judeans want to kill Jesus. But when Jesus, having waited for Lazarus to die, finally sets out for Bethany, the others set out with him. If Thomas' statement of 11:16 reflects the disciples' prevailing mood ("Let us also go to die with him"), then it was a grim group indeed that struck out for Bethany that day.

Imagine how puzzling Jesus' initial behavior must have been to the disciples, Lazarus' sisters, and perhaps to poor Lazarus himself as he lay dying. Upon learning of his beloved friend's illness and possessing the power to heal him, Jesus does *nothing*. And although Martha reveals a profound trust and belief in Jesus, perhaps there is also some anger in her words of greeting to Jesus: "Lord, if you had been here, my brother would not have died" (11:21; see also Mary's greeting in 11:32).

Proclaim Jesus' prayer to his Father slowly, but with strength and boldness.

Let the words "Lazarus, come out!" be the loudest words of this reading, but don't shout them. Look up at the assembly when you deliver them. Pause before and after you speak them.

Jesus **said** to her,
"Did I **not** tell you that if you **believe**
you will see the glory of **God**?"
So they took **away** the stone.
And Jesus **raised** his eyes and said,
"Father, I **thank** you for hearing me.
I know that you **always** hear me;
but because of the **crowd** here I have said this,
that they may **believe** that **you** sent **me**."
And when he had said this,
he cried out in a loud voice,
"**Lazarus**, **come out!**"
The dead man came out,
tied **hand** and **foot** with burial bands,
and his face was **wrapped** in a **cloth**.
So Jesus said to them,
"**Untie** him and let him **go**."

Now **many** of the Jews who had come to **Mary**
and **seen** what he had done began to **believe** in him.

[Shorter: John 11:3–7, 17, 20–27, 33b–45]

John reports that the raising of Lazarus was such a powerful sign to the Jews that the chief priests plot to murder not only Jesus but Lazarus as well (12:9–11). The raising of Lazarus, the last of Jesus' signs in John's Gospel, appears to have had its intended effect of fostering belief in Jesus (12:11; see also 20:30–31).

PALM SUNDAY OF THE LORD'S PASSION

Lectionary #37

GOSPEL AT THE PROCESSION   Matthew 21:1–11

A reading from the holy Gospel according to Matthew

When Jesus and the disciples drew near **Jerusalem**
and came to **Bethphage** on the **Mount** of **Olives**,
Jesus sent two disciples, saying to them,
"Go into the village opposite you,
and **immediately** you will find an **ass** tethered,
and a **colt** with her.
Untie them and bring them here to me.
And if **anyone** should say anything to you, reply,
'The **master** has **need** of them.'
Then he will **send** them at once."
This happened so that what had been spoken through the prophet
might be **fulfilled**:
    *Say to daughter **Zion**,*
    *"**Behold**, your king **comes** to you,*
        *meek and riding on an **ass**,*
        *and on a **colt**, the **foal** of a **beast** of **burden**."*

The disciples went and did as Jesus had **ordered** them.
They brought the **ass** and the **colt** and laid their **cloaks** over them,
and he **sat** upon them.
The very large crowd spread their **cloaks** on the **road**,
while others cut **branches** from the **trees**
and **strewed** them on the **road**.

Bethphage = BETH-faje

Zion = ZI-yon
Proclaim the fulfilled words of scripture as well as the scriptural words of the celebrating crowd in a clear, bold tone of voice.
foal = fohl

PROCESSION GOSPEL | **In the Gospel of Matthew, even seemingly insignificant details of Jesus' life fulfill scripture. After the incarceration of John the Baptist, Matthew reports that Jesus' relocation to Capernaum, a fishing village of the Galilee, fulfills scripture (4:14–16). And in at least one instance we cannot identify the source of the prophecy Matthew says Jesus fulfills (Matthew 2:23). We even find Matthew's understanding of Jesus' role in the fulfillment of scripture on Jesus' own lips in this Gospel: "Do not think that I have come to abolish the law or the** prophets. I have come not to abolish but to fulfill" (Matthew 5:17).

It has been previously observed that Matthew understands Jesus' ministry to be the fulfillment of scripture. All four of the New Testament Gospels see Jesus in this way. But Matthew has a characteristic way of informing his readership that something Jesus did or said happened in fulfillment of scripture. In today's reading, we find a typical example of this verbal formula. Jesus has instructed two of his disciples to go into the nearby village of Bethphage, untie two animals to be found there, and bring them back to Jesus. "This happened," Matthew writes, "so that what had been spoken through the prophet might be fulfilled: 'Say to daughter Zion, "Behold, your king comes to you, meek and riding on an ass, and on a colt, the foal of a beast of burden." ' " The prophet Matthew has in mind is Zechariah. Zechariah 9:9 supplies the principal image of the victorious ruler seated on an animal. The original historical context of Zechariah 9—14 cannot be determined with any precision. But it is quite likely that this portion of the book was written later and by a different author than the first eight chapters. In any

The crowds preceding him and those following
kept crying out and saying:
"**Hosanna** to the **Son** of **David**;
blessed is **he** who **comes** in the **name** of the **Lord**;
hosanna in the **highest**."
And when he **entered** Jerusalem
the whole **city** was shaken and asked, "**Who is this**?"
And the crowds replied,
"**This** is **Jesus** the **prophet**, from **Nazareth** in **Galilee**."

Lectionary #38

READING I   Isaiah 50:4–7

A reading from the Book of the Prophet Isaiah

The Lord GOD has **given** me
a **well-trained** tongue,
that I might know how to **speak** to the **weary**
a **word** that will **rouse** them.
Morning after **morning**
he **opens** my **ear** that I may **hear**;
and I have **not** rebelled,
have **not** turned back.

I gave my **back** to those who **beat** me,
my **cheeks** to those who **plucked** my beard;
my **face** I did **not** shield
from **buffets** and **spitting**.

Margin notes

Hosanna = Ho-SAN-nah

Emphasize both the city's question and the crowd's answer.
Nazareth = NAH-zah-reth
Galilee = GAL-li-lee

Emphasize the occurrences of the word "not."

Let the punctuation mark brief pauses in your delivery.

event, the prophecy of Zechariah 9:9–17 concerns the advent of a king of David's royal line.

If one looks at Matthew's account of Jesus' entry into Jerusalem next to the other three evangelists' accounts of the same events (Mark 11:1–11; Luke 19:28–40; John 12:12–19), one finds in Matthew a very interesting and unique feature. Matthew has Jesus sit on two animals while the other three evangelists portray him sitting on one only. What is the reason for this difference, and how does one sit on two pack animals at the same time anyway?

Most biblical scholars would probably call Zechariah 9:9–14 poetry. Among the most basic features of Hebrew poetry is "parallelism." Rather than relying on rhyming (as in much poetry in English), or on the number and arrangement of vowels in a line (as in ancient Greek and Latin poetry), Hebrew poetry relies to large extent on parallelism. All this means is that the first of a pair of lines expresses an idea or an image that is then taken up and repeated, completed, reflected, inverted, or even interpreted in the second line. To put it another

way, parallel lines of Hebrew poetry speak with each other.

In Hebrew, it is pretty clear that Zechariah 9:9 is an example of parallelism. Our Bible translates the text of Zechariah 9:9 directly from the Hebrew: "See, your king shall come to you; a just savior is he, Meek, and riding on an ass, on a colt, the foal of an ass." Our Bible's translation of the Old Testament passage holds that Zechariah was not talking about two different animals any more than he was talking about two different kings.

The Lord **GOD** is my **help**,
> therefore I am **not** disgraced;
I have set my **face** like **flint**,
> knowing that I shall **not** be put to shame.

READING II   Philippians 2:6–11

A reading from the Letter of Saint Paul to the Philippians

Christ Jesus, though he was in the **form** of God,
> did not regard **equality** with God
> something to be **grasped**.
Rather, he **emptied** himself,
> taking the form of a **slave**,
> coming in **human** likeness;
> and found **human** in appearance,
> he **humbled** himself,
> becoming obedient to the point of **death**,
> even **death** on a **cross**.
Because of this, God **greatly exalted** him
> and bestowed on him the **name**
> which is above **every** name,
> that at the name of **Jesus**
> **every** knee should bend,
> of those in **heaven** and on **earth** and **under** the earth,
> and **every** tongue **confess** that
> **Jesus Christ** is **Lord**,
> to the **glory** of **God** the **Father**.

Proclaim this part of the reading slowly, emphasizing each word of the phrase "Rather, he emptied himself."

Briefly pause and look out at the assembly when you read the words "even death on a cross."
Pause between verses 8 and 9, stressing the words "Because of this."

Emphasize in particular the occurrences of the word "every."

Slow down, look up, and emphasize each word of the phrase "Jesus Christ is Lord."

Matthew, however, thought that the two pack animals of Zechariah 9:9 were not parallel images, with the second image reflecting the first, but actually referred to two separate animals on which Jesus sat. In this he differs from the other three evangelists, each of whom depicts Jesus' entry on a single animal. This bothered some early Christian biblical interpreters. One early harmonization of Matthew's account of the triumphal entry with those of the other three evangelists claimed that Jesus did ride on both animals, just not at the same time; he rode now on one, now on the other, all the way into Jerusalem.

Although Matthew often identifies things Jesus says and does as the fulfillment of scripture, he does not *always* do so. This is the case in Matthew 21:9, which originally comes from Psalm 118: "Blessed is he who comes in the name of the Lord." For Matthew, the fulfillment of scripture is so deeply embedded in the person and work of Jesus of Nazareth that he simply cannot, or does not see the need, to point it out in every instance.

READING I   "Sing to the Lord a new song, his praise from the end of the earth: Let the sea and what fills it resound, the coastlands, and those who dwell in them" (Isaiah 42:10). One of the delights of reading Isaiah 40—66 is that delight itself is one of the themes of these chapters: delight in the vindication of Israel, delight in creation, delight in Jerusalem, delight in the history of Israel in light of new experience, delight in the ways of Israel's God.

Isaiah 40—55 includes a set of so-called "servant songs" (42:1–9; 49:1–7; 50:4–11; 52:13—53:12; see commentary I, Baptism

PASSION   Matthew 26:14—27:66

The Passion of our Lord Jesus Christ according to Matthew

Judas Iscariot = JU-das Is-CAR-i-ot

(1) One of the **Twelve**, who was called **Judas Iscariot**,
   went to the chief priests and said,
   "**What** are you **willing** to **give** me
   if I hand him over to you?"
They paid him thirty pieces of **silver**,
   and from **that** time on he looked for an **opportunity**
      to hand him **over**.

(2) On the **first** day of the **Feast** of **Unleavened Bread**,
   the disciples **approached** Jesus and said,
   "**Where** do you want us to prepare
   for you to eat the **Passover**?"
He said,
   "**Go** into the **city** to a certain **man** and **tell** him,
   'The **teacher** says, "My appointed time draws **near**;
   in **your** house I shall celebrate the **Passover**
      with my **disciples**."'"
The disciples then **did** as Jesus had **ordered**,
   and **prepared** the **Passover**.

(3) When it was **evening**,
   he reclined at **table** with the **Twelve**.
And while they were **eating**, he said,
   "**Amen**, I **say** to you, **one** of you will **betray** me."
Deeply **distressed** at this,
   they began to say to him one after another,
   "**Surely** it is not **I**, Lord?"

Emphasize the shock and surprise of the disciples' denials.

---

of the Lord, January 13). At 49:3 the text identifies this servant as Israel, but elsewhere the servant's identity is not at all clear. Indeed, we need not suppose that in each case the author had the same people or person in mind. This is true of today's reading as well. Some have seen the servant as a single person, a prophet perhaps, tormented for speaking unpopular truths. Others have envisioned a band of prophets or a group of men and women abused for their unwelcome public testimony.

For Catholics entering Holy Week, the servant's experience of violence at the hands of hostile people brings immediately to mind Jesus' Passion. The way of the cross is not just a painful death, but also a gauntlet of humiliation: spitting, blows, insults, taunts, and mockery. All four evangelists report that the jeers of those who earlier welcomed Jesus as a king pummel his ears in the last minutes of his life.

If one would enjoy delight's brilliant coloring of so much of Isaiah 40—66, one must also pay heed to these chapters' grim hues in their portrayal of the suffering of God's faithful ones.

READING II As they got up from their last supper together and headed toward Gethesemane, Jesus and his disciples sang hymns. Colossians 3:16 and Ephesians 5:19−20 mention the singing of hymns in worship. And in his first letter to the Church at Corinth, after admonishing the Corinthians for an excessive, and perhaps competitive, practice of speaking in tongues, Paul suggests the following program of worship: "When you assemble, one has a psalm, another an instruction, a revelation, a tongue, or an interpretation. Everything should be done for building up." The "psalm"

He said in reply,
    "He who has dipped his **hand** into the **dish** with me
    is the **one** who will **betray** me.
The Son of Man indeed **goes**, as it is **written** of him,
    but **woe** to that **man** by whom the **Son** of **Man** is **betrayed**.
It would be **better** for that man if he had **never** been born."
Then **Judas**, his **betrayer**, said in reply,
    "**Surely** it is not **I**, Rabbi?"
He answered, "**You** have **said** so."

(4) While they were **eating**,
    Jesus took **bread**, said the **blessing**,
    broke it, and **giving** it to his disciples said,
    "**Take** and **eat**; **this** is my **body**."
Then he took a **cup**, gave **thanks**, and **gave** it to them, saying,
    "**Drink** from it, **all** of you,
    for **this** is my **blood** of the **covenant**,
    which will be **shed** on behalf of **many**
    for the **forgiveness** of **sins**.
I tell you, from **now on** I shall **not** drink this **fruit** of the **vine**
    until the **day** when I **drink** it with you **new**
    in the **kingdom** of my **Father**."
Then, after singing a **hymn**,
    they went out to the **Mount** of **Olives**.

(5) Then **Jesus** said to them,
    "**This** night **all** of you will have your **faith** in me **shaken**,
    for it is **written**:
        *I will **strike** the **shepherd**,*
            *and the **sheep** of the **flock** will be **dispersed**;*
    but after I have been **raised up**,
    I shall go **before** you to **Galilee**."

Emphasize both Judas' denial and Jesus'
knowing reply.
Rabbi = RAH-bye

Slow down to emphasize the words of
institution.

Emphasize especially the words "all
of you."

Galilee = GAL-li-lee

would have almost certainly been sung or chanted.

Some biblical scholars are convinced that we possess not only evidence in the New Testament that Christians sang, but also bits and pieces of actual Christian hymns used in worship. Today's reading is one such example (see also John 1:1–14; Colossians 1:15–20; 1 Timothy 3:16; Hebrews 1:3; 1 Peter 1:18–21; 2:21–25; 3:18–21). While Paul neither calls this section of Philippians a hymn nor suggests that it was ever sung, its sophistication, unusual vocabulary, and other stylistic features set it off from the surrounding text as an uncommonly elevated piece of writing.

Philippians 2:6 presents one of the most famous challenges of Greek translation in the New Testament. There are two main ways to translate the verse, each yielding a very different meaning than the other. The first possibility is the one supplied by our Bible. Here, Christ is one "who, though he was in the form of God, did not regard equality with God something to be grasped." The second possibility goes something like this: "who, because he was in the form of God, did not think it robbery to be equal to God."

These translations do not describe situations within the Godhead that are essentially contradictory. The choice of one over the other has to do with what one thinks Paul wants to emphasize. Does Paul emphasize Jesus' decision to humble himself by taking on human form? Or does Paul emphasize the equality between the divine natures of Father and Son?

From You to Us

Proof of God's existence

I strongly disagree with Marvin Moore's assertion that we cannot offer proof of God's existence. Given the most favorable assumptions, the probability of putting together a simple cell by random processes can be shown to be less than $10^{240,000}$. Borel, the great Russian probabilist, says that events with probabilities less than 10^{50} never occur. Conclusion: Evolution and a material explanation are false. Thus we can be sure we live in a universe created by a loving God and He is the God of the Bible.

Jerry Olsen, email

Editor's response: The most that statistical evidence might prove about God is that He is very intelligent and powerful. It cannot prove that He is loving or that He is the God of the Bible.

Why many Christians keep Sunday

Here are several reasons why most Christians worship on Sundays: On the first day of the week Jesus rose and Mary worshiped Him. Jesus broke bread with His disciples on the first day of the week. The day of Pentecost was on the first day of the week. And Paul collected church offerings on this day.

Glenn Beauchamp, Auckland, New Zealand

Editor's response: Those points are all true, but not one of them says that the first day of the week replaced the seventh as the Sabbath.

A different picture of Jesus

Regarding the article "Jesus as Warrior" [August 2000], what a choice piece of material to read! I've often wondered why this picture of Jesus is never spoken or written about. This article gets cut out and put in my scrapbook of articles to read when I need to remember all the faces of my God.

Darlene M. Parker, Idaho Falls, Idaho

Praying for a miracle

I have never seen the issue of prayer and miracles addressed as well as it was by Randy Maxwell in "Praying for a Miracle" [February 2001]. People so often want to know why their prayers were not answered. Perhaps we should rather be happily surprised when they are answered, especially just the way we want them.

Sally Brebart, Saco, Maine

I attended a church where one woman stood before the congregation and told how she "prayed away" a migraine headache. Yet another member was dying of brain cancer. I wonder what he was thinking during her testimony as he sat quietly in the pew.

Richard Lasseter, Valdosta, Georgia

Punishment of the wicked

You say that the wicked will not be punished in everlasting fire. But speaking of the wicked, Mark 9:44 says that "their worm dieth not and the fire is not quenched" (KJV).

Jason Roberts, email

Editor's response: According to Jesus, it's the worm that doesn't die. Are you suggesting that maggots are immortal? A fire that is quenched is deliberately put out. Fires that are not quenched go out when all the fuel is burned up. Mark 9:44 does not persuade us to believe the doctrine of eternal punishment.

The importance of baptism

Concerning the article "Is Baptism Necessary for Salvation?" [February 2001], the Bible never teaches that baptism is symbolic. Baptism of water and Spirit is the very act of being born again. You cannot believe your way into Christ; you must be baptized into Christ.

Tom Arnold, Niles, Michigan

Editor's response: If baptism is absolutely essential for salvation, then salvation is not all of faith but depends partly on works.

Praise God for leading me to all the answers in His Word that I asked for on the subject of whether baptism is necessary for salvation. I was confronted with this issue recently by a friend, and I needed some biblical facts to work with. Two days later a Christian friend gave me your *Signs of the Times*® magazine, and it had all the correct answers.

Ty Wright, Frankfort, Indiana

We welcome your reaction to any of the articles or columns in this issue. Please keep your comments to 250 words or less. We reserve the right to edit for grammar, punctuation, and space. All letters to the editor become the property of *Signs of the Times*® Address all letters to *Signs* Letters, P.O. Box 5353, Nampa, ID 83653-5353 or fax them to (208) 465-2531. You can also email letters to <letters.signs@pacific press.com>.

SIGNS OF THE TIMES® (ISSN 0037-5047). Published monthly by Pacific Press® Publishing Association, 1350 North Kings Road, Nampa, ID 83687-3193, U.S.A.

U.S.A. SUBSCRIPTIONS: Rate when purchased in the U.S.A. and mailed within the U.S.A. and its territories: $18.95 (U.S.) annually. Single copy, $2.50. To other countries, $21.95 (U.S.) annually. Single copy, $3.00 (U.S.). Periodicals postage paid at Nampa, Idaho. Vol. 128, No. 4.

POSTMASTER: Send address changes to SIGNS OF THE TIMES® P.O. Box 5353, Nampa, ID 83653-5353.

CANADIAN SUBSCRIPTIONS: Rate when purchased in Canada and mailed within Canada: $27.95 (CDN.) annually (includes GST). Single copy, $3.50 (CDN.). To countries outside Canada (except U.S.A.): $30.95 (CDN.). Publications Mail Agreement Number 1650327.

CANADA POST: Send address changes and return undeliverable copies to Alberta ABC, I-194 College Avenue, College Heights, AB T4L 2G1.

Copyright © 2001 by Pacific Press® Publishing Association, a Seventh-day Adventist institution. Printed in the United States of America.

Christian countries most free

Countries with a Christian majority are among the freest in the world, according to a recent survey by the human rights group Freedom House. The survey tracked religious freedom in 75 countries, noting how well each country protects rights such as the right to worship, appoint leaders, have schools, adopt or abandon a religion or belief, and promote one's faith.

No historically Christian country other than communist Cuba was ranked "unfree." And no historically Islamic or Hindu country was ranked "free." There are exceptions: Jordan and some African Islamic countries would probably have been ranked "free" or "mostly free" if included in the survey. And then there's Yugoslavia and Serbia. —*National Catholic Register*

Lutherans, Methodists aim at full communion

The Evangelical Lutheran Church in America and The United Methodist Church are preparing for a new round of talks aimed at a relationship of full communion. Each church has appointed a chair and four other members to the dialogue, the first meeting of which is scheduled for Sept. 6-9, 2001, at The Iliff School of Theology, Denver. In preparation for that meeting, members of the dialogue will be asked to explore the status of Scripture or the status of doctrine in their respective church bodies.

U.S. Lutherans and United Methodists previously held dialogues in 1977–79 and 1981. These dialogues resulted in common statements on baptism and the office of bishop. —ELCA News Service

Chilean law establishes religious liberty

Chile has taken a major step toward providing full religious liberty for all its citizens. It has begun to implement a law, passed in 1999, that grants Protestants and other religious bodies equality with Roman Catholics. Lee Iverson, an American attorney living in Santiago, says the law supplies the basis for the case-by-case challenges that will bring about true religious equality. —*Christianity Today*

Texas Baptists pull funds

In a strong reaction to conservative control over the national Southern Baptist Convention (SBC), delegates to the Texas state Baptist convention have voted by at least a 3-to-1 margin to slash by $4.3 million funding for six Southern Baptist Convention seminaries. They also voted to defund completely the SBC's Ethics and Religious Liberty Commission and to eliminate all but $10,000 (down more than $700,000) for the SBC Executive Committee.

The $4.3 million diverted from the seminaries will go instead to three Texas Baptist schools. Another $1 million plus will be redirected to Texas-based projects such as Hispanic ministry and human welfare programs. The Texas Baptist Convention will continue to provide funding to the SBC's International Mission Board ($12 million) and North American Mission Board ($5.5 million).

—Episcopal News Service and *Christian Century*

Methodist church to give away $56 million

Members of the United Methodist Church in St. Mary's, Georgia, voted that a $60 million bequest be spent almost entirely on others. They decided to put $2.8 million into an endowment fund that will generate about $100,000 a year in income for the 352-member church—the amount that the congregation's benefactor had given the church annually for the past several years. The money will be used for missions and special projects. Of the remaining bequest, some $16 million will be given away up front, and the bulk of the estate, about $40 million, will be lodged with a church foundation to support non-profit causes: a retirement home, a children's home, youth programs, and mission projects. The congregation voted down a recommendation from an advisory board to set aside $4 million for a future building program or capital funds campaign for themselves.

—United Methodist News Service

Canadians Committing to Mission Service

During 1992 ▨ During 1999 ▮

Source: *Christian week*

Long term (more than four years)
3,100
2,600

Moderate term (one to four years)
100
420

Short term (two weeks to one year)
2,500 (1996)
3,200

"Do what you can, and God will increase your ability."
—Christian Service, *page 15*

ILLUSTRATIONS BY THE JUSTINEN CREATIVE GROUP

Marvin Moore

Love the Sinner, Hate the Sin

One of the articles in last month's *Signs of the Times®* told the story of a father who became enraged when he discovered that his teenage son was gay.[1] The father yelled at the boy in front of his school friends and told him never to come back home. The author—an adult who observed the entire episode—was naturally shocked.

Five years later she ran into the boy's father at their hometown post office. The encounter was awkward at first, because they both knew she knew. However, she tried to put him at ease, and soon, in a stumbling way, he acknowledged that he loved his son and truly did miss him in spite of his objections to the young man's lifestyle.

While the reaction of the father in the story was extreme, it illustrates the difficulty that conservative Christians face in dealing with the fact that our culture—at least a major segment of it—accepts homosexuality as normal. And it particularly illustrates the difficulty that conservative Christian parents face when they discover that one of their children is gay.

We at *Signs of the Times®* agree with the conservative Christian view that homosexual practice is morally wrong. We derive that understanding from the Bible. However, the Bible also teaches that all human beings are created by God, and that He loves all of us. Jesus said that God makes His sun shine on the just and the unjust, His rain to fall on the righteous and the wicked.[2] Obviously, while we may hate the sin, God makes us responsible for loving the sinner. So how can we do that in our relationship with gays? I'd like to offer four suggestions.

Be friends. People whom the religious elite of Jesus' day considered to be sinners actually loved to be around Jesus. And the reason is simple: He made them feel welcome in His presence. So smile a lot. Be relaxed and friendly around your gay friends. Follow Jesus' example: Do everything you can to make them feel welcome when they're around you.

Avoid condemnation. Jesus said, " 'God did not send his Son into the world to condemn the world, but to save the world through him.' "[3] While the biblical principle that we are to warn sinners of their evil ways[4] is important, it needs to be applied with a lot of patience, love, and prayer. Remember that condemnation has as much to do with attitude as it does with words. So spend at least as much of your prayer time

asking God to give you the right attitude toward your gay friends and relatives as you do praying directly for them.

Also, keep in mind that loving the sinner while hating the sin is a principle that's best lived rather than talked. Gay people tend to be turned off by it, in part I'm sure because it's a subtle form of condemnation.

Be honest. If you follow the first two principles, you may have a chance to discuss homosexuality with your gay friends. It's best to wait for the opportunity to present itself naturally. When it does, you can be respectfully honest about your convictions. Some gays may condemn you for disagreeing with their interpretation of the Bible. If that happens, it's OK to respectfully stand your ground and expect them to accept you as much as you accept them.

Offer help. Christian young people who discover that they are gay often have great feelings of shame and guilt and wish desperately that they could change. Conventional wisdom in the gay community says that change from a homosexual to a heterosexual orientation is impossible. However, since the Bible clearly condemns homosexual activity, then to claim that change is impossible is to deny the power of the gospel. Keep in mind, though, that this change doesn't come easily. While prayer must be a part of the process, that alone is seldom enough. It takes the help of committed Christians who understand the change process and how to lead gay people through it. That's why the Bible says that those who are struggling with sinful issues need the help of spiritual people.[5]

However, this area of counseling is so specialized that it's best left to those who are trained to do it. I recommend that you put your friends or relatives in touch with a reputable Christian organization that has had significant success in helping homosexuals and lesbians to make the change.

A prayerful application of these principles will help you to relate to your gay friends in a positive Christian way.

> *While the biblical principle that we are to warn sinners of their evil ways is important, it needs to be applied with a lot of patience, love, and prayer.*

---

[1]Judy Gulley, "We Still Talk," March 2001, 30.
[2]Matthew 5:45. [3]John 3:17. [4]Ezekiel 3:18, 19. [5]Galatians 6:1.

Marvin Moore
Editor

God's Help Line

My husband and I are owners/operators of a semi. What with fuel prices being the highest in history and the company with which we had a contract not giving decent paying loads, we were about to lose our 1996 Freightliner condo.

Before going to bed in the wee hours of March 17, I had a long talk with God. "God," I prayed, "we need help again. I have called every loan and mortgage company I can find. All of them have turned us down. Lord, we're fixin' to lose our means of support. Please help us find a way to save the truck.

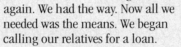

Iris Niemann

"One more thing, Lord. Somewhere in Texas is my crack-addicted son. Please help him remember he has a mother who loves him. Thank You. In Jesus' name. Amen."

My husband arrived home just as I was starting my day.

"What are we going to do when they take our truck?" he asked miserably. I could tell by the sound of his voice that he was getting very discouraged.

"Honey—" I began. That was as far as I got before the phone began to ring. The loan officer of the place where our truck is financed was on the line.

"I'm going out on a limb here," Kim said. "I have an offer for you that my supervisor has already approved. If you two will send us $1,000 before March 24, we'll move the January,

February, and March payments to the end of the note. We'll move your due date to the fourth of each month, give you a 10-day grace period, and give you until May 4 to make your next payment. Deal?"

I gasped! I was like a ricocheting bullet bouncing off the walls.

"Thank You, God! Oh, Kim, this is great. Oh, this is wonderful. Thank You! Oh, praise God—He came through for us."

When I hung up, I told my flabbergasted husband everything. He was nearly as ecstatic as I was. God had come through for us again. We had the way. Now all we needed was the means. We began calling our relatives for a loan.

Around two o'clock my husband's sister Maggie called. "I just got my bank statement," she said. "I've got a little over $1,000 in my account. I know it's not a lot, but if it will help, ya'll are more than welcome to it."

"Oh, Maggie," I cried. "God has spoken to you too." Then I told her about my call from Kim.

"I'm so glad," she replied. "As I lay down last night, all I said was 'Lord, I sure wish I could help those two.' I never expected an answer like this."

For the second time that day, I was bouncing off the walls. God had also provided the means.

While I was preparing for bed a few hours later, the phone rang again.

"Hello," I answered. The line was open but no one spoke.

"Hel-lo-o," I shouted.

"Mom," came the reply. "It's me, your youngest."

"Oh, son," I sobbed. "God has heard my prayers again. Where are you? Are you all right?"

"Yes, yes, Mom," Billy said. "I'm in Houston, in a half-way house. I, uh, I had some trouble, but I'm clean now. I go to meetings six times a week. I have a good job, and God is helping me get my life back together. I love you, Mom. Thank you for praying for me. Please

"What are we going to do when they take our truck?"

keep it up. I still have a long way to go."

While other people were wearing funny green hats with shamrocks and drinking green beer and celebrating Saint Patrick's Day, I was once again bouncing off the walls and shouting, "Thank You, God. Thank You for all Your miracles."

•*Iris Niemann writes from Joelton, Tennessee.*

We invite you to share with others how God's grace has made a difference in your life: a prayer answered, a victory gained, His guidance just when you needed it—in short, any inspirational spiritual experience. Submissions should be 650 to 700 words long. We will pay $50 for each entry we accept. Address all correspondence to Amazing Grace, Signs of the Times,® P.O. Box 5353, Nampa, ID 83653-5353. Please send a photograph of yourself. Enclose a self-addressed, stamped envelope if you want us to respond. We reserve the right to edit for grammar, punctuation, and length.

Twisted Values

Tiger Woods gets twice as much money from a box of Wheaties featuring his picture as do the farmers who grow the wheat to make the cereal in the box.
—*U.S. Catholic*

Go Figure

Iceland—where the capital's mean temperature year-round is 41 degrees, snow falls 100 days of the year and torrential gales and blinding fog are frequent, and volcanoes have produced 33 percent of the world's lava in the past 500 years. Iceland, of all places, is the happiest country on earth. Its citizens express higher rates of satisfaction and contentment than do those of any other country, including the United States.
—*U.S. Catholic*

Oops. Whew!

A study conducted a decade ago suggested that left-handers died nine years earlier than do right-handed folk. Researchers had found less than the expected number of lefties among those over age 65. A new study has accounted for the dearth: apparently, a significant number of elderly right-handers were really lefties who had been made to switch in childhood.
—*U.S. News & World Report*

Who's Keeping Watch?

Amusement park rides sent 7,260 people to the emergency room last year, and six people died. The number of injuries was up 95 percent from the previous year, although attendance rose by only 7 percent.   —*U.S. News & World Report*

Deadly Heritage

Nineteen percent of drug abusers in treatment programs were introduced to drug use by a parent or older sibling. Less than 1 percent were introduced to drugs by a pusher.   —*Time*

PHOTO BY ROBERT LANDAU/CORBIS

100 Years Ago in *Signs*

Ministers may do their work faithfully and well, yet it will amount to very little if parents neglect their work. It is to a lack of Christianity in the home life that the lack of power in the church is due. Until parents take up their work as they should, it will be difficult to arouse the youth to a sense of their duty. If religion reigns in the home, it will be brought into the church. The parents who do their work for God are a power for good. As they restrain and encourage their children, bringing them up in the nurture and admonition of the Lord, they bless the neighborhood in which they live. And the church is strengthened by their faithful work.

There's Strength in Numbers

According to John Hoffman of Brigham Young University, profession of faith in God has little positive impact on gambling addiction, while attendance at religious services has a notable effect on the problem.
—*Religion Watch*

It's Not Fair!

While nearly 80 percent of married men and women—and 70 percent of divorced or separated men—said they were able to save money out of their current incomes, only 59 percent of divorced or separated women said they managed to do so. And less than 40 percent of divorced or separated female retirees, compared with 64 percent of divorced or separated men, said they had enough money to live comfortably.
—*Modern Maturity*

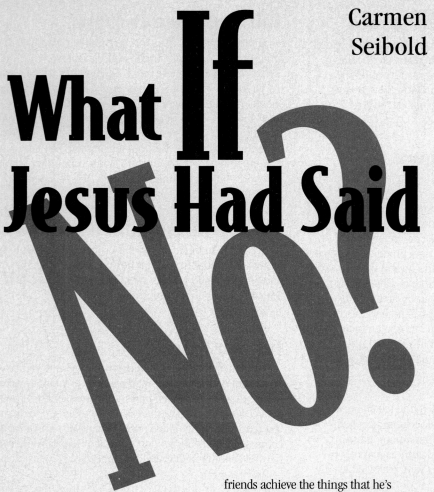

What If Jesus Had Said No?

Carmen Seibold

EVER WONDER what your life would be like if you'd made different choices? What if you'd chosen a different career? What if you hadn't gone on that first date? What if you had moved to Paris? What if you had made different friends? What if you had more, fewer, or no children? And what of that job or investment you passed up? Maybe you'd be happier or wealthier or somehow better off if you'd done things differently.

What if?

Frank Capra's classic film *It's a Wonderful Life* portrays one man asking the "what if" question about his life—and experiencing the answer. George Bailey is an all-American guy who longs for adventure. But whenever he's about to follow his dream, he's held back by a family or national crisis. Each time, he gives up what he wants to do in order to do the right thing.

George watches his brother and friends achieve the things that he's wanting and chafes against his own mundane existence. Finally, feeling trapped by responsibilities, George wishes that he'd never been born. In answer to his wish, an angel comes to show George what life without him would have been like for his family and community.

If George had never lived he wouldn't have been around to save his little brother's life, so the boy would never have grown up to become a war hero. George wouldn't have been there to encourage the town floozy to do better, so she would have done worse. He wouldn't have wedded Mary and had a family, so she would have ended up sadly alone. And if George hadn't been there to fight the greedy banker, Mr. Potter, their hometown would have lost its wholesomeness and many hardworking families would have lost their homes. George Bailey's life, it turns out, was crucial to the town of Bedford Falls.

George Bailey is just a character in a story. But he provides us with a pretty good metaphor for understanding the most important life of all. Jesus Christ's life was crucial to our planet. However, at one time He, too, questioned His life and what He was doing for others. He reached a distressing point where He wondered whether the pain and struggle was worth it. And because of His choice, the world has never been the same.

The setting for Jesus' greatest conflict was Jerusalem at the time of Passover. The holiday—the festival of freedom—evoked both celebration and mourning. God had freed His people at one time, but now they were under foreign rule again. Every Jewish woman, man, and child prayed at Passover that God would save them once more.

The disciples had arranged the Seder, the Passover ritual meal commemorating the Exodus. As twilight tossed out its first star, Jesus sat down to eat that Last Supper with the Twelve. At its center was the roasted lamb, sacrificed as a substitute for human death. The bread and the wine, over which every Jewish holiday blessing is still said, Jesus appropriated as symbols of His sacrifice and the forgiveness of sin.

Threads of meaning were winding and weaving together. This Passover there would be deliverance again—a deliverance even more central to human hopes and fears than release from slavery. In fact, the first Passover, glorious as it was, was a mere foretaste of this new freedom that God was shaping.

When Jesus and His disciples had finished the Seder, they walked out the city gates and climbed the Mount of Olives to an area called Gethsemane (which was probably an orchard rather than our notion of a garden). There, Jesus' sacrifice took place. No, He didn't die there, but He did make His decision to die as a ransom for humanity's sins. The Crucifixion couldn't take Jesus' life—He had to surrender it.

That choice took Jesus through the loneliest, most severe anguish anyone has ever experienced. In their most poignant scenes, the Gospels describe Jesus as truly struggling on that fateful night. His struggle proved that His humanity was not merely a disguise for His divinity. If it were, the decision to become the Substitutionary Sacrifice for our sins would not have been so crushing.

Jesus' sacrifice took place in Gethsemane. There He chose to die for humanity's sins. There He accepted crucifixion.

You see, suffering and dying are common to human beings. A divine being could have faced these challenges unscathed and unshaken. But somehow in this mysterious, glorious melange of humanity and divinity that is Jesus Christ, the divine could only serve as the currency for forgiveness, while the human must bear the cost.

At the Passover meal, Jesus was clear about His mission. He knew what His death would mean.[1] But that night He needed to pray for the strength to say Yes to it. The enormity of bearing all the sins of humanity filled Him with "anguish and dismay,"[2] and He asked Peter, James, and John to stay awake and pray while He struggled.

"He went on a little, [and] fell on his face in prayer."[3] Ellen White described Jesus' agony at Gethsemane this way:

The guilt of fallen humanity He must bear. Upon Him who knew no sin must be laid the iniquity of us all. So dreadful does sin appear to Him, so great is the weight of guilt which He must bear, that He is tempted to fear it will shut Him out forever from His Father's love. Feeling how terrible is the wrath of God against transgression, He exclaims, "My soul is exceeding sorrowful, even unto death."[4]

In the updated language of a modern Bible translation, His expression of pain is possibly even sadder: " 'My heart is ready to break with grief.' "[5]

He who had always acted and spoken with confidence in His oneness with God now is overcome with human anguish. He pleads for His own deliverance, His own exodus: " 'My Father, if it is possible, let this cup pass me by. Yet not as I will, but as thou wilt.' "[6] In his Gospel, Luke the physician reports that Christ's sweat "was like clots of blood falling to the ground."[7] Desperate for some support, He goes to Peter, James, and John, but they've abandoned Him for sleep.

Three times Jesus prays His heartbreaking prayer, shrinking from the unimaginable sacrifice.[8]

The awful moment had come—that moment which was to decide the destiny of the world. The fate of humanity trembled in the balance. Christ might even now refuse to drink the cup apportioned to guilty man. It was not yet too late. . . . He might say, Let the transgressor receive the penalty of his sin, and I will go back to My Father. Will the Son of God drink the bitter cup of humiliation and agony? Will the innocent suffer the consequences of the curse of sin, to save the guilty?[9]

A third time, according to Matthew, Jesus searched out His closest companions and found them oblivious to His suffering. But now time has run out. A mob is already gathering about them, and Judas betrays his Lord with a kiss.

In this moment of turmoil and danger, Jesus makes His final choice. Someone whips out a sword to defend

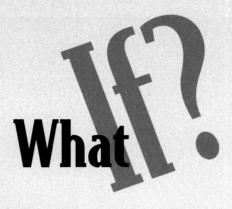

What If?

Him, but He objects. " 'Do you suppose that I cannot appeal to my Father, who would at once send to my aid more than twelve legions of angels?' "[10] He has made His decision. He is the Sacrifice, the Passover Lamb to be slain for sinners. Escape is only a prayer away, but Jesus stays to undergo death for every woman, man, and child. " 'This is the cup the Father has given me; shall I not drink it?' "[11]

From this decision follow the terrible events of the rest of that night and the following day. And from it also follows the miracle of the Resurrection, for "through him God chose to reconcile the whole universe to himself, making peace through the shedding of his blood upon the cross—to reconcile all things, whether on earth or in heaven, through him alone."[12]

What if He had said No? Without the salvation thus provided, we'd be captives to sin and its wages. There would be no promise of eternal life. Our lives would have no ultimate meaning, nor would our relationships. Grief and suffering would be unrelieved by hope. We'd have no irrefutable evidence that God is a loving God.

In *It's a Wonderful Life*, George comes to see that the choices he made have paid off. His life, though hard at times, has contributed to the happiness of many others. In Gethsemane, Jesus could have chosen an easier path. He could have said No to suffering the penalty for our sins. But He said Yes, and it will take us all eternity to begin to grasp why He considered us worth the pain He suffered. Truly, though, with His death the universe became wonderful.

What would your life be like if you had made different choices? I don't

know that about my own life, but I do know this one thing: The details we wonder and worry about are much less important than we sometimes think because Christ has taken care of the big picture. Because of His death, the "what if" questions about our own lives have an incredibly wonderful answer—"all things work together for good to them that love God."[13]

Christ promises us a happy ending, one He's already purchased with His blood. Knowing that—and believing it!—doesn't just tell us about the future. When given to Christ, our lives begin to take on the colors and flavors of eternal life now. "Taste, . . . and see that the Lord is good."[14]

When we are Christ's people, our joys need not be clouded by the knowledge that they won't last. Instead, they can soar because we know there's even more joy ahead. Our grief need never be the grief of despair, of those who have no hope.[15] We can live abundant lives[16] because there's a safety net under us. We can live joyful lives[17] because with God there are second chances.

What if Jesus hadn't said Yes to giving us all this and heaven too? We needn't let the alternative trouble us—He did. That's reality.

It really *is* a wonderful life!

---

[1]See Matthew 26:26-28. [2]Matthew 26:37. All Scripture quotations not credited otherwise are from The New English Bible. [3]Matthew 26:39.
[4]Ellen G. White, *The Desire of Ages* (Nampa, Idaho: Pacific Press, 1940), 685.
[5]Matthew 26:38. [6]Matthew 26:39. [7]Luke 22:44. [8]See Matthew 26.
[9]White, 690.
[10]Matthew 26:53. [11]John 18:11. [12]Colossians 1:20. [13]Romans 8:28, KJV. [14]Psalm 34:8. [15]1 Thessalonians 4:13. [16]John 10:10. [17]John 15:11.

What's your response to this article? Share it with us; see page 3 for instructions.

•*Carmen Seibold writes from Worthington, Ohio.*

You Are Special to God

Jamie Buckingham

S **EVERAL YEARS AGO** Fred Craddock was lecturing at Yale University. He told of going back one summer to Gatlinburg, Tennessee, to take a short vacation with his wife. One night they found a quiet little restaurant where they looked forward to a private meal—just the two of them.

While they were waiting for their meal, they noticed a distinguished-looking, white-haired man moving from table to table, visiting guests. Craddock whispered to his wife, "I hope he doesn't come over here." He didn't want the man to intrude on their privacy.

But the man did come by their table. "Where you folks from?" he asked amicably.

"Oklahoma."

"Splendid state, I hear, although I've never been there. What do you do for a living?"

"I teach homiletics at the graduate seminary of Phillips University."

"Oh, so you teach preachers, do you. Well, I've got a story I want to tell you." And with that he pulled up a chair and sat down at the table with Dr. Craddock and his wife. Craddock said he groaned inwardly. *Oh, no, here comes another preacher story. It seems everyone has one.*

The man stuck out his hand. "I'm Ben Hooper. I was born not far from here across the mountains. My mother wasn't married when I was born, so I had a hard time. When I started school, my classmates had a name for me, and it wasn't a very nice name. I used to go off by myself at recess and during lunchtime because the taunts of my playmates cut so deeply.

"What was worse was going downtown on Saturday afternoon and feeling every eye burning a hole through me. They were all wondering just who my father was.

"When I was about 12 years old, a new preacher came to our church. I would always go in late and slip out early. But one day the preacher said the benediction so fast I got caught and had to walk out with the crowd. I could feel every eye in church on me. Just about the time I got to the door, I felt a big hand on my shoulder. I looked up, and the preacher was looking right at me. 'Who are you, son? Whose boy are you?' he asked.

"I felt the old weight come on me. It was like a big, black cloud. Even the preacher was putting me down.

"But as he looked down at me, studying my face, he began to smile a big smile of recognition. 'Wait a minute,' he said, 'I know who you are. I see the family resemblance. You are a son of God.'

"With that he slapped me across the rump and said, 'Boy, you've got a great inheritance. Go and claim it.' "

The old man looked across the table at Fred Craddock and said, "That was the most important single sentence ever spoken to me." With that he smiled, shook the hands of Craddock and his wife, and moved on to another table to greet old friends.

Suddenly, Fred Craddock said, he remembered that the people of Tennessee had elected an illegitimate to be their governor. His name was Ben Hooper.

Although we have been born in iniquity and although we have chosen to go our own way, through the blood of Jesus Christ we are saved—not only from our past, but from the fear of failure in our present and from powerless living in our future as well. That's what it means to be chosen by God.

We have a great inheritance. The power for living that comes to us from God enables us to go and claim it.

•Adapted from Jamie Buckingham's Power for Living *(Arthur S. DeMoss Foundation, 1999). Used by permission of the Arthur S. DeMoss Foundation.*

You Can't

Clifford Goldstein

In **1982, FULL-PAGE ADS** in twenty of the world's most prestigious and influential newspapers proclaimed, "The Christ is now here!" According to the paper-and-ink promo (which cost half a million dollars) Christ was back on earth, living in quiet obscurity, but would soon make Himself manifest to the world. Of course, the ads ran 19 years ago—and this returned Christ has yet to make His grand appearance.

Christ's return, of course, is not the controverted point. On the contrary, it's because Christians almost universally believe He will return that the other problem has arisen—that of those claiming to be the returned Christ. Except for this widely held belief, these charlatans would deceive no one.

The brazen ad campaign wasn't the first time some have claimed that Christ has returned—nor, no doubt, will it be the last. From the earliest days of the Christian church through the twentieth century, numerous souls have claimed to be the returned Christ. And thousands upon thousands of people have believed them, often with disastrous results.

None of this should be surprising, however. On the contrary, it should be expected, if for no other reason than that the Lord Jesus Himself explicitly warned about it. He said, " 'False Christs and false prophets will appear and perform great signs and miracles to deceive even the elect—if that were possible.' "[1]

According to Jesus, then, not only would there be false christs, but these imposters would fool many people. Time and again, history has proved both parts of this remarkable prediction true.

Yet none need be deceived, because the Bible clearly explains the manner of His coming—and if the Bible is crystal clear about anything, it's crystal clear about this: Christ's return will be one outrageously unmistakable event.

An unmistakable happening

Jesus Himself stressed that His return would be a worldwide phenomenon, one that hardly lends itself to imitation. In the very context in which He warned about deception, He said,

> "If anyone tells you, 'There he is, out in the desert,' do not go out; or, 'Here he is, in the inner rooms,' do not believe it. For as lightning that comes from the east is visible even in the west, so will be the coming of the Son of Man."[2]

Christ compared the manner of His return with lightning streaking from one end of the sky to the other. That's not a quiet, hidden advent in which He reveals Himself to a select few in some out-of-the-way location. On the contrary, the whole world sees this event.

Revelation 6:15-17 also describes His return—again in language that, if accepted, would spare anyone from the deceptions that have captured thousands:

> The kings of the earth, the princes, the generals, the rich, the mighty, and every slave and every free man hid in caves and among the rocks of the mountains. They called to the mountains and the rocks, "Fall on us and hide us from the face of him who sits on the throne and from the wrath of the Lamb! For the great day of their wrath has come, and who can stand?"

Besides being visible, Christ's return will be noisy. The apostle Paul depicted an event that hardly seems ordinary or easy to fake:

> The Lord himself will come down from heaven, with a *loud command,* with the *voice of the archangel* and with the *trumpet call of God,* and the dead in Christ will rise first. After that, we who are still alive and are left will be caught up together with them in the clouds to meet the Lord in the air. And so we will be with the Lord forever.[3]

If these texts reveal anything, they reveal that Christ's return will be, to say the least, noisy.

Hard to duplicate

In addition to being noisy and visible to everyone, Christ's return will result in an event that would be very hard to duplicate—even for the trickiest, most demonic impersonator. At His return the righteous dead are resurrected. Then they and the righteous living all go off to heaven.

The passage I just quoted above says that the dead will rise and with the living will go to "meet the Lord in the air." In another place where Paul was

Miss It

also writing about what happens at the Second Coming, he said:

> Listen, I tell you a mystery: We will not all sleep, but we will all be changed—in a flash, in the twinkling of an eye, at the last trumpet. For the trumpet will sound, the dead will be raised imperishable, and we will be changed. For the perishable must clothe itself with the imperishable, and the mortal with immortality. When the perishable has been clothed with the imperishable, and the mortal with immortality, then the saying that is written will come true: "Death has been swallowed up in victory."[4]

The dead are raised and brought to life, the living are instantly transformed (exchanging mortality for immortality), and both are taken to heaven with Christ. When that happens, and only when that happens—along with all the other signs—can one be sure that Christ has, indeed, returned. Until then, the careful Christian should beware.

Scripture sets forth another unmistakable mark of Christ's return: the death of the wicked. In Revelation 19, John described it in figurative language, picturing Jesus as a warrior mounted on a white horse and leading the armies of heaven. He said that at Jesus' coming, with the exception of the righteous, "kings, generals, and mighty men, . . . and . . . all people, free and slave, small and great" will be "killed with the sword that came out of the mouth of the rider on the horse."[5]

The resurrection of the righteous dead and the death of the unrighteous

living at Christ's return testify to another important truth. There's a notion that somehow, after Jesus comes back, the righteous and the unrighteous will live together on the earth, at least for a time. But the Bible makes it clear that there will be at that time a final and irrevocable separation between these two groups.

In His parable of the fishnet, Jesus Himself noted that just as fishermen sort the good fish from the bad, so a similar separation will happen at His coming:

> "The kingdom of heaven is like a net that was let down into the lake and caught all kinds of fish. When it was full, the fishermen pulled it up on the shore. Then they sat down and collected the good fish in baskets, but threw the bad away. This is

how it will be at the end of the age. The angels will come and separate the wicked from the righteous."[6]

Finally, Christ's return will be accompanied by incredible convulsions of nature, including a terrible earthquake that will leave the planet in ruins. Revelation 16:18 speaks of an earthquake like none that "has ever occurred since man has been on the earth, so tremendous was the quake." And yet this is just one of many devastating eruptions in nature that will herald the second coming of Christ.

Christ's return will be accompanied by numerous events: the righteous dead are raised from their graves, the righteous living are given immortality, and both are taken to heaven while the earth (temporarily) is left in ruins. The whole world will see His coming, the whole world will hear it, the evil will be slain, and there will be convulsions of nature on a scale never before seen.

In short, Christ's return is one outrageously unmistakable event—one that you certainly won't sleep through to read about in the morning newspaper.

---

[1]Matthew 24:24. [2]Matthew 24:26, 27. [3]1 Thessalonians 4:16, 17, emphasis supplied. [4]1 Corinthians 15:51-54. [5]Revelation 19:18, 21. [6]Matthew 13:47-49.

•Clifford Goldstein writes from Silver Spring, Maryland.

Beyond
Words and

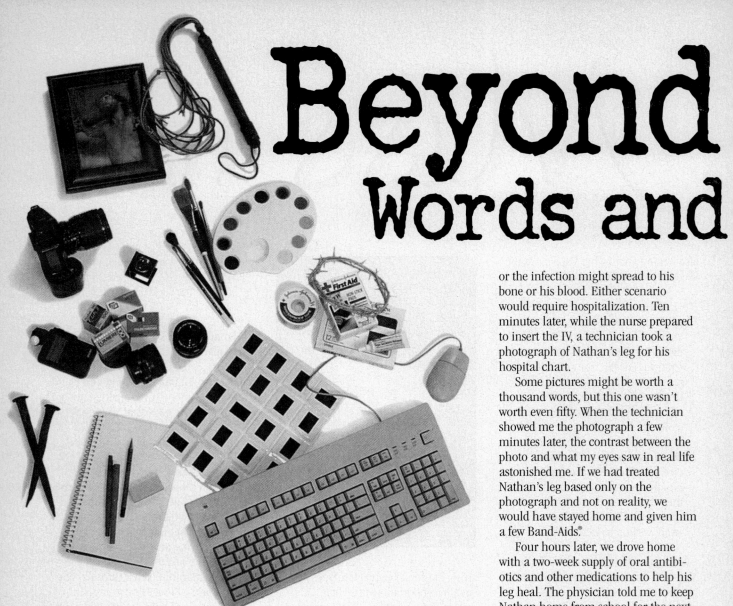

or the infection might spread to his bone or his blood. Either scenario would require hospitalization. Ten minutes later, while the nurse prepared to insert the IV, a technician took a photograph of Nathan's leg for his hospital chart.

Some pictures might be worth a thousand words, but this one wasn't worth even fifty. When the technician showed me the photograph a few minutes later, the contrast between the photo and what my eyes saw in real life astonished me. If we had treated Nathan's leg based only on the photograph and not on reality, we would have stayed home and given him a few Band-Aids.®

Four hours later, we drove home with a two-week supply of oral antibiotics and other medications to help his leg heal. The physician told me to keep Nathan home from school for the next ten days.

Less than real

After Nathan went to bed, I sat at my computer to unwind. As I stared at the blank screen, my mind replayed the procession of events from the moment I first saw his wound to our visit to the emergency room. I relived my gnawing fear as the doctor attended to Nathan's infection. Then my thoughts anchored on the photograph and how different it had been from reality.

While I pondered the contrast, my eyes drifted from the computer to the painting on my wall of Christ's crucifixion. Talk about a contrast between replica and reality! How insipid the painting seemed when set against Calvary.

R ECENTLY, our 15-year-old son went on a weekend mission trip to Mexico. The moment he walked into the house upon his return, he began chattering about his experience with an enthusiasm I thought he reserved only for computer gaming. His excitement continued through dinner as he painted vivid word-pictures of the homes he and the other members of our church had built for two impoverished families, the children they met, the food they ate, the bugs they chased. Then, as we got up from the table, he added, "By the way, I cut my leg two days ago." He pulled at his pants leg to give me a look. "What do you think?"

When I saw his wound, he had no trouble guessing my thoughts. I've been a nurse a long time, but I've never seen such a mass of angry, reddish-blue pustules as those that covered his shin. It was hard to know where the infection stopped and healthy skin began. A thin, yellow fluid had seeped from an open, inch-wide blister and tracked down into his sock. I bent closer and caught a faint whiff of foul odor.

"Put on your coat," I told him. "We're going to the emergency room."

Shortly after we arrived, a physician examined Nathan's leg. He prodded, poked, and murmured an occasional "That's interesting" to no one in particular. Then he looked at us and announced the bad news. Nathan needed intravenous antibiotic therapy

Richard Maffeo

Pictures

Christ's crucifixion began with flogging. Soldiers fashioned leather whips studded with small rocks and bone fragments. Standing on either side of Christ, they swung the lashes against His back, and every blow ripped open new wounds. His muscles and tendons quickly turned into a mass of quivering, bleeding flesh. Most prisoners died of shock and blood loss long before being nailed to the cross.

After the beating, soldiers forced Jesus to drag His cross to the execution site. There they laid it on the ground and threw Him down onto it. The seven-inch spikes hammered through His wrists and feet tore through exquisitely sensitive nerves, sending bolts of electrifying pain through His limbs.

As Christ hung between heaven and earth, gravity restricted the natural movement of His respiratory muscles, forcing Him to push against His feet and flex His arms just to breathe. But doing so only intensified the strain on His ravaged nerves, and each breath forced His back against the splintered wood, reopening the raw wounds. Every breath, every movement, every moment on the cross inflamed His physical anguish.

But that was not all. Adding to the physical torture the Son of God suffered was the immeasurable spiritual loneliness He endured. When God's only begotten Son, the Lamb "who had no sin," became sin for us,[1] the Father turned His back on Him for the first time in eternity. Sensing this, Jesus cried aloud, " 'My God, my God, why have you forsaken me?' "[2]

The painting on my wall is done in rich tones. With consummate skill, the artist has drawn the figure of Christ and attempted to capture His pain. But how could anyone ever do that? Just as the emergency-room photograph could not touch the gravity of Nathan's wound, neither could ten thousand paintings or as many sermons or books adequately portray the death of God's Son. Only the Holy Spirit can unveil to our hearts the reality of Calvary. Only He can cause us to understand why Christ permitted Himself to be mauled so we could be forgiven.

How I long to mature in my understanding of that truth—that the details of His death will become to me exquisitely more astonishing . . . and impel my thanks.

---

[1]2 Corinthians 5:21. [2]Matthew 27:46.

•*Richard Maffeo writes from San Diego, California.*

Mother's Midnight

Voya Vitorovich as told to Ann Vitorovich

A **BRIGHT, WHITE** full moon lit up the night sky and cast an eerie glow over the fields of ripening feed corn and the stubble of already harvested wheat. A lone figure—a woman, short and stocky—walked in the middle of the road with a sack slung over her left shoulder and a long walking stick in her right hand. In the sleeping silence of the Yugoslavian village, the soft footfalls of her sandal-shod feet and the tap of her walking stick on the gravel road resonated in repetitive staccato rhythm.

Under cover of darkness

It was Mother. In her dark kerchief, dress, sweater, and woolen stockings, her figure merged with the warm, black September night. From time to time she stopped to shift the heavy sack from one shoulder to the other. Then she resumed her journey to her friend Mila's house. No one at home knew of her mysterious trips.

Somewhere in the distance a cock crowed at the midnight moon. The night air, tinged with the subtle scent of ripe corn, smelled fresh and clean. Mother breathed it in deeply. She had come to cherish these special quiet times alone in the darkness with her God. In her imagination, the two of them were the only ones in the world awake and about their business.

Ahead on her left loomed a long stockade fence that enclosed a trio of houses, where three brothers lived with their families. As she neared the first house, dogs that belonged to Zivadin, the youngest of the brothers, started a chorus of bays and barks. Soon the dogs that belonged to the other brothers joined in.

Suddenly, the clatter of chains froze Mother in her tracks. She watched as seven dogs leaped nimbly over the fence and onto the road, each dragging behind it its chain.

That night, a terrible toothache had kept Zivadin awake. Hearing the racket, he peered out a window and saw the dogs running toward the dark figure of a woman. He saw her raise her stick overhead and the dogs stop barking and then line up as if at attention, their ears perked and their tails standing upright.

I can't believe this! the astonished man thought. *How did those dogs get out? And who is that woman?*

Zivadin rubbed his eyes as if he could erase the puzzling picture. Then he pressed his nose against the windowpane again. "Why, that looks like—no, it can't be," he muttered to himself. "It *is*. It's Mara Vitorovich!"

As he continued to watch, the woman kept walking. When she had passed his and his brothers' property, the dogs resumed their barking. Then, one by one, they leaped back over the fence, their chains clanging and bumping after them.

Zivadin's head seemed to throb even more intensely. He ladled a dipper of water from the covered bucket in the

Why was Mother making surreptitious midnight

ILLUSTRATION BY CONSUELO UDAVE

Errand

trips to Mila's house? And what was she carrying in the sack slung over her back?

corner of his bedroom, swallowed two aspirin, and returned to the window. There, on a patch of grass below his window, lay his two dogs, as peaceful and limpid as lambs. "It was a dream; I'm hallucinating!" he groaned, holding his jaw and lying down beside his still-sleeping wife.

By 1:30 a.m. Mother had returned home. She checked on her twins sleeping soundly in the crib made especially for them, then on her two girls. Finally she went to bed as though nothing unusual had happened.

Was it a dream?

With wheat harvest coming to an end, the grinding season was in full swing. Farmers brought their new wheat to our steam-powered mill. In heavily laden horse-drawn wagons or oxcarts they came, depositing loads, each tagged with the owner's name and specifying the type of flour desired—fine, medium, coarse; white, whole wheat.

Hundreds of sacks weighing from 110 to 220 pounds rose in crisscross layers to the open-beam ceiling of the upper platform of the mill. Other sacks of fresh-milled flour waited on the lower platform for pickup. Soon the corn harvest would begin; the mill would continue working around the clock through December.

Around midmorning, an unshaven and tired-looking Zivadin walked to the mill and stopped in the doorway on the lower level. Father, looking distinguished in his black-on-black, braid-bound woolen jacket and gray britches, was rubbing some flour between his fingers to test its texture. When Zivadin spotted Father, he started to call out, changed his mind, and turned to leave. He stopped at the threshold of the platform and then turned back.

He fidgeted nervously, and his small eyes stared blankly at the wall while his lips moved in silent rehearsal of his speech. Earlier that morning, when he had related his tale of the night before to his two brothers, they had laughed. "Absurd! You're imagining things!" they had pronounced. "Where would Mara be going in the middle of the night? And what would she be carrying? Now, don't embarrass yourself by telling Ilija."

But Zivadin was determined. "Mara

will tell the truth," he assured himself.

"Good morning, Zivadin," Father greeted him cheerily when he noticed him standing just outside the open doorway, deep in thought and empty-handed. "What brings you here, my friend?"

"Ilija," Zivadin began timidly, "I came because something strange happened last night. I scarcely believe it myself." He dropped his eyes. "It's about your wife, Mara."

"My Mara?" Ilija asked, surprise in his voice.

"Last night I had a terrible toothache and couldn't sleep. Something happened around midnight." Zivadin related to Father what he believed he had seen. "My brothers say I was hallucinating. They told me not to bother you," he concluded. Then he added emphatically, "I'm not crazy, Ilija." His eyes focused fervently on Ilija. "I must ask Mara. Whatever she says I'll believe, and I apologize in advance if I'm wrong."

Father smiled good-naturedly. "Mara was with me and my boys until nine o'clock last night. Yesterday was the twins' first birthday, you know. The mill has been running around the clock, so last night I slept here, as I often do during peak season. But," he chuckled, "Mara was definitely home last night sleeping with the children." His reply was casual and confident.

"Whoa, boy!" Another heavily loaded wagon drew up to the platform, catching Father's attention.

"Mara should be here any minute to get some flour. You can ask her yourself," Father said, turning toward his customers.

What really happened?

Within a few minutes Mother came through the side door carrying an empty round wooden container. She was dressed in a navy-blue suit dress, kerchief, and stockings, wisps of blond curls peering out from under her kerchief.

"Mara," Father called to her, "Zivadin wants to ask you something."

Mother placed the container on the wood floor beside a six-foot-square wooden tub filled with flour. It contained the miller's portion, paid as a fee by each farmer for having his grain

ground. She smiled sweetly at Zivadin and walked toward him.

Zivadin's eyes darted back and forth. He spoke in low tones. "Mara, this is very embarrassing, but for my own sanity, I have to ask you something." He clenched his hands until his fingertips turned red. "Around midnight last night I saw a woman walking on the road in front of my house. It looked like you, Mara."

"Yes, Zivadin, it was me," Mother answered straightforwardly.

Overhearing Mother's reply, Father dropped the sack he was lifting and whirled around, his tanned face a picture of disbelief.

"Ilija, I was going to tell you . . ." Mother's voice was apologetic as she turned to her husband. "I've been paying my tithe to the church—the 10 percent of income God requires." Seeing the questioning look on Father's face, she forged ahead. "I have no income, Ilija. You provide well for all my needs." She looked appreciatively at him. "But I wanted to give my own tithe and offerings to church. So Mila and I came up with a plan. We estimated the benefit I receive for my living expenses as well as the value of my labor. We decided it would be fair for me to take 25 pounds of flour from our bin twice a month and sell it. So every second Wednesday I take a sack to Mila's house. She sells it at half price to the poor and gives me the money. That's where I was going last night."

When Mother finished, Father was still staring at her. He looked confused and unsure of what to say. Then he asked, his voice subdued, "How long have you been doing this?"

"Seven months," she replied.

Mother turned to Zivadin. "Last night when those dogs ran toward me, I nearly panicked. Then I remembered that I was doing God's business. So I raised my stick and said sternly, 'Satan, you have sent these dogs. In the name of Jesus Christ, I command you dogs to stop barking!' And they did!"

Zivadin's face lit up like a lantern. "You are a holy woman, Mara. I feel like a new man. Now my brothers will believe me. I'm OK; I'm not crazy!" He

shook her hand vigorously and then grabbed Father's. "Thank you! Thank you!"

In God's hands

Father and Mother remained alone, his figure towering over her. "Mara, Mara," he repeated, shaking his head. "I don't begrudge your helping the poor. We have much, and you know I am fair in my business dealings." Mother nodded agreement. "You're a God-fearing woman, Mara. But I can't get used to some of your ways." Mother smiled her understanding and began loading flour into her container while Father watched her thoughtfully.

The next year, when the golden brown heads of wheat hung heavily from their stems, awaiting harvest, a sudden hailstorm hit the fertile plains of Macva. Just before the storm reached our fields, it divided. Looping around our fields, it came back together on the other side of them. Everywhere around us ripened wheat lay smashed to the ground, some fields destroyed totally. Our wheat fields remained intact, along with portions of the fields that bordered ours.

From surrounding towns, people came to see and to marvel, Zivadin among them. For months afterward he related to anyone who would listen the story of Mother's midnight ordeal with the watchdogs. "Mara's God saved their fields because Mara was faithful and generous," he told them.

And Father looked on in wonder while Mother read to all who came the promise in Malachi 3:10, 11:

"Bring the whole tithe into the storehouse, that there may be food in my house. Test me in this," says the Lord Almighty, "and see if I will not throw open the floodgates of heaven and pour out so much blessing that you will not have room enough for it. I will prevent pests from devouring your crops, and the vines in your fields will not cast their fruit," says the Lord Almighty.

•*Voya and Ann Vitorovich live in Sebring, Florida.*

Carol Cannon

Part One:
When You No It All

Recently, one of my sons emailed me a large file that included a number of photographs. When I tried to download the file, my little laptop computer hummed and blinked busily for five or ten minutes and then posted a message that said, "Shame on you—the file is too big."

I called my son, who obligingly divided the file in two and sent the material again. But I couldn't download the smaller files either. I deleted the offending file, but it reappeared and I still couldn't open it. I deleted it again, emptied the "trash," and logged off. But when I logged on later, the message was back in my mailbox! I deleted it again, and it re-appeared again. I couldn't make that file go away.

Being technologically challenged (you wouldn't have guessed that, would you!), I had no idea what was wrong. Finally, it occurred to me to call for tech support. The technician explained that my system was log-jammed— the oversized file was too big to budge.

Negaholism is sort of like that. Traumatic experiences create painful feelings that, left unexpressed, build up and cause a backlog of emotions that get stuck in the pipeline and recycle themselves endlessly.

The most obvious and irritating symptom of addiction to misery is chronic complaining. In *A Co-dependent's Guide to the Twelve Steps,* Melody Beattie describes this habit from personal experience: "I had little to offer friends except my perpetual complaints about the misery of my life. Most of my friendships centered around shared stories of victimization. . . . I had no feelings that I was aware of. I had no needs that I was aware of. I prided myself in my ability to endure needless suffering, deprive myself, and go without."

Negaholics are grievance collectors. They never forget an insult. Years after the fact, they can describe an offense in detail—when and where it happened and what the offender was thinking, feeling, and wearing. Because they can read minds, they know exactly what the other person's motives are. Unfortunately, they think their assumptions are reality and respond accordingly.

Misery addicts not only collect grievances, they are offense-seeking missiles! Because they don't feel right unless they're being wronged, they set friends, relatives, employers, and co-workers up to persecute them so they can feel good, virtuous, or normal. The only way misery addicts' friends and family can satisfy them is to offend them. In other words, the only way they can get it "right" is to be "wrong." That's why it's so difficult to be in a relationship with a negaholic. It's crazy-making.

There's a character in the Winnie the Pooh tales who is negativity personified—remember the donkey named Eeyore who looks at the bleak side of everything? If there's a picnic being planned, he knows it will rain. When the wind blows, he's sure his house will fall down. If there's a party scheduled, he probably won't be invited. He "doesn't deserve attention," "isn't worth much," and on and on. Eeyore never runs out of things to be unhappy about; he's the archetype for addiction to misery.

Assuming the worst is what negaholics do best. They await disaster, anticipate unhappiness, expect abuse or abandonment, and assume that everybody is against them. They seek out troublesome situations and then worry themselves sick. If they can't find something personal to fret about, they obsess about someone else's problems. They'll settle for almost anything: the mayor's morality, a friend's impending divorce, the pastor's grammar, the school board's unfair policies, the qualifications of the police chief, or the status of society in general.

Clearly, negaholism is not an enjoyable addiction. Unlike other addictions, which promise pleasure at first, misery addiction is *never* pleasurable. It's familiar and therefore reassuring, but it's never *fun.* Consequently, misery addicts have difficulty seeing their behavior as addictive. When confronted by the habitual nature of their problem, they whine, "How can I be addicted to *misery*? I don't *enjoy* being unhappy!" This is a real double bind, which seems a little unfair. (Uh-oh, we'd better not go there!)

Next month I'll discuss how to break the chronic misery habit.

• *Carol Cannon is the clinical director at The Bridge, a treatment center for addictive disorders in Bowling Green, Kentucky. Her column is a regular feature in* Signs.

Enrich Your *Life* With

Patricia L. Fry

I **RECALL MY MOTHER** asking me, when I was small and wanted another helping of mashed potatoes, "What's the magic word?" After dishing up the potatoes, she'd ask, "What do you say?" Of course, she was trying to instill in me the habit of saying Please and Thank you.

Do you always remember to apply the manners your parents taught you? Or are you often too busy to say Thank you? Appreciation is more than just a courteous expression of respect. A sincere Thank you connects people. When you feel the spirit of thankfulness, you are blessed. When you express it, you're sharing that blessing with others, and they are uplifted.

Too often we let generous gestures go by without responding to them. You may declare to yourself, "That was sweet of Jill to include my son when she took her kids to the zoo." Or "I really love the book Jill gave me for my birthday." But if you keep those good feelings and thoughts to yourself, you're denying Jill the opportunity to experience them.

Express your gratitude

In our family, birthday and holiday celebrations are big events. Because things can get hectic, we make sure that each gift given that day is noted. On Christmas, for example, we take turns opening gifts so we can acknowledge each one. We've also established the habit of writing personal Thank-you notes after the gathering. This gives us a chance to express our special appreciation to the hosts and to those who brought thoughtful gifts.

Be creative when expressing your gratitude. Send a picture of yourself wearing the blouse your mom gave you for your birthday. Videotape your family opening gifts from the long-distance grandparents, and send the tape to them. You might even, like one of my daughters, give a small gift as a Thank you for a kindness.

A friend's 12-year-old granddaughter visited our family last fall. When I noticed that she didn't have a camera, I bought her a disposable one so she could record her California trip. When she returned to Oklahoma, her grandmother had duplicate pictures made and sent me copies as a Thank you.

A friend of mine recently sent me a note of appreciation on her own birthday. She said that she wanted to acknowledge those who had made a positive difference in her life throughout the year. Now, don't you know that made my day?

Sometimes we touch someone without knowing it. A few years ago a friend wrote thanking me for saving her life. I didn't know what she was talking about until she wrote about a night ten years earlier when I'd stopped at her apartment unannounced. She said, "I was just about to swallow a handful of pills and drink them down with a bottle of wine when you knocked on my door." She said that my visit that evening and our conversation made her realize that there were people who cared about her. That was enough to convince her not to end her life after all.

Procrastination aborts many Thank you's. So does lack of preparation. So, stock up on blank note cards and pretty postage stamps. Buy cards at discount stores, yard sales, or thrift stores. Carry a few in your car, tuck some in your desk drawer at work, and put a box of them in plain sight at home.

Some people have trouble thinking of something to write. Here are some ideas:

• Write what you want that person to know: that you received the item, that you appreciate it, and that you recognize the thought that went into it, for example.

• Express your feelings about the gift or gesture. Are you pleased? Happy? Joyful? Surprised? Excited?

• Tell how you will use it. You might say, "I can't wait for my next golf game so I can wear my new shirt." Or "The little pansy pillow is absolutely stunning on my blue sofa."

• Say something about that person's generosity, sense of style, or thoughtfulness.

Here's a sample Thank-you note:

What a surprise to receive a copy of *Home Gardener Magazine* in the mail today! You couldn't have given me a more appropriate gift because, as you know, we're replanting our backyard this spring. Every month when my magazine arrives, I'll think of you with fondness. Thank you for a very special gift.

Appreciate the positive

Sometimes we're quick to point out the negative and we forget to acknowledge the positive. Instead of saying to yourself or someone else, "The neighbors' home is looking really nice since they replaced the siding and painted," tell the neighbors themselves. Give them the gift of appreciation. Let them know that someone notices and cares.

Several years ago, I owned some property that the renters were not keeping up. No matter how I tried to make it look nice and to motivate them to do the same, the place was an

Gratitude

eyesore. When I'd just about given up, I received a very unkind letter from an anonymous neighbor who made all sorts of ugly comments about the condition of the property. That spurred me into serious action. I went on a cleaning rampage. But I heard nothing at all from the neighborhood once the place was cleaned up. What a nice gesture it would have been if the anonymous letter-writer had sent some sort of positive acknowledgment.

Thank you's aren't just for personal use. Express your gratitude with clients, associates, and others. I do a lot of networking. It's my nature to pass along bits of useful information to colleagues. Few of them respond beyond the initial Thanks, however. Recently, a fellow author called to thank me for arranging the contact that resulted in a book review in a prestigious magazine. What a wonderful feeling to know that my effort was appreciated.

Thankfulness is learned. I believe it starts at home. When my own children were small, they received handmade dresses from their great-grandmother. I explained to them that great-grandma must sure think they're special because she made the dresses just for them. Only then did they begin to understand the concept of expressing gratitude.

As they got older, we'd all sit down together and write Thank-you notes after receiving gifts. Because kids can learn as much about thankfulness through giving as through receiving, I encouraged my young daughters to

Delay aborts many Thank you's, so stock up on blank note cards and pretty stamps.

experience the joy in giving, too. They have generously passed this gift along to their children. What we've discovered is that children who give are more appreciative and less focused on what they're getting.

In this fast-paced world, one of the things we tend to leave behind is our manners. Let's reawaken them by incorporating that simple little phrase, Thank you, into our everyday thoughts and deeds.

So, express your gratitude. Not only

will it make someone's day, it will enrich your own life.

Please tell us what you think about this article. Thank you! (See page 3 for instructions.)

•Patricia L. Fry is the author of Creative Grandparenting Across the Miles *and* Ideas for Sharing Love, Faith and Family Traditions. *She writes from Ojai, California.*

John Rosemond

Good Rules

Rules are social boundaries. They outline the limits of acceptable behavior and preserve the stability of human environments. For children, rules are as necessary to healthy development as are stimulation, good food, and sunshine.

When the rules of a game are clear, the players know what moves are available and can predict with some degree of certainty what moves the other players will make. Rules organize the game. They reduce uncertainty and anxiety.

So it is with children. When rules are present, children know what is and is not allowed and can predict their parents' behavior. On the other hand, when rules are unclear or enforced sporadically, children can't predict what their parents will do next. Under these circumstances, they become anxious, insecure, and sometimes even physically sick.

Good rules should meet four basic requirements:

1. All rules should be stated clearly. No dressing or garnishing is necessary, nor is a complicated explanation. If you must explain, make the explanation brief and to the point: 25 words or less.

Older children understand reasons and like to argue about them. If parents argue back, the basic issue—that parents set rules and children abide by them— becomes confused. If a child wants to argue, say, "I will not argue. You will have to do as you are told."

Some parents feel guilty about making straightforward demands on their children, so they disguise their demands as requests that require "yes" as the only acceptable answer. "Will you take out the garbage?" is really a rule if the child has no choice but to take out the garbage. Phrased as a question, however, the rule is unclear. The garbage sits in the kitchen, the parents become upset, and the child becomes increasingly confused.

2. Rules should be clearly defined. What is meant by "clean up your room"? Parents think their children know, but a child's idea of clean is never the same as a parent's. Only Sylvia's mother knows exactly what she wants when she tells Sylvia to clean up her room. To reduce uncertainty and confusion, define tasks specifically, as in, "You must make up your bed, fold your clothes, put them in your dresser, and put your books back on the shelf before you can go outside." If a

chore must be done every day, making a list of the steps involved will eliminate many unnecessary arguments. When a rule is defined clearly, it is easier to enforce.

3. Rules about chores should be reasonable. A child's day should not be filled with chores. There should be plenty of time for rest, study, and play. Before assigning a chore, be sure the child is able to do it. If the child is capable but needs some initial guidance, break the task down into small steps and teach one step at a time.

For instance, most five-year-olds don't know how to make beds, but they can be taught. First, have Sylvia watch you make the bed while you describe each step. Then have her help you. Over several days, let her do more and more of the job until she does it alone.

4. Parents should make only rules that they can and will enforce. When rules are made, children will break them. Children *must* break new rules to be sure that they *are* rules. If their parents fail to enforce them, they are *not* rules. If this happens frequently, the relationship between parent and child becomes tense and uncomfortable. When parents say, "I've tried everything and nothing works," they really mean they haven't enforced their rules.

Some parents attempt to enforce too many rules. These parents are usually found in hectic pursuit of their children, making up "don't's" while the children try desperately to escape. Don't invent rules on the run. Concentrate on enforcing only two or three at a time. You will be surprised at how quickly other things seem to fall into place once this is accomplished.

We live by rules because without them there would be no freedom. When parents make good rules and enforce them, they create a relaxed emotional climate in which their children are free to be OK.

•Family psychologist John Rosemond is director of the Center for Affirmative Parenting, Gastonia, North Carolina. For information on his parenting newsletter, call (800) 525-2778. His award-winning Web site is <www.rosemond.com>.

Lethal Air

Raymond O. West

A FEW MONTHS AGO a father in his mid-thirties zipped himself and his 13-year-old son into their two-person tent. Because it was cold, they brought in a source of heat. Now snug and warm, they said goodnight—for the final time. The next morning other campers, noting no activity and getting no response to their calls, unzipped the flaps and found them lifeless. Dad's mistake—a charcoal grill still smoldering and generating effusive quantities of carbon monoxide.

Far too many people die in tents and campers unaware that the air enclosed is lethal—deadly because of carbon monoxide (CO).

Remember, life depends on oxygen. The trillions of tiny cells that are in our bodies depend for their lives on the constant delivery of oxygen. Delivery, courtesy of crimson hemoglobin, is regular and dependable—dependable until that scarlet hemoglobin greedily binds the oxygen, refusing to give it up to the cells. And that's exactly the scenario when CO taints the air around us.

CO is a sneaky, invisible, and odorless gas, void of irritants that might give its deadly presence away. A silent stalker. A quiet killer. No wonder then that no other agent causes more unintentional poisoning. It's not that it produces no symptoms. It does, but the symptoms—nausea, headache, and dizziness—are easily dismissed as "flu" or "just a virus" that will be gone by morning.

The common denominator that underlies CO poisoning is incomplete combustion of carbon-based fuels like gasoline, propane, and charcoal. These days even kids will respect a closed garage when motors are running. Machinery like lawn mowers, garden tillers, diesel generators and the like all suffuse the air with CO. As do, of course, cars and trucks. Especially trucks. Generally not appreciated though are the perils of portable gas stoves, charcoal grills, camp heaters, and even lanterns.

So then, have we covered all the dangers? Not completely, for most fatalities occur in the home. If living quarters are enclosed and heated against outside chills and if the source of warmth is other than electrical, then breathe with care. And that snug little camper top latched tight to the bed of your pickup truck demands scrutiny. Enclosed, it sits all too close to an engine that burns gasoline, propane, or diesel. All of these spew forth CO like a smoke stack. So, whether parked in the campground or speeding down the Interstate—no people, no pets in the camper shell when the engine is running. Never!

Think of it. One thousand needless deaths each year could be prevented if we would pay a little more respect to this unforgiving killer. Should we be buying carbon monoxide detectors? Yes, one or more for every home in America.

•Raymond O. West, M.D., M.P.H., prepares this column as a community service of the Seventh-day Adventist Church. © General Conference of Seventh-day Adventists.

John McVay

Everyone Needs a

A **FEW DAYS AGO** my wife made a gentle complaint about the latest conglomeration of sticks and earth my 12-year-old son had built back in the trees. When she left, he offered an interesting defense. He averred, "But, Dad, everyone needs a sanctuary!"

It struck me as odd that he would use that word, *sanctuary.* I would have expected *fort* or even *castle.* But *sanctuary?*

His statement seemed as true to me as the word felt misplaced. We all do indeed need a sanctuary—a place where we feel utterly and completely safe. A place where we belong, where we have a sure and rightful place. A center from which we live our lives.

My dictionary says the word *sanctuary* means in part a "place recognized as holy; church, temple, tabernacle, holy place, holy of holies."[1] Much of this language evokes the tabernacle that was central to the worship of the children of Israel as they wandered in the wilderness. This sanctuary was a mobile structure that they built according to divine instructions, one that they dismantled and moved with them from place to place. It had a courtyard, and within the courtyard a tent-like tabernacle that was divided into two compartments. The first compartment, the larger of the two, was called the Holy Place. The second, inner compartment was called the Most Holy Place.

This portable sanctuary was no hovel of sticks and earth. Crafted of rich fabrics and precious metals, it was a magnificent structure. Yet, as different as this building might have been from my son's fort, it served a similar purpose. It provided a place where one could feel utterly and completely safe. Through the offering of sacrifices and the ministry of priests, sinners experi-enced forgiveness. Because of it, the author of Hebrews could write that the "good news," the gospel, was pro-claimed to those wilderness pilgrims.[2]

An enduring place of safety

While I toured my son's fort, I listened to the lilt in his voice as he described its features. To my adult eye the structure seemed crude and senseless. But to him it possessed considerable meaning. It was his sanctuary. I let my memory scan the years and recall a few of the rough places of refuge I had constructed as a boy. They came to mind with surprising clarity, and I experienced afresh the sense of pride and safety that I found in them.

It has been decades since I built my last fort. And yet the need for a central place of safety and meaning remains. Again and again the Bible invites us to find such an enduring place of safety. One such passage is the fourth chapter of Revelation. John, its author, sees a door standing open in the heavens, a graphic invitation into the Great Beyond. A trumpet-like voice beckons, " 'Come up here.' " In vision John is drawn into the vortex of this sky portal and finds himself at the center of it all—the throne room in God's sanctuary, the heavenly model for Israel's tabernacle[3]:

> At once I was in the spirit, and
> there in heaven stood a throne,
> with one seated on the throne!
> And the one seated there looks like
> jasper and carnelian, and around
> the throne is a rainbow that looks
> like an emerald.[4]

As John begins to describe the scene, his language is quite static. He could be describing a photograph. A still picture. Though the shutter speed is slow, the picture is clear. No motion blurs it. The

A sanctuary is a place—like our home—where

Sanctuary

we feel utterly safe. The Bible describes another sanctury for us, one that's in heaven.

photo must be in color, though, for hues of jasper, carnelian, and emerald enrich the scene.

John continues by noting: "Around the throne are twenty-four thrones, and seated on the thrones are twenty-four elders, dressed in white robes, with golden crowns on their heads."[5] A still picture, still. No one has moved. No one has spoken. Yet we readers have begun to suspect that these beings—especially

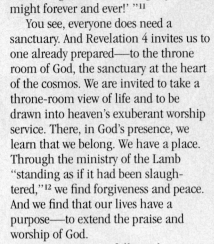

the One seated on the throne—are fully alive and poised for action. We are beginning to sense a suppressed energy.

Action!

Let the action begin! Into the quiet solemnity of the static photo blasts and blazes a high-powered sound-and-light show. Lightning flashes from the throne. Peals of loud, low thunder reverberate through the immense rooms. Seven torches blaze incandescent light. And all of it reflects off the

glassy surface of a crystalline sea. This is a static photograph no more!

As the action builds, John continues: "Around the throne, and on each side of the throne, are four living creatures, full of eyes in front and behind: the first living creature like a lion, the second living creature like an ox, the third living creature with a face like a human face, and the fourth living creature like a flying eagle."[6] Repetitively and continuously—yet without the slightest hint of disinterest and boredom—these four sing their one-stanza hymn of praise to the Occupant of the throne they encircle: " 'Holy, holy, holy, the Lord God the Almighty, who was and is and is to come.' "[7]

Amidst the fury of the sound-and-light show, the pace of the unfolding drama increases as these four living creatures trigger the greatest action sequence one could imagine—worship! Their exaltation spreads in widening circles, a boulder of praise dropped into a cosmic sea. The brief hymn they sing calls forth the worship of the 24 enthroned elders, who cast their crowns before the throne and sing their own exalted song.[8]

Then, in view of the unfolding drama centered in the Lamb, the four living creatures and the 24 elders unite to sing a "new song" of praise.[9] This inspires another wave of worship in which the creatures and elders are joined by "many angels surrounding the throne" who number "myriads of myriads and thousands of thousands."[10] Finally, "every creature in heaven and

on earth and under the earth and in the sea, and all that is in them" are caught up in worship. They sing, " 'To the one seated on the throne and to the Lamb be blessing and honor and glory and might forever and ever!' "[11]

You see, everyone does need a sanctuary. And Revelation 4 invites us to one already prepared—to the throne room of God, the sanctuary at the heart of the cosmos. We are invited to take a throne-room view of life and to be drawn into heaven's exuberant worship service. There, in God's presence, we learn that we belong. We have a place. Through the ministry of the Lamb "standing as if it had been slaughtered,"[12] we find forgiveness and peace. And we find that our lives have a purpose—to extend the praise and worship of God.

So I invite you to follow John through the open door to find what we each need—a sanctuary.

Since, then, we have a great high priest who has passed through the heavens, Jesus, the Son of God, let us hold fast to our confession. For we do not have a high priest who is unable to sympathize with our weaknesses, but we have one who in every respect has been tested as we are, yet without sin. Let us therefore approach the throne of grace with boldness, so that we may receive mercy and find grace to help in time of need.[13]

[1]*The Concise Oxford Dictionary,* 7th ed. (Oxford: Clarendon Press, 1982), 926.

[2]See Hebrews 4:2. [3]See Hebrews 8:1-7. [4]Revelation 4:2, 3. All Scripture quotations are from the New Revised Standard Version. [5]Revelation 4:4. [6]Revelation 4:6, 7. [7]Revelation 4:8. [8]Revelation 4:9-11. [9]Revelation 5:9, 10. [10]Revelation 5:11. [11]Revelation 5:13. [12]Revelation 5:6. [13]Hebrews 4:14-16.

What is your response? Tell us about it; see page 3 for instructions.

•*John McVay is the dean of the Seventh-day Adventist Theological Seminary at Andrews University, Berrien Springs, Michigan.*

ILLUSTRATION BY LARS JUSTINEN

Sandra Doran

How Protective Should I Be?

Q: I am confused about the concept of the "over-protective mother." How can you tell when to back off and let your children experience the consequences of their own actions? If a ship is sinking, do you just watch it go down?

A: You have brought up a topic that clearly is connected to a very vulnerable spot within your heart. Evidently, someone has accused you of being an "over-protective mother." You are left in a difficult place. Do you stand back and watch your child sink deeper and deeper into an ongoing problem, or do you take control, with fears of over-doing it and making the problem worse?

As a mother, you face the difficult challenge of sorting through all the well-meaning advice that surrounds you like a swarm of gnats on a May morning. From the time your first child enters the world you are met with a medley of experts on everything from breast-feeding to appropriate discipline. As you seek to do "the right thing," it is all too easy to try to please the chorus of voices rather than listen to your own heart.

I agree that over-involved parents can strip their children of power, leaving them with little motivation or desire to accomplish their own goals. But I am also aware that terms like "over-protective parent" can be used disparagingly by people with an agenda. How well I remember sitting at a conference table, trying in vain to convince a group of "professionals" that my son needed further testing to identify some of his learning struggles. I was only being an over-protective mother, they all agreed. He was fine. I only needed to back off and allow him to blossom without any further parental meddling.

Maybe so, but this "over-protective mother" was not satisfied with glib answers. My quest for understanding led me to quit my job as the administrator of a school, negotiate my way by train and subway system into a city I'd never entered, deposit myself on the campus of an institution of higher education,

and emerge four years later with a doctoral degree and enough knowledge to change my son's life.

I have known "over-protective mothers" who have stayed up all night on the last day of the marking period, working through stacks of homework papers with children who have come dangerously close to losing it when left to their own devices. I have known "over-protective mothers" who have fought with, cried over, cajoled, coaxed, pleaded, taught, bought, bribed, baby-stepped their errant sons and daughters back to wholeness, success, the narrow path.

I become concerned when I hear terms like "over-protective mother" being thrown around by those who profess to know it all. Until you have watched a child struggle unsuccessfully to read, received the horrifying news that your daughter has been caught downtown smoking pot, found a notebook full of suicidal messages, you will never know what it means to give your all to win a child back.

Over-protective mother? I say, Follow your heart. Don't ignore the warning signs. If the ship is sinking, seek the help of the experts, not the heckling mob yelling one-liners from the shore.

In what ways are you being accused of being "over-protective"? Why do you feel a need to step in and help your child? In what areas does he seem to be struggling? Is he having academic difficulties? Emotional problems? Social issues? A spiritual conflict? Then go to the ends of the earth to find people and information and methods that will help you help your son. Don't be deterred by labels that are meant to humiliate you as you respond to the red flags that signal that the ship is indeed going down.

Sometimes, an "over-protective mother" is all that stands between a child and self-destruction. Stand your ground. Do your homework. Find ways to empower your child. Connect him to sources of help. And when it is time, get out of the way.

•Sandra Doran's book, Gathering, *co-authored with her sister Dale Slongwhite and published by Pacific Press, is listed as a valuable resource by #1 best-seller Cheryl Richardson in her new book,* Life Makeovers.

Dialogue

Dear *Signs*:

I have done some comparison with various Bible translations, and thus Alden Thompson's article "Which Bible Is Best for You?" [January 2001] interested me. Satan has a counterfeit Bible—the New International Version [NIV]—from which a number of texts have been omitted that are in the King James Version [KJV]. Among these are Matthew 17:21, Mark 7:16, Luke 17:36, and others. We need to be aware, because Satan uses all methods of deception.

—Darren C. Yates, email

You raise a very important issue: Can modern translations that differ significantly from the King James Version be trusted? The answer is Yes.

The task of the Bible translator is to produce a version of the Bible that is as true to the original language as possible. However, this task is complicated by the fact that over the past several hundred years scholars have found many ancient manuscripts of the Bible, both Greek and Hebrew, and minor differences exist among these manuscripts. One common difference is that certain verses in one set of manuscripts are missing in others. So which manuscripts are right—those that include these verses or those that leave them out?

The easy way to decide would be to include everything that's in every manuscript. That way we would be certain to get all of God's Word. Keep in mind, however, that scribes hand-copied these manuscripts a letter at a time, often taking a year or more to produce one Bible. And sometimes they made mistakes. Some scribes accidentally left out a few words or sentences, which they wrote in the margin. However, scribes also are known to have written comments in the margins of their Bibles that later scribes assumed were verses that had been accidentally omitted, and they put them in as part of the Bible they were copying.

Of course, none of these words in the margins include explanatory notes that say "Oops—I left out these words" or "This is a comment, not a part of the Bible." So the modern translator has to figure out which is which. It would be nice if we today had manuscripts that were known to be the very ones that were written by Isaiah, Paul, and John, but we don't. So translators generally assume that the more ancient manuscripts are probably the most accurate, being closest to the original. And of course, scholars today have access to a vast number of very ancient Bible manuscripts that were not available to the King James translators.

With this background, let's examine a couple of the Bible verses that are

Scholars today have access to a vast number of very ancient Bible manuscripts that were not available to the King James translators.

found in the KJV but not in the NIV.

One that you mentioned is Matthew 17:21, which says: "Howbeit this kind goeth not out but by prayer and fasting" (KJV). A Bible commentary that I use quite often points out that textual evidence is divided over whether Matthew actually wrote these words. Thus, their omission in the NIV is not a satanically inspired plot to change the Bible. There are valid reasons for leaving them out.

A couple of other points add credibility to the conclusion that the NIV translators were not trying to undermine God's Word: (1) They put the missing words in a footnote, and (2) they included them in Mark 9:29, where textual evidence favors keeping them. You'll find the same situation with many other verses in the KJV that the NIV leaves out, including Matthew 18:11 and Luke 19:10; Mark 7:16 and Matthew 11:15; and Luke 17:36 and Matthew 24:40.

Most of these omissions are doctrinally insignificant. However, 1 John 5:7 in the KJV has great doctrinal significance, yet nearly all modern translations either omit it altogether or put it only in footnotes. This verse in the KJV says: "For there are three that bear record in heaven, the Father, the Word, and the Holy Ghost: and these three are one." These words support the doctrine of the Trinity unequivocally. However, the earliest Greek manuscripts to include them date to the 1500s—a millennium and a half after John wrote his letter! Prior to that, they appear only in Latin manuscripts. Scholars today are almost unanimously agreed that the words crept into the Latin as a marginal note and should not be included in today's Bible versions.

Differences do exist among scholars, of course, over which manuscripts are the most reliable. However, I believe I am safe in saying that the vast majority of today's Bible translators do their very best to give God's people the most accurate translation possible. So when in doubt over a particular reading in the NIV, your best approach is to compare with several other translations.

Marvin Moore
Editor

Dialogue flourishes where opinions differ—so when you disagree with a Signs® author's or editor's understanding of Scripture or with views expressed in Dialogue itself, drop us a line. Send your letters to Dialogue, Signs of the Times,® P.O. Box 5353, Nampa, ID 83653-5353, or email them to us at: <letters.signs@pacificpress.com>. Please restrict questions to 100 words or less. We reserve the right to edit questions for grammar, punctuation, and space.

Radio and TV Highlights for April

Signs of the Times® is pleased to announce the program titles for April of several radio and TV broadcasts that we highly recommend. The *TV Guide* will list the stations in your area that carry the TV programs. You can also call 800 SDA PLUS (732-7587) for information about the airing time and station in your area for any of these programs—or look up the various programs and their schedules via <www.adventistmedia.org/>.

The Voice of Prophecy Radio Program
Weekend broadcast with Lonnie Melashenko

March 31/April 1: The Word Became Flesh
April 7/8: Job: The Devil's Punching Bag
April 14/15: Folded Graveclothes
April 21/22: Psalms: God's Hymnbook
April 28/29: What's Next?

The Voice of Prophecy Radio Program
Daily broadcast with Lonnie Melashenko

April 2-6: Out . . . and Then Back In!
April 9-13: Is That God's Voice I Hear?
April 16-20: "Shut Up!"
April 23-27: Getting a Brain Transplant

It Is Written
Sunday telecast with Mark Finley

April 1: Conspiracies vs. God's Plan
April 8: Breaking the Bible Code
April 15: The Original Passion Play
April 22: Little Lies, Big Disasters
April 29: When Your Heart Follows Your Eyes

Lifestyle Magazine
Sunday telecast with Dan Matthews

(Trinity Broadcasting Network stations; see sources listed above for commercial channel schedule.)

April 5/7: Caring for Aging Parents
April 12/14: Recovering From Abuse
April 19/21: Stories of Survival
April 26/28: Making Corporations Act Responsibly

SIGNS OF THE TIMES® is published by the Seventh-day Adventist Church. Adventists believe the Bible to be the authoritative Word of God, Jesus to be their all-sufficient Savior, the seventh-day Sabbath to be a continuing reminder of His love, and the promise of His soon return to be their greatest hope and joy.

Staff Members

Editor
Marvin Moore

Associate Editor
David C. Jarnes

Editorial Secretary
Helen Stiles

Art Direction and Design
Merwin Stewart

Marketing and Sales
Dale E. Galusha

Circulation
Warren Riter

Copy Preparation
Deanna Davis, director
Wendy Perla
Kelly Reed

SIGNS OF THE TIMES® accepts manuscripts from freelance writers. Writer's guidelines are available on our Web site (see below) or write to us for guidelines and a free sample copy of the magazine at P.O. Box 5353, Nampa, ID 83653. Please enclose SASE with three first-class stamps.

Unless otherwise noted, all verses cited are from the New International Version.

Subscriptions

U.S.A. SUBSCRIPTIONS: Rate when purchased in the U.S.A. and mailed within the U.S.A. and its territories: $18.95 (U.S.) annually. Single copy, $2.50 (U.S.). To other countries, $21.95 (U.S.) annually. Single copy, $3.00 (U.S.).

To order, call 1-800-545-2449 or write to *SIGNS OF THE TIMES®,* P. O. Box 5353, Nampa, ID 83653. Periodicals postage paid at Nampa, Idaho. Vol. 128, No. 4.

CANADIAN SUBSCRIPTIONS: Rate when purchased in Canada and mailed within Canada: $27.95 (CDN.) annually (includes GST). Single copy, $3.50 (CDN.). To countries outside Canada (except U.S.A.): $30.95 (CDN.). To order, call 1-800-765-6955 or write to *SIGNS OF THE TIMES®* at nearest address below:

I-194 College Ave.
College Heights, AB T4L 2G1

1626 McCallum Road
Abbotsford, BC V2S 5H4

Box 398
Oshawa, ON L1H 7L5

940 CH Chambly
Longueuil, PQ J4H 3M3

For change of address within the U.S.A. and Canada, call 1-800-545-2449 Monday through Thursday or email us at <order.signs@pacificpress.com>.

All subscriptions are prepaid. If you did not order *SIGNS OF THE TIMES®,* it is being sent as a gift from a friend. You will not be billed.

Email

Letters to the editor:
<letters.signs@pacificpress.com>
Prayer requests:
<prayer.signs@pacificpress.com>
Subscriptions/address changes:
<order.signs@pacificpress.com>
Web home page:
<http://www.pacificpress.com/signs>

The List

Judie Gulley

MY STUPID LIST. Why did I even bother?

I pulled my school bus up to the high school, shut the engine off, then turned and ripped the piece of paper from the wall beside me. It was quiet on the bus. The kids behind me knew they were in trouble. And they knew why.

"Does anyone ever read this?" I asked, holding the paper up.

Nothing. What did I expect?

I put up a different list every year. "Rules to Live By" I call them. This year number one was "Say one nice thing to your mom." Number two was "Give your teacher a compliment." It was number five I was interested in. "Be a friend to someone who needs one." I stabbed at it with my finger. "Do any of you know what this says?"

No one looked.

"What gives you the right," I fumed, "to make life miserable for someone else? Do any of you have a clue what it's like to get on this bus every morning and face brats who have nothing better to do than make you feel bad?"

I looked at the leaders of the pack: Jennie Schmidt, Brett Jackson, Ryan Fedders, and maybe Sarah Blake. None of them troublemakers. But they'd gone down a major step in my estimation this past year.

All because of Tommy Flynn.

When Tommy and his mother moved into our district, I'd heard they were poor. He stepped into the bus that first morning and looked at me, his thin lips curved into a shy smile, and I knew the rumors were true.

He was small, frail looking, his pale blue eyes too big for the pinched, drawn face. His shaggy hair and worn clothes weren't those of a fashion rebel. He wore them that way from necessity.

I felt the stares from the back, the whispers a little too loud. I hated to send him back there.

"Hi, I'm Tom Flynn," he said, looking at me to see if anyone was listening.

"Hi, I'm Tom Flynn," a high-pitched, whiny voice from the back mimicked him. Both of us pretended not to notice.

"I'm glad to meet you, Tom," I said. Then I hesitated, looking up into the overhead mirror. He understood.

"In the back?"

"You can sit here with the little kids if you like."

"That's OK ," he said. "Got to get it over with sooner or later."

This gentle boy had been in new schools before—probably every time the rent was overdue. In the mirror I watched him walk to the back.

Jennie Schmidt wrinkled her nose and scattered her books across the seat next to her. One by one, the rest of them did the same.

"One of you move over," I said— and then added in a tone I reserved for special occasions, "Now!"

"O-o-oh, bus driver's pet," someone snickered. But they moved. Pink patches appeared on Tom's cheeks as he sat down. I wanted to strangle every one of the ringleaders.

It didn't get any better. I tried to keep my mouth shut, tried to let Tom fight it through on his own. Maybe one of them would show a little compassion. But it soon became apparent nothing was going to change. They teased, taunted, and made fun. Through it all, Tom was quiet and withdrawn.

Then one day Tom wasn't waiting outside his ramshackle farmhouse. I made my furious speech when we got to the school yard. Afterwards, all I saw were impatient glances, shuffling papers, eyes rolling with mock disgust. I crumpled my list into a ball and threw it on the floor as I reached for the door handle.

Jan Adams, the school counselor, was standing outside.

"Tom Flynn is sick," she said. I could tell by her expression that it wasn't a little cold and fever. "He's in Trinity Hospital," she added. "You might want to tell your kids."

I was in Tommy's room when some of them came to see him. Funny, they were as pale as he was. They sat next to him . . . tried to make small talk . . . to make themselves feel better. It was sad the way Tommy tried to comfort them.

He died a month later. We found out he'd been diagnosed with leukemia just before he'd moved to our town.

For a long time, it was hard for me to talk to the high schoolers in the back. But I noticed something going on. I saw them putting their heads together, whispering, glancing my way. No grins and giggles. Serious stuff. When they saw I was looking, they pretended to be doing nothing.

Then one morning when I stopped at the high school, Brett stood and leaned across the aisle to talk to a middle-school boy.

"Brett, what's the holdup?" I called. Startled, Brett jumped. Something clattered to the floor. Pennies, dimes, and quarters rolled under the seats and to the front of the bus, some falling into the step well. The bus grew quiet as the last of the coins clattered and clicked and stopped.

Dark eyes big with anticipation, Brett

Tommy was new, small, frail looking, and obviously poor. And kids can be so mean—especially when they sense vulnerability.

knelt and began raking coins into a pile.

"What's going on?" I said again, keeping my voice as level as I could.

Brett glanced back at his partners in crime. They were silent. Finally he shrugged.

"It's number eight," he said.

What was this kid talking about?

"We had a lot of trouble with number five, so we thought we'd try number eight."

He pulled a crumpled bit of paper from his pocket and held it out. The list. I smoothed the paper, my fingers shaking.

Number eight: "Do something nice for someone and don't let anyone know." I looked up. My confusion must have shown on my face.

Brett shrugged again. "Tom's mother couldn't afford a tombstone," he said.

I looked at them, Brett and Jennie and Ryan and Sarah. Saw the guilt and sorrow in their eyes.

Then I went back to my seat and taped the crumpled piece of paper back to the wall.

•*Judie Gulley writes from Orion, Illinois.*

ILLUSTRATION BY BARBARA KIWAK

The Practice of Forgiveness

Victor M. Parachin

him had they struck his head.

The following day, Charlotte police arrested two teens. They said they had been target practicing with their pellet guns and never intended to shoot anyone. Their arrest might have been the end of this story except for Hyde's compassion and forgiveness combined with his passion about running.

When the teens called Hyde to apologize, he accepted the apology, forgave them, and suggested they get together for a jog in McAlpine Park. "I love the park, which has a sort of magic to it with its mix of young people, old people, and middle-aged people, and I didn't want that destroyed by what happened to me," he said.

So, six days after the incident, the three met at McAlpine for a 5-K. The teens had trouble keeping up. "He's no jogger, he's a real runner," one teen joked. The other noted, "He thanked us for coming and for taking responsibility. Considering what we did, he was pretty nice. I probably couldn't have done that!"

Hyde's response to the shooting was creative, compassionate, forgiving, and, ultimately, resulted in healing. He does not harbor anger or bitterness toward the teens. His gentle, compassionate response has had a powerful impact on them, dissolving any fear or anxiety they might have felt toward him. And all three can feel good about spending time in McAlpine Park.

What author Marianne Williamson said is true: "The practice of forgiveness is our most important contribution to the world." So ask yourself, Whom do I need to forgive today?

For **THE PAST TWO DECADES,** Dan Hyde, of Charlotte, North Carolina, has been running marathons. He routinely logs forty to fifty miles a week in training, so his five-mile run through McAlpine Creek Park in Charlotte is not unusual. However, as he was completing that run recently, he felt two pellets slam into the back of his legs. Members of a cross-country team running nearby stopped to help and called 911. Soon Hyde, a 43-year-old engineer, was in the hospital, where doctors removed the pellets and sent him home with both legs bandaged. A police sergeant told Hyde he was "lucky" because the pellets could have killed

•Victor M. Parachin writes from Tulsa, Oklahoma.

Peter is absolutely certain that he will not betray Jesus. Stress the word "never" in his denial.

Gethsemane = Geth-SEM-mah-nee

Zebedee = ZEH-beh-dee

Deliver Jesus' words throughout this reading in a bold, confident tone. But as Jesus first begs his Father to spare him the way of the cross, and then resigns himself to his Father's will, try to bring out Jesus' humanity. Try to bring out the fear and desperation Jesus must be feeling, and then the sadness and resignation to his fate in a flatter, quieter, less emotional tone.

Use either a sad or irritated tone of voice to reflect Jesus' disappointment in his sleeping disciples.

Peter **said** to him in reply,
  "Though **all** may have their **faith** in you **shaken**,
  mine will **never** be."
Jesus **said** to him,
  "**Amen**, I **say** to you,
  this very night before the **cock** crows,
  you will deny me **three** times."
Peter **said** to him,
  "Even though I should have to **die** with you,
  I will **not** deny you."
And all the disciples spoke **likewise**.

Then Jesus came with them to a place called **Gethsemane**,
  and he **said** to his disciples,
  "**Sit here** while I go over there and **pray**."
He took along **Peter** and the two sons of **Zebedee**,
  and began to feel **sorrow** and **distress**.
Then he **said** to them,
  "My **soul** is **sorrowful** even to **death**.
Remain here and keep **watch** with me."
He advanced a little and fell **prostrate** in **prayer**, saying,
  "My **Father**, if it is **possible**,
  let this cup **pass** from me;
  yet, not as **I** will, but as **you** will."
When he **returned** to his **disciples** he found them **asleep**.
He said to **Peter**,
  "So you could **not** keep watch with me for **one hour**?
Watch and **pray** that you may **not** undergo the **test**.
The **spirit** is **willing**, but the **flesh** is **weak**."
Withdrawing a **second** time, he prayed **again**,
  "My **Father**, if it is not possible that this cup **pass**
  without my **drinking** it, **your will** be **done**!"

The first option, which we find in our Bible, is the more likely of the two. Look at 2:7–8. What do they describe? They describe Jesus' emptying of himself and taking on a slave's form. They describe his willing acceptance of death on a cross. These verses do not stress Jesus' equality with God, but rather the consequence of Jesus' decision to humble himself.

In 2:9, the hymn's whole perspective shifts. In 2:6 – 8, we read of Jesus' voluntary acceptance of a slave's form, human like-ness, and even death on one of the crueler tools of execution human ingenuity ever devised. In 2:9, we find ourselves no longer with Jesus in earthly humiliation, but from God's vantage, who exalts Jesus from the lowly stature he adopted to a position of lordship over the cosmos.

Some biblical scholars do not think Paul wrote Philippians 2:6–11, believing the hymn was a traditional and popular one in use in the Churches. They suggest Paul included the text in his letter because it was well known and helped him to make his point about the importance of self-sacrificial love in the Church. Others think Paul freely adapted what was originally a Jewish hymn to wisdom *(sophia)* or reason *(logos)*. These are possible but unnecessary explanations. Paul was capable of beautiful and ele-vated writing. Witness his praise of love in 1 Corinthians 13. Very few imagine that Paul did not write 1 Corinthians 13, which has many of the same stylistic features as Philippians 2:6–11. And the theme of

Then he **returned** once more and found them **asleep**,
    for they could **not** keep their eyes open.
He **left** them and withdrew **again** and prayed a **third** time,
    saying the same thing again.
Then he returned to his disciples and said to them,
    "Are you still **sleeping** and taking your **rest**?
Behold, the **hour** is **at hand**
    when the **Son** of **Man** is to be handed over to **sinners**.
Get up, let us **go**.
Look, my **betrayer** is at **hand**."

(6) While he was still speaking,
    Judas, one of the **Twelve**, arrived,
        accompanied by a large crowd, with **swords** and **clubs**,
        who had come from the **chief priests** and the **elders**
            of the **people**.
His betrayer had arranged a **sign** with them, saying,
    "The man I shall **kiss** is **the one**; arrest **him**."
Immediately he went over to **Jesus** and said,
    "**Hail**, **Rabbi**!" and he **kissed** him.
Jesus **answered** him,
    "**Friend**, **do** what you have **come** for."
Then stepping forward they laid **hands** on Jesus and **arrested** him.
And **behold**, one of those who **accompanied** Jesus
    put his **hand** to his **sword**, drew it,
    and **struck** the high priest's servant, cutting off his **ear**.
Then Jesus said to him,
    "**Put** your **sword** back **into** its **sheath**,
    for **all** who take the **sword** will **perish** by the **sword**.
Do you **think** that I cannot **call** upon my **Father**
    and he will not **provide** me at this **moment**
    with more than **twelve legions** of **angels**?

Rabbi = RAH-bye

Deliver Judas' lines as though he were truly cheerful and happy to see his beloved rabbi. This will effectively communicate his hypocrisy to the assembly.

Bring out Jesus' anger at his disciple's swordplay.

Philippians 2:6–11 fits very well in a letter urging to "complete my joy by being of the same mind, with the same love, united in heart, thinking one thing. Do nothing out of selfishness or out of vainglory; rather, humbly regard others as more important than yourselves, each looking out not for his own interests, but [also] everyone for those of others" (Philippians 2:2–4).

The theme of Philippians is the need for self-sacrifice. Paul presents himself as an example in this regard. He writes from prison. But far from being unhappy about this, Paul claims, "my situation has turned out rather to advance the Gospel, so that my imprisonment has become well known in Christ throughout the whole praetorium and to all the rest, and so that the majority of the brothers, having taken encouragement in the Lord from my imprisonment, dare more than ever to proclaim the word fearlessly" (Philippians 1:12–14). This is no overnight stay in jail. Paul faces the possibility of death as 1:20–22 reveal. Although Paul faces death and has questioned the motives of some who preach Christ, he still manages to keep things in perspective: "What difference does it make, as long as in every way, whether in pretense or in truth, Christ is being proclaimed? And in that I rejoice" (Philippians 1:18). Christ and the local Churches are bigger and more important than Paul is. He can set aside his fears and resentments in order to concentrate on what is truly important: the proclamation of the Gospel.

But then **how** would the **Scriptures** be **fulfilled**
   which **say** that it **must** come to pass in this way?"
At that hour Jesus said to the **crowds**,
   "Have you **come out** as against a **robber**,
   with **swords** and **clubs** to **seize** me?
Day after **day** I sat **teaching** in the temple area,
   yet you did **not** arrest me.
But **all** this has come to **pass**
   that the **writings** of the **prophets** may be **fulfilled**."
Then **all** the disciples **left** him and **fled**.

Caiaphas = CAI-ah-phas

(7) Those who had **arrested** Jesus led him away
   to **Caiaphas** the high priest,
   where the **scribes** and the **elders** were **assembled**.
Peter was **following** him at a **distance**
   as far as the high priest's courtyard,
   and going inside he sat down with the **servants**
      to see the **outcome**.

Sanhedrin = San-HEH-drin

The **chief priests** and the entire **Sanhedrin**
   kept **trying** to obtain **false** testimony against **Jesus**
   in order to **put** him to **death**,
   but they found **none**,
   though **many** false witnesses came forward.
Finally **two** came **forward** who **stated**,
   "This man said, 'I can **destroy** the temple of God
   and within **three days** rebuild it.'"
The high priest **rose** and **addressed** him,
   "Have you no answer?
What are these men **testifying** against you?"
But Jesus was **silent**.

Pause briefly before and after you deliver the line "But Jesus was silent."

Thus, Paul presents himself to the Philippians in a way that is similar to his presentation of Christ in today's reading. For the local Churches and the Gospel, has Paul given up his freedom, and perhaps his life, just as Christ emptied himself, took a slave's form, and died on a cross for others. Paul offers both Christ and himself in imitation of Christ as examples to the Philippians of the need for Christians, the members of Christ's body, to place others' interests before their own.

PASSION More than a third of the Gospel of Matthew (8 chapters out of 28) is given over to the deeds, words, and events of the last week of Jesus' earthly life. Today's reading covers nearly two chapters and is almost entirely given over to the events of a single evening and following day of that week. All four evangelists slow down their narration to a relative snail's pace in order to recount what happened to Jesus in the final days, hours, and minutes of his life.

The word "passion" derives from the Greek word *paschō*, which means "experience" or "undergo," but also "suffer." Matthew's description of the final hours of Jesus' life is an account of both what Jesus underwent and what he suffered—a passion in both senses of the word. It is a dreadful story. In less than a week, the people who welcomed Jesus into the city with waving palms and psalms on their lips become a mob baying for blood, willing to take upon

Raise your voice to communicate the high priest's rage and the hostility of the mockery Jesus suffers.

Prophesy = PROF-uh-sī

Gal-li-LAY-an
Proclaim Peter's denials with increasing levels of emotion. Deliver the first denial in a calm and rational tone, but use a tone of irritation for the second denial and one of anger and desperation for the final denial.

Nazorean = Nah-zo-RAY-an

Then the **high priest** said to him,
  "I **order** you to tell **us under oath** before the **living God**
  whether **you** are the **Christ**, the **Son** of **God**."

Jesus **said** to him in reply,
  "**You** have said so.
But **I** tell you:
  From now on you will see 'the **Son** of **Man**
    seated at the **right hand** of the **Power**'
    and '**coming** on the **clouds** of **heaven**'."
Then the high priest tore his robes and said,
  "He has **blasphemed**!
What further need have we of **witnesses**?
You have now **heard** the **blasphemy**;
  what is **your** opinion?"
They said in reply,
  "He **deserves** to **die**!"
Then they **spat** in his face and **struck** him,
  while some **slapped** him, saying,
  "**Prophesy** for us, Christ: who is it that **struck** you?"

(8) Now **Peter** was sitting outside in the **courtyard**.
One of the **maids** came over to him and **said**,
  "You **too** were with **Jesus** the **Galilean**."
But he **denied** it in front of **everyone**, saying,
  "**I** do **not** know what you are **talking** about!"
As he went out to the gate, **another** girl saw him
  and said to those who were there,
  "**This** man was with **Jesus** the **Nazorean**."
Again he **denied** it with an **oath**,
  "**I** do **not know** the **man**!"

themselves and their children the guilt of Jesus' murder (Matthew 27:25). The Roman authorities appear almost powerless (27:24). Against the advice of his own wife (27:19) and in seeming opposition to his conscience (27:18, 23), Pontius Pilate does not sentence Jesus to die, but rather tries to absolve himself of responsibility before turning him over to the crowd (27:24).

The accounts of Jesus' Passion in the Gospels open onto many possible avenues of exploration. But one theme deserves special attention: the meaning of Jesus' identity as the Son of Man. We encounter it in three separate verses of this reading (26:24, 45, 64). In Matthew's Gospel, as in the other three, "Son of Man" is among the most important designations or titles of Jesus. But while the meaning of "Son of Man" is key to Matthew's understanding of who Jesus is, what he does, and why he must undergo his Passion, the title is still somewhat obscure.

In the book of Ezekiel, "son of man" is the name by which God calls the prophet Ezekiel. The precise Hebrew phrase is *ben-adam,* as in the prophet's inaugural vision when God addresses Ezekiel, who lies as though dead before the divine throne: "Son of man, stand up! I wish to speak with you" (Ezekiel 2:1). In Ezekiel, "son of man" simply calls readers' attention to the prophet's humanity in relation to God's divinity (see also Job 25:6). For this reason, many Bibles translate *ben-adam* in Ezekiel as "mortal."

In some later strains of Judaism, "son of man" changed quite radically in meaning. In Daniel 7—12, a prophet reports multiple

A little later the bystanders came over and said to Peter,
"**Surely** you **too** are one of them;
even your **speech** gives you away."
At that he began to **curse** and to **swear**,
"I do **not know** the **man**."
And **immediately** a cock crowed.
Then Peter remembered the **word** that Jesus had spoken:
"Before the **cock** crows you will deny me **three times**."
He went out and began to **weep bitterly**.

When it was **morning**,
all the chief **priests** and the **elders** of the people
took **counsel** against Jesus to put him to **death**.
They **bound** him, led him **away**,
and handed him over to **Pilate**, the governor.

Pilate = PI-lat

(9) Then **Judas**, his **betrayer**, seeing that **Jesus** had been
condemned,
deeply **regretted** what he had done.
He **returned** the thirty pieces of silver
to the chief priests and elders, saying,
"I have **sinned** in betraying **innocent blood**."
They said,
"**What** is that to **us**?
Look to it yourself."
Flinging the money into the temple,
he **departed** and went off and **hanged** himself.
The chief priests **gathered** up the money, but said,
"It is not lawful to deposit this in the temple treasury,
for it is the **price** of **blood**."
After consultation, they used it to buy the potter's field
as a burial place for **foreigners**.

Judas is clearly sorry and repentant, although the priests couldn't care less. Deliver Judas' lines in a tone of sorrow and regret, but the high priests' with sharpness and an air of superiority.

visions, including the spectacle of "One like a son of man coming, on the clouds of heaven" to receive "dominion, glory, and kingship" and the service of "nations and peoples of every language." The "one like a son of man" receives all this from an enthroned and white-haired figure the prophet calls the "Ancient One" (Daniel 7:12–14). In Daniel's original literary context, the "Ancient One" likely represented Israel's God, while the "one like a son of man" most probably represented the archangel Michael, who elsewhere in Daniel appears in a military and leadership capacity in God's service (10:13, 21; 12:1). But in the cryptic world of Daniel, the precise identity of the "one like a son of man" remains mysterious, never being spelled out in so many words.

The scene of Daniel 7:12–14 provided some Jews, and later early Christians, with an important prophetic witness to the belief that, at some point in the future, a supernatural figure, "the son of man," possessing God-given authority to wield righteous power would arrive in Israel. Early Christians identified this "son of man" with Jesus. In Matthew's account of the Passion, after the high priest asks Jesus "tell us . . . whether you are the Messiah, the Son of God," Jesus replies, quoting Daniel 7:13: "You have said so. But I tell you: From now on you will see 'the Son of Man seated at the right hand of the Power' and 'coming on the clouds of heaven'" (Matthew 26:63–64; see also Mark 14:61–62; Luke 22:67–70). In Jesus Christ, the

That is why that field even today is called the **Field** of **Blood**.
Then was **fulfilled** what had been **said** through **Jeremiah**
the **prophet**,
And they took the thirty pieces of silver,
the value of a man with a price on his head,
a price set by some of the Israelites,
and they paid it out for the potter's field
just as the Lord had commanded me.

(10) Now **Jesus** stood before the governor, who **questioned** him,
"Are **you** the **king** of the **Jews**?"
Jesus said, "**You** say so."
And when he was **accused** by the chief **priests** and **elders**,
he made no answer.
Then **Pilate** said to him,
"Do you not **hear** how many things they are **testifying**
against you?"
But he did not **answer** him **one** word,
so that the governor was greatly **amazed**.

Now on the occasion of the **feast**
the governor was accustomed to **release** to the crowd
one prisoner whom they wished.
And at that time they had a **notorious** prisoner called **Barabbas**.
So when they had assembled, Pilate said to them,
"Which one do you want me to **release** to you,
Barabbas, or **Jesus** called **Christ**?"
For he knew that it was out of **envy**
that they had handed him over.

Pilate speaks seven times. The first six times are questions he directs either to Jesus or the crowds. Make sure you proclaim the questions *as* questions, raising the tone of your voice at the end of each line.

Barrabas = Bar-RAH-bas

evangelists believed they had found Daniel's mysterious "one like a son of man."

But there is more to Matthew's portrait of Jesus as the Son of Man than claims to power and authority, for the Passion is also about weakness, suffering, and death, which seems the very opposite of power and authority. In Matthew's Gospel, Jesus three times refers to his Passion by predicting that the Son of Man must endure suffering and death (17:12, 22–23; 20:18–19). The idea that the Son of Man must suffer and die

in addition to exercising power likely comes from the decision of early Christian interpreters to read Zechariah 12:10–14 and Daniel 7:12–14 in light of the experience of Jesus, even combining these passages in places. Of the evangelists, the only one to quote Zechariah 12:10 in relation to Jesus' Passion is John (see John 19:37). But in Matthew 24:30, Jesus borrows critical Greek vocabulary from the Greek text of Zechariah 12:10–14, which describes the

mourning of many at the death of the one "thrust through" in 12:10, before he quotes Daniel 7:13 (see also Revelation 1:7, where Daniel 7:13 and Zechariah 12:10–14 are also brought together).

Why does Matthew apparently "cut and paste" scripture like this? And why should it matter to us? For Matthew, the confirmation of the Church's proclamation that Jesus is the Christ rests upon the testimony of scripture and Jesus' fulfillment of it. Repeatedly we learn from Matthew that Jesus said or

While he was still **seated** on the bench,
   his wife sent him a **message**,
    "Have **nothing** to do with that **righteous** man.
I suffered **much** in a dream today because of him."
The chief **priests** and the **elders persuaded** the crowds
   to ask for **Barabbas** but to destroy **Jesus**.
The governor said to them in **reply**,
   "Which of the two do you want me to **release** to you?"
They answered, "**Barabbas**!"
Pilate said to them,
   "Then what shall I do with **Jesus** called **Christ**?"
They all said,
   "Let him be **crucified**!"
But he said,
   "**Why**? What **evil** has he done?"
They only shouted the louder,
   "Let him be **crucified**!"

When Pilate saw that he was not succeeding at **all**,
   but that a **riot** was breaking out instead,
   he took **water** and **washed** his hands in the sight of the crowd,
   saying, "I am **innocent** of this man's blood.
Look to it yourselves."
And the whole people said in reply,
   "His **blood** be upon **us** and upon our **children**."
Then he released **Barabbas** to them,
   but **after** he had Jesus **scourged**,
   he **handed** him over to be **crucified**.

(11) Then the soldiers of the governor took Jesus
   inside the **praetorium**
   and gathered the whole cohort around him.

praetorium = pray-TOR-ee-um

did something in order to fulfill scripture (1:22; 2:15, 17, 23; 4:14; 8:17; 12:17; 13:14, 35; 21:4, 9). Jesus has come to "fulfill" Jewish law, not to abolish it (5:17). More to the point of this reading is Jesus' statement that, if he wished, he could powerfully protect himself from his fate, but that scripture can be fulfilled in no other way (26:54, 56). In every aspect of his life—birth, life, work, Passion, death, and Resurrection—Matthew's Jesus fulfills scripture. Matthew wants his readers to understand that the Son of Man, simultaneously holding otherworldly power and being submissive in solitary weakness, is Jesus. But Matthew also wants his readers to believe that this conviction arose not merely from the testimony of the disciples, but because the disciples' testimony can be shown to be in profound agreement with the testimony of scripture.

Jesus is being mocked here. Deliver these lines as taunts, in a derisive and sarcastic tone of voice.

They **stripped** off his clothes
and threw a scarlet military cloak about him.
Weaving a **crown** out of **thorns**, they placed it on his head,
and a **reed** in his right hand.
And kneeling before him, they **mocked** him, saying,
"**Hail**, **King** of the **Jews**!"
They **spat** upon him and took the reed
and kept **striking** him on the head.
And when they had **mocked** him,
they **stripped** him of the cloak,
dressed him in his own clothes,
and led him off to **crucify** him.

Cyrenian = Sy-REN-i-an

(12) As they were going out, they met a **Cyrenian** named Simon;
this man they pressed into service
to carry his cross.

Golgatha = GOL-go-tha

And when they came to a place called **Golgotha**
—which means **Place** of the **Skull**—,
they gave Jesus **wine** to drink mixed with gall.
But when he had tasted it, he refused to drink.
(13) After they had **crucified** him,
they divided his garments by casting lots;
then they sat down and kept watch over him there.
And they placed over his head the **written charge** against him:
This is **Jesus**, the **King** of the **Jews**.
Two revolutionaries were **crucified** with him,
one on his **right** and the other on his **left**.
Those passing by reviled him, shaking their heads and saying,
"You who would **destroy** the temple and **rebuild** it
in three days,
save yourself, if you are the **Son** of **God**,
and **come down** from the **cross**!"

Likewise the chief **priests** with the **scribes** and **elders**
   mocked him and said,
   "He saved **others**; he cannot save himself.
So **he** is the **king** of **Israel**!
Let him **come down** from the **cross** now,
   and we will **believe** in him.
He **trusted** in God;
   let him **deliver** him now if he **wants** him.
For he said, 'I am the **Son** of **God**.'"
The revolutionaries who were crucified with him
   also kept **abusing** him in the same way.

(14) From noon onward, darkness came over the whole land
   until three in the afternoon.
And about three o'clock Jesus **cried out** in a loud voice,
   "Eli, Eli, lema sabachthani?"
   which means, *"My God, my God, why have you forsaken me?"*
Some of the bystanders who heard it said,
   "**This** one is calling for **Elijah**."
Immediately one of them **ran** to get a sponge;
   he soaked it in **wine**, and putting it on a **reed**,
   gave it to him to **drink**.
But the rest said,
   "**Wait**, let us **see** if Elijah comes to **save** him."
But **Jesus** cried out again in a **loud voice**,
   and **gave up** his spirit.

[Here all kneel and pause for a short time.]

And **behold**, the veil of the sanctuary
   was **torn** in **two** from **top** to **bottom**.

**Raise your voice when you deliver Jesus'
cry of desolation.**

**Eli, Eli, lema sabachthani = EL-li EL-li LE-ma
Sah-bac-TAH-ni**

Elijah = El-LI-jah

Pause for several seconds here.

Look up and make eye contact with the assembly when you proclaim, slowly and clearly, the centurion's confession of faith.

Magdalene = MAG-dah-len

The earth **quaked**, rocks were **split**, tombs were **opened**,
   and the bodies of many saints who had fallen asleep
      were **raised**.
And coming forth from their tombs after his resurrection,
   they **entered** the holy city and **appeared** to many.
The **centurion** and the **men** with him who were
      keeping watch over Jesus
   feared greatly when they saw the **earthquake**
   and **all** that was happening, and they said,
   "**Truly**, **this** was the **Son** of **God**!"
(15) There were many **women** there, looking on from a distance,
   who had **followed** Jesus from **Galilee**, ministering to him.
Among them were **Mary Magdalene** and **Mary**
      the mother of James and Joseph,
   and the **mother** of the sons of Zebedee.

When it was **evening**,
   there came a rich man from **Arimathea** named **Joseph**,
   who was **himself** a disciple of **Jesus**.
He went to **Pilate** and asked for the body of **Jesus**;
   then Pilate ordered it to be handed over.
Taking the body, Joseph **wrapped** it in clean linen
   and **laid** it in his new tomb that he had **hewn** in the rock.
Then he rolled a **huge stone** across the entrance to the tomb
      and departed.
But **Mary Magdalene** and the **other Mary**
   remained sitting there, facing the tomb.

(16) The next day, the one following the day of preparation,
   the chief **priests** and the **Pharisees**
   gathered before Pilate and said,
   "Sir, we remember that this impostor while still alive said,
   'After **three days** I will be **raised up**.'

Arimathea = Ar-rih-mah-THE-ah

Pharisees = PHAR-i-sees

Give orders, then, that the grave be secured until the **third day**,
    lest his **disciples** come and **steal** him and say to the people,
    'He has been **raised** from the **dead**.'
This **last** imposture would be worse than the **first**."
Pilate said to them,
    "The guard is **yours**;
    go, **secure** it as **best** you can."
So they went and secured the tomb
    by fixing a **seal** to the stone and setting the **guard**.

[Shorter: Matthew 27:11–54]

HOLY THURSDAY: MASS OF THE LORD'S SUPPER

Lectionary #39

READING I   Exodus 12:1–8, 11–14

A reading from the Book of Exodus

The LORD said to **Moses** and **Aaron** in the land of **Egypt**,
"This month shall stand at the head of your calendar;
    you shall reckon it the first month of the year.
Tell the **whole** community of Israel:
    On the tenth of this month **every one** of your families
        must **procure** for itself a **lamb**, one apiece for **each** household.
If a family is **too small** for a **whole** lamb,
    it shall **join** the nearest household in procuring one
    and shall **share** in the lamb
    in proportion to the number of persons who partake of it.
The **lamb** must be a year-old **male** and without **blemish**.
You may take it from either the **sheep** or the **goats**.
You shall keep it until the fourteenth day of this month,
    and then, with the **whole assembly** of **Israel** present,
    it shall be **slaughtered** during the evening twilight.
They shall take some of its blood
    and apply it to the two **doorposts** and the **lintel**
    of every house in which they **partake** of the **lamb**.
That **same night** they shall eat its roasted **flesh**
    with **unleavened bread** and **bitter herbs**.

Aaron = AIR-ron

READING I   In today's reading, we read instructions for the celebration of a domestic Jewish liturgy, the Passover. The roots of the Passover, like those of a great many spring feasts around the world in herding and farming societies, lie in the ritual petition to the gods for freedom from transgression and guilt incurred in the past year and for a prosperous season. Distinguishing the Passover from other ritual celebrations from Israel's ancient Middle Eastern cultural environment is Passover's association with Israel's flight from Egyptian slavery and its exclusive relationship with its God.

It may be hard to proclaim, and for the assembly to take to heart, a passage in which God announces the intention to destroy the firstborn of Egypt. It may help to know that this detail of the Exodus stems from a religious environment in which the first produce of farm, field, and home belonged to the gods (Exodus 13:2; Leviticus 3:13). Slaughtered animals and other offerings could be made to "stand in" for a human victim. This religious context does not eliminate the horror of the narrative, but it has something to do with why we find the narrative in our Bibles in the first place.

In Luke 12:35, Jesus quotes Exodus 12:11 ("Gird your loins and light your lamps") as an example of the kind of readiness his disciples should maintain as they wait in expectation of the Son of Man. In Jesus' example, Israel's escape from Egyptian slavery is conceived anew as the exodus of Jesus' followers from the turmoil of the end of days that will accompany the return of the son of Man (Luke 12:40).

"**This** is how you are to **eat** it:
with your **loins girt**, **sandals** on your **feet** and your **staff**
in **hand**,
you shall **eat** like those who are in **flight**.
It is the **Passover** of the LORD.
For on this **same night** I will go through **Egypt**,
striking down **every** firstborn of the land, both **man** and **beast**,
and executing **judgment** on all the **gods** of **Egypt**—I, the LORD!
But the **blood** will mark the houses where you are.
Seeing the **blood**, I will pass over you;
thus, when I **strike** the land of **Egypt**,
no destructive blow will come upon **you**.

"**This day** shall be a **memorial feast** for you,
which **all** your generations shall celebrate
with **pilgrimage** to the LORD, as a **perpetual institution**."

Read this line slowly and in a firm tone of voice.

READING II   1 Corinthians 11:23–26

A reading from the first Letter of Saint Paul to the Corinthians

Brothers and **sisters**:
I received from the **Lord** what I **also** handed on to **you**,
that the **Lord Jesus**, on the night he was **handed over**,
took **bread**, and, after he had **given thanks**,
broke it and said, "**This** is my **body** that is for **you**.
Do this in **remembrance** of **me**."
In the **same** way also the cup, **after** supper, saying,
"**This cup** is the **new covenant** in my **blood**.

Emphasize the chain of transmission from "the Lord" to Paul to the Corinthians.

READING II   In this reading Paul hands on to the Corinthians a tradition he says he received "from the Lord." The tradition should be a familiar one, for we hear something nearly identical spoken by priests in the Mass during the consecration (see also Matthew 26:26–29; Mark 14:22–25; Luke 22:19–20).

But why does Paul hand on this tradition to the Corinthians in this letter? It is not as though he is telling them about the Eucharist for the first time. Back up to 11:17

and you will get a better view of the issue at hand. In the Church at Corinth, people have supplied their own food at the Eucharist. The well-off bring plenty of food and wine, while the poor of the Church get little or nothing. Paul disapproves of the way the Corinthians have been celebrating the Eucharist: some have plenty to eat, and even too much to drink, while others starve. And so Paul reminds his addressees of the character of the ritual meal on which their tradition is based.

The problems at the Eucharist are one instance of the general problem of division in the Corinthian Church. If we back up even further to the letter's beginning, we may recall that the report Paul received about the Corinthian Church had to do with the existence of factions and rivalries among its members. To this situation of division Paul addresses his wish "that there be no divisions among you" (1 Corinthians 1:10). Paul perceives divisions about Church leadership, sexual relations, lawsuits, marriage,

Look up at the assembly as you proclaim the concluding clause, emphasizing the word "you."

Do this, as often as you **drink** it, in **remembrance** of me."
For as **often** as you **eat** this **bread** and **drink** the **cup**,
    you **proclaim** the **death** of the **Lord** until he **comes**.

GOSPEL   John 13:1–15

A reading from the holy Gospel according to John

Before the feast of **Passover**, Jesus **knew** that his hour had come
    to **pass** from **this world** to the **Father**.
He **loved** his own in the world and he **loved** them to the **end**.
The devil had already induced **Judas**, son of **Simon** the **Iscariot**,
    to hand him over.
So, during supper,
    fully aware that the Father had put **everything** into his power
    and that he had **come** from **God** and was **returning** to **God**,
    he **rose** from supper and **took off** his outer garments.
He took a **towel** and tied it around his **waist**.
Then he poured **water** into a **basin**
    and began to **wash** the disciples' **feet**
    and **dry** them with the towel around his **waist**.
He came to **Simon Peter**, who said to him,
    "**Master**, are **you** going to wash **my** feet?"
Jesus answered and said to him,
    "What I am doing, you do **not** understand now,
    but you **will** understand later."
Peter said to him, "You will **never** wash my feet."
Jesus answered him,
    "**Unless** I wash you, you will have **no inheritance** with me."

Read this line slowly and deliberately, emphasizing the word "loved."

Judas Iscariot = JU-das Is-CAR-iot

Peter has three lines in this reading. In the first one, Peter cannot believe his ears. Jesus wash *his* feet? It ought to be the other way around! Raise your voice to communicate Peter's shock and disbelief. In the second one, raise your voice again, but this time with a firm tone to indicate Peter's refusal. In the third, however, Peter has completely changed his mind in the space of a heartbeat. Deliver it cheerfully and with a broad smile (his abrupt and total change of mind is a little humorous).

chastity, eating meat offered to idols, male and female attire in worship, and spiritual gifts. To this list we can add the way the Corinthians celebrated the Eucharist.

In view of the Corinthians' divisions, an exasperated Paul asks them early in his letter (1 Corinthians 1:13): "Is Christ divided?" The Corinthians' behavior suggests that they think he has been. The appropriate answer, of course, is "no."

GOSPEL Before John narrates Jesus' removal of his garments in order to wash his disciples' feet, he takes great care to point out that Jesus is fully aware "that his hour had come to pass from this world to the Father" (John 13:1). Jesus washes his disciples' feet, therefore, in the shadow cast by his coming death.

Even the act of Jesus' removal of his garments calls to mind his death. In the speech about the Good Shepherd, Jesus says that he is "the good shepherd," and that "A good shepherd lays down his life for the sheep" (10:11). The Greek verb for "lay down" *(tithēmi)* is the same one conveying the action of Jesus' "taking off" of his outer garments. This might not seem like much at first (the verb is quite common and has a range

Simon Peter said to him,
  "Master, then not only my **feet**, but my **hands**
    and **head** as well."
Jesus said to him,
  "Whoever has **bathed** has no **need**
    except to have his feet **washed**, for he is **clean** all over;
  so **you** are clean, but not **all**."
For he **knew** who would betray him;
  for this reason, he said, "**Not all** of you are clean."

So when he had **washed** their feet
  and put his **garments** back on and reclined at **table** again,
  he said to them, "Do you **realize** what I have done for you?
You call me '**teacher**' and '**master**,' and **rightly so**, for indeed I am.
If I, therefore, the **master** and **teacher**, have washed **your** feet,
  you ought to wash one **another's** feet.
I have given you a **model** to follow,
  so that as **I** have done for **you**, **you** should **also** do."

of meanings), but there are other considerations leading to this conclusion. The Good Shepherd speech (John 10:11–18) is John's explanation of the reason for—and redemptive power of—Jesus' approaching death. Jesus life is not taken from him. It is something he lays down himself: "No one takes it from me, but I lay it down on my own. I have power to lay it down, and power to take it up again" (John 10:18). Jesus dies on the cross

in John much as he removes his clothing: he lays down his life in an act of service to others, but it is always his to lay down and to take up as he wishes. In addition to this, we also have the Greco-Roman idea of the body as a garment. (Paul offers us a stellar example of this idea in 2 Corinthians 5:1–10.)

That Jesus foreshadows his redemptive death by taking off his garments probably helps account for the note of mystery in Jesus' explanation of his behavior to Peter:

"What I am doing, you do not understand now, but you will understand later" (John 13:7). Peter only sees Jesus getting ready to wash his feet; Jesus knows that his deed of service is a symbol foreshadowing what he will yet achieve by the cross.

GOOD FRIDAY OF THE LORD'S PASSION

Lectionary #40

READING I   Isaiah 52:13—53:12

A reading from the Book of the Prophet Isaiah

In your preparation of this reading, you may notice that sometimes one clause restates or somehow reflects the immediately previous one. Emphasize the main words and ideas shared by such clauses, pausing briefly between them.

See, my **servant** shall **prosper**,
    he shall be **raised high** and **greatly exalted**.
Even as **many** were **amazed** at him—
    so **marred** was his look **beyond** human semblance
    and his appearance **beyond** that of the sons of man—
so shall he **startle** many nations,
    because of him **kings** shall stand **speechless**;
for those who have **not** been told shall **see**,
    those who have **not** heard shall **ponder** it.

Read these rhetorical questions slowly and clearly, making eye contact with the assembly as you do so.

Who would **believe** what we have heard?
    To whom has the arm of the LORD been **revealed**?
He grew up like a **sapling** before him,
    like a **shoot** from the parched earth;
there was in him **no** stately bearing to make us **look** at him,
    nor **appearance** that would **attract** us to him.
He was **spurned** and **avoided** by people,
    a man of **suffering**, accustomed to **infirmity**,
one of those from whom people hide their faces,
    spurned, and we held him in **no** esteem.

Emphasize the following occurrences of the words "we," "our," "him," and "his," making eye contact with the assembly as you proclaim them.

Yet it was **our** infirmities that he bore,
    our sufferings that he endured,
while we thought of him as **stricken**,
    as one **smitten** by God and **afflicted**.

READING I   Isaiah 40—55 seems to reflect, in general, the situation of the Babylonian exile community as it witnessed Cyrus of Persia rise to challenge their Babylonian captors (mid-sixth century BC). The mood is one of rising hope that God is using Cyrus as a tool to free the captives and allow them to return home. The esteem of Cyrus is so great that one oracle names Cyrus God's "anointed," which is a title that, when applied to monarchs, elsewhere in the Old Testament always means a king of Israel or Judah (Isaiah 45:1; see also 44:24–28).

The belief that God was acting through Cyrus, however, was probably not universal among the captives. Indeed, some may have hoped that Cyrus would not succeed, preferring life in Babylon as it was to any further turmoil. The servant's suffering in today's reading may have happened in the course of disagreements within the exile community concerning God's regard for the people in light of the hard fact of Jerusalem's destruction, God's strength against the gods of Babylon, and whether God could and would ever act to restore the people to their homeland.

One of the features setting off Isaiah 40—55 from 1—39 and 56—66 is the presence of four so-called "servant songs"

But he was pierced for **our** offenses,
    crushed for **our** sins;
upon him was the **chastisement** that makes **us** whole,
    by **his** stripes **we** were healed.
We had **all** gone astray like sheep,
    each following his **own** way;
but the LORD laid upon **him**
    the **guilt** of us **all**.

Though he was **harshly** treated, he **submitted**
    and opened **not** his mouth;
like a **lamb** led to the **slaughter**
    or a **sheep** before the **shearers**,
he was **silent** and opened **not** his mouth.
Oppressed and **condemned**, he was taken away,
    and who would have thought any **more** of his **destiny**?
When he was **cut off** from the land of the living,
    and **smitten** for the sin of his people,
a **grave** was assigned him among the **wicked**
    and a **burial** place with **evildoers**,
though he had done **no** wrong
    nor spoken **any** falsehood.
But the LORD was **pleased**
    to **crush** him in **infirmity**.

If he gives his **life** as an **offering** for **sin**,
    he shall see his **descendants** in a **long life**,
    and the **will** of the LORD shall be **accomplished** through **him**.

Because of his affliction
    he shall see the **light** in fullness of days;

(Isaiah 42:1–9; 49:1–7; 50:4–11; 52:13—53:12). In some cases the servant is almost unmistakably an individual (42:1–4; 50:4–11; 52:13—53:12). In another, the servant is Israel itself (49:1–7). The shifting identity of the servant back and forth from unnamed individuals to Israel and back again tells us that the meaning of "servanthood" to the prophet who composed these oracles will always remain somewhat elusive.

But there are some things we can know. The Hebrew phrase *ebed Yahweh*, "servant of the Lord," is a posthumous description of Moses in Deuteronomy 34:5 and is used many times of him in the book of Joshua (1:1, 13, 8:31, 33; 11:12; 12:6; 13:8; 14:7; 18:7; 22:4–5; see also 2 Kings 18:12 and 2 Chronicles 1:3). It is also a posthumous description of Joshua, son of Nun, Moses' designated successor (Joshua 24:29; Judges 2:8). There is a strong connection of Moses with prophecy

in Deuteronomy and in the historical books of Joshua, Judges, 1 and 2 Samuel, and 1 and 2 Kings, to which Deuteronomy is closely related (see Deuteronomy 18:15, 18; 34:10). It was probably in association with Deuteronomy's description of a future "prophet like Moses" that the notion of the prophetic servant was born. In Isaiah 50:4–11 and 52:13—53:12, the servant is almost certainly a prophetic figure. The person who

through his **suffering**, my servant shall **justify many**,
and their **guilt** he shall **bear**.
Therefore I will **give** him his **portion** among the **great**,
and he shall **divide** the spoils with the **mighty**,
because he **surrendered** himself to **death**
and was **counted** among the **wicked**;
and he shall **take away** the sins of **many**,
and win **pardon** for their **offenses**.

READING II   Hebrews 4:14–16; 5:7–9

A reading from the Letter to the Hebrews

Brothers and **sisters**:
Since we have a **great high priest** who has **passed**
through the **heavens**,
Jesus, the **Son** of **God**,
let us **hold fast** to our confession.
For we do **not** have a **high priest**
who is **unable** to **sympathize** with our **weaknesses**,
but one who has **similarly** been tested in **every way**,
yet **without sin**.
So let us **confidently** approach the **throne** of **grace**
to receive **mercy** and to find **grace** for timely help.

In the days when **Christ** was in the **flesh**,
he offered **prayers** and **supplications** with loud **cries** and **tears**
to the **one** who was able to **save** him from **death**,
and he was **heard** because of his **reverence**.

Emphasize this phrase especially.

Pause briefly before this line and look up as you proclaim them.

composed today's passage may have had a particular prophet in mind, perhaps a community of prophets, who suffered before and during the Babylonian captivity for prophesying what the people of Jerusalem and Judah, later captives, did not want to hear.

Biblical scholars often call this reading "the song of the suffering servant." The voice in the opening and closing verses of this passage is God's (52:13 – 15; 53:11–12). In between another voice takes over. It is the voice of someone who, along with everyone, once despised and avoided the servant, but has come to realize the great importance of his mission. The great insight of the voice of 53:1–10 is that although everyone previously imagined this wretched servant to have been cursed by God, he was in fact suffering on their behalf: "Yet it was *our* infirmities that he bore, *our* sufferings that he endured, while we thought of him as stricken, as one smitten by God and afflicted. But he was pierced for *our* offenses, crushed for *our* sins, upon him was the chastisement that makes us whole, by his stripes we were healed" (Isaiah 53:4–5).

From very early days, Christians have interpreted Isaiah 52:13—53:12 as a prophecy of Jesus Christ. In the Acts of the Apostles, a disciple called Philip is sent by an angel to meet an official from the court of Queen Candace of Ethiopia on the road from Jerusalem to Gaza. The official, returning home from a pilgrimage to Jerusalem, is reading Isaiah aloud. "Do you understand what you are reading?" Philip asks the Ethiopian. "How can I, unless someone instructs me?" he replies, inviting Philip to sit with him in his chariot. The Ethiopian,

Son though he was, he learned **obedience** from what he **suffered**;
  and when he was made **perfect**,
  he became the **source** of eternal **salvation** for **all** who
    obey him.

PASSION John 18:1—19:42

The Passion of our Lord Jesus Christ according to John

Kidron = Kid-RON

(1) Jesus went out with his disciples across the **Kidron valley**
  to where there was a **garden**,
  into which **he** and his **disciples** entered.
Judas his **betrayer** also knew the place,
  because **Jesus** had often met there with his **disciples**.
So **Judas** got a band of **soldiers** and **guards**
  from the chief **priests** and the **Pharisees**
  and went there with **lanterns**, **torches**, and **weapons**.

Judas = JU-das
Pharisees = PHAR-i-sees

Jesus, knowing **everything** that was going to happen to him,
  went out and said to them, "**Whom** are you looking for?"
They answered him, "**Jesus** the **Nazorean**."
He said to them, "**I AM**."
Judas his betrayer was also with them.
When he said to them, "**I AM**,"
  they turned **away** and **fell** to the ground.
So he again asked them,
  "**Whom** are you looking for?"
They said, "**Jesus** the **Nazorean**."
Jesus answered,
  "I **told** you that **I AM**.
So if you are looking for me, let these men go."

Nazorean = Nah-zoh-RAY-an
Pause before and after your proclamation
of "I AM" in this line. Raise your voice,
delivering these words in a strong, bold
tone.

Philip finds, is reading Isaiah 53:7–8. "I beg you, about whom is the prophet saying this?" asks the Ethiopian. "About himself, or about someone else?" Acts continues: "Then Philip opened his mouth and, beginning with this scripture passage, he proclaimed Jesus to him" (Acts 8:26–35). While the Ethiopian's questions testify to the difficulty noted above in identifying the servant, Philip's reply demonstrates that Luke, at least, had an answer.

And thus it is not a little surprising, given how well this reading suits Jesus' final hours, that the evangelists do not quote it as they quote the psalms in their accounts of Jesus' Passion. Jesus' silence before his accusers, his scourging, his humiliating death, his subsequent vindication by God, and his disciples' belated comprehension of his death's meaning all square very well with Isaiah 52:13—53:12.

READING II We know that the author of Hebrews, along with his audience, was not associated with Jesus during his ministry, but rather learned of Jesus through the testimony of others (Hebrews 2:3–4). He knew enough about his audience to describe their courage in the face of persecution and harassment (Hebrews 10:32–34). Otherwise, he has little specific to say about them. The closing greeting from "those from Italy" has suggested to some scholars that the author sent this text to Christians in Italy, perhaps Rome (Hebrews 13:24). The letter's traditional name and the subjects the writer addresses suggest that his intended recipients were probably Jewish Christians for the most part. The Greek used in the letter to the Hebrews is elegant and polished.

Malchus = MAL-kus

Proclaim Jesus' word of rebuke to Peter in a tone of irritation to communicate that Jesus is upset with what Peter has done.

Annas = AN-nas
Caiaphas = CAI-ah-phas

Ask the gatekeeper's question with a hint of suspicion.
Proclaim Peter's first reply in a calm tone of voice.

This was to **fulfill** what he had said,
   "I have not lost **any** of those you gave me."
(2) Then **Simon Peter**, who had a **sword**, drew it,
   struck the high priest's slave, and cut off his right ear.
The slave's name was Malchus.
Jesus said to Peter,
   "Put your **sword** into its **scabbard**.
Shall I not **drink** the cup that the Father **gave** me?"

So the band of **soldiers**, the **tribune**, and the **Jewish guards**
      seized Jesus,
   bound him, and brought him to **Annas** first.
He was the father-in-law of **Caiaphas**,
   who was high **priest** that year.
It was **Caiaphas** who had counseled the **Jews**
   that it was **better** that **one man** should die
      rather than the **people**.

(3) **Simon Peter** and another disciple followed **Jesus**.
Now the **other** disciple was known to the high priest,
   and he entered the courtyard of the high priest with **Jesus**.
But **Peter** stood at the gate outside.
So the **other** disciple, the **acquaintance** of the high priest,
   went out and spoke to the gatekeeper and brought Peter in.
Then the maid who was the gatekeeper said to Peter,
   "**You** are not one of this man's disciples, **are** you?"
He said, "I am **not**."
Now the **slaves** and the **guards** were standing
      around a charcoal fire
   that they had **made**, because it was **cold**,
   and were **warming** themselves.
Peter was also standing there keeping warm.

There is much, however, that we cannot know about Hebrews. We neither know the author's name nor anything significant about him. Where he was when he wrote the letter, we cannot say. Neither do we know precisely when he wrote it: any time from the second half of the first century to the first half of the second is possible.

The subject of this reading falls under the general heading of Christology, the study of the person and work of Jesus Christ. The New Testament is laden not only with different perspectives on Christology, but also with a variety of different kinds of evidence testifying to who Jesus was and is, what he did and does. Unlike the evangelists, our author is not all that interested in what Jesus did during his human life. Jesus' earthly life is not the basis of his Christology. He does not, for example, recite the miraculous circumstances of Jesus' birth, say much about what Jesus said, or describe any specific miracles, healings, signs, and wonders Jesus performed during the span of his earthly ministry as proof that Jesus is the Christ. Neither does our author found his Christology on any personal revelation he received from Jesus. Our author's Christology emerges instead from his exegesis of Old Testament texts, which he clearly believes not only *concern* Jesus, but even *speak with Jesus' voice*. If we read Hebrews 2:11–14, for example, we find that the author believes the speaker of Psalm 21:23 and Isaiah 8:17–18 to have been Jesus himself. This conviction of the author's is founded on his belief

(4) The high **priest** questioned **Jesus**
    about his **disciples** and about his **doctrine**.
Jesus answered him,
    "I have spoken **publicly** to the world.
I have **always** taught in a synagogue
    or in the temple area where **all** the Jews gather,
    and in **secret** I have said **nothing**. Why ask **me**?
Ask those who **heard** me what I **said** to them.
They know what I said."
When he had **said** this,
    one of the temple guards standing there **struck** Jesus and said,
    "Is **this** the way you answer the **high priest**?"
Jesus **answered** him,
    "If I have spoken **wrongly**, **testify** to the wrong;
    but if I have spoken **rightly**, **why** do you strike me?"
Then **Annas** sent him bound to **Caiaphas** the high priest.

Now **Simon Peter** was standing there keeping **warm**.
And they said to him,
    "**You** are not one of his disciples, are you?"
He denied it and said,
    "I am **not**."
One of the slaves of the high priest,
    a relative of the one whose ear Peter had cut off, said,
    "**Didn't** I see you in the **garden with** him?"
Again Peter denied it.
And **immediately** the cock crowed.

(5) Then they brought **Jesus** from **Caiaphas** to the **praetorium**.
It was **morning**.
And they themselves did **not** enter the praetorium,
    in order **not** to be defiled so that they could eat the **Passover**.

Again, proclaim the questions to Peter in a slightly suspicious tone.

Deliver Peter's denial in a worried or irritated tone.

that God's prior speech through the prophets has been more recently followed ("in these last days") by God's speech through "a son" (Hebrews 1:2).

In Hebrews 1 and 2, the author argues on the basis of scripture for Jesus' superiority to the angels. He points out that Jesus has not only been more greatly exalted by God, but has also become more like human beings than they. Jesus' ability to help

human beings, our author writes, has to do with his being like them and undergoing tests and trials like theirs: "he had to become like his brothers in every way, that he might be a merciful and faithful high priest before God to expiate the sins of the people. Because he himself was tested through what he suffered, he is able to help those who are being tested" (Hebrews 2:17–18).

As the author has compared Jesus to the angels, so also does he compare Jesus' Crucifixion to the annual sacrifice of the high priest on the Day of Atonement in the Jerusalem temple: "For we do not have a high priest who is unable to sympathize with our weaknesses, but one who has similarly been tested in every way, yet without sin." What is new, however, is the description of Jesus as "high priest" (Hebrews 4:15). But Jesus' sacrifice, in every way, is

Pilate = PI-lat

Pilate is the highest legal authority in this reading. Jesus' fate lies with him. Proclaim his early questions and statements with a judge's calm, with the cool of someone who has seen it all.

So **Pilate** came out to them and said,
  "What **charge** do you bring against this man?"
They answered and said to him,
  "If he were not a **criminal**,
  we would not have handed him over to you."
At this, Pilate said to them,
  "Take him **yourselves**, and judge him according to **your** law."
The Jews answered him,
  "We do not have the **right** to execute **anyone**, "
  in order that the word of Jesus might **be fulfilled**
  that he said indicating the kind of **death** he would die.
So **Pilate** went back into the praetorium
  and summoned **Jesus** and said to him,
  "Are **you** the **King** of the **Jews**?"
Jesus answered,
  "Do **you** say this on your own
  or have **others** told you about me?"
Pilate answered,
  "**I** am not a Jew, **am** I?
Your own **nation** and the chief **priests** handed you over to me.
What have you done?"
Jesus answered,
  "**My** kingdom does not belong to **this** world.
If my kingdom **did** belong to this world,
  my attendants would be **fighting**
  to keep me from being handed over to the Jews.
But as it is, **my** kingdom is not here."
So Pilate said to him,
  "Then you **are** a king?"
Jesus answered,
  "**You** say I am a king.

superior to the high priest's. While the high priest must offer sacrifices repeatedly to atone for sin in the temple, which our author considers but a copy of heavenly reality, Jesus the high priest needed only to offer himself once as a sacrifice in order to atone for all human sin.

It is Jesus' superiority both to the earthly high priest and to the sacrifices he offers that leads the author to his description of Jesus as a "high priest according to the order of Melchizedek" (Hebrews 5:6, 10; Psalm 110:4;

see also 6:20; 7:17). The Lectionary does not include either 5:6 or 5:10, but there is little hope in grasping the author's meaning without examining these verses.

The description of Jesus in these terms is an example of the author's Christ-centered exegesis of the Old Testament. According to Genesis 14:18–20, Melchizedek was a priest of Salem to whom Abraham gave a tithe. The passage quoted in Hebrews 5:6 comes originally from Psalm 110:4, which in turn refers to the figure mentioned in Genesis 14:18–20. The author repeatedly quotes Psalm 110 (Hebrews 1:13; 5:6; 7:17) and even more often

refers to it without quoting it directly. This psalm was important not only to the Christology of Hebrews, but also to the Christology of other early Christian writers (see Matthew 22:44; Mark 12:36; Luke 20:42; Acts 2:34; 1 Corinthians 15:25). The typical interpretation of Psalm 110 in Hebrews and the Gospels is that it is a report by King David of something God the Father says directly to Jesus: "Like Melchizedek you are a priest forever" (Psalm 110:4).

For **this** I was born and for **this** I came into the world,
> to **testify** to the **truth**.
Everyone who belongs to the truth listens to my **voice**."
Pilate said to him, "**What** is **truth**?"

(6) When he had **said** this,
> he **again** went out to the Jews and said to them,
"I find **no** guilt in him.
But you have a **custom** that I release **one** prisoner
> to you at **Passover**.
Do you want me to **release** to you the **King** of the **Jews**?"
They cried out again,
> "Not **this one** but **Barabbas**!"
Now Barabbas was a revolutionary.

(7) Then **Pilate** took **Jesus** and had him scourged.
And the soldiers wove a **crown** out of **thorns**
> and placed it on his **head**,
> and **clothed** him in a **purple cloak**,
> and they came to him and said,
"**Hail**, **King** of the **Jews**!"
And they **struck** him repeatedly.
Once more Pilate went out and said to them,
> "Look, I am **bringing** him out to you,
> so that you may know that I find **no** guilt in him."
So Jesus came out,
> wearing the **crown** of **thorns** and the **purple cloak**.
And he said to them, "**Behold, the man**!"
When the chief priests and the guards saw him they cried out,
> "**Crucify** him, **crucify** him!"
Pilate said to them,
> "Take him **yourselves** and crucify him.

Barrabas = Bar-RAH-bas

Deliver the soldiers' words in a sarcastic, mocking tone.

With these words, Pilate is presenting Jesus to the crowds as an object of mockery and humiliation: he has been "crowned" and vested in royal purple. Proclaim Pilate's words to the crowds in the sarcastic tone of the soldiers, for he is joining in their public sport with Jesus.

Proclaim the chief priests' words emphatically here.

In Hebrews 7, our author explains why this designation of Jesus makes Jesus superior to the high priest in Jerusalem. Abraham, the father of Israel, great-grandfather of Levi from whom all priests are descended, tithed to Melchizedek. Through Abraham the temple priesthood has already given a sign of Jesus' superiority by tithing to Melchizedek. The author's reasoning goes like this: *because* all priests are descended from Abraham, and *because* Abraham tithed to Melchizedek (Genesis 14:18-20), and *because* God the Father made Jesus a high priest of this order (Psalm 110:4), *therefore*

Jesus is a heavenly priest of an order and power far superior to the powers and orders of earthly priests.

PASSION | John's account of Jesus' Passion is rich in detail, intricate in structure, and profound in theological meaning. In the space available only a few aspects of John's unique Christology can be examined. There is *great* profit in slow, repeated readings of this passage in your preparation to deliver it.

In John 18:5–6, Jesus' reply of "I am" knocks his would-be captors to the ground. In Greek, Jesus' response is *ego eimi*, which means either "I am he" or simply "I am." What is it about Jesus' terse response that literally floors his enemies?

There are a number of points in the Gospel of John where Jesus speaks the phrase "I am" *(ego eimi)* with a predicate. Take, for example, 6:35 and 6:51 ("*I am* the bread of life") or 15:1 and 15:5 ("*I am* the true vine") (see also 8:12; 9:5; 10:7, 9, 11, 14, 11:25; 14:6; 15:1, 5; 18:5, 7).

Here, John reveals a new dimension of his depiction of Pilate: cowardice. Add a note of panic and desperation to your proclamation of these questions.

Caesar = SEE-zer

Gabbatha = GAH-Bah-tha

I find **no** guilt in him."
The Jews answered,
   "**We** have a **law**, and according to that **law** he ought to **die**,
    because he **made himself** the **Son** of **God**."
Now when Pilate heard this statement,
   he became even **more** afraid,
    and went back into the **praetorium** and said to Jesus,
   "**Where** are you **from**?"
Jesus did **not** answer him.
So **Pilate** said to him,
   "Do you not speak to **me**?
Do you not know that I have **power** to **release** you
   and I have power to **crucify** you?"
Jesus answered him,
   "You would have **no** power over me
   if it had not been given to you from **above**.
For this reason the one who handed me over to you
   has the **greater** sin."
Consequently, Pilate tried to **release** him; but the Jews cried out,
   "If you **release** him, you are **not** a Friend of Caesar.
Everyone who makes himself a **king** opposes **Caesar**."

When Pilate heard these words he **brought** Jesus out
   and **seated** him on the judge's bench
    in the place called **Stone Pavement**, in Hebrew, **Gabbatha**.
It was preparation day for **Passover**, and it was about noon.
And he said to the Jews,
   "**Behold**, your **king**!"
They cried out,
   "**Take** him **away**, **take** him **away**! **Crucify** him!"

There are also places where Jesus says, "I am" in reference to himself, but without a predicate. At the end of one long, heated, and quite ugly argument, the Jews reject Jesus' statement that "Abraham your father rejoiced to see my day; he saw it and was glad." "You are not yet fifty years old," they object, "and you have seen Abraham?" To this Jesus replies, "before Abraham came to be, *I am*" (8:56–58). In John 6:20, 8:24, 28, 13:19, and 18:5, 7, "I am" *(ego eimi)* is used similarly.

By this strange phrase, John is quietly informing his readers of the divinity of Jesus. To see how, it will help to look at Exodus 3. In this chapter, God introduces himself to Moses and gives him a message for the Israelites. Moses asks God whom he should say gave him the message. God replies, "I AM WHO I AM." He said further, "Thus you shall say to the Israelites, 'I AM has sent me to you' " (Exodus 3:13–15). In Hebrew, the original language of Exodus, God's words are a play on his Hebrew name, Yahweh, which comes from the verb "to be."

In John's Gospel, Jesus' use of "I am" in reference to himself signifies that Jesus shares in God's own name. We see this on powerful display in John 18:5. These "I am" sayings emerge from John's unique Christology, which holds that Jesus is so extraordinarily close to the Father that the language of equality (5:18) and unity (10:30) with the Father adequately expresses it. In John's Gospel, moreover, Jesus is called "God" *(theos)* three times (1:1, 18; 20:28), which is quite unusual in the New Testament.

Pilate said to them,
"Shall I **crucify** your king?"
The chief priests answered,
"We have **no king** but **Caesar**."
Then he handed him over to them to be crucified.

(8) So they took Jesus, and, carrying the cross **himself**,
he went out to what is called the **Place** of the **Skull**,
in Hebrew, **Golgotha**.
There they **crucified** him, and with him two others,
one on either side, with **Jesus** in the middle.
Pilate also had an inscription written and put on the cross.
It read,
"**Jesus** the **Nazorean**, the **King** of the **Jews**."
Now **many** of the Jews read this inscription,
because the place where Jesus was **crucified** was near the **city**;
and it was written in **Hebrew**, **Latin**, and **Greek**.
So the chief **priests** of the **Jews** said to **Pilate**,
"Do not write 'The **King** of the **Jews**,'
but that he **said**, 'I am the **King** of the **Jews**'."
Pilate answered,
"**What** I have **written**, I have **written**."

When the soldiers had **crucified** Jesus,
they **took** his **clothes** and **divided** them into four shares,
a share for each soldier.
They also took his **tunic**, but the tunic was **seamless**,
woven in **one piece** from the top down.
So they said to one another,
"Let's not **tear** it, but cast lots for it to see **whose** it will be,"

Golgatha = GOL-gah-tha

In the context of the importance of these "I am" statements, two of Peter's three denials of Jesus take on special importance. Peter is first charged with being one of Jesus' disciples by the high priest's gatekeeper. "I am not," he replies (18:17). Charged again, he denies it: "I am not" (18:25). Peter's denials thus resonate with Jesus' "I am" sayings, such that they become not only denials of discipleship, but also rejections of God.

Like the other three evangelists, John believes that Jesus fulfills scripture. Twice in his narration of Jesus' Passion, John explains that something happens to Jesus "in order that the passage of scripture might be fulfilled" (19:24) and "so that the scripture passage might be fulfilled" (19:36; see also 12:38; 13:18; 15:25; 17:12). But in today's Gospel, John puts an intriguing twist on the language of fulfillment. In both 18:9 and 18:32, what are fulfilled are not words of

scripture, but words Jesus himself has previously spoken in John's Gospel. In 18:9, we learn that Jesus' demand that his enemies set free his disciples fulfills words he has only just spoken in 17:12: "I guarded them, and none of them was lost except the son of destruction, in order that the scripture might be fulfilled." And in 18:32 we find that the conversation between Pilate and the Jews about Jesus' execution fulfills what Jesus

Clopas = Klo-PAS

John portrays Jesus as in command of his situation, even as he dies on the cross. Continue to deliver his words clearly and boldly.

in order that the passage of Scripture might be **fulfilled**
   that says:
      They **divided** my garments among them,
         and for my vesture they **cast lots.**
This is what the soldiers did.
Standing by the cross of Jesus were his **mother**
   and his mother's sister, **Mary** the wife of **Clopas**,
   and **Mary** of **Magdala**.
When **Jesus** saw his **mother** and the disciple there whom he **loved**
   he said to his **mother**, "**Woman**, **behold**, your **son**."
Then he said to the **disciple**,
   "**Behold**, your **mother**."
And from that hour the disciple took her into his home.

After this, aware that **everything** was now **finished**,
   in order that the **Scripture** might be **fulfilled**,
   Jesus said, "I **thirst**."
There was a **vessel** filled with **common wine**.
So they put a **sponge** soaked in **wine** on a sprig of **hyssop**
   and put it up to his **mouth**.
When Jesus had taken the wine, he said,
   "It is **finished**."
And bowing his head, he handed over the **spirit**.

[Here all kneel and pause for a short time.]

Pause for several seconds here.

Now since it was preparation day,
   in order that the **bodies** might not **remain** on the **cross**
      on the **sabbath**,
      for the **sabbath** day of that **week** was a **solemn** one,
      the **Jews** asked **Pilate** that their **legs** be **broken**
      and that they be taken **down**.

sabbath = SAB-uth

has earlier said about "the kind of death he would die." (This "kind of death" is, of course, crucifixion, the preferred Roman capital punishment for slaves, common criminals, and people guilty of sedition.) The earlier saying to which 18:32 refers occurs in 12:32. Here, at the conclusion of his public ministry, Jesus says, "And when I am lifted up from the earth, I will draw everyone to myself." This "lifting up" has a double meaning. On the one hand, the Greek verb translated by "lifted up" *(hupsoō)* refers to Jesus' exaltation to the Father. On the other hand, it refers to Jesus' physical "lifting up" on the cross. The following verse makes it clear: "He said this indicating the kind of death he would die" (12:33).

John is placing the words of Jesus recorded in this Gospel on the same level of authority as the scriptural passages Jesus elsewhere fulfills. Because the Gospel of John is canonical scripture for us, we may not at first see what is so interesting about this. But if we pause and reflect that there was no New Testament canon when John wrote, and that scripture for him was mostly composed of texts we find in the Old Testament, we may begin to see what a bold and revolutionary move John has made toward the inclusion of Christian writings among the texts of scripture.

So the soldiers came and **broke** the legs of the **first**
  and then of the **other** one who was crucified with **Jesus**.
But when they came to **Jesus** and saw that he was **already dead**,
  they did **not** break his legs,
  but one soldier thrust his **lance** into his **side**,
  and immediately **blood** and **water** flowed out.
An **eyewitness** has **testified**, and his testimony is **true**;
  he **knows** that he is speaking the **truth**,
  so that **you also** may come to **believe**.
For this happened so that the **Scripture** passage might be **fulfilled**:
  *Not a **bone** of it will be **broken**.*
And again **another** passage says:
  *They will **look** upon him whom they have **pierced**.*

Pause before and after you proclaim this verse. Emphasize in particular the phrase "you also may come to believe," making eye contact with the assembly as you do so.

Arimathea = Ar-i-mah-THEE-a

After this, **Joseph** of **Arimathea**,
  secretly a disciple of **Jesus** for fear of the **Jews**,
  asked **Pilate** if he could remove the body of **Jesus**.
And Pilate permitted it.
So he came and took his body.

Nicodemus = Nic-o-DEE-mus

Nicodemus, the one who had first come to him at **night**,
  also came bringing a mixture of **myrrh** and **aloes**
  weighing about one **hundred** pounds.
They **took** the body of Jesus
  and **bound** it with **burial cloths** along with the **spices**,
  according to the **Jewish burial custom**.
Now in the place where he had been **crucified** there was **a garden**,
  and in the **garden** a new **tomb**, in which **no one**
    had yet been **buried**.
So they laid **Jesus** there because of the Jewish preparation day;
  for the **tomb** was close by.

EASTER VIGIL

Lectionary #41

READING I   Genesis 1:1—2:2

A reading from the Book of Genesis

In the **beginning**, when **God** created the **heavens** and **the earth**,
> the earth was a formless **wasteland**, and **darkness**
>> covered the **abyss**,
> while a **mighty wind** swept over the **waters**.

Then **God** said,
> "**Let** there be **light**," and there was **light**.
God saw how **good** the light was.
God then separated the **light** from the **darkness**.
God called the light "**day**" and the darkness he called "**night**."
Thus **evening** came, and **morning** followed—the **first** day.

Then **God** said,
> "Let there be a **dome** in the middle of the **waters**,
> to separate **one** body of water from the **other**."
And so it **happened**:
> God made the **dome**,
> and it separated the **water above** the dome
>> from the **water below** it.
God called the dome "**the sky**."
Evening came, and **morning** followed—the **second** day.

Then **God** said,
> "Let the **water** under the **sky** be gathered into a single **basin**,
> so that the dry land may **appear**."

Make eye contact with the assembly each time you proclaim God's perception of the goodness of Creation, emphasizing the word "good."

Pause briefly between your proclamation of the events of each day of Creation.

READING I   For centuries, many Jews and Christians, including Catholics, held that Moses himself had composed the Pentateuch, the first five books of the Bible: Genesis, Exodus, Leviticus, Numbers, and Deuteronomy. We find this belief present, for example, in John's Gospel, when Jesus challenges a hostile crowd with refusing to accept legitimate testimony about him: "For if you had believed Moses, you would have believed me, because he wrote about me. But if you do not believe his writings, how will you believe my words?" For John, Moses was the unquestioned author of the Pentateuch.

Few modern Catholic interpreters now agree that Moses himself actually wrote these books. Together with many Protestant biblical scholars, most Catholic biblical scholars discern four major strands of writing woven together in the Pentateuch. Each strand has a different author or authors, contains different text and traditions, and emerges from a particular historical period. One of those strands is designated "P" for "Priestly" because of its authors' keen interest in religious ritual and law. We neither know the priestly authors' names nor have any certainty about when they wrote.

And so it **happened**:
> the **water** under the **sky** was gathered into its **basin**,
> and the **dry land** appeared.

God called the dry land "the **earth**,"
> and the basin of the water he called "the **sea**."

God saw how **good** it was.

Then **God** said,
> "Let the **earth** bring forth **vegetation**:
> **every** kind of **plant** that bears **seed**
> and **every** kind of **fruit** tree on **earth**
> that bears **fruit** with its **seed** in it."

And so it **happened**:
> the **earth** brought forth **every kind** of **plant** that bears **seed**
> and **every kind** of fruit tree on **earth**
> that bears **fruit** with its **seed** in it.

God saw how **good** it was.

Evening came, and **morning** followed—the **third** day.

Then **God** said:
> "Let there be **lights** in the **dome** of the **sky**,
> to separate **day** from **night**.

Let them mark the fixed times, the **days** and the **years**,
> and serve as **luminaries** in the **dome** of the **sky**,
> to shed **light** upon the **earth**."

And so it **happened**:
> God made the two **great lights**,
> the **greater** one to govern the **day**,
> and the **lesser** one to govern the **night**;
> and he made the **stars**.

God set them in the **dome** of the **sky**,
> to shed **light** upon the **earth**,
> to govern the **day** and the **night**,
> and to separate the **light** from the **darkness**.

This reading, which begins our Bible, is most likely from the P source. One of the reasons scholars have argued for this reading's origin among priests has to do with the seven-day period of Creation. The period of the world's Creation matches the liturgical week of Israel, in which one day of rest followed six days of labor. In this reading, the Sabbath week is the organizing principle of the entire universe.

Lying well in the background of this reading is a creation myth found among a number of the peoples of the ancient near east. In this myth, a god fights a battle with the forces of chaos, often symbolized by water, which he wins. From the god's victory emerge the earth and order throughout the universe. We observe this theme in today's

reading. The waters, as we see in Genesis 1:2, are already there. The creation of the dome of the sky gathers the waters into their proper places so that dry land can appear.

To envision our authors' account of Creation, it helps to momentarily set aside what we may know of science. Imagine the sky not as the realm of refracted light and atmosphere, but as a "dome" against which the waters above are always pressing. From time to time, God opens gates in the sky to

God saw how **good** it was.
Evening came, and **morning** followed—the **fourth** day.

Then **God** said,
  "Let the water **teem** with an abundance of **living creatures**,
  and on the **earth** let birds fly beneath the **dome** of the **sky**."
And so it **happened**:
  God created the great **sea monsters**
  and **all** kinds of swimming creatures with which
    the water **teems**,
  and **all** kinds of **winged birds**.
God saw how **good** it was, and God **blessed** them, saying,
  "Be **fertile**, **multiply**, and **fill** the water of the seas;
  and let the birds **multiply** on the earth."
Evening came, and **morning** followed—the **fifth** day.

Then **God** said,
  "Let the **earth** bring forth **all** kinds of **living creatures**:
  cattle, **creeping** things, and **wild animals** of all kinds."
And so it **happened**:
  God made **all** kinds of wild animals, **all** kinds of cattle,
  and **all** kinds of creeping things of the **earth**.
God saw how **good** it was.
Then **God** said:
  "Let us make **man** in **our image**, after **our likeness**.
Let them have **dominion** over the **fish** of the **sea**,
  the **birds** of the **air**, and the **cattle**,
  and over **all** the wild animals
  and **all** the creatures that **crawl** on the **ground**."
God created **man** in **his image**;
  in the **image** of God he created **him**;
  male and **female** he created **them**.

Slow down to emphasize this verse, letting the punctuation mark brief pauses.

permit the waters above to rain down on the earth (see, for example, Genesis 7:11). Imagine also that the earth lies flat beneath this dome, like a plate beneath a bowl, surrounded by water. The stars of the sky are not flaming balls of gas millions of light years away, but just "lights" of some unspecified distance. The earth does not orbit the sun, nor does the moon orbit the earth. Rather, the sun and moon rise and set over the earth (Genesis 1:14–18) in order to

distinguish and govern the light, day, and night that have already been created (Genesis 1:3–5). This was how the authors of this reading understood the construction of the universe and their own place in it.

The creation of human beings marks the final act in this reading. As God did with the light, the dome of the sky, the earth, vegetation, the stars, the sun, the moon, sea creatures, and land animals, now God creates human beings. But humans are different from all other pieces of God's "very

good" creation (Genesis 1:31; see also 1:4, 10, 12, 18, 21, 25), for "God created man in his image; in the divine image he created him; male and female he created them" (Genesis 1:27). No other creature bears God's "image" and shares God's "likeness."

According to our authors, and traditional Catholic teaching, the male and female human beings are the height of God's creative work, unique among everything God has made: "Being in the image of God

God **blessed** them, saying:
  "Be **fertile** and **multiply**;
  fill the earth and **subdue** it.
Have **dominion** over the **fish** of the **sea**, the **birds** of the **air**,
  and **all** the living things that **move** on the **earth**."
God **also** said:
  "See, I give you **every** seed-bearing plant **all over** the **earth**
  and **every** tree that has **seed-bearing fruit** on it to be your **food**;
  and to **all** the animals of the **land**, **all** the birds of the **air**,
  and **all** the living creatures that **crawl** on the **ground**,
  I give **all** the green plants for **food**."
And so it **happened**.
God looked at **everything** he had made, and he found it
    very good.
Evening came, and **morning** followed—the **sixth** day.

Thus the **heavens** and the **earth** and **all** their array
    were completed.
Since on the **seventh** day God was **finished**
  with the **work** he had been **doing**,
  he **rested** on the seventh day from **all** the work
    he had undertaken.

[Shorter: Genesis 1:1, 26–31a]

Emphasize the words "very good."

READING II   Genesis 22:1–18

A reading from the Book of Genesis

God put Abraham to the test.
He called to him, "**Abraham**!"
"**Here** I am," he replied.

---

the human individual possesses the dignity of a person, who is not just something, but someone. He is capable of self-knowledge, of self-possession and of freely giving himself and entering into communion with other persons. And he is called by grace to a covenant with his Creator, to offer him a response of faith and love that no other creature can give in his stead" (CCC, #357).

READING II In Genesis 12:1–3, God tells Abram to leave his land, family, and home behind and go where God tells him. And Abram, at the age of 75, goes: "Abram went as the LORD directed him" (Genesis 12:4). Genesis records nothing about what Abram may have thought or felt about what God told him to do. We read only that he did it.

In today's reading, we find Abraham, formerly Abram (see Genesis 17:5), showing the same kind of obedience to a call from God. But what God now commands is far more terrible than the order of Genesis 12:1–3. We also know that Abraham loves the son God demands that he kill. Worse still, God calls attention to the father's love: "Take your son Isaac, your only one, whom you love, and go" (Genesis 22:2). As Abraham

Read these words slowly, letting the
commas mark pauses.
Issac = EYE-zac
Moriah = Mo-RYE-ah

Then God said:
"Take your son **Isaac**, your **only** one, whom you **love**,
and go to the land of **Moriah**.
There you shall offer him up as a **holocaust**
on a **height** that I will **point out** to you."
Early the next morning Abraham **saddled** his donkey,
took with him his son **Isaac** and **two** of his **servants** as well,
and with the **wood** that he had cut for the **holocaust**,
set out for the place of which God had told him.

On the third day **Abraham** got sight of the place from afar.
Then he said to his **servants**:
"Both of you stay **here** with the donkey,
while the boy and I go on over **yonder**.
We will **worship** and then come back to you."
Thereupon Abraham took the **wood** for the **holocaust**
and **laid** it on his son Isaac's shoulders,
while he himself carried the **fire** and the **knife**.
As the two walked on together, Isaac spoke
to his father Abraham:
"**Father**!" Isaac said.
"**Yes**, son," he replied.
Isaac continued, "**Here** are the **fire** and the **wood**,
but where is the **sheep** for the **holocaust**?"
"**Son**," Abraham answered,
"God **himself** will provide the **sheep** for the **holocaust**."
Then the two continued going **forward**.

When they **came** to the **place** of which **God** had **told** him,
Abraham built an **altar** there and arranged the **wood** on it.
Next he **tied up** his son **Isaac**,
and put him on top of the **wood** on the **altar**.

This verse contains an innocent question of
Abraham's beloved son, yet also a horrible
question in light of what God has asked
Abraham to do. Proclaim it in the exuberant
tones of a child, clearly marking it as a
question by raising your voice at the end
of the sentence.

prepares for his journey, chopping wood and saddling his beast, he is in possession of horrible knowledge. He has no way of knowing that God will spare his son. As in Genesis 12:4, we do not read what Abraham thought or felt during the three days he journeyed with Isaac and his slaves, when he prepared the altar, when he tied up his child, and when he lifted the knife above his head to kill his only son. We read only that he does it.

The sacrifice of children was a religious practice found among some of the peoples in the ancient Mediterranean. In 2 Kings 3:27, we read of a Moabite king who sacrifices his son in the face of military defeat. Centuries later, the people of the North African city of Carthage, who were descended from Israel's seagoing neighbors, sacrificed children in desperation as Roman armies closed around them. Exodus 13:15

and Deuteronomy 12:29–31 and 18:9–12 explicitly forbid this abhorrent practice. But in Jeremiah 7:31 and Ezekiel 16:20, we find the accusation of child sacrifice leveled at citizens of the kingdom of Judah itself. Abraham's sacrifice of Isaac is not so foreign to Israel as one at first might think.

In its original form, this story may have been associated with a particular holy site, explaining its evolution from a place of human sacrifice to one in which animals

Then he **reached out** and took the **knife** to **slaughter** his son.
But the LORD's **messenger** called to him from heaven,
    "**Abraham**, **Abraham**!"
"Here I am," he answered.
"Do **not** lay your hand on the boy," said the messenger.
"Do not do the **least thing** to him.
I know now how **devoted** you are to **God**,
    since you did **not** withhold from me your **own beloved son**."
As Abraham looked about,
    he spied a **ram** caught by its horns in the thicket.
So he went and took the **ram**
    and offered it up as **a holocaust** in place of his **son**.
Abraham named the site **Yahweh-yireh**;
    hence people now say, "On the **mountain** the LORD will see."

Again the LORD's messenger called to **Abraham** from heaven
        and said:
    "I **swear** by **myself**, declares the LORD,
    that because you **acted** as you **did**
    in not withholding from me your **beloved son**,
    I will bless you **abundantly**
    and make your descendants **as countless**
    as the **stars** of the **sky** and the **sands** of the **seashore**;
    your descendants shall take **possession**
    of the gates of their **enemies**,
    and in your descendants **all** the nations of the earth
        shall find **blessing**—
    all this because you obeyed my **command**."

[Shorter: Genesis 22:1–2, 9a, 10–13, 15–18]

Yahweh-yireh = YAH-weh yir-EH

came to be substituted for human victims. It may also have provided a reason for the kind of animal the priests of the site demanded. But in its present form, this story is about Abraham's fidelity to God: "I know now how devoted you are to God, since you did not withhold from me your own beloved son" (Genesis 22:12).

READING III The likely historical context for Israel's original presence in, and exodus from, the land of Egypt is the reign of the so-called *Hyksos* in Egypt. In the first centuries of the second millennium BC, settlers from Asia, including Canaan, entered Egypt in droves. Eventually, these foreigners dominated southern Egypt. Their rulers, the Hyksos, were eventually

overthrown and forced into Canaan in the mid-sixteenth century BC. Many historians argue that probably among these migrants were the ancestors of Israel. Some scholars, however, suppose that the Exodus actually took place over several centuries. According to this understanding, the Exodus may be better described as a series of migrations

Proclaim God's words in a strong, bold tone of voice.

Pharoah = PHAY-roh

READING III   Exodus 14:15—15:1

A reading from the Book of Exodus

The LORD said to **Moses**, "**Why** are you crying out to me?
Tell the **Israelites** to go **forward**.
And you, lift up your staff and, with hand outstretched
    over the sea,
      split the **sea** in **two**,
    that the Israelites may pass through it on dry land.
But I will make the Egyptians so **obstinate**
    that they will go in after them.
Then I will receive **glory** through **Pharaoh** and **all** his army,
    his **chariots** and **charioteers**.
The **Egyptians** shall **know** that I am the LORD,
    when I receive **glory** through **Pharaoh**
    and his **chariots** and **charioteers**."

The angel of God, who had been **leading** Israel's camp,
    now **moved** and went around **behind** them.
The **column** of **cloud** also, leaving the **front**,
    took up its place **behind** them,
      so that it came **between** the camp of the **Egyptians**
    and that of **Israel**.
But the cloud now became **dark**, and thus the night **passed**
    without the rival camps coming any closer together
      all night long.

Then Moses stretched out his **hand** over the **sea**,
    and the LORD swept the **sea**
    with a **strong** east **wind** throughout the **night**
    and so **turned** it into **dry land**.

---

than as a one-time departure. The migrants brought their traditions and stories of their wanderings to Canaan, where they resettled and intermarried with the local populations. In time, their traditions and stories were woven together into a narrative of national origin.

The biblical account of the Exodus is as much about God's reputation in Egypt as it is about the rescue of Israel from slavery.

Were Pharaoh's heart not repeatedly hardened against the Israelites (Exodus 4:21; 7:3, 13–14, 22; 8:15, 19, 32; 9:7, 12, 34–35; 10:1, 20, 27; 11:10; 14:4, 8), the people might have required fewer acts of divine power to rescue them. But God has something to prove: "I will lay my hand on Egypt and by great acts of judgment I will bring the hosts of my people, the Israelites, out of the land of Egypt, *so that the Egyptians may learn that I am the LORD,* as I stretch out my hand against

Egypt and lead the Israelites out of their midst" (Exodus 7:4–5). The victory of Israel over its foes is, first and foremost, the victory of Israel's God.

READING IV   The image of the captive people of Judah as "a wife forsaken and grieved in spirit, a wife married in youth and then cast off" is a harsh and disturbing image. It is harsher still when

When the **water** was thus **divided**,
  the Israelites marched into the **midst** of the **sea** on **dry land**,
  with the **water** like a **wall** to their **right** and to their **left**.

The **Egyptians** followed in pursuit;
  all Pharaoh's horses and chariots and charioteers
    went after them
  right into the **midst** of the **sea**.
In the night watch just before dawn
  the LORD cast through the column of the **fiery cloud**
  upon the Egyptian force **a glance** that threw it into a panic;
  and he so **clogged** their chariot wheels
  that they could hardly drive.
With that the Egyptians sounded the **retreat** before Israel,
  because the LORD was **fighting** for them against the **Egyptians**.

Then the LORD told **Moses**, "Stretch out your hand over the **sea**,
  that the **water** may flow **back** upon the **Egyptians**,
  upon their **chariots** and their **charioteers**."
So Moses stretched out his **hand** over the **sea**,
  and at **dawn** the sea **flowed back** to its normal **depth**.
The **Egyptians** were fleeing head on toward the **sea**,
  when the LORD hurled them into its **midst**.
As the **water** flowed back,
  it covered the **chariots** and the **charioteers**
    of Pharaoh's **whole** army
  which had followed the **Israelites** into the sea.
Not a **single one** of them escaped.
But the **Israelites** had marched on **dry land**
  through the **midst** of the **sea**,
  with the **water** like a **wall** to their **right** and to their **left**.
Thus the LORD **saved Israel** on that **day**
  from the **power** of the **Egyptians**.

Look up at the assembly as you slowly deliver this line, pausing before and after it.

one considers that a woman thus rejected by her husband in ancient Israel or Judah would have had little (if any) chance at survival outside of prostitution and begging. A wife "forsaken" and "cast off" was often as good as dead. The decision by her husband (God) to take her back does not erase a sense of grave injustice, even cruelty. Why does the prophet use such an image?

This prophecy dates to the period of the Babylonian captivity, which was a profound religious crisis for the people taken captive. They reasoned that if God's holy city of Jerusalem lay in ruins, and the temple built for the worship of God had been plundered and destroyed (in 587 or 586 BC), what use was there in continuing to serve God? Perhaps God was too weak to withstand the Babylonians and their gods, or perhaps God had finally rejected Judah and its people,

abandoning them permanently to their enemies, as the kingdom of Israel had been to the Assyrians 130 years before the Babylonians finally stormed into Jerusalem.

But by the middle of the sixth century BC, the captives' religious crisis became more complex. With the rise of Cyrus of Persia (present-day Iran), Babylon was on shakier footing. The fall of Babylon, and with it the prospect of the captives' return,

When **Israel** saw the **Egyptians** lying **dead** on the **seashore**
and beheld the **great power** that the LORD
had **shown** against the Egyptians,
they feared the LORD and **believed** in him
and in his servant **Moses**.

Then **Moses** and the **Israelites** sang this **song** to the LORD:
I will **sing** to the LORD, for he is gloriously **triumphant**;
horse and **chariot** he has **cast** into the **sea**.

READING IV   Isaiah 54:5–14

A reading from the Book of the Prophet Isaiah

The **One** who has become your **husband** is your **Maker**;
his **name** is the LORD of **hosts**;
your **redeemer** is the **Holy One** of **Israel**,
called **God** of **all** the **earth**.
The LORD calls you back,
like a wife **forsaken** and **grieved** in spirit,
a wife **married** in **youth** and then **cast off**,
says your **God**.
For a **brief** moment I **abandoned** you,
but with great **tenderness** I will take you back.
In an **outburst** of **wrath**, for a **moment**
I hid my **face** from you;
but with enduring **love** I take **pity** on you,
says the LORD, your **redeemer**.

seemed increasingly likely. For many captives this was doubtless a cause for joy. But it did not necessarily settle previous doubts. Why had God abandoned Judah in the first place? Was the hand of God now at work at improving the captives' situation?

Isaiah 40—55 is, broadly speaking, a sustained reply to these questions. The anonymous prophet who composed the majority of these oracles understood the captivity as temporary punishment for the people's sins, and interpreted Cyrus' rise and Babylon's instability as proof of God's oncoming intervention on the people's behalf in honor of ancient covenants. Certainly not all captives agreed that God was now at work on their behalf. Isaiah 50:10–11 probably reflects the opposition some supporters of the new theology, including perhaps the anonymous prophet himself, encountered from their countrymen in Babylon.

In this context, the image of the wife once-forsaken, but received back by her newly affectionate husband becomes somewhat easier to comprehend. And while this reading mentions no reason for the husband's severity, we find a clear reason in the similar and equally disturbing image of Isaiah 50:1. Here, God speaks as a husband and father who has divorced his wife and sold his child into slavery: "Where is the bill of divorce with which I dismissed your mother? Or to which of my creditors have I sold you? It was for your sins that you were sold, for your crimes that your mother was dismissed." Similarly, in Isaiah 40:2, we read that Jerusalem's "service is at an end, her

Noah = NOH-wah

Emphasize the coordination of the days of
Noah with the author's present day.

Emphasize the word "never" in this line.

carnelians = kar-NEEL-yuns

carbuncles = KAR-bunk-ulz

Emphasize the word "All" in this line.

Read the final verse slowly, emphasizing
the words in bold.

This is for me like the days of **Noah**,
    when I **swore** that the **waters** of **Noah**
    should never again deluge the earth;
so I have sworn **not** to be **angry** with you,
    or to **rebuke** you.
Though the **mountains** leave their place
    and the **hills** be **shaken**,
my **love** shall **never** leave you
    nor my **covenant** of **peace** be **shaken**,
    says the LORD, who has **mercy** on you.
O afflicted one, **storm-battered** and **unconsoled**,
    I lay your **pavements** in **carnelians**,
    and your **foundations** in **sapphires**;
I will make your **battlements** of **rubies**,
    your **gates** of **carbuncles**,
    and all your **walls** of **precious stones**.
All your children shall be **taught** by the LORD,
    and **great** shall be the peace of your **children**.
In **justice** shall you be **established**,
    far from the **fear** of **oppression**,
    where **destruction** cannot come near you.

READING V   Isaiah 55:1–11

A reading from the Book of the prophet Isaiah

Thus says the LORD:
All you who are **thirsty**,
    come to the **water**!

---

guilt is expiated; indeed, she has received from the hand of the LORD double for all her sins." The captives' suffering has been payment for sin.

The image of God as a husband casting aside the wife of his youth, or as that of a father dissolving his family, is *supposed* to disturb readers. And it is by such potent imagery that the prophet speaks to the magnitude and enormity of what God now does for the captives. Reaching back through Israel's history, past David, past Moses and the Exodus, back beyond even Abraham, the prophet takes hold of the time of Noah and holds it up, comparing God's present promise with the covenant cut with Noah, and through him with all humanity (Genesis 9:9–17): "This is for me like the days of Noah, when I swore that the waters of Noah should never again deluge the earth; so I have sworn not to be angry with you, or to rebuke you" (Isaiah 54:9).

READING V In the Old Testament, a covenant is an agreement, a kind of contract, in which two or more parties agree to do, or not to do, certain things. In Hebrew one typically "cuts" a covenant. In 1 Kings 5:26, we read that "there was peace between Hiram and Solomon, since they were parties to a treaty." In 1 Kings 5:15–32, the covenant's mutual obligations are spelled out: Solomon supplies food to Hiram in exchange for logs of Lebanon cedar. The

Be sure to use your voice to indicate the speaker's question here.

You who have **no money**,
   come, receive **grain** and **eat**;
come, without paying and without cost,
   drink **wine** and **milk**!
Why spend your **money** for what is **not bread**,
   your **wages** for what **fails** to **satisfy**?
Heed me, and you shall eat **well**,
   you shall **delight** in rich fare.
Come to me heedfully,
   listen, that you may have **life**.
I will **renew** with you the everlasting covenant,
   the **benefits** assured to **David**.
As I made him a **witness** to the **peoples**,
   a **leader** and **commander** of **nations**,
so shall you summon a **nation** you knew **not**,
   and **nations** that knew you not shall **run** to you,
because of the LORD, your **God**,
   the **Holy One** of **Israel**, who has **glorified** you.

Seek the LORD while he may be **found**,
   call him while he is **near**.
Let the **scoundrel** forsake his way,
   and the **wicked** man his thoughts;
let him **turn** to the LORD for **mercy**;
   to our **God**, who is generous in **forgiving**.
For **my** thoughts are not **your** thoughts,
   nor are **your** ways **my** ways, says the LORD.
As **high** as the **heavens** are above the **earth**,
   so **high** are **my** ways above **your** ways
   and **my** thoughts above **your** thoughts.

Read this line slowly, making eye contact with the assembly.

Hebrew word for "treaty" here is *berit*, which is the same word we find in today's reading (Isaiah 55:3). In Joshua 24:1–28, Joshua makes a covenant *(berit)* with the people of Israel at Shechem to obey God's ordinances in exchange for the land of Canaan (Joshua 24:25). Isaiah can speak of a "covenant with death" cut by Jerusalem's haughty ruling elites, by which Isaiah means that these rulers are a threat to their subjects' survival (28:15, 18).

God's covenant with David, like God's covenants with Noah (Genesis 6:18; 9:8–17), Abraham (Genesis 15:1–21; 17:1–22), and Moses, is binding not only on David, but also on his descendants. In exchange for David's fidelity to God, God promises to sustain his royal line (see 2 Samuel 7:8–16; 1 Kings 8:23–26; Psalm 89:27–37). In this reading, the prophet likens Israel's new relationship with God in terms of the covenant with

David. As David once received the respect of nations and commanded them, so also will the descendants of the captives enjoy similar international status and renown.

READING VI The introduction to Baruch identifies its author as "Baruch, son of Neriah," who "wrote in Babylon, in the fifth year (on the seventh day of the month, at the time when the Chaldeans

For just as from the **heavens**
    the **rain** and **snow** come **down**
and do not **return** there
    till they have **watered** the **earth**,
    making it **fertile** and **fruitful**,
giving **seed** to the one who **sows**
    and **bread** to the one who **eats**,
so shall **my** word be
    that goes **forth** from my **mouth**;
my word shall not **return** to me **void**,
    but shall do **my will**,
    achieving the **end** for which I **sent** it.

READING VI   Baruch 3:9–15, 32 — 4:4

Baruch = bah-ROOK

A reading from the Book of the Prophet Baruch

Proclaim this question slowly, as though it were a series of questions.

Hear, O Israel, the **commandments** of **life**:
    listen, and know **prudence**!
How is it, Israel,
    that **you** are in the **land** of your **foes**,
    grown **old** in a foreign **land**,
defiled with the **dead**,
    accounted with those **destined** for the **netherworld**?
You have **forsaken** the **fountain** of **wisdom**!
    Had you **walked** in the **way** of **God**,
    you would have dwelt in **enduring peace**.

took Jerusalem and burnt it with fire)" (Baruch 1:1–2). It is highly unlikely, however, that Baruch, son of Neriah, who worked as Jeremiah's scribe and helper (see Jeremiah 32:1–25; 36:1–32; 43:1–7; 45:1–5), is the actual author of this text. There are a number of telling signs that the contents of this book were written much later than the fall of Jerusalem in the sixth century BC. Today's reading was likely written in the first century BC in Hebrew, but shortly after translated into Greek.

This reading is an example of a kind of Jewish religious writing biblical scholars call "wisdom literature." Wisdom (in Hebrew, *hochma*; in Greek, *sophia*) is the grand subject of this literature. Wisdom is often personified as a divine female creature (hence, "she" in this reading), sometimes assisting God in the work of creation (Proverbs 8), sometimes protecting Israel (Wisdom 10—19). Divine wisdom is an important precursor to the idea of the divine Word, or *logos*, in John's Gospel (see John 1:1–18). Wisdom literature, as we find it in Job, Proverbs, Ecclesiastes, Wisdom, Sirach, and so on, is actually concerned with a great many themes, including the cultivation of virtue, wonder at the design of creation,

Read this verse slowly and clearly.

Learn where **prudence** is,
> where **strength**, where **understanding**;
that you may know also
> where are **length** of **days**, and **life**,
> where **light** of the **eyes**, and **peace**.
Who has found the **place** of **wisdom**,
> who has entered into her **treasuries**?

The One who knows **all** things knows her;
> he has **probed** her by his **knowledge**—
the One who **established** the earth for all **time**,
> and **filled** it with four-footed **beasts**;
> he who **dismisses** the **light**, and it **departs**,
> **calls** it, and it **obeys** him trembling;
before whom the **stars** at their **posts**
> **shine** and **rejoice**;
when he calls them, they **answer**, "**Here** we are!"
> **shining** with **joy** for their **Maker**.
Such is our **God**;
> no **other** is to be compared to him:
he has **traced** out the **whole way** of **understanding**,
> and has given her to **Jacob**, his **servant**,
> to **Israel**, his **beloved** son.

Since then she has **appeared** on earth,
> and **moved** among **people**.
She is the **book** of the **precepts** of **God**,
> the **law** that **endures forever**;
all who cling to her will **live**,
> but those will **die** who **forsake** her.
Turn, O Jacob, and **receive** her:
> **walk** by her **light** toward **splendor**.

---

questions about the justice of human suffering, the proper aim of human life, the celebration of the beauty of wisdom, and many other topics as well.

The text today is a hymn or poem associating wisdom *(sophia)* with "the commandments of life" and "the book of the precepts of God, the law that endures forever" (Baruch 3:9; 4:1). The sentiment is close to that of Sirach 15:1, which commences a chapter celebrating the joys of seeking wisdom: "he who is practiced in the law will come to wisdom."

READING VII Many of us are familiar with the idea that what is legal and what is ethical or moral are not necessarily identical—that one can follow the letter of the law but still be ethically or morally in the wrong. This idea would have made little sense to the prophet Ezekiel. He did not separate ethics and morality from the letter of Israel's law because he was convinced that the people's obedience to law was the one and only foundation for its ethical and moral behavior.

According to Ezekiel, the people's great sin and the reason for its punishment by God through the Babylonians is its worship of other gods: "Therefore, as I live, says the Lord GOD, because you have defiled my sanctuary with all your detestable abominations, I swear to cut you down. I will not look upon you with pity nor have mercy" (Ezekiel 5:11; see also 6:1— 8:18; 14:1–11; 16:1–63; 23:1–49). Today's reading begins with God's retribution for Israel's worship of other gods: "Therefore I poured out my fury upon them (because of the blood which they

Give **not** your glory to **another**,
    your **privileges** to an **alien race**.
Blessed are we, O Israel;
    for what pleases **God** is **known** to us!

READING VII   Ezekiel 36:16–17a, 18–28

A reading from the Book of the Prophet Ezekiel

The **word** of the LORD came to me, saying:
    Son of **man**, when the house of **Israel** lived in their **land**,
    they defiled it by their conduct and deeds.
Therefore I **poured out** my **fury** upon them
    because of the **blood** that **they** poured out on the **ground**,
    and because they **defiled** it with idols.
I **scattered** them among the nations,
    dispersing them over foreign lands;
    according to their **conduct** and **deeds** I judged them.
But when they came among the nations wherever they came,
    they served to **profane** my holy name,
    because it was said of them: "**These** are the **people** of the LORD,
    yet they had to **leave** their land."
So I have **relented** because of my holy name
    which the house of Israel **profaned**
    among the **nations** where they **came**.

Emphasize this basis for God's action.

Therefore say to the house of Israel: **Thus** says the **Lord GOD**:
    Not for **your** sakes do I act, house of Israel,
    but for the **sake** of **my holy name**,
    which you **profaned** among the nations to which you **came**.

---

poured out on the ground, and because they defiled it with idols" (Ezekiel 36:18).

    Some prophets, while attacking Israelite idolatry in their own times, hold up an earlier period, often Israel's Exodus from Egypt, as a shining example of what the people's relationship with God once was and could be again. For example, the prophet Hosea (who lived in the eighth century BC) contrasts Israel's innocent days in Egypt with the idolatry of the northern kingdom: "When

Israel was a child I loved him, out of Egypt I called my son. The more I called them, the farther they went from me, sacrificing to the Baals and burning incense to idols" (Hosea 11:1). For Hosea, the time in Egypt was Israel's golden age. Ezekiel, however, recalls no golden age at all. There is no period of Israel's history to hold up as a shining example. Israel, in his view, was idolatrous from its very infancy (see Ezekiel 23:3).

In other words, Ezekiel has precious little confidence in Israel's capacity ever to deserve God's favor. In today's reading, therefore, there should be little surprise in finding that the reason for Israel's future ingathering from the nations has nothing to do with God's regard for Israel, but rather God's regard for God ("Not for your sakes do I act, house of Israel, but for the sake of my holy name"), and that the people require nothing less than spiritual transplant surgery

I will prove the **holiness** of my great name,
    profaned among the nations,
    in whose midst you have **profaned** it.
Thus the **nations** shall **know** that I am the LORD,
    says the Lord GOD,
    when in **their** sight I prove my **holiness** through you.
For I will **take** you **away** from among the nations,
    gather you from all the foreign lands,
    and **bring you back** to your **own** land.
I will sprinkle **clean water** upon you
    to **cleanse** you from all your **impurities**,
    and from **all** your idols I will **cleanse** you.
I will give you a **new heart** and place a **new spirit** within you,
    taking from your bodies your **stony** hearts
    and giving you **natural** hearts.
I will put **my** spirit within you and make you **live** by my **statutes**,
    careful to **observe** my **decrees**.
You shall **live** in the **land** I gave your **fathers**;
    you shall be **my** people, and I will be **your** God.

Proclaim this verse slowly and in a bold, clear tone of voice.

("A new heart I will give you, and a new spirit I will put within you; and I will remove from your body the heart of stone and give you a heart of flesh").

EPISTLE Nowhere in Paul's letters, or indeed in the New Testament, do we find what a Christian Baptism looked like. The *Didache,* a Syrian text from the late first or early second century, and the *Apostolic Tradition,* which contains Roman traditions from the turn of the third century, are the earliest Christian texts containing baptismal liturgies. Although the New Testament likely contains bits and pieces of baptismal rituals, what we chiefly have in the New Testament are theological interpretations of Baptism.

In this reading, Paul interprets Baptism as believers' participation in Jesus Christ's death, burial, and Resurrection. Working with a set of opposing ideas (burial and raising, death and new life, death and Resurrection, slavery to sin and freedom from sin, dying to sin and living for God), Paul holds up the rite of Baptism as a ritual death through which one must pass to new life in the Resurrection.

Critical to Paul's interpretation of Baptism is his understanding that the baptized person dies to the powers of sin and death. These are not new subjects; rather, they continue Paul's discussion in Romans 5. The problem, as Paul sees it in Romans 5:12–21, is that the sway of sin and death requires some greater power, namely grace, to overcome them. This grace is more than

EPISTLE Romans 6:3–11

A reading from the Letter of Saint Paul to the Romans

Brothers and **sisters**:
Are you **unaware** that **we** who were **baptized** into **Christ Jesus**
    were **baptized** into his **death**?
We were **indeed** buried with him through **baptism** into **death**,
    so that, just as **Christ** was **raised** from the **dead**
    by the **glory** of the **Father**,
    we **too** might live in **newness** of **life**.

For if we have **grown** into **union** with him
        through a **death** like his,
    we shall also be **united** with him in the **resurrection**.
We know that our **old** self was **crucified** with him,
    so that our **sinful body** might be done away with,
    that we might **no longer** be in **slavery** to **sin**.
For a **dead** person has been **absolved** from sin.
If, then, we have **died** with **Christ**,
    we **believe** that we shall also **live** with him.
We **know** that **Christ**, **raised** from the **dead**, dies **no more**;
    death no longer has **power** over him.
As to his **death**, he died to **sin once** and for **all**;
    as to his **life**, he **lives** for **God**.
Consequently, **you too** must think of **yourselves**
        as being **dead** to **sin**
    and **living** for God in **Christ Jesus**.

Make sure you raise the tone of your voice to indicate Paul's rhetorical question.

Note that Paul is contrasting opposites: the realm of sin and death with the realm of spirit and life. Take care to emphasize this contrast throughout the reading.

sufficient to do this and comes through Christ. But how do Christ's followers get access to it? Baptism is Paul's answer, or at least part of his answer. By being entombed together with Christ in Baptism (Romans 6:4; see also Colossians 2:12), the individual may be raised to a new life like Christ's over which sin and death no longer hold sway.

GOSPEL Mark and Luke record that the women came to the tomb carrying spices, which were for the anointing of Jesus' body. John and Matthew do not tell us why the women (in John's case, it is only Mary Magdalene) arrive at the tomb. All four evangelists agree that a woman or women were the first to learn, quite early in the morning, that the tomb where Jesus' body had been was now empty. Mark, Luke, and John report that when the women arrived, they found the stone blocking the entrance of the tomb rolled away or, in John's case, removed (Mark 16:1–4; Luke 24:1–2; John 20:1). Of the evangelists, only Matthew depicts the rolling away of the stone.

sabbath = SAB-uth

Magdalene = MAG-dah-len

Proclaim the words of the angel in a clear, strong voice.

Galilee = GAL-ih-lee

Proclaim Jesus' words in a softer, gentler tone, and more slowly than the angel's.

GOSPEL   Matthew 28:1–10

A reading from the holy Gospel according to Matthew

After the **sabbath**, as the first day of the week was **dawning**,
    Mary Magdalene and the **other** Mary came to see the **tomb**.
And behold, there was a great **earthquake**;
    for an **angel** of the **Lord** descended from **heaven**,
    approached, **rolled back** the stone, and **sat** upon it.
His appearance was like **lightning**
    and his clothing was **white** as **snow**.
The guards were **shaken** with fear of him
    and became like **dead men**.
Then the **angel** said to the women in reply,
    "Do **not** be afraid!
I know that you are seeking **Jesus** the **crucified**.
He is **not** here, for he has been **raised** just as he said.
Come and **see** the place where he **lay**.
Then go **quickly** and tell his **disciples**,
    'He has been **raised** from the **dead**,
    and he is going **before** you to **Galilee**;
    there you will see him.'
    Behold, I have **told** you."
Then they went away **quickly** from the tomb,
    fearful yet **overjoyed**,
    and ran to **announce** this to his **disciples**.
And behold, **Jesus** met them on their way and greeted them.
They approached, embraced his feet, and did him homage.
Then Jesus said to them, "Do **not** be afraid.
Go tell my **brothers** to go to **Galilee**,
    and **there** they will see me."

In today's reading, the women receive two commissions. The angel gives them the first one: "go quickly and tell his disciples, 'He has been raised from the dead, and he is going before you to Galilee; there you will see him' " (Matthew 28:7). Jesus gives them the second one: "Go tell my brothers to go to Galilee, and there they will see me" (Matthew 28:10).

The angel and Jesus tell the women to do almost exactly the same thing. One important difference, however, is that where the angel says "his disciples," Jesus says "my brothers." Earlier in Matthew, Jesus calls his disciples and members of the Church "brothers" (most clearly in 18:15–35; other possibilities are 5:22–24, 47; 23:8; 25:40). We also find Jesus redefining family in quite radical terms in Matthew 12:46–50:

"whoever does the will of my Father in heaven is my brother and sister and mother" (Matthew 12:50). Jesus' designation of the disciples as his brothers in Matthew 28:10 signifies that, whatever the remaining strength of previous family bonds, the Church is the new family of God.

EASTER SUNDAY

Lectionary #42/46

READING I   Acts 10:34a, 37–43

A reading from the Acts of the Apostles

Judea = Ju-DEE-ah

Galilee = GAL-li-lee

Nazareth = NAH-zah-reth

Pause and make eye contact with the assembly when you proclaim this line.

Peter proceeded to speak and said:
"You **know** what has happened all over **Judea**,
    beginning in **Galilee** after the **baptism**
    that **John** preached,
    how God anointed **Jesus** of **Nazareth**
    with the **Holy Spirit** and **power**.
He went about doing **good**
    and **healing** all those **oppressed** by the **devil**,
    for **God** was **with** him.
We are **witnesses** of **all** that he did
    both in the country of the **Jews** and in **Jerusalem**.
They put him to **death** by **hanging** him on a **tree**.
This man **God** raised on the **third day** and **granted**
        that he be **visible**,
    not to **all** the people, but to **us**,
    the **witnesses** chosen by **God** in **advance**,
    who **ate** and **drank** with him after he **rose** from the **dead**.
He commissioned **us** to **preach** to the **people**
    and **testify** that he is the one appointed by **God**
    as **judge** of the **living** and the **dead**.
To him **all** the prophets bear witness,

Emphasize the word "everyone" in this line.

    that **everyone** who believes in him
    will receive **forgiveness** of sins through his **name**."

READING I   Luke records that Peter spoke these words in the coastal city of Cesarea to Cornelius, a Roman army officer, who was joined on the occasion by his family and close friends (10:1–2, 24). Peter and Cornelius form quite an unlikely pair (see commentary II, Acts 10:34–38, January 13). They have been brought together not by natural or typical circumstances, but by visions each man has received. When Cornelius describes his vision of the man who told him to summon

Peter from Joppa, Peter at last understands the meaning of his own vision concerning clean and unclean foods: "In truth," Peter says in 10:34-35, "I see that God shows no partiality. Rather, in every nation whoever fears him and acts uprightly is acceptable to him." What Peter has seen is that a Gentile's failure to observe Jewish dietary law is no impediment to membership in the fellowship of the Church. The Church is large enough to include both Jews and Gentiles.

Peter's speech (one might almost as easily call it a homily) refers extensively to personal experience. But it is a collective personal experience, shared also by the other members of Jesus' inner circle. Thus Peter does not speak in terms of "I" and "me," but of "we" and "us." "*We* are witnesses," he says, concerning Jesus' ministry and Crucifixion (10:39). Jesus appeared not to everyone, "but to us, the witnesses chosen by God in advance, who ate and drank with him after he rose from the dead"

This reading contrasts the opposite realms of what is "above" and "on earth." Emphasize these contrasted opposites.

READING II   Colossians 3:1–4

A reading from the Letter of Saint Paul to the Colossians

Brothers and **sisters**:
If then you were **raised** with **Christ**, seek what is **above**,
    where **Christ** is seated at the **right hand** of God.
Think of what is **above**, **not** of what is on **earth**.
For you have **died**, and your life is **hidden** with **Christ** in **God**.
When **Christ** your **life** appears,
    then **you too** will appear with him in **glory**.

Or:

READING II   1 Corinthians 5:6b–8

A reading from the first Letter of Saint Paul to the Corinthians

Brothers and **sisters**:
Do you **not know** that a little **yeast** leavens all the **dough**?
Clear out the old yeast,
    so that you may become a **fresh** batch of dough,
    inasmuch as you are **unleavened**.
For our **paschal lamb**, **Christ**, has been **sacrificed**.
Therefore, let us **celebrate** the feast,
    not with the **old** yeast, the yeast of **malice** and **wickedness**,
    but with the **unleavened bread** of **sincerity** and **truth**.

Paul is "laying down the law" to the Corinthians in this chapter. Proclaim his words in a strong, sharp tone.

Pause briefly before and after you proclaim the phrase "For our paschal lamb, Christ, has been sacrificed." Make eye contact with the assembly when you proclaim it.

(10:41; see Luke 24:41–43). Jesus "commissioned *us* to preach to the people and testify that he is the one appointed by God as judge of the living and the dead" (10:42).

In this speech, Peter and the apostles are not the only witnesses to Jesus. Peter also claims the prophets as witnesses, whose recorded oracles and books he claims support what he says of Jesus. Not only the apostles (Acts 3:18; 13:27; 28:23), but also Jesus himself (Luke 18:31; 24:25, 27; 24:44), call on the testimony of "the prophets" to proclaim the truth and significance of Jesus' life, ministry, Passion, death, and Resurrection.

There is a choice of second readings today. Speak with the liturgy coordinator or homilist to find out which one will be used.

READING II   **COLOSSIANS.** Eschatology" is a kind of belief, thought, or speculation about the end of days and the world to come. Jesus' movement and the earliest Church built themselves around the eschatological belief that the end of days was fast approaching, that God would very soon intervene in the world and bring a sudden end to human history and society.

In many of our New Testament texts we can discern a kind of tension on the subject of eschatology. On the one hand, the end of days lies in the future: Christ has not yet returned. But on the other hand, the Resurrection of Christ, the gift of the Holy Spirit, and the birth of the Church suggest that the end of days has already commenced. When Paul, for example, warns the Corinthians that "the appointed time has grown short" and advises them to adopt a more stringent sexual morality, he does so on the basis of an eschatological belief: "For the present form of this world is passing

GOSPEL John 20:1–9

A reading from the holy Gospel according to John

On the **first** day of the week,
    Mary of **Magdala** came to the **tomb early** in the morning,
    while it was **still dark**,
    and saw the **stone** removed from the tomb.
So she **ran** and **went** to **Simon Peter**
    and to the **other** disciple whom Jesus **loved**, and told them,
    "They have **taken** the **Lord** from the **tomb**,
    and we **don't know** where they put him."
So **Peter** and the **other** disciple went out and came to the **tomb**.
They both **ran**, but the **other** disciple ran **faster** than Peter
    and arrived at the tomb **first**;
    he bent **down** and saw the **burial** cloths there, but did
      not go in.
When **Simon Peter** arrived after him,
    he went into the **tomb** and saw the **burial** cloths there,
    and the **cloth** that had covered his **head**,
    not with the burial cloths but **rolled up** in a separate place.
Then the **other** disciple **also** went in,
    the one who had arrived at the tomb **first**,
    and he **saw** and **believed**.
For they did **not yet understand** the **Scripture**
    that he **had** to **rise** from the **dead**.

Magdala = MAG-duh-luh

Unaware of Jesus' Resurrection, Mary believes his body has been stolen. Raise your voice slightly and use an emotional tone of voice to communicate how upset she is.

Look up and pause briefly before slowly and clearly proclaiming the words "and he saw and believed."

away" (1 Corinthians 7:29–31). Although the world yet remains in its present form, Christ's Resurrection, the first proof of the coming end, proves that it cannot remain so for long. Thus, Paul advises the Corinthians to prepare themselves for an eschatological future he sees as coming to pass now.

In this reading, our author sees the end of days in both present and future terms. As Paul does in his letter to the Romans, our author conceives of baptism as a kind of death and rebirth that together conform the believer to Jesus Christ. Already "raised with Christ," the addressees enjoy the new

life now: "for you have died, and your life is hidden with Christ in God."

And yet the present enjoyment of the new life awaits some final consummation that has not yet arrived. "When Christ your life appears, then you too will appear with him in glory" (Colossians 3:4). To this we can compare Paul's description of the end of days in 1 Corinthians 15:51–52, Philippians 3:20–21, 1 Thessalonians 4:13–17, and other places in our New Testament describing the glorified state of Jesus' followers in the age yet to come.

1 CORINTHIANS. The precise background to today's reading is somewhat indelicate. In the Corinthian Church there appears to have been, as Paul puts it, "a man living with his father's wife" (1 Corinthians 5:1). How Paul came by this fascinating information we can only guess, although perhaps "Chloe's people" let slip this tidbit as they revealed to Paul the existence of the various factions in the Corinthian Church (1 Corinthians 1:11–12).

In 1 Corinthians 1—4, Paul accuses the Corinthians of being spiritually pretentious,

Lectionary #46

AFTERNOON GOSPEL   Luke 24:13–35

A reading from the holy Gospel according to Luke

That **very day**, the **first** day of the week,
    two of Jesus' disciples were going
    to a **village** seven miles from Jerusalem called **Emmaus**,
    and they were **conversing** about **all** the things
        that had occurred.
And it happened that while they were **conversing** and **debating**,
    Jesus himself drew near and walked with them,
    but their eyes were **prevented** from recognizing him.
He **asked** them,
    "What are you **discussing** as you walk along?"
They stopped, looking **downcast**.
One of them, named Cleopas, said to him in reply,
    "Are you the **only** visitor to Jerusalem
    who does **not** know of the things
    that have **taken place** there in these days?"
And he replied to them, "What **sort** of things?"
They said to him,
    "The things that happened to **Jesus** the **Nazarene**,
    who was a **prophet** mighty in **deed** and **word**
    before **God** and **all** the people,
    how our chief **priests** and **rulers** both handed him over
    to a sentence of **death** and **crucified** him.
But we were **hoping** that he would be the one to **redeem Israel**;
    and besides all this,
    it is now the **third day** since this took place.

Emmaus = eh-MAY-us

Clearly proclaim Jesus' questions to his disciples as questions, raising the tone of your voice at the end of each one.
Cleopas = KLEE-oh-pus
The disciples can scarcely believe their new companion knows nothing about what has just happened in Jerusalem. Proclaim Cleopas' question so as to communicate his disbelief.

---

arrogant, inconsistent, and boastful when, in his view, they have actually very little to be proud of. What good things the Corinthians have, Paul says, they have received from Christ through Paul: "Who confers distinction upon you? What do you possess that you have not received? But if you have received it, why are you boasting as if you did not receive it?"

Most of 1 Corinthians 1—4 addresses the Corinthians' spiritual pride in general terms. In 1 Corinthians 5, Paul turns to a specific case. Paul calls the sexual relationship between the man and his stepmother *porneia*. This is a Greek word meaning "sexual immorality," "sexual sin," or even "sexual deviance." But sex is the common denominator. How can the Corinthians be so proud of themselves and puffed up if they tolerate *porneia* in their midst? While Paul will later compromise on certain matters pertaining to marriage and sexual ethics (see 1 Corinthians 7), in 1 Corinthians 5:5 he commands the Corinthians to expel the man.

Some Bible translations seek to give the impression that it is the man's flesh that will be destroyed. More likely, Paul conceives of "the flesh" here in theological terms and in opposition to "the spirit," such as we find in Romans 8, 1 Corinthians 3:3, Galatians 5:13 – 23, and elsewhere. If the Corinthians would truly be the community of spirit they have boastfully claimed to be, then they must first expunge the flesh among them. Like a little leaven in a lump of dough, their toleration of a little flesh in the form of *porneia* can spoil their community.

Some **women** from our group, however, have **astounded** us:
  they were at the **tomb** early in the morning
  and did **not** find his body;
  they came back and reported
  that they had indeed seen a **vision** of **angels**
  who announced that he was **alive**.
Then some of those with us went to the **tomb**
  and found things **just** as the women had described,
  but **him** they did not **see**."
And he said to them, "Oh, how **foolish** you are!
How **slow** of **heart** to believe **all** that the prophets spoke!
Was it not **necessary** that the **Christ** should **suffer** these things
  and enter into his **glory**?"
Then beginning with **Moses** and **all** the **prophets**,
  he interpreted to them what referred to him
  in **all** the **Scriptures**.
As they approached the **village** to which they were going,
  he gave the **impression** that he was going on farther.
But they urged him, "**Stay with us**,
  for it is nearly evening and the day is almost over."
So he went in to stay with them.
And it happened that, while he was with them at table,
  he took **bread**, said the **blessing**,
  broke it, and **gave** it to **them**.
With that their **eyes** were **opened** and they **recognized** him,
  but he **vanished** from their sight.

Emphasize this verse, proclaiming it slowly but forcefully, making eye contact with the assembly as you do so.

There is a choice of Gospels today. Speak with the liturgy coordinator or homilist to find out which one will be used.

GOSPEL The identity of "the disciple whom Jesus loved" is, at best, a mystery. We meet him in 13:23, reclining at dinner with Jesus. Perhaps because this disciple is lying nearest to Jesus, or perhaps because everyone knew that Jesus was closest to this man out of all of his disciples, Peter asks the beloved disciple to discover whom among them will betray Jesus. In 19:26, we meet him again when Jesus, dying on the cross, entrusts his mother into the disciple's care. And in 21:24 (see also 21:20–23), we find that the beloved disciple provided the essential testimony on which John's Gospel is based. Today we meet him again as he races with Peter to the empty tomb.

John narrates the race in a curious way. He records that the beloved disciple ran faster than Peter and arrived at the tomb first (20:4). But he is also careful to point out that the beloved disciple did not then enter the tomb, but rather looked inside to see Jesus' linen burial garments (20:5). John tells us that Peter, despite his late arrival, enters the tomb first, noting a few more details than the beloved disciple (20:6–7). Finally, the beloved disciple enters: "and he saw and believed" (20:8). With the exception of the entry, John presents the beloved disciple as first in all things at the empty tomb: arrival, seeing, and belief.

But what does the beloved disciple believe? Upon seeing the tomb's interior, does he immediately believe that Jesus has risen from the dead? If so, then 20:9 explains something about the beloved disciple's belief. The disciples have not yet understood

Proclaim these verses in a hopeful and excited tone of voice. The disciples' recognition of Jesus in the breaking of the bread is the first hint they have received that he is not dead, but alive.

Then they said to each other,
  "Were not our hearts **burning** within us
  while he **spoke** to us on the **way** and opened the **Scriptures**
    to us?"
So they set out at once and returned to **Jerusalem**
  where they found gathered together
  the **eleven** and those with them who were saying,
  "The **Lord** has **truly** been **raised** and has appeared to **Simon**!"
Then the two recounted
  what had taken place on the way
  and how he was made **known** to them in the **breaking** of **bread**.

that scripture (which scripture we cannot be sure) informs of Christ's Resurrection. The belief of the beloved disciple is therefore founded not on scripture, but on the empty tomb. Unlike Thomas in 20:19–29, who demands evidence of Jesus' wounds, the beloved disciple does not need to see Jesus in order to believe.

AFTERNOON GOSPEL In both Luke and John, the first people to see Jesus after his Resurrection do not recognize him. In John's Gospel, Mary

Magdalene is not only the first to discover the stone rolled away from the tomb (John 20:1), but also the first to see the risen Christ. But she mistakes him for a gardener. It is only when Jesus calls her by name— "Mary!"—that she recognizes him, responding, "Rabbouni!" This scene recalls Jesus' words about the good shepherd, to whom the sheep respond when he calls them "by name" (John 10:3).

In today's Gospel, two disciples are walking to the village of Emmaus while talking and perhaps arguing about all that happened during the last few days of Jesus'

life. Jesus himself falls in with them, "but their eyes were prevented from recognizing him" (Luke 24:16). Once they get over their shock at their new companion's ignorance about what happened to Jesus, they reveal their dashed hopes: "we were hoping that he would be the one to redeem Israel" (24:21). To this Jesus replies on the basis of scripture that things had to happen as they did. But still they do not recognize him. Only after they have sat down to supper and their companion, now their guest, reenacts their last meal together (Luke 22:19) do they at last recognize him.

Lectionary #43

READING I   Acts 2:42–47

A reading from the Acts of the Apostles

They **devoted** themselves
    to the **teaching** of the **apostles** and to the **communal** life,
    to the **breaking** of **bread** and to the **prayers**.
Awe came upon **everyone**,
    and many **wonders** and **signs** were done through the **apostles**.
All who believed were **together** and had **all** things in **common**;
    they would **sell** their **property** and **possessions**
    and **divide** them among **all** according to each one's need.
Every day they devoted themselves
    to meeting **together** in the **temple** area
    and to **breaking bread** in their **homes**.
They ate their **meals** with **exultation** and **sincerity** of **heart**,
    praising God and enjoying **favor** with **all** the people.
And **every** day the Lord **added** to their **number**
    those who were being **saved**.

Pause and look up at the assembly before you proclaim this line.

READING I   At several points in Acts, Luke summarizes the situation, character, and customary activities of the early Church. Acts contains three "big" summaries of at least three verses in length (2:42–47; 4:32–35; 5:12–16) and seven "little" summaries, all no longer than a single verse except in one case (1:14; 6:7; 9:31; 12:24; 16:5; 19:20; 28:30–31).

One feature common to most of the summaries, big and little, is a reference to the growth of the Church. Examples are Acts 6:7 ("The word of God continued to spread, and the number of the disciples in Jerusalem increased greatly"), 12:24 ("But the word of God continued to spread and grow"), and 19:20 ("Thus did the word of the Lord continue to spread with influence and power"). We find a statement similar to these in today's reading: "And every day the Lord added to their number those who were being saved" (2:47).

Also characteristic of the summaries, though occurring less frequently than references to the expansion of the Church, is the Greek word *homothumadon*. We find it in today's reading. It means "all together" in a spatial sense, or being "of one accord" or "of the same mind." We find it used in the second sense in the summaries of 1:14, 2:46, and 5:12, while the same idea is expressed in the summary of 4:32–35: "The community of believers was of one heart and mind" (4:32). The word well applies to this community, depicted as single-minded in its pursuit of teaching, fellowship, and prayer, but also sharing all property in common and freely distributing money and goods among its members according to their needs (2:45; 4:32).

Proclaim this reading slowly, enunciating clearly and looking up at the assembly as much as possible.

READING II   1 Peter 1:3–9

A reading from the first Letter of Saint Peter

Blessed be the **God** and **Father** of our **Lord Jesus Christ**,
    who in his **great mercy** gave us a **new birth** to a **living hope**
    through the **resurrection** of **Jesus Christ** from the **dead**,
    to an inheritance that is **imperishable**, **undefiled**,
      and **unfading**,
    kept in heaven for **you**
    who by the **power** of **God** are **safeguarded** through **faith**,
    to a **salvation** that is ready to be **revealed** in the final time.
In **this** you **rejoice**, although now for a little while
    you may have to **suffer** through various trials,
    so that the **genuineness** of your faith,
    more **precious** than **gold** that is **perishable** even though
      tested by **fire**,
    may prove to be for **praise**, **glory**, and **honor**
    at the **revelation** of **Jesus Christ**.
Although you have **not** seen him you **love** him;
    even though you do **not** see him **now** yet **believe** in him,
    you **rejoice** with an **indescribable** and **glorious joy**,
    as you attain the **goal** of your **faith**, the **salvation** of your **souls**.

READING II   The first letter of Peter is addressed "to the chosen sojourners of the dispersion in Pontus, Galatia, Cappadocia, Asia, and Bithynia." The territory encompassing these regions is a large chunk of north-central Asia Minor (present-day Turkey).

The author's designation of his recipients as "chosen sojourners of the dispersion" in 1:1 and his transmission of greetings from "the chosen one at Babylon" in 5:13 reveal an understanding of the Church as the successor to Israel and, like Israel under Babylon, scattered beyond the confines of

heaven, its true home. Babylon, by the beginning of the Christian era, was no longer a great power, but only a tiny, unimportant place. The name is almost certainly code for Rome, whose authority was beyond question throughout the world known to the author.

The author refers in today's reading, which is taken from the letter's opening lines, to "various trials" suffered by the addressees (1:6; see also 2:20; 3:14; 4:1, 12–13; 5:9). The author does not tell us much about these trials. We do have, however, a letter written by a Roman governor of

Bithynia (one of the regions mentioned in 1 Peter 1:1) to the emperor Trajan sometime between 111 and 113 AD. In this letter, the governor, whose name is Pliny, asks Trajan about what his policy should be toward those accused of being Christian. In the course of his preliminary investigations, Pliny reveals that he has tortured some of the Christians' female leadership in order to find out what they believed. He also reveals that there was no shortage of people stepping forward to denounce others as Christians. Perhaps these are the kind of trials the author of 1 Peter has in mind.

GOSPEL John 20:19–31

A reading from the holy Gospel according to John

On the evening of that **first** day of the week,
    when the doors were **locked**, where the **disciples** were,
    for **fear** of the **Jews**,
    Jesus came and stood in their **midst**
    and said to them, "**Peace** be **with** you."
When he had **said** this, he showed them his **hands** and his **side**.
The disciples **rejoiced** when they **saw the Lord**.
Jesus **said** to them again, "**Peace** be **with** you.
As the **Father** has **sent** me, **so I** send **you**."
And when he had **said** this, he **breathed** on them
      and said to them,
    "**Receive** the **Holy Spirit**.
Whose **sins** you **forgive** are **forgiven** them,
    and whose **sins** you **retain** are **retained**."

Thomas, called **Didymus**, one of the **Twelve**,
    was **not** with them when Jesus came.
So the **other** disciples **said** to him, "**We** have **seen the Lord**."
But he **said** to them,
    "**Unless** I see the **mark** of the **nails** in his **hands**
    and put my **finger** into the **nailmarks**
    and put my **hand** into his **side**, I will **not** believe."

Didymus = DID-uh-mus

Proclaim this line in an excited and joyful tone.

Thomas, because he has not also seen the Lord, cannot share the disciples' excitement and joy. Use a skeptical tone of voice as you deliver his conditions for belief.

GOSPEL   Docetism was the name given to an early Christian belief that Jesus did not actually possess a physical body, but only seemed to do so (*dokeō* means "seem" or "appear"). Some of the roots of docetism can be found in the philosophy of Plato, whose idea of the soul's immortality distinguished soul, mind, intellect, and matter. Docetic Christology was popular among so-called Gnostic Christians, many of whom held that the material world was bad, or even evil, and that only the

world of the Spirit was of any consequence. They did not call themselves Gnostics as far as we know, but were given that name in the modern period due to their orthodox opponents' reports that they claimed to possess an esoteric and secret knowledge (*gnōsis* means "knowledge").

If the material world, including all human flesh and blood, was bad, then it followed from this that Christ could not have had a physical body. He could not have suffered pain. And he could not have died on the cross. To the so-called Gnostics, Christ's

body, his suffering, and his death only seemed to occur. Orthodox believers challenged these beliefs, affirming Jesus' full humanity along with his full divinity.

In today's reading, supporters of docetism could point to Jesus' sudden appearance behind locked doors and that even though he invites Thomas to examine his wounds, John does not say that Thomas did. But orthodox opponents could argue, having already pointed out Jesus' bodily fatigue in Samaria (4:6) and heartfelt weeping over

Deliver Thomas' reply with the same
excited joy the disciples exuded earlier.

Emphasize especially the word "not" in
this line.
Pause briefly here.

Look up at the assembly, proclaiming this
line slowly and clearly.

Now a week later his disciples were **again** inside
    and **Thomas** was with them.
Jesus came, although the doors were locked,
    and stood in their midst and said, "**Peace** be **with** you."
Then he said to Thomas, "**Put** your finger **here** and **see** my hands,
    and **bring** your **hand** and put it into my **side**,
    and do **not** be unbelieving, but **believe**."
Thomas answered and said to him, "My **Lord** and my **God**!"
Jesus said to him, "Have you come to **believe**
    because you have **seen** me?
Blessed are those who have **not** seen and have **believed**."

Now, Jesus did many other signs in the presence of his disciples
    that are **not** written in this book.
But **these** are written that **you** may come to **believe**
    that **Jesus** is the **Christ**, the **Son** of **God**,
    and that through this **belief** you may have **life** in his **name**.

Lazarus (11:35), that if Jesus' wounds were
not actual, physical wounds on an actual,
physical body, then Jesus was trying to
deceive Thomas, which he would never
have done. The humanity of Jesus was a
subject on which the orthodox victors in this
struggle were prepared to compromise.

3RD SUNDAY OF EASTER

Lectionary #46

READING I   Acts 2:14, 22–33

A reading from the Acts of the Apostles

Then **Peter** stood up with the **Eleven**,
    raised his voice, and **proclaimed**:
"**You** who are **Jews**, indeed **all** of you staying in **Jerusalem**.
Let this be **known** to **you**, and **listen** to my words.
You who are **Israelites**, **hear** these words.
Jesus the **Nazarene** was a man commended to you by **God**
    with **mighty deeds**, **wonders**, and **signs**,
    which God **worked** through him in your midst,
        as you yourselves know.
This man, delivered up by the **set plan** and **foreknowledge**
    of **God**,
    you **killed**, using **lawless** men to **crucify** him.
But **God** raised him **up**, **releasing** him from the **throes** of **death**,
    because it was **impossible** for him to be **held** by it.
For **David** says of him:
    *I saw the **Lord** ever before me,*
        *with him at my right hand I shall **not** be **disturbed**.*
    *Therefore my **heart** has been **glad** and my **tongue** has **exulted**;*
        *my **flesh**, too, will **dwell** in **hope**,*
    *because **you** will **not abandon** my **soul** to the **netherworld**,*
        ***nor** will you **suffer** your **holy one** to see **corruption**.*
    *You have made **known** to me the **paths** of **life**;*
        *you will **fill** me with **joy** in your **presence**.*

Proclaim Peter's speech in a clear, bold tone. (This is the first public proclamation about Jesus in Acts!)

Nazarene = naz-uh-REEN

Pronounce each word of this line slowly and firmly.

READING I   The Acts of the Apostles contains many speeches. We need not suppose that Luke had access to a stenographer's notes when he wrote them all down. Ancient standards for the composition of history allowed for a writer to compile what facts and information he had about his subjects, and then to craft what a person might well have said at a particular time and place. The Greek historian Thucydides gave the first explicit description of this principle. Thucydides' successors followed suit, such that Josephus, in his *Jewish Antiquities,* composed speeches for Moses and other Israelites not found anywhere in the Bible. Luke works in this tradition of historical writing. What Peter declares in today's reading is what Luke's personal knowledge, sources, and research led him to believe Peter would have likely said on this occasion.

Today's reading comes from the first major public speech by an apostle in Acts. We might perhaps call Jesus' last words to his disciples a speech (1:7–8), and certainly also Peter's words at the selection of Judas' replacement (1:15–17, 20–22). But these are fairly short in length and delivered to Jesus' followers. By contrast, Peter's speech is

Pause between the end of the scripture quotation and the resumption of Peter's own words.

"My **brothers**, one can **confidently** say to you
  about the patriarch David that he **died** and was **buried**,
  and his **tomb** is in our midst to this **day**.
But since he was a **prophet** and **knew** that God had sworn
    an **oath** to him
  that he would set one of his descendants upon his **throne**,
  he **foresaw** and **spoke** of the resurrection of the **Christ**,
  that **neither** was he abandoned to the **netherworld**
  nor did his flesh see **corruption**.
God raised this Jesus;
  of this **we** are **all witnesses**.
Exalted at the right hand of God,
  he received the promise of the **Holy Spirit** from the **Father**
  and poured him forth, as you **see** and **hear**."

Pronounce the first four words slowly and firmly, then look up and make eye contact with the assembly.

READING II   1 Peter 1:17–21

A reading from the first Letter of Saint Peter

Beloved:
If you invoke as **Father** him who judges **impartially**
  according to each one's works,
  conduct yourselves with **reverence** during the time
    of your sojourning,
  realizing that you were **ransomed** from your futile conduct,
  handed on by your ancestors,
  not with **perishable** things like **silver** or **gold**
  but with the **precious blood** of Christ
  as of a spotless unblemished **lamb**.

Look up and stress the phrase beginning with the words "realizing that you."

Read slowly to bring out the contrast between the words "perishable things" and "precious blood of Christ."

---

quite long, spanning 22 verses (Acts 2:14–36), and is addressed to outsiders. Luke presents it as the first public proclamation of Jesus Christ by the Church to those outside its fellowship.

Luke records that some Jews and others from foreign parts have witnessed the effects of the reception of the Holy Spirit by the disciples at the feast of Pentecost and concluded that the disciples are drunk (2:1–13). Peter's speech is a reply to them.

Peter interprets the gift of the Spirit as fulfillment of the prophecy of Joel 2:28–32 (Acts 2:17–21), reminds the Jews about Jesus of Nazareth and blames them for his death (2:22–24), and interprets Jesus' Resurrection as the fulfillment of passages from the psalms (Acts 2:25–35).

READING II   The New Testament contains more than one understanding of the meaning of Jesus' death and Resurrection. One of the most common is the idea that Jesus atoned for human sin by dying on the cross. Interpretations of Jesus' death as sacrifice, or the likening of Jesus to a sacrificial victim, express this idea. We see it developed extensively in the letter to the Hebrews, where the author understands Jesus as both priest *and* offering. We also see it in this reading, where the author describes Jesus' blood as having ransomed the letter's addressees, and likens him to an unblemished lamb. (The absence of blemish was a common requirement for the acceptability of a sacrificial offering. See, for example, Leviticus 22:17 – 25.)

He was **known** before the **foundation** of the **world**
   but **revealed** in the final time for **you**,
   who through him believe in **God**
   who **raised** him from the **dead** and gave him **glory**,
   so that your **faith** and **hope** are in **God**.

GOSPEL   Luke 24:13–35

A reading from the holy Gospel according to Luke

That **very** day, the **first** day of the week,
   two of Jesus' **disciples** were going
   to a village seven miles from Jerusalem called **Emmaus**,
   and they were **conversing** about **all** the things
      that had occurred.
And it happened that while they were **conversing** and **debating**,
   Jesus himself drew near and walked with them,
   but their eyes were **prevented** from recognizing him.
He asked them,
   "**What** are you **discussing** as you walk along?"
They stopped, looking **downcast**.
One of them, named Cleopas, said to him in reply,
   "Are you the **only** visitor to **Jerusalem**
   who does **not** know of the things
   that have taken place there in these days?"

Emmaus = eh-MAY-us

Clearly proclaim Jesus' questions to his disciples as questions, raising the tone of your voice at the end of each one.

Cleopas = KLEE-oh-pus

The disciples can scarcely believe their new companion knows nothing about what has just happened in Jerusalem. Proclaim Cleopas' question so as to communicate his disbelief.

In the past week's commentary on 1 Peter 1:3–9 (see commentary II, Second Sunday of Easter, March 30), some language was pointed out that showed the author of 1 Peter applying the language of the Babylonian captivity to the spiritual exile of Christians in the Roman world. Today we may see more such language. When the author advises his addressees, "conduct yourselves with reverence during the time of your sojourning," he again describes the era of the Church as a time of "sojourning" *(paroikia)*, an allusion to Israel's experience in Babylon.

The author also urges his addressees to compare the people they were before their conversions to who they are in the present. And he invites them to consider that while they were still hostage to their prior ways of life, God nevertheless purchased their freedom. The image is strongly reminiscent of Isaiah 62:11–12, where the prophet describes the end of the exile in Babylon as the ransom of slaves by God (see also Romans 5:6–11).

GOSPEL   In Matthew's Gospel, Jesus first appears to his disciples in Galilee (Matthew 28:16–20). In Mark, an angel tells the women who arrive at Jesus' tomb only to find the stone rolled away and the tomb empty: "He [Jesus] is going before you to Galilee; there you will see him, as he

Nazarene = naz-uh-REEN

And he replied to them, "What sort of things?"
They said to him,
     "The things that happened to **Jesus** the **Nazarene**,
     who was a **prophet mighty** in **deed** and **word**
     before **God** and **all** the **people**,
     how our chief **priests** and **rulers** both handed him over
     to a sentence of **death** and **crucified** him.
But we were **hoping** that he would be the one to **redeem** Israel;
     and besides all this,
     it is now the **third day** since this took place.
Some **women** from our group, however, have **astounded** us:
     they were at the **tomb** early in the morning
     and did **not** find his body;
     they came back and reported
     that they had indeed seen a **vision** of **angels**
     who **announced** that he was alive.
Then some of those with us went to the **tomb**
     and found things **just** as the **women** had **described**,
     but him they did **not** see."
And he said to them, "Oh, how **foolish** you are!
How **slow** of **heart** to **believe** all that the **prophets** spoke!
Was it not **necessary** that the Christ should **suffer** these things
     and enter into his **glory**?"
Then beginning with **Moses** and **all** the **prophets**,
     he interpreted to them what referred to him
     in **all** the **Scriptures**.
As they approached the village to which they were going,
     he gave the impression that he was going on farther.
But they urged him, "**Stay** with us,
     for it is nearly evening and the day is almost over."
So he went in to **stay** with them.

Emphasize this verse, proclaiming it slowly but forcefully, making eye contact with the assembly as you do so.

told you" (Mark 16:7). In Luke and John, however, Jesus first appears to his followers in the vicinity of Jerusalem (Luke 24; John 20:11–29). An additional detail Luke and John share, and which is quite important in today's reading, is that Jesus' followers do not at first recognize him after he has been raised from the dead. In John, Mary Magdalene thinks Jesus is a gardener until he calls her by name (John 20:11–18; see also John 10:1–6). And in Luke, two disciples do not recognize that their companion on the road is Jesus until he breaks bread with them (Luke 24:13–35).

One thing Jesus learns from his disciples on their journey together is that he did not live up to their expectations. While the disciples agree that Jesus was "a prophet mighty in deed and word before God and all the people," his arrest and execution put an end to their greater wish: "But we were hoping that he would be the one to redeem Israel" (Luke 24:19–21).

The kind of redeemer these disciples have in mind was probably a political messiah, someone who would restore Israel's independence and reestablish its monarchy as in the days of king David (see also Acts 1:6). Some Jews in Jesus' day hoped for precisely such a messiah. The disciples do not as yet understand that Jesus is a redeemer different than they have expected, someone come not for Israel only, but for all peoples.

And it **happened** that, while he was **with** them at table,
   he took **bread**, said the **blessing**,
   broke it, and **gave** it to them.
With that their eyes were **opened** and they **recognized** him,
   but he **vanished** from their sight.
Then they said to each other,
   "Were not our hearts **burning** within us
   while he **spoke** to us on the way and opened the **Scriptures**
     to us?"
So they set out at once and **returned** to Jerusalem
   where they found **gathered together**
   the **eleven** and those with them who were saying,
   "The **Lord** has **truly** been **raised** and has **appeared** to **Simon**!"
Then the two recounted
   what had taken place on the way
   and how he was **made known** to them in the **breaking** of **bread**.

Proclaim these verses in a hopeful and excited tone of voice. The disciples' recognition of Jesus in the breaking of the bread is the first hint they have received that he is not dead, but alive.

4TH SUNDAY OF EASTER

Lectionary #49

READING I   Acts 2:14a, 36–41

A reading from the Acts of the Apostles

Then **Peter** stood up with the **Eleven**,
    raised his voice, and **proclaimed**:
"Let the whole house of **Israel** know for **certain**
    that **God** has made both **Lord** and **Christ**,
    this **Jesus** whom you **crucified**."

Now when they **heard** this, they were **cut** to the **heart**,
    and they asked **Peter** and the other **apostles**,
    "**What** are we to **do**, my brothers?"
Peter **said** to them,
    "**Repent** and be **baptized**, **every one** of you,
    in the name of **Jesus Christ** for the **forgiveness** of your **sins**;
    and you will receive the **gift** of the **Holy Spirit**.
For the **promise** is **made** to **you** and to your **children**
    and to **all** those far off,
    whomever the Lord our God will **call**."
He **testified** with many other arguments,
    and was **exhorting** them,
    "**Save** yourselves from this **corrupt** generation."
Those who **accepted** his message were **baptized**,
    and about **three thousand** persons were **added** that day.

Peter has just brought this audience to repentance. Deliver its line in a regretful, even sorrowful tone.

Proclaim this line in a strong, firm tone of voice, looking up at the assembly as you proclaim the phrase "every one of you."

READING I   This reading contains the conclusion of the first public speech by an apostle in Acts (see commentary I, Third Sunday of Easter, April 6). Having proclaimed that Jesus of Nazareth fulfills scripture, Peter urges his audience to repent and be baptized, promising them the same Holy Spirit that he himself has just received (2:1–4). This is interesting, because it was only in the previous chapter that the disciples, still confused, ask Jesus, "Lord,

are you at this time going to restore the kingdom to Israel?" But one chapter later, Peter seems to understand a great deal that he has previously given no hint of knowing.

Luke has actually been laying the foundations of this scene for some time. In Luke 24:25–27, the risen Jesus explains to two of his disciples on the basis of scripture that he had to suffer, die, and rise precisely as he did. In Luke 24:45, the evangelist reports that the risen Jesus "opened their [the disciples'] minds to understand the scriptures" by way of showing them that "repentance and

forgiveness of sins is to be proclaimed in his [the Messiah's] name to all the world, beginning from Jerusalem" (24:46–47). The disciples can bear witness to all of this. In Acts 1:8, in answer to his disciples' hopeful query about the restoration of the Israelite monarchy, Jesus ignores the substance of their question, replying, "you will receive power when the holy Spirit comes upon you, and you will be my witnesses in Jerusalem, throughout Judea and Samaria, and to the ends of the earth."

READING II 1 Peter 2:20b–25

A reading from the first Letter of Saint Peter

Beloved:
If you are **patient** when you **suffer** for doing what is good,
  this is a **grace** before God.
For to **this** you have been called,
  because Christ **also** suffered for you,
  leaving **you** an **example** that you should **follow** in his **footsteps**.
*He committed **no sin**, and **no deceit** was found in his **mouth**.*

When he was **insulted**, he returned **no insult**;
  when he **suffered**, he did **not threaten**;
  instead, he handed **himself** over to the one who judges justly.
He himself bore **our** sins in his body upon the **cross**,
  so that, **free** from sin, **we** might live for **righteousness**.
By his wounds **you** have been healed.
For you had gone **astray** like **sheep**,
  but you have **now** returned to the **shepherd** and **guardian**
    of your **souls**.

Look up as you proclaim this line, emphasizing the pronouns in particular.

Only with the advent of the Church at Pentecost does Peter at last understand and proclaim what has previously baffled him and his fellow disciples.

READING II   Back up and read 1 Peter 2:18 to the end of today's reading. While the idea that suffering conforms a Christian to Christ may have a broad application, here the author addresses slaves in particular. He encourages them to

model themselves on Christ's example, willingly accepting even ill treatment by a master's hand.

If this seems shocking, consider this: slavery was the way of the ancient world. The status a Christian enjoyed in the Church, whether or not he or she was a slave, would probably not translate into a similar status in society at large. What would it have mattered to a non-Christian slave owner had a slave stated, "There is neither Jew nor Greek, there is neither slave nor free person,

there is not male and female; for you are all one in Christ Jesus" (Galatians 3:28)?

Recall that this author refers to some kind of trial—harassment perhaps, if not outright persecution. Let the Church not suffer, the author reasons, due to opponents' discovery of some pretext or other for claiming that the Church teaches slaves to disobey and stirs up social unrest. If the Church must suffer, let it suffer for its testimony about Jesus and the hope of Resurrection (3:14–17).

GOSPEL   John 10:1–10

A reading from the holy Gospel according to John

Jesus said:

"**Amen**, **amen**, I say to you,
    whoever does not enter a sheepfold through the **gate**
    but climbs over **elsewhere** is a **thief** and a **robber**.
But whoever enters through the **gate** is the **shepherd** of the **sheep**.
The **gatekeeper** opens it for him, and the **sheep** hear his voice,
    as the shepherd calls his **own** sheep by **name**
        and **leads** them out.
When he has driven out **all** his **own**,
    he walks **ahead** of them, and the sheep **follow** him,
    because they **recognize** his **voice**.
But they will **not** follow a stranger;
    they will run **away** from him,
    because they do **not recognize** the voice of **strangers**."
Although Jesus **used** this figure of speech,
    the **Pharisees** did not realize what he was trying to **tell** them.

So Jesus said again, "**Amen**, **amen**, I say to you,
    I am the **gate** for the **sheep**.
All who came before me are **thieves** and **robbers**,
    but the **sheep** did not **listen** to them.
I am the **gate**.
Whoever enters through me will be **saved**,
    and will **come in** and **go out** and **find pasture**.
A thief comes **only** to **steal** and **slaughter** and **destroy**;
    I came so that they might have **life**
        and have it more **abundantly**."

Proclaim this reading slowly. Pause briefly at each comma or semicolon, and a longer duration at each period.

GOSPEL   Mark's Gospel begins with the proclamation of John the Baptist. Matthew's Gospel starts well before John the Baptist with a genealogy of Jesus reaching all the way back to Abraham. Luke concentrates on neither time nor history, but rather on place, commencing his Gospel's narrative (after its introduction) in the Jerusalem temple. John's Gospel takes us all the way back before Creation: "In the beginning was the Word, and the Word was with God, and the Word was God" (John 1:1).

    There are several words in John's Gospel that have definitions specific to the Gospel itself. "Darkness," "night," "light," and "sight" are some of these (see Gospel commentary, Fourth Sunday of Lent, March 2). "World" is another. In today's reading, we encounter John's keen sense of irony: "the world came to be through him, but the world did not know him" (1:9). Sometimes John describes the world in positive terms (3:16–17; 4:42; 6:33, 51; 12:19). Often, however, he describes "the world" in highly negative terms, as a realm characterized by its opposition to, even hatred of, Jesus (7:7; 8:23; 12:31; 14:17, 27, 30; 15:18–19; 16:20, 33; 17:9, 14, 16, 25).

    The Greek word our Bible translates as "overcome" is *katalambanō* (see John 1:5). It means both "overcome" and "comprehend." While John 12:35 suggests that "overcome" is the word's main sense here, both of its meanings come together nicely in the English word "apprehend." This is a fitting verb to describe what the darkness cannot accomplish where the light is concerned. Ignorance and hostility toward Jesus go together in John's Gospel, where public reactions to Jesus in Judea begin with confusion followed by vigorous, sometimes hostile, and finally deadly opposition.

5TH SUNDAY OF EASTER

Lectionary #52

READING I   Acts 6:1–7

A reading from the Acts of the Apostles

As the **number** of disciples continued to **grow**,
    the **Hellenists** complained against the **Hebrews**
    because their **widows**
    were being **neglected** in the daily distribution.
So the **Twelve** called together the **community** of the disciples
        and said,
    "It is not **right** for us to **neglect** the **word** of **God**
        to serve at table.
Brothers, select from among you seven **reputable** men,
    filled with the **Spirit** and wisdom,
    whom we shall **appoint** to this task,
    whereas **we** shall devote **ourselves** to prayer
    and to the **ministry** of the word."
The proposal was **acceptable** to the **whole** community,
    so they chose **Stephen**, a man filled with **faith**
        and the **Holy Spirit**,
    also **Philip**, **Prochorus**, **Nicanor**, **Timon**, **Parmenas**,
    and **Nicholas** of **Antioch**, a convert to **Judaism**.
They presented these men to the **apostles**
    who **prayed** and laid **hands** on them.

Hellenists = HEL-len-ists

Proclaim the list of the seven slowly, without rushing.

Prochorus = PRO-chor-us
Nicanor = NI-can-nor
Timon = TEE-moan
Parmenas = Par-men-AS
Antioch = AN-ti-ock

READING I   In today's reading, Luke records the first instance of major disagreement between factions in the Church. As did the account of Ananias and Sapphira in Acts 5:1–11, today's reading complicates the idyllic portrait of the Church offered in the summaries of 2:42–47 and 4:32–35.

In today's reading we meet several groups of people: disciples, Hellenists, Hebrews, widows, the 12 apostles, and a group of seven Hellenist men who are individually named. Luke defines the Church as a whole as "the community of the disciples."

Whether a "widow" was a title designating a vowed celibate woman, or simply meant a woman whose husband was dead, Luke here depicts a widow as a woman depending on those of her particular faction to provide for her from the generosity of the Church (on widows in the Church, see 1 Timothy 5).

"The twelve" appear to have status in the Church that is sufficiently separate and authoritative from the disciples that they are able to convene a general assembly and excuse themselves from table service. Whether Luke means that "the seven" (see Acts 21:8) were selected to be counterparts of the 12 apostles, or to occupy positions beneath them, one cannot say with any certainty.

Pause briefly here.

The **word** of **God** continued to **spread**,
and the **number** of the **disciples** in Jerusalem increased **greatly**;
even a large group of **priests** were becoming **obedient**
to the faith.

READING II   1 Peter 2:4–9

A reading from the first Letter of Saint Peter

Beloved:
Come to him, a **living** stone, **rejected** by human beings
but **chosen** and **precious** in the sight of **God**,
and, **like** living stones,
let **yourselves** be built into a **spiritual** house
to be a **holy priesthood** to offer **spiritual sacrifices**
acceptable to **God** through **Jesus Christ**.
For it says in Scripture:
*Behold, I am laying a **stone** in **Zion**,*
*a **cornerstone**, **chosen** and **precious**,*
*and **whoever** believes in it shall **not** be put to shame.*
Therefore, its value is for you who have *faith*,
but for those **without** faith:
*The stone that the builders **rejected***
*has become the **cornerstone**,*
and
*a stone that will make people **stumble**,*
*and a rock that will make them **fall**.*
They stumble by disobeying the **word**, as is their **destiny**.

Zion = ZI-yon

There are four quotations from the Old Testament in this reading. Take care to proclaim them with a clear and dignified tone.

It is hard to tell whom Luke means by the terms "Hebrews" and "Hellenists." But because Luke does not mention the reception of the Holy Spirit by non-Jews until the Church reaches Samaria in Acts 8, and then with greater elaboration in Acts 10, it is likely that he believes the Jerusalem Church was composed exclusively of Jewish Christians prior to the persecution and scattering of the disciples described in Acts 8:1–4.

The significant differences between these two groups of Jewish Christians were probably of language (the Hellenists likely spoke Greek, while the Hebrews probably spoke Aramaic and/or Hebrew) and culture (the Hellenists probably hailed from the Mediterranean Jewish Diaspora, perhaps including Greek-speaking areas of Palestine, while the Hebrews came from Jerusalem, Judea, and Galilee).

READING II In Matthew, Mark, and Luke, Jesus delivers a parable about a landlord's judgment upon some people who rent his vineyard, abuse his slaves, and finally kill his son. The thinly veiled theme of this parable is that the mistreatment of the prophets and the eventual murder of Jesus by Jews will lead to God's rejection of them and his election of others, presumably Gentiles, in their place. In all three Gospels, Jesus concludes his parable with the words of Psalm 118:22: "The stone that the builders rejected has become the cornerstone; by the Lord has this been done, and it is wonderful in our eyes" (Matthew 21:42; see Mark 12:10; Luke 20:17).

Pause briefly between each of these descriptions of the Church. Emphasize the word "you," looking out at the assembly as you do so.

You are "a **chosen race**, a royal **priesthood**,
a **holy** nation, a people of his **own**,
so that you may announce the **praises**" of him
who called you out of **darkness** into his wonderful **light**.

GOSPEL   John 14:1–12

A reading from the holy Gospel according to John

Jesus said to his **disciples**:
"Do **not** let your hearts be troubled.
You have faith in **God**; have **faith** also in **me**.
In my Father's house there are **many** dwelling places.
If there were not,
would I have told you that I am going to prepare
a place for you?
And if I go and prepare a place for you,
I will come **back** again and take you to **myself**,
so that where **I** am **you** also may be.
Where **I** am going **you** know the way."
Thomas said to him,
"Master, we do **not** know where you are going;
how can we know the **way**?"

Pause briefly here to highlight Thomas' question.

Before anyone found prophecies of Christ contained within it, Psalm 118 was a royal hymn celebrating the reign and military victories of a king of Judah. In Jesus' mouth, Psalm 118:22, which may have also been a popular proverb, prophesies God's construction of a new people out of unlikely materials. Later in Acts, Peter preaches before the Sanhedrin (a sort of supreme Jewish council of religious elites) that Jesus himself was the stone rejected by the members of the Sanhedrin when they crucified him (Acts 4:10–11). In today's reading,

the author identifies both Jesus and the Church with the rejected cornerstone. The Church, by patiently undergoing its present trials (1 Peter 1:6; 2:20; 3:14; 4:1, 12–13; 5:9), conforms itself to the example of Christ's endurance of suffering.

GOSPEL Today's Gospel selection explores a topic closely related to the meaning of belief in John's Gospel: seeing God (see also Gospel commentary, March 2, Fourth Sunday of Lent).

In 1:18, we read that "No one has ever seen God. The only Son, God, who is at the Father's side, has revealed him." As this verse suggests, and as 6:46 makes clear, this "no one" does not include Jesus. Later, Jesus tells his Judean questioners that "the Father who sent me has testified on my behalf. But you have never heard his voice nor seen his form" (5:37). John records no reply to this claim by Jesus' questioners.

In today's reading, Jesus tells his disciples that "From now on you do know him [the Father] and have seen him." But Philip

Jesus said to him, "I am the **way** and the **truth** and the **life**.
No one comes to the Father **except** through me.
If you **know me**, then you will **also** know **my Father**.
From now on you **do** know him and have **seen** him."
Philip said to him,
    "Master, **show** us the Father, and **that** will be **enough** for us."
Jesus said to him, "Have I been **with** you for so long a time
    and you still do **not** know me, Philip?
Whoever has seen me has seen the **Father**.
How can you say, '**Show** us the **Father**'?
Do you **not** believe that **I** am in the **Father**
        and the **Father** is in **me**?
The words that **I** speak to you I do **not** speak on my **own**.
The **Father** who **dwells** in **me** is doing his **works**.
Believe me that **I** am in the **Father** and the **Father** is in **me**,
    or else, **believe** because of the **works** themselves.
Amen, **amen**, I say to you,
    whoever believes in me will do the **works** that I do,
    and will do **greater** ones than these,
    because I am going to the **Father**."

is still confused, asking Jesus to show the Father to him and the disciples. Jesus replies, "Have I been with you for so long a time and you still do not know me, Philip? Whoever has seen me has seen the Father." Seeing the Father, according to John, is a matter of seeing Jesus, and to a lesser extent seeing his works (14:7–11).

In John's Gospel, Jesus' principal revelation is that he reveals the Father. This is the main content of his teaching and the ultimate disclosure of his signs. Those who can "see" are those who believe. Those who either cannot or will not see that Jesus reveals the Father are those who do not believe.

6TH SUNDAY OF EASTER

Lectionary #55

READING I   Acts 8:5–8, 14–17

A reading from the Acts of the Apostles

Samaria = Sah-MAR-I-ah

Philip went down to the city of **Samaria**
    and proclaimed the **Christ** to them.
With **one accord**, the crowds paid attention
        to what was said by Philip
    when they **heard** it and **saw** the signs he was doing.
For unclean spirits, crying out in a loud voice,
    came out of many possessed people,
        and many paralyzed or crippled people were **cured**.
There was **great joy** in that city.

Pause here briefly. The setting is changing
from Samaria to Jerusalem.

Now when the **apostles** in **Jerusalem**
    heard that Samaria had accepted the word of God,
    they sent them **Peter** and **John**,
    who went **down** and **prayed** for them,
    that they might **receive** the **Holy Spirit**,
    for it had not yet **fallen** upon **any** of them;
        they had only been **baptized** in the name of the **Lord Jesus**.
Then they laid **hands** on them
    and they **received** the Holy Spirit.

READING I   In Acts 8:1, we read about a "severe persecution" of the Church in Jerusalem. Everyone except for the apostles, by whom Luke probably means "the twelve" (Luke 6:13–16; Acts 1:13, 15–26), fled Jerusalem. Despite the admittedly painful circumstances of persecution, Luke almost certainly understands the historical event of the Church's spread to have been set in motion and guided by God.

Acts 8 introduces us to Philip. Luke cannot mean that he is the Philip who was also one of the 12 apostles (Luke 6:14; Acts 1:13). Luke states that the apostles did not

leave Jerusalem during the persecution and it is very unlikely that he means "the apostles" not to include "the twelve" (8:1). Acts 21:8–9 finds "Philip the evangelist, who was one of the seven" (see Acts 6:5) and his four virgin prophetess daughters hosting Paul at their home in the coastal city of Cesarea. It is presumably this Philip whose exploits Luke narrates in Acts 8.

In today's reading, Philip proclaims Christ in Samaria (due north of Judea), does signs, and effects cures of the infirm and lame. In Samaria, Philip demonstrates the power Peter has already displayed in

Jerusalem (Acts 3:1–10), although on its sheer scale Philip's healing mission in Samaria is more reminiscent of Jesus than of Peter's healing of a single man (Luke 4:40; 5:15; 6:17–19; 7:18–23; 9:11).

In Acts 8:14–17, Luke makes explicit the order of ritual by which people entered the Church: proclamation, Baptism, laying on of hands, and reception of the Holy Spirit. Luke does not consistently maintain this order in Acts (see, for example, Acts 10:44–48).

READING II   1 Peter 3:15–18

A reading from the first Letter of Saint Peter

Beloved:

Sanctify **Christ** as **Lord** in your **hearts**.
Always be ready to give an **explanation**
   to **anyone** who asks you for a **reason** for your **hope**,
   but do it with **gentleness** and **reverence**,
   keeping your **conscience** clear,
   so that, when you are **maligned**,
   those who **defame** your good **conduct** in **Christ**
   may **themselves** be put to shame.
For it is **better** to **suffer** for doing **good**,
   if that be the **will** of **God**, than for doing **evil**.
For Christ **also** suffered for sins once,
   the **righteous** for the sake of the **unrighteous**,
   that he might **lead** you to **God**.
Put to **death** in the **flesh**,
   he was brought to **life** in the **Spirit**.

Emphasize the word "Always" in this line.

Pause briefly here. Slow down, stressing the words "gentleness" and "reverence."

Pause before you deliver this line. Emphasize the likeness of the Christians' suffering to Christ's, stressing the word "also" and looking up and making eye contact with the assembly as you proclaim.

READING II   In this reading, the author urges his addressees to remain in constant readiness to speak in defense of their faith. More precisely, Christians must be ready to provide an explanation *(apologia)* "to anyone who asks you for a reason for your hope" (3:15). In the New Testament and much early Christian literature, "hope" is shorthand for the promise of the resurrection. What the author is exhorting his addressees to do, therefore, is to stand ready to defend core Christian beliefs.

But the manner of the defense matters as much to the author as its content. The tone must be one of "gentleness and reverence." Otherwise, one will only aid one's opponents. The context suggests a public forum of some sort, perhaps even a courtroom setting, in which the charge might have ranged from sedition to simply "being Christian." If the latter seems unlikely, consider that in 110–111 AD the Roman governor of the province of Bithynia (one of the provinces to which the author addresses this letter in 1:1) wrote to the emperor asking if simply being Christian was sufficient reason to punish a person.

The author acknowledges that even if one gives an opponent no basis for accusation beyond Christian "hope," one might still suffer anyway. Provided one has not eagerly sought after such suffering, such a person is blessed, because suffering innocently for what is right imitates Christ's Passion.

GOSPEL   All four Gospels report that Jesus and his disciples enjoyed a meal and a time of fellowship on the night before he died. What sets John apart from Matthew, Mark, and Luke is his

GOSPEL   John 14:15–21

A reading from the holy Gospel according to John

Jesus said to his **disciples**:
"If you **love** me, you will **keep** my commandments.
And I will ask the **Father**,
    and he will give you **another** Advocate to be with you **always**,
    the Spirit of **truth**, whom the **world** cannot **accept**,
    because it neither **sees** nor **knows** him.
But **you** know him, because he **remains** with **you**,
    and will be **in** you.
I will **not** leave you orphans; I will **come** to you.
In a little while the **world** will no longer **see** me,
    but **you** will see me, because **I** live and **you** will live.
On that day **you** will realize that **I** am in my **Father**
    and **you** are in **me** and **I** in **you**.
Whoever has my commandments and **observes** them
    is the one who **loves** me.
And **whoever** loves **me** will be **loved** by my **Father**,
    and **I** will **love** him and **reveal** myself to him."

Jesus' discourses in John present the Gospel reader with a special challenge, for they are often complicated and highly repetitive. Therefore, read them slowly, pausing frequently, and stressing the words in bold.

inclusion of an extensive "farewell discourse" delivered by Jesus to his disciples (John 14—17). Except for the Sermon on the Mount (Matthew 5:1—7:29), Jesus does not speak at such length in one physical location at any other point in the Gospels.

Jesus delivers several variations on a phrase we find in 14:19: "In a little while the world will no longer see me, but you will see me, because I live and you will live." But in 16:10 we read, "I am going to the Father and you will no longer see me," and

in 16:16, "A little while and you will no longer see me, and again a little while later and you will see me." What is Jesus trying to tell to his disciples?

Jesus' repeated and seemingly contradictory versions of this phrase progressively reveal to John's readership how Jesus explained to his disciples that he, despite his physical absence, would remain powerfully alive among his followers. In today's Gospel, Jesus promises that "another Advocate," "the Spirit of Truth," will come to his disciples. This Spirit will testify to the disciples

about Jesus, helping them to recall all he spoke when he was present (14:26; 15:26). Indeed, Jesus *must* leave for the Advocate to come (16:7).

Jesus and the Advocate, whom the Catholic Church has traditionally identified with the Holy Spirit, are closely identified in John's Gospel. John calls the Spirit "*another* Advocate," while in 1 John 2:1 the author identifies "Jesus Christ the righteous one" as the Church's "Advocate with the Father."

ASCENSION OF THE LORD

Lectionary #58

READING I   Acts 1:1–11

A reading from the beginning of the Acts of the Apostles

Theophilus = thee-OFF-uh-lus

In the first book, **Theophilus**,
   I dealt with **all** that Jesus did and taught
   until the day he was taken up,
   after giving instructions through the **Holy Spirit**
   to the **apostles** whom he had **chosen**.
He presented himself **alive** to them
   by many **proofs** after he had **suffered**,
   appearing to them during **forty days**
   and speaking about the **kingdom** of **God**.
While **meeting** with them,
   he **enjoined** them not to **depart** from Jerusalem,
   but to wait for "the **promise** of the **Father**
   about which you have **heard** me **speak**;
   for John **baptized** with **water**,
   but in a few days you will be **baptized** with the **Holy Spirit**."

Raise the tone of your voice to indicate the disciples' hopeful question.

When they had gathered **together** they asked him,
   "**Lord**, are you at this time going to **restore**
       the kingdom to **Israel**?"
He answered them, "It is not for you to know the **times**
       or **seasons**
   that the Father has established by his **own** authority.

If the Ascension of the Lord is celebrated next Sunday, today's readings are used in place of those for the Seventh Sunday of Easter.

READING I   In today's Gospel, Luke introduces the second half of his work, the first half being the Gospel according to Luke. In Acts 1:2, Luke identifies Jesus' Ascension ("the day he was taken up") as the end of what he calls in the previous verse "the first book," that is, the Gospel of Luke.

Note the disciples' question in Acts 1:6. "Lord," they ask, "are you at this time going to restore the kingdom to Israel?" The question reminds one of the shattered hope about Jesus expressed by the two disciples whom Jesus meets on the road to Emmaus: "But we were hoping that he would be the one to redeem Israel" (Luke 24:21). In both cases, the disciples' greatest hope is Israel's restoration and redemption. They likely suppose, as many first-century Jews did, that a true messiah was someone who would throw off the yoke of Israel's oppressors and bring

back the rule of a monarch like David, or even of one of his descendants.

Despite Jesus' Passion, death, and Resurrection, and despite the scriptural education he has given his disciples about who he is, why things had to happen to him as they did, and what the disciples must yet undergo and do (Luke 24:25–27, 44–48; Acts 1:4–5), the disciples still do not understand that Jesus is not a royal messiah with his eye solely on Israel. Even though Jesus has clearly informed them of it, the disciples cannot yet imagine that Jesus' eye ranges

Judea = Ju-DEE-ah
Samaria = Sah-MAR-I-ah

Galilee = GAL-ih-lee

But you will receive **power** when the **Holy Spirit** comes upon you,
    and you will be my **witnesses** in **Jerusalem**,
    throughout **Judea** and **Samaria**,
    and to the **ends** of the **earth**."
When he had **said** this, as they were looking on,
    he was **lifted up**, and a **cloud** took him from their **sight**.
While they were looking **intently** at the sky as he was going,
    suddenly two men dressed in **white garments**
        stood **beside** them.
They said, "**Men** of **Galilee**,
    why are you **standing** there looking at the **sky**?
This **Jesus** who has been taken up from you into **heaven**
    will **return** in the same way as you have **seen** him
        going into heaven."

READING II Ephesians 1:17–23

A reading from the Letter of Saint Paul to the Ephesians

This reading is quite long and rather complicated. Let the commas mark brief pauses.

Brothers and **sisters**:
May the **God** of our **Lord** Jesus Christ, the **Father** of **glory**,
    give you a **Spirit** of **wisdom** and **revelation**
    resulting in **knowledge** of him.
May the eyes of your hearts be **enlightened**,
    that you may know what is the **hope** that belongs to his **call**,
    what are the **riches** of **glory**
    in his **inheritance** among the holy ones,
    and what is the surpassing **greatness** of his **power**
    for **us** who **believe**,
    in accord with the **exercise** of his great **might**,

much further, even "to the ends of the earth" (Acts 1:8; see also 13:47).

READING II Although Paul himself probably did not write Ephesians, someone quite familiar with his work and reputation did. The author of Ephesians in today's reading demonstrates his mastery of one of the most important themes of Paul's letters: the Church as the body of Christ.

In 1 Corinthians, which Paul certainly had a hand in composing, Paul urges the Corinthians at every turn to heal their many divisions. One of the ways he does this is by likening the Corinthian Church to a body: "As a body is one though it has many parts, and all the parts of the body, though many, are one body, so also Christ" (1 Corinthians 12:12). This was a common metaphor ancient Greek orators used when exhorting the citizens of a city or members of a council to remember the unity and interdependence underlying their individual variety.

The author of the Ephesians, as we see from today's reading, also thinks of the Church as Christ's body (see also 4:4, 12, 16; 5:29–30). But his understanding of the Church is somewhat more grand and exalted than what Paul reveals in his letters. In Ephesians 3:8–10 one reads that Paul was made an apostle "so that the manifold wisdom of God might now be made known through the Church to the principalities and authorities in the heavens." The Church lives and bears witness to God through Christ not only on earth, but also in spiritual places as well. In Ephesians, the author emphasizes that Christ's body, the Church, inhabits both earth and heaven, time and eternity.

which he worked in **Christ**,
raising him from the **dead**
and seating him at his **right hand** in the **heavens**,
far above every **principality**, **authority**, **power**, and **dominion**,
and **every** name that is **named**
not only in **this** age but also in the **one** to **come**.
And he put **all** things beneath his feet
and gave him as **head** over **all** things to the **church**,
which is his **body**,
the **fullness** of the one who fills **all** things in every way.

GOSPEL Matthew 28:16–20

A reading from the holy Gospel according to Matthew

The eleven **disciples** went to **Galilee**,
to the mountain to which **Jesus** had **ordered** them.
When they **saw** him, they **worshiped**, but they **doubted**.
Then Jesus **approached** and **said** to them,
  "All **power** in **heaven** and on **earth** has been **given** to me.
Go, therefore, and make **disciples** of **all** nations,
  baptizing them in the name of the **Father**,
  and of the **Son**, and of the **Holy Spirit**,
  teaching them to observe **all** that I have commanded you.
And behold, I am **with** you **always**, until the **end** of the **age**."

Galilee = GAL-ih-lee

Pause briefly before the phrase "but they doubted."

Proclaim the words of the risen Christ in a clear, bold tone.

Emphasize in particular the word "always" in this line.

GOSPEL **When Jesus commissions the apostles in the Gospel of Matthew**, he begins by saying, "Do not go into pagan territory or enter a Samaritan town. Go rather to the lost sheep of the house of Israel" (10:6). In 15:21–28, a Canaanite woman begs for healing. Jesus eventually heals her, but not before initially rebuffing her, saying, "I was sent only to the lost sheep of the house of Israel" (15:24).

But there are hints in Matthew's Gospel that Jesus will not always confine himself to Israel. In Matthew 8:5, a centurion comes to Jesus and asks him to heal his servant.

The centurion demonstrates such faith in Jesus that Jesus replies, "Amen, I say to you, in no one in Israel have I found such faith. I say to you, many will come from the east and the west, and will recline with Abraham, Isaac, and Jacob at the banquet in the kingdom of heaven, but the children of the kingdom will be driven out into the outer darkness, where there will be wailing and grinding of teeth" (8:10–12). Not only does this passage anticipate the Church's mission to the Gentiles, but it also reflects an antipathy for Jews, which probably owes more to the friction between synagogue and Church

in Matthew's own day than Jesus' authentic sentiment.

In today's reading, the risen Christ commissions his disciples once again: "Go, therefore, and make disciples of all nations, baptizing them in the name of the Father, and of the Son, and of the holy Spirit" (28:19). While the earthly Jesus focused his ministry mainly on Israel, the risen Christ greatly expands the scope of the disciples' ministry, such that no ethnic criteria need impede the work of the universal Church.

7TH SUNDAY OF EASTER

Lectionary #59

READING I   Acts 1:12–14

A reading from the Acts of the Apostles

After **Jesus** had been taken up to **heaven** the **apostles**
    returned to **Jerusalem**
    from the mount called **Olivet**, which is near **Jerusalem**,
    a sabbath day's journey away.

When they entered the city
    they went to the upper room where they were staying,
    Peter and **John** and **James** and **Andrew**,
    Philip and **Thomas**, **Bartholomew** and **Matthew**,
    James son of **Alphaeus**, **Simon** the **Zealot**,
    and **Judas** son of **James**.
All these devoted themselves with **one accord** to **prayer**,
    together with some **women**,
    and **Mary** the mother of **Jesus**, and his **brothers**.

Olivet = OL-ih-vet
sabbath = SAB-uth

Proclaim this list slowly, enunciating each
name clearly.
Bartholomew = bar-THOL-uh-myoo
Alphaeus = AL-phae-us
Zealot = ZEL-ut
Judas = JU-das

READING II   1 Peter 4:13–16

A reading from the first Letter of Saint Peter

Beloved:
Rejoice to the extent that you share in the **sufferings** of Christ,
    so that when his **glory** is **revealed**
    you may **also rejoice** exultantly.

Look up and make eye contact with the
assembly as you proclaim in a cheerful
tone, "so that when his glory is revealed
you may also rejoice exultantly."

If the Ascension of the Lord is celebrated
today, please see pages 160–162 for the
appropriate readings.

READING I — With the Ascension of
Jesus, the nucleus of his
ministry remains together in Jerusalem. This
nucleus is composed of the 11 remaining
disciples (see Luke 6:13–16), some unnamed
women (see Luke 8:1–3), Jesus' mother, and
Jesus' brothers. By staying in Jerusalem, the
group adheres to Jesus' final instruction, the
last of his words Luke records in his Gospel:

"stay in the city until you are clothed with
power from on high" (Luke 24:49; see also
Acts 1:7–8). The disciples' clothing "with
power from on high" refers to the Baptism of
the Holy Spirit at Pentecost (Acts 2:1–4).

The presence of Jesus' family among
his disciples is interesting. Except for the
story of Jesus' infancy and youth, the only
time Luke mentions Jesus' mother and
brothers is an occasion when they arrive to
visit with Jesus. Indeed, in Luke's account
of Jesus' ministry in Jerusalem, there seems
to have been little room for family at all.
Thus, it may come as something of a sur-

prise to find Jesus' mother and brothers
among his core followers in Jerusalem.

Acts contains a number of summaries
describing the growth of the Church and the
customary activity of its membership.
Today's reading contains the first of these
summaries, depicting the disciples' devo-
tion to communal prayer (Acts 1:14; see also
2:42–47; 4:32–35; 5:12–16; 6:7; 9:31; 12:24;
16:5; 19:20; 28:30–31). It should not be missed
that prayer is the formative activity of the
group that will shortly become the Church.
Before public preaching, healings, missions,

If you are **insulted** for the name of **Christ**, **blessed** are you,
    for the **Spirit** of **glory** and of **God** rests upon you.
But let **no** one among you be made to **suffer**
    as a **murderer**, a **thief**, an **evildoer**, or as an **intriguer**.
But **whoever** is made to **suffer** as a **Christian**
    should **not** be ashamed
    but **glorify** God because of the **name**.

GOSPEL   John 17:1–11a

A reading from the holy Gospel according to John

Jesus raised his eyes to **heaven** and said,
"**Father**, the **hour** has **come**.
Give **glory** to your **son**, so that your **son** may glorify **you**,
    just as you gave him **authority** over **all** people,
    so that your **son** may give eternal **life** to **all** you gave him.
Now **this** is eternal life,
    that they should **know** you, the **only** true God,
    and the **one** whom you **sent**, **Jesus Christ**.
I glorified you on **earth**
    by accomplishing the **work** that you **gave** me to do.
Now glorify **me**, Father, with **you**,
    with the **glory** that I had with you **before** the world **began**.

Jesus is praying to his Father in the presence of his disciples. Proclaim these words slowly and with the dignity appropriate for public prayer.

imprisonments, and martyrdoms, there is first a community of prayer.

READING II It may come as a surprise that the word "Christian" occurs only three times in the New Testament. From Acts 11:26 we discover that it was in the Syrian city of Antioch "that the disciples were first called Christians" (see also Acts 26:28). Today's reading from 1 Peter is the third of these three occasions.

First Peter mentions "trials" (*peirasmos*; 1:6; 4:12-13) and contains additional evidence (2:20; 3:14; 4:1; 5:9) that the addressees of this letter may be undergoing some kind of harassment, if not outright persecution. We know that some Christians suffered persecution in the Roman province of Bithynia, one of the regions to which 1 Peter is addressed, in the second decade of the second century (see commentary II, Second Sunday of Easter, March 30). But attempts by scholars to link the situation assumed by 1 Peter to this or another specific instance of harassment or persecution have yielded nothing certain.

The Greek of 4:16 is admittedly a little ambiguous, but our Bible doesn't do a very good job with it. "The name" in question, while it could be "Christ" (see 4:14), is more likely "Christian." Although in Acts 5:41 the disciples rejoice "that they had been found worthy to suffer dishonor for the sake of the name," meaning "Jesus," this is not what 1 Peter 4:16 means. The Greek of this verse is better translated, "but if someone suffers as a Christian, let him not be shamed, but let him glorify God with this name." The name of "Christian," when someone suffers as one, is not a source of shame as when someone condemned as a "murderer," "thief," "evildoer," or "intriguer" suffers (4:15). On

"I **revealed** your name to those whom you gave me
   out of the world.
They **belonged** to you, and you **gave** them to me,
   and **they** have **kept** your **word**.
Now they know that **everything** you gave me is from you,
   because the **words** you gave to me I have **given** to them,
   and they **accepted** them and **truly** understood
      that I **came** from you,
   and **they** have **believed** that **you** sent me.
I **pray** for them.
I do **not** pray for the **world** but for the **ones** you have **given** me,
   because **they** are **yours**, and **everything** of **mine** is **yours**
   and **everything** of yours is **mine**,
      and I have been **glorified** in **them**.
And now I will **no longer** be in the **world**,
   but **they** are in the **world**, while I am **coming** to you."

the contrary, bearing the name of "Christian" is a means by which the righteous sufferer glorifies God.

| GOSPEL | The word "glory" has several meanings. In the Old Testament, sometimes God's "glory" refers to fame, honor, esteem, or reputation God wins through mighty acts of power (see, for example, Exodus 14:17–18). But sometimes "the glory of the Lord" signifies a kind of shining, visible presence of God. We read in Exodus 24:17 that when God's glory settled on Mount Sinai, "to the Israelites the glory of the LORD was seen as a consuming fire on the mountaintop."

The completed work the Father sent Jesus to do, and by which Jesus glorifies the Father, was his call of followers and ministry of signs in John 1—11. The signs, whose purpose is to lead to belief (20:30–31), are routinely called "works" (see 10:37–38).

Another of the things Jesus' glorification means in John's Gospel is his Crucifixion and Resurrection. This is especially the case in John 12, which is important for understanding today's reading. In 12:16, Jesus' glorification appears to be clearly identified with Jesus' Crucifixion and Resurrection (see also 7:39). Verse 23 refers to "the hour" of Jesus' glorification, much as we read in today's reading: "Father, the hour has come. Give glory to your son, so that your son may glorify you" (17:1). The way Jesus will glorify God is by laying down his life and taking it up again (see John 10:18). The cross will be the means by which he is "lifted up" in both a literal, physical sense, and in the figurative sense of being gloriously exalted (12:32–33).

PENTECOST: VIGIL

Lectionary #62

READING I   Genesis 11:1–9

A reading from the Book of Genesis

The **whole world** spoke the **same** language, using the
  same words.
While the people were migrating in the **east**,
  they came upon a **valley** in the land of **Shinar** and **settled** there.
They said to one another,
  "**Come**, let us mold **bricks** and harden them with **fire**."
They used **bricks** for **stone**, and **bitumen** for **mortar**.
Then they said, "**Come**, let us **build** ourselves a **city**
  and a **tower** with its **top** in the **sky**,
  and so make a **name** for ourselves;
  otherwise we shall be **scattered** all over the earth."

The **LORD** came down to see the **city** and the **tower**
  that the people had **built**.
Then the LORD said: "If **now**, while they are **one** people,
  all speaking the **same** language,
  they have started to do this,
  nothing will later stop them from doing
    whatever they **presume** to do.
Let us then go **down** there and **confuse** their language,
  so that **one** will not **understand** what **another** says."
Thus the LORD **scattered** them from there all over the earth,
  and they **stopped** building the city.

Shinar = Shi-NAR

Proclaim humanity's words in an eager and enthusiastic tone.
bitumen = bih-TOO-mun

Really emphasize the word "nothing" in this verse. The emphasis will spotlight God's dread of what a united humanity might have achieved.

There is a choice of first readings today. Speak with the liturgy coordinator or homilist to find out which one will be used.

READING I   **GENESIS.** In today's reading, God confuses humanity's speech in order to block the effects of its skill and ingenuity. Why? Are not human beings parts of the "very good" creation? Have they not been appointed stewards of the world God has made? Why frustrate their collective talent?

Consider God's shocked question to Eve after she and Adam have earned expulsion from paradise ("Why did you do such a thing?") and God's anguished question to Cain after his murder of Abel ("What have you done! Listen: your brother's blood cries out to me from the soil!"). It seems that the appointed stewards of creation are not working out as originally intended. From the incident in the garden with the serpent and the fruit of the tree of good and evil, to the first murder, to the worldwide wickedness

that leads God to regret creating human beings (Genesis 6:5–7), the human record is a poor one. It is no surprise, therefore, if one detects worry, or even fear, as God contemplates what humans may do if they pool their skills: "If now, while they are one people, all speaking the same language, they have started to do this, nothing will later stop them from doing whatever they presume to do" (Genesis 11:6).

Some readers of this passage may be confused when God says, "Let us then go down and there confuse their language"

Babel = BA-bel

That is why it was called **Babel**,
     because there the **LORD** confused the speech of **all** the world.
It was from **that** place that he **scattered** them all over the **earth**.

Or:

READING I   Exodus 19:3–8a, 16–20b

A reading from the Book of Exodus

Moses went up the **mountain** to **God**.
Then the **LORD** called to him and said,
"Thus shall you say to the **house** of **Jacob**;
     tell the **Israelites**:
     You have seen for yourselves how I treated the **Egyptians**
     and how I bore you up on **eagle** wings
     and brought you here to **myself**.
Therefore, if you hearken to my **voice** and keep my **covenant**,
     you shall be my **special possession**,
     dearer to me than all other people,
     though all the **earth** is **mine**.
You shall be to me a **kingdom** of **priests**, a **holy nation**.
That is what you must tell the Israelites."
So **Moses** went and summoned the **elders** of the people.
When he set before them
     all that the LORD had **ordered** him to **tell** them,
     the people all answered **together**,
"**Everything** the LORD has said, we will **do**."

Read God's words slowly in a strong, bold tone of voice.

Emphasize the word "if" in this verse. This is important, for Israel's election depends on whether or not it keeps the terms of the covenant agreement.

Pause here at the end of God's speech.

Emphasize the word "Everything" in this verse. Make eye contact with the assembly as you proclaim, slowly and with emphasis on each word, "we will do!"

(Genesis 11:7). Who beside God is included in this "us"? As did many other peoples in the ancient near east, ancient Israelites often conceived of God as a king surrounded by a heavenly court of angels and divine beings. God likely directs the plural address of 11:7 to members of this heavenly court. For a clearer view of this religious conception, see 1 Kings 22:19–22.

EXODUS. "Everything the LORD has said, we will do" (see also Joshua 24). This is a big promise, particularly because God has not yet explained with precision Israel's end

of the covenant. And yet Israel is not simply stepping out on faith alone, for Israel, by this point in Exodus, has some experience with God. The one to whom Israel makes this promise has already rescued it from Egypt in spectacular fashion.

The covenant cut between God and Israel at Sinai is a covenant primarily of law (on covenants, see commentary V, Easter Vigil, March 22). God's selection of Israel as "my special possession, dearer to me than all other people" is not a free gift with any strings attached. The condition of God's selection is that Israel must "hearken

to my voice and keep my covenant" (Exodus 19:5). Israel's willing observance of the particular rules and customs found in the law confirms the nation's unique theological identity (this law takes up much of the remainder of Exodus, Leviticus, Numbers, and Deuteronomy). Subsequent biblical writers, such as the composers and editors of Deuteronomy, Joshua, Judges, 1 and 2 Samuel, and 1 and 2 Kings, will interpret the future success and failure of Israel largely in terms of the degree to which its people remain faithful to the covenant.

On the **morning** of the third day
   there were peals of **thunder** and **lightning**,
   and a **heavy cloud** over the **mountain**,
   and a very loud **trumpet** blast,
   so that **all** the people in the camp **trembled**.
But **Moses** led the people out of the **camp** to meet **God**,
   and they **stationed** themselves at the **foot** of the mountain.
Mount Sinai was all wrapped in **smoke**,
   for the LORD came down upon it in **fire**.
The smoke **rose** from it as though from a **furnace**,
   and the whole mountain trembled **violently**.
The trumpet blast grew **louder** and **louder**,
    while **Moses** was **speaking**,
   and **God** answering him with **thunder**.

When the LORD came **down** to the **top** of Mount Sinai,
   he summoned **Moses** to the **top** of the **mountain**.

Or:

Sinai = SYE-nye

Pause, then look up at the assembly as you proclaim the final words of the reading.

READING I   Ezekiel 37:1–14

A reading from the Book of the Prophet Ezekiel

The **hand** of the LORD came **upon** me,
   and he **led** me **out** in the **spirit** of the LORD
   and set me in the **center** of the **plain**,
   which was now filled with **bones**.
He made me **walk** among the bones in every direction
   so that I saw **how many** they were on the **surface** of the **plain**.

Ancient Jews and Christians studied with great interest the biblical account of Moses' ascent up Mount Sinai to receive the law. A century or so before the birth of Christ, a Jewish playwright composed a play containing a scene where Moses tells of a dream in which God handed him a crown and scepter and vacated the divine throne for him. Later Christian writers, probably encouraged by the earlier work of a Jewish scholar, Philo of Alexandria, interpreted Moses' ascent up the mountain to be a type or example of the soul's ascent to God.

EZEKIEL. Ezekiel's vision of the valley of dry bones symbolizes the situation of Israel in exile. "Our bones are dried up, our hope is lost, and we are cut off" expresses the captives' sentiments in light of their city's destruction, the many thousands of injuries and deaths, the hard fact of captivity itself, and God's seeming refusal or perhaps, still worse, inability to bring any relief. But the bones' despair, like that of the exiles, will not last forever. By the words of the prophet, God gives the bones sinew and

breath, which prefigures the restoration of the kingdom of Judah and the service of the temple under God's protection and care.

Today's reading was an early proof-text Christians used in support of the doctrine of the Resurrection of the dead. In Acts, Paul's mention of the Resurrection leads some among his non-Christian audience to scoff at him. But Christians differed among themselves about the Resurrection, as 1 Corinthians 15 makes plain (see especially 1 Corinthians 15:12–19). Irenaeus of Lyon, who lived during the second century, quotes

Look up and emphasize the bones' dryness in this verse. Pause briefly before and after this line.

Prophesy = PROF-uh-sī

sinews = SIN-yooz

prophesied = PROF-uh-sīd
prophesying = PROF-uh-sī-ing

Emphasize the word "prophesy" in this verse.

How **dry** they were!
He asked me:
    Son of **man**, can these **bones** come to **life**?
I answered, "Lord GOD, you **alone** know that."
Then he said to me:
    Prophesy over these bones, and say to them:
    Dry bones, **hear** the **word** of the LORD!
Thus says the **Lord GOD** to these **bones**:
    See! I will bring **spirit** into you, that you may come to **life**.
I will put **sinews** upon you, make **flesh** grow over you,
    cover you with **skin**, and put **spirit** in you
        so that you may **come** to **life** and **know** that I am the LORD.
I, Ezekiel, prophesied as I had been **told**,
    and even as I was **prophesying** I heard a **noise**;
    it was a **rattling** as the **bones** came **together**, **bone** joining **bone**.
I saw the **sinews** and the **flesh** come upon them,
    and the **skin** cover them, but there was no **spirit** in them.
Then the LORD said to me:
    Prophesy to the spirit, **prophesy**, son of man,
    and **say** to the **spirit**: Thus says the Lord GOD:
    From the four winds come, **O spirit**,
    and **breathe** into these **slain** that they may come to **life**.
I **prophesied** as he **told** me, and the **spirit** came into them;
    they came **alive** and stood **upright**, a vast army.
Then he said to me:
    Son of **man**, these **bones** are the whole house of **Israel**.
They have been **saying**,
    "Our **bones** are **dried** up,
    our **hope** is **lost**, and we are **cut off**."

today's reading to demonstrate that the God who created human beings will also raise them after death (*Against Heresies*, 15.1).

In Hebrew, *ruah* is the word for "wind," "breath," and "spirit." The multiple meanings of this word sometimes pose a problem for Bible translators. In Genesis 1:2, for example, the "wind" on the waters might just as easily be translated as "spirit." In Ezekiel 37:9, "breath," "winds," and "spirit" are all translations of *ruah* in its various forms.

JOEL. The theme of this reading, and indeed the major theme of the book of the prophet Joel, is the "Day of the Lord, the great and terrible day." In ancient Israel and Judah, the Day of the Lord (Joel 3:4) was conceived as a time of suffering, when Israel, Judah, or another people would come under God's judgment for its sins and transgressions. It seems that invading armies were the chief means by which God was believed to exercise judgment. The prophet Amos

offers one of the earliest biblical expressions of this notion from the eighth century BC. Like Joel, Amos imagines the Day of the Lord as great turmoil (5:18): "Woe to those who yearn for the day of the LORD! What will this day of the LORD mean for you? Darkness and not light!"

Today's reading became very important to some strains of Judaism and early Christianity. Among Christians, understandings of the Day of the Lord underwent profound changes: no longer was the Day of the

Slow down to emphasize these verses, using a bold tone of voice.

Therefore, **prophesy** and say to them: **Thus** says the **Lord GOD**:
    O my **people**, I will **open** your **graves**
    and have you **rise** from them,
    and **bring** you **back** to the **land** of **Israel**.
Then you shall **know** that I am the LORD,
    when I **open** your **graves** and have you **rise** from them,
    O my **people**!
I will put my **spirit** in you that you may **live**,
    and I will **settle** you upon your **land**;
    thus **you** shall **know** that I am the LORD.
I have **promised**, and I will **do** it, says the LORD.

Or:

READING I   Joel 3:1–5

Proclaim this reading slowly, and in a strong tone of voice.

prophesy = PROF-uh-sī

A reading from the Book of the Prophet Joel

Thus says the LORD:
I will pour out my **spirit** upon all **flesh**.
Your **sons** and **daughters** shall **prophesy**,
    your **old men** shall **dream dreams**,
    your **young men** shall **see visions**;
even upon the **servants** and the **handmaids**,
    in those days, I will pour out my **spirit**.
And I will work **wonders** in the **heavens** and on the **earth**,
    blood, **fire**, and columns of **smoke**;
the **sun** will be turned to **darkness**,
    and the **moon** to **blood**,

Lord simply a day of pain and suffering at the hands of foreign invaders, but a day of worldwide supernatural upheaval when Christ, the Son of Man, would return in glory. In Acts 2:17–21, which records the first public proclamation of the Gospel by the Church, today's reading is the first piece of scripture quoted. The apostle Peter, the preacher, proclaims Joel's words to an international audience in Jerusalem (see Acts 2:5, 9–11), explaining to them that the apparently

strange behavior of the disciples is not evidence of drunkenness, but rather of the nearness of the Day of the Lord.

READING II   At some points in these verses Paul's meaning is somewhat obscure. What are we to make, for example, of a "groaning" creation? And how does creation's groaning relate to the interior groaning of believers awaiting "the redemption of our bodies" (Romans 8:22–23)?

Paul has earlier spoken of the redemption "in Christ Jesus," meaning that Christ's death on the cross is the means by which people are released from the authority of sin. Later, Paul will pair death with sin as powers to which people are subject absent God's freely given redemption (Romans 5:12–14). But in Romans 8 we learn that redemption is not just a human affair, but something won for all of creation. It is plain from Romans 8:19 that human beings have a central role to

Pause briefly here. Emphasize especially
the word "everyone" in this verse.
Zion = ZI-yon

at the **coming** of the **day** of the LORD,
 the **great** and **terrible** day.
Then **everyone** shall be rescued
 who calls on the name of the LORD;
for on **Mount Zion** there shall be a **remnant**,
 as the LORD has said,
and in **Jerusalem** survivors
 whom the LORD shall **call**.

READING II Romans 8:22–27

A reading from the Letter of Saint Paul to the Romans

Brothers and **sisters**:
We know that **all** creation is **groaning** in labor pains
 even until now;
 and not only that, but **we ourselves**,
 who have the **firstfruits** of the **Spirit**,
 we **also** groan within ourselves
 as we wait for **adoption**, the **redemption** of our **bodies**.
For in **hope** we were **saved**.
Now **hope** that sees is **not** hope.
For **who hopes** for what **one sees**?
But if we **hope** for what we do **not** see, we wait with **endurance**.

In the **same** way, the **Spirit** too comes to the **aid** of our **weakness**;
 for we do **not** know how to **pray** as we **ought**,
 but the **Spirit himself** intercedes with inexpressible **groanings**.

**Make eye contact with the assembly as
you proclaim this verse.**

**Look up at the assembly as you ask this
question. Make sure to raise the pitch of
your voice at the end of the sentence to
indicate that it is a question.**

---

play in this drama of redemption ("For creation awaits with eager expectation the revelation of the children of God"), and we learn that "the sufferings of this present time" (8:18), "futility" (8:20), and "slavery to corruption" (8:21) affect the whole of creation.

 Whatever Paul's specific meaning, it is clear that creation's relief, the time of "glory" (8:21), has not yet arrived. In this intervening period between the cross and the glory to come, the era of the Church, Christians have received the gift of the Spirit. Paul here mentions two main roles of the Spirit: teacher

and intercessor. The Spirit, therefore, not only brings Christians' petitions before God, but first shows Christians how to pray rightly. Christian prayer, as Paul states the case here, does not function without the aid and guidance of the Spirit.

GOSPEL In John's Gospel, Jesus' "glorification" is closely related to his Crucifixion and Resurrection. We see this especially in John 12:20–36, where Jesus speaks in a cryptic and veiled way about the death to follow his completed

ministry: "The hour has come for the Son of Man to be glorified" (12:23). If we are used to thinking of Jesus' Crucifixion as a glorious event, we may miss how jarring is John's concept of glorification: the means to Jesus' glorification involves a form of death that is intentionally humiliating and degrading. Where is the glory here? Aren't the hard wood and nails of the cross glory's utter opposites?

 Had Jesus' cross been the end of him, there would be no glory to speak of. But the cross is not the end. Like the miraculous

And the one who **searches hearts**
  knows what is the **intention** of the **Spirit**,
because he intercedes for the **holy** ones
  according to God's will.

GOSPEL   John 7:37–39

A reading from the holy Gospel according to John

On the **last** and **greatest** day of the **feast**,
  Jesus stood up and exclaimed,
  "Let **anyone** who thirsts **come** to **me** and **drink**.
As Scripture says:
  *Rivers of living water will **flow** from within him*
    *who **believes** in me.*"

He said this in reference to the **Spirit**
  that those who came to **believe** in him were to receive.
There **was**, of course, **no** Spirit **yet**,
  because Jesus had **not yet** been **glorified**.

Jesus is making a public proclamation in the crowded temple precincts. Do not yell, but proclaim his words in a very bold and strong tone of voice.

Pause between Jesus' words and the words of the narrator. When you proclaim the narrator's words, look up at the assembly and use a milder, softer tone of voice than the one you use to proclaim Jesus' speech.

signs he performs (2:11; 11:4, 40), Christ's Resurrection reveals his glory and the glory of the Father. John's language of glory aims not so much *at* as *through* the cross to the new life beyond.

In today's reading, we find in the narrator's aside a useful explanation of Jesus' declaration in the Jerusalem temple on the last day of the Festival of Tabernacles, also called Sukkoth (see 7:2, 10, 14). John interprets Jesus' words in today's reading as testimony to a Spirit not yet present in the

world, a Spirit that will only come after Jesus has died and risen. And this is exactly the sequence John offers. In John 20:19–23, the risen Christ appears to his disciples, commissions them, breathes on them, and says, "Receive the holy Spirit" (20:22). The cross precedes the Resurrection, and the Resurrection precedes the Spirit.

PENTECOST: DAY

Lectionary #63

READING I   Acts 2:1–11

A reading from the Acts of the Apostles

When the time for **Pentecost** was **fulfilled**,
  they were **all** in one place together.
And suddenly there came from the **sky**
  a noise like a **strong driving wind**,
  and it **filled** the **entire** house in which they were.
Then there appeared to them **tongues** as of **fire**,
  which **parted** and came to rest on **each one** of them.
And they were **all filled** with the **Holy Spirit**
  and began to **speak** in different tongues,
  as the Spirit **enabled** them to proclaim.

Now there were **devout Jews** from **every** nation under heaven
  staying in **Jerusalem**.
At this sound, they gathered in a large crowd,
  but they were **confused**
  because **each** one heard them speaking in his **own** language.
They were **astounded**, and in **amazement** they asked,
  "Are not **all** these people who are speaking **Galileans**?
Then **how** does **each** of us hear them in his **native language**?
We are **Parthians**, **Medes**, and **Elamites**,
  inhabitants of **Mesopotamia**, **Judea** and **Cappadocia**,

---

Pentecost = PEN-teh-cost

Pause briefly before you read this verse. Then look up and stress the word "suddenly."

Pause briefly here. Our attention moves from the disciples to those outside, who, like ourselves, are looking in on them.

Read this list slowly, emphasizing each name and pausing briefly between them.

Galileans = Gah-lih-LEE-ans
Parthians = PAR-thee-ans
Medes = MEEDS
Elamites = EE-lah-mites
Mesopotamia = Meh-soh-pah-TAY-mee-ya
Judea = Ju-DEE-ah
Cappadocia = Cah-pah-DOH-see-ah

READING I According to Acts, the reception of the Holy Spirit by Jesus' disciples in Jerusalem on the feast of Pentecost marks the beginning of the Church. Wind, fire, and proclamation in many tongues are the visible signs of this new thing the Spirit is bringing into existence. This event has long been predicted. In Luke's Gospel, before Jesus has called a single disciple or even been baptized, John the Baptist prophesies that "one mightier than I is coming. I am not worthy to loosen the thongs of his sandals. He will baptize you with the holy Spirit and fire" (Luke 3:16;

see also Matthew 3:11, Mark 1:7–8; Acts 11:16). Much later, after Jesus has concluded his ministry, died, and risen, he instructs his disciples to remain in Jerusalem "until you are clothed with power from on high" (Luke 24:49). And lastly, included among Jesus' final words to his disciples in Acts, there is a promise: "But you will receive power when the holy Spirit comes upon you" (Acts 1:8).

Based on Acts 2:7, the people upon whom the Spirit comes are Galileans, men and women who followed Jesus south to Jerusalem from the rural north. The idea that such a gaggle of yokels should, together and

at the same time, burst out speaking a sizeable percentage of the world's tongues shocks the international crowd of witnesses. The great variety of languages the disciples speak is an important detail of the story. Here, Luke informs us that the Church was "catholic" (that is, universal) at its very inception. The Church was not born Galilean, Jewish, or, for that matter, Roman. It will take some time for the Church in Acts to spread any farther than Jerusalem, but Pentecost foreshadows its future international reach, just as Jesus predicts in his concluding words to his disciples: "you will

Pontus = PON-tus
Phrygia = FRIH-jee-ah
Pamphylia = Pam-FU-lee-ya
Cyrene = SYE-reen
Cretans = CREE-tans

Pontus and **Asia**, **Phrygia** and **Pamphylia**,
Egypt and the districts of **Libya** near **Cyrene**,
as well as travelers from **Rome**,
both **Jews** and **converts** to Judaism, **Cretans** and **Arabs**,
yet we hear them speaking in our **own** tongues
of the **mighty** acts of **God**."

READING II   1 Corinthians 12:3b–7, 12–13

A reading from the first Letter of Saint Paul to the Corinthians

Brothers and sisters:
No one can say, "**Jesus** is **Lord**," except by the **Holy Spirit**.

There are **different** kinds of **spiritual gifts** but the **same** Spirit;
    there are **different** forms of **service** but the **same** Lord;
    there are **different** workings but the **same** God
    who produces **all** of them in **everyone**.
To **each** individual the manifestation of the Spirit
    is given for some benefit.

As a **body** is **one** though it has **many** parts,
    and **all** the parts of the body, though **many**, are **one body**,
    so also **Christ**.
For in **one Spirit** we were **all** baptized into **one body**,
    whether **Jews** or **Greeks**, **slaves** or **free persons**,
    and we were **all** given to drink of **one** Spirit.

Pause briefly between Paul's expressions of difference and sameness.

Look up at the assembly and proclaim clearly and slowly, emphasizing each word of the phrase "so also Christ."

Emphasize each occurrence of the word "one." It will help you drive home Paul's support and encouragement of unity in the Church.

---

be my witnesses in Jerusalem, throughout Judea and Samaria, and to the ends of the earth" (Acts 1:8).

READING II   Paul states the general problem of the Church at Corinth in the first chapter of the letter. "For it has been reported to me about you . . . that there are rivalries among you. I mean that each of you is saying, 'I belong to Paul,' or 'I belong to Apollos,' or 'I belong to Kephas,' or 'I belong to Christ.' Is Christ divided? Was Paul crucified for you? Or were you baptized in the name of Paul?" The answer Paul expects

to these questions is "no." And yet the Corinthians, in Paul's view, have been acting as though Christ is divided. Much of 1 Corinthians, including today's reading, is Paul's prescription for the healing of the Church body.

A body is not a body, says Paul, unless basic unity underlies its diversity. The different kinds of "spiritual gifts," "service," and "workings" respectively depend on "the same Spirit," "the same Lord," and "the same God" (1 Corinthians 12:4–6). The body of Christ has many members, but without

membership in a single whole these members cease to exist.

Paul's conception of the Church as a body has deep roots in Greek political thought. It was common for a Greek orator to compare a city to a body when exhorting its citizens to pursue some common aim. What sets Paul's use of this traditional comparison apart from non-Christian predecessors is the source of the Church's unity. Like a city, the Church has its variety supplied by its members. But unlike a city, the Church finds the source of its unity in a God whose very nature is also unity.

GOSPEL John 20:19–23

A reading from the holy Gospel according to John

On the **evening** of that first day of the week,
  when the doors were **locked**, where the disciples were,
  for **fear** of the **Jews**,
    Jesus came and stood in their midst
    and said to them, "**Peace** be with **you**."
When he had said this, he showed them his **hands** and his **side**.
The disciples **rejoiced** when they saw the Lord.
Jesus said to them again, "**Peace** be with **you**.
As the **Father** has sent **me**, so **I** send **you**."
And when he had said this, he **breathed** on them
    and said to them,
  "**Receive** the **Holy Spirit**.
Whose sins you **forgive** are **forgiven** them,
and whose sins you **retain** are **retained**."

Emphasize both occurrences of the word "Peace," making eye contact with the assembly as you do so.

GOSPEL In John 20:19, the evangelist makes clear that Jesus appears to his disciples and gives to them the Holy Spirit on the evening of Easter. Yet in today's first reading, it is the feast of Pentecost, 50 days after Easter, that is the occasion for the gift of the Holy Spirit. While this discrepancy has troubled some biblical interpreters, it need not trouble us, for John stands apart from the other three evangelists in many respects, including chronology. While the other three evangelists record that Jesus came once to Jerusalem during his ministry, John records that Jesus made multiple visits (John 2:13; 5:1; 7:10; 12:12–19). While the other three evangelists record that Jesus was killed on Passover, John records that he was killed the day before Passover (John 19:14, 31, 42).

What both this Gospel selection and today's first reading share is the disciples' reception of the Spirit in Jerusalem and their commissioning or commencement of their mission to the world. In Acts, the gift of the Spirit immediately precedes the first public proclamation of Jesus Christ to the world by the Church (Acts 2:14–41); in John, Jesus commissions the disciples before giving the Holy Spirit to them (John 20:21–22).

The specific commission of the disciples in John 20:21 ("As the Father has sent me, so I send you") recalls Jesus' final prayer before his Passion: "As you sent me into the world, so I sent them into the world" (John 17:18). Although the reunion of Jesus with his disciples is joyous, the task he gives them is perilous. This peril is particularly clear in the case of Peter, whose pastoral commission in John 21:15–19 also alludes to his martyrdom.

MOST HOLY TRINITY

Lectionary #164

READING I   Exodus 34:4b–6, 8–9

Sinai = SYE-nye

Emphasize God's repeated declarations of "the Lord."

Moses intercedes for Israel after the unfortunate episode with the golden calf in Exodus 32. Proclaim his words in a calm, respectful tone of voice, the tone of someone asking an important favor of a superior.

A reading from the Book of Exodus

Early in the morning **Moses** went up **Mount Sinai**
    as the **LORD** had commanded him,
    taking along the two stone tablets.

Having come down in a cloud, the **LORD** stood with **Moses** there
    and proclaimed his name, "**LORD**."
Thus the **LORD** passed before him and cried out,
    "**The LORD, the LORD**, a **merciful** and **gracious** God,
    slow to **anger** and **rich** in **kindness** and **fidelity**."
Moses at once **bowed down** to the ground in **worship**.
Then he said, "If I find **favor** with you, **O Lord**,
    do come along in our **company**.
This is **indeed** a stiff-necked people;
    yet **pardon** our **wickedness** and sins,
    and **receive** us as your own."

READING I In today's reading, Moses makes a second attempt at mediating a covenant between God and Israel. An earlier attempt did not work out so well. While Moses was up on Sinai, his brother Aaron fashioned an idol, a golden calf, at the request of the Israelites: "Come, make us a god who will be our leader; as for the man Moses who brought us out of the land of Egypt, we do not know what has happened to him" (Exodus 32:1). When Moses returns to camp from the heights and sees what has happened in his absence, he angrily smashes the tablets of the covenant

before swiftly punishing the people for their wrongdoing (Exodus 32:15–28).

Despite God's rage at the people's behavior, Aaron's complicity in it, and Moses' destruction of "tablets that were made by God, having inscriptions on them that were engraved by God himself," God does not give up on Israel and its designated leaders. Neither does Moses quit his thankless task of mediating God's instructions to the people. Moses continues to intercede for the people in today's reading, even as God continues to seek them, instructing Moses to make another two tablets, ascend

the mountain again, and receive new terms of covenantal agreement (34:1–3, 10).

"The Lord" in Hebrew is God's name, Yahweh (34:5–6). At a very early time in their history, Israelites decided God's name was too holy to pronounce. Today many Jews pronounce *Adonai* ("Lord") in place of *Yahweh* when speaking or reading Hebrew. God's emphatic repetition of this personal name before Moses, Israel's mediator, as Moses bows in supplication, highlights that God's authority over Israel occurs within the context of an intensely personal relationship.

A reading from second Letter of Saint Paul to the Corinthians

Brothers and **sisters**, **rejoice**.
 Mend your ways, **encourage** one another,
 agree with one another, **live** in peace,
 and the **God** of **love** and peace will be with **you**.
Greet one another with a **holy kiss**.
All the holy ones **greet** you.

The **grace** of the **Lord Jesus Christ**
 and the **love** of **God**
 and the **fellowship** of the **Holy Spirit** be with **all** of you.

Pause briefly between each of Paul's instructions.

READING II Second Corinthians is most likely a combination of several letters, or pieces of letters, composed by Paul for the Church at Corinth. Paul's relationship with this Church was often rocky. The command, "mend your ways" is one of Paul's closing instructions to this Church at the rockiest period of this relationship for which we have direct literary evidence.

Second Corinthians 10:1—13:13 is one of several letters the early Church combined into what we today call 2 Corinthians; 10:1—13:13 responds to what Paul considers to be a very serious challenge to himself and

his apostolate. Someone at Corinth has accused Paul of inconsistency: while he writes quite powerful letters, this critic has observed, Paul makes a weak personal impression (2 Corinthians 10:10). Moreover, questions about Paul have intensified with the arrival of new people at Corinth. Like Paul, they are Jewish. Like Paul, they call themselves "ministers" *(diakonoi)* and "apostles" *(apostoloi)* (2 Corinthians 11:22–23; 11:5, 13, 12:11). If Paul's treatment of these people is somewhat angry and sarcastic, keep in mind that there was plenty of blame to go around.

Never conceding his inferiority to these newcomers, Paul argues that his perceived deficits are actually assets. Paul argues that his weakness, for example, actually confirms his apostolate, for his weakness makes him like Christ (2 Corinthians 12:1–13). The Corinthians, Paul argues, ought never to have joined the newcomers in their criticism; instead, they should have commended him to them (2 Corinthians 12:11). To mend their ways, the Corinthians should confess their wrongs and acknowledge that Paul, who evangelized them in the first place, is indeed a valid apostle.

A reading from the holy Gospel according to John

God **so** loved the world that he gave his **only Son**,
    so that **everyone** who **believes** in him might **not** perish
    but might have **eternal life**.
For God did **not** send his Son into the world
        to **condemn** the world,
    but that the world might be **saved** through him.
Whoever believes in him will **not** be condemned,
    but whoever does **not** believe has **already** been condemned,
    because he has **not** believed in the **name** of the **only**
        Son of God.

Emphasize the word "everyone" in this line.

Emphasize the word "not."

GOSPEL   One of the features setting Christianity apart from many of the religions of the ancient world is the emphasis its adherents placed upon "belief." Worshippers of the Greek god Apollo, for example, did not need to "believe" that Apollo was the son of Zeus and could cure diseases in order to worship in one of the temples dedicated to him. In contrast, earliest Christian evangelization challenged the world to believe in a seemingly incredible story: "Christ died for our sins in accordance with the scriptures; that he was buried; that

he was raised on the third day in accordance with the scriptures" (1 Corinthians 15:3–4).

In John's Gospel, belief in Jesus usually means believing that what Jesus says *about himself* is true. And chief among the things Jesus says about himself is that his Father sent him into the world. "This is the work of God," Jesus informs 5,000 people whom he has just miraculously fed, "that you believe in the one he sent" (John 6:29). Twice Jesus prays to his Father that groups of people "may believe that you sent me" ("the crowd" in 11:42 and "the world" in 17:21). In today's reading, we read what are

the stakes of belief and disbelief in Jesus as John sees them: "Whoever believes in him will not be condemned, but whoever does not believe has already been condemned" (John 3:18). John offers no compromise on this standard here or anywhere else in his Gospel. But today's reading also attests to God's great love for the world, the greatest proof of which is the Father's sending of Jesus Christ.

MOST HOLY BODY AND BLOOD OF CHRIST

Lectionary #167

READING I	Deuteronomy 8:2–3, 14b–16a

A reading from the Book of Deuteronomy

Moses said to the **people**:
"Remember how for forty years now the LORD, your GOD,
  has directed **all** your journeying in the desert,
  so as to **test** you by **affliction**
  and find out whether or not it was your **intention**
  to keep his **commandments**.
He therefore let you be **afflicted** with hunger,
  and then **fed** you with **manna**,
  a food **unknown** to you and your **fathers**,
  in order to **show** you that not by bread alone does one **live**,
  but by **every word** that comes forth
    from the **mouth** of the LORD.

"Do **not** forget the LORD, your God,
  who **brought** you out of the **land** of **Egypt**,
  that place of **slavery**;
  who guided you through the **vast** and **terrible** desert
  with its **saraph serpents** and **scorpions**,
  its **parched** and **waterless** ground;
  who brought forth **water** for you from the **flinty rock**
  and **fed** you in the **desert** with **manna**,
  a food **unknown** to your fathers."

Emphasize the word "you," making eye contact with the assembly two or three times as you proclaim it.

saraph = sah-RAPH

manna = MAH-nah

READING I In Exodus 16, manna from heaven is God's answer to the complaints of the hungry Israelites. In today's reading, we learn God intended the manna's relief of Israel's hunger to educate its people "that not by bread alone does man live, but by every word that comes forth from the mouth of the LORD" (Deuteronomy 8:3). In the book of Wisdom (16:26), the author similarly claims that the miraculous food taught Israel "that it is not the various kinds of fruits that nourish man, but it is your [God's] word that preserves those who believe you!"

In the accounts of Jesus' temptation in Matthew 4:1–11 and Luke 4:1-13, Deuteronomy 8:3 figures quite prominently. Corresponding to Israel's 40 years in the wilderness are Jesus' 40 days in the desert. Corresponding to Israel's testing in the desert is Jesus' testing *(peirazō)* by the devil, which is often called his temptation. To the devil's command that he turn rock into bread, Jesus replies, "It is written: 'One does not live by bread alone, but by every word that comes forth from the mouth of God' " (Matthew 4:4; see Luke 4:4). Unlike Israel in the course of its desert wandering, Jesus does not require God's forgiveness. He easily passes his test.

If Israel's fidelity to God through 40 years of desert hardship was a test, what grade might Israel have deserved? There was the idolatrous incident of the golden calf (Exodus 32), the rebellion of Korah (Numbers 16), and a great deal of complaining along the way (Exodus 14:11; 15:24; 16:2; 17:3; Numbers 11:1; 12:1–2; 14:2; 17:6; 21:5). Whatever grade Israel might have *deserved,* what it *received* was the tough but steadfast love of God.

READING II   1 Corinthians 10:16–17

A reading from the first Letter of Saint Paul to the Corinthians

Brothers and **sisters**:
The cup of **blessing** that we **bless**,
   is it **not** a participation in the **blood** of **Christ**?
The **bread** that we **break**,
   is it **not** a participation in the **body** of **Christ**?
Because the loaf of bread is **one**,
   we, though **many**, are **one body**,
   for we **all** partake of the **one loaf**.

Make sure to clearly raise the pitch of your voice at the end of both of these questions. Pause between the clause prior to each question and the question itself, then look up at the assembly as you the question.

GOSPEL   John 6:51–58

A reading from the holy Gospel according to John

Jesus said to the **Jewish crowds**:
   "I am the **living bread** that came down from **heaven**;
   whoever eats this **bread** will live **forever**;
   and the **bread** that I will **give**
   is my **flesh** for the **life** of the **world**."
The Jews **quarreled** among themselves, saying,
   "**How** can **this man** give us his **flesh** to eat?"
Jesus said to them,
   "**Amen**, **amen**, I say to you,
   unless you eat the **flesh** of the **Son** of **Man** and **drink** his **blood**,
   you do **not** have life within you.

Jesus is explaining the Eucharist to a group that does not as yet understand him. Proclaim his words slowly, in a clear, calm tone of voice.

Raise the pitch of your voice to indicate this question.

Slow down and emphasize this line, looking up and making eye contact with the assembly as you do so.

READING II This reading provides a very brief glimpse into one of the more fascinating pieces of moral and ethical reasoning in the New Testament. The basic issue of these chapters is whether it is right or wrong to eat meat previously offered in sacrifice to idols. The issue was an important one for Christians in antiquity, because a large percentage of the meat on sale at any point in time in an urban meat "market" (1 Corinthians 10:25) came from pagan sacrifices. Could Christians eat such food?

Paul openly confronts this issue in 1 Corinthians 8:1–13 and returns to it in 10:25–29. In between he provides examples, both personal (9:1–27) and scriptural (10:1–11), showing how important it is to restrain one's freedom when the good of others is at stake. Because he agrees "there is no idol in the world" and "there is no God but one," Paul concludes that Christians are indeed free to eat food offered to idols (1 Corinthians 8:4).

Whether Christians *should* eat meat offered to idols, however, is a question separate from whether they *may*. Paul realizes that some Corinthians still associate eating meat with the pagan religious festivals and rites for which the meat was sacrificed in the first place (1 Corinthians 8:7). If some Christians at Corinth, for whom eating meat sacrificed to idols has no pagan association, are harming the consciences of those for whom such meat has pagan associations, then no Corinthian Christian should eat such meat. Period. The unity of the community demands it.

The unity of the Church at Corinth, as Paul points out repeatedly in this letter, is founded upon God's own unity (1 Corinthians 1:10–13; 8:4, 6; 10:17; 12:4–31; 15:20–28). This

Whoever **eats** my **flesh** and **drinks** my **blood**
  has eternal life,
  and I will **raise** him on the last day.
For my **flesh** is **true food**,
  and my **blood** is **true drink**.
Whoever **eats** my **flesh** and **drinks** my **blood**
  remains in **me** and I in **him**.
Just as the living Father **sent** me
  and I have **life** because of the Father,
  so also the one who **feeds** on me
  will have life **because** of me.
This is the bread that came down from **heaven**.
Unlike your ancestors who **ate** and **still died**,
  whoever eats this bread will live **forever**."

is so in matters both small and large. The Church encounters its own unity and the unity of God, as we read today, in the sacrament of the Eucharist: "the loaf of bread is one, we, though many, are one body, for we all partake of the one loaf" (1 Corinthians 10:17).

GOSPEL All four evangelists include an account of Jesus miraculously feeding 5,000 people, the only one of Jesus' Galilean miracles to be found in all four Gospels (Matthew 14:15–21; Mark 6:35–44; Luke 9:12–17; John 6:1–13). Both Matthew and Mark record an additional

feeding of 4,000 (Matthew 15:32–38; Mark 8:1–9). According to Matthew, these feedings educate the disciples about the importance of keeping away from the teachings of the Pharisees (Matthew 16:5–12). According to Mark, the disciples' reaction to the feedings demonstrates only their continued ignorance of Jesus' greatness (Mark 8:14–21).

John stands somewhat apart from the other three Gospels. For example, the feeding of the 5,000 in John, along with Jesus' cryptic description of himself as "the bread of life," commences an argument between Jesus and Jews (John 6:35, 48). The Jews'

irritation and confusion is clear from today's reading (6:52; see also 6:41–42). The majority of his disciples, upon hearing Jesus describe himself as the bread of life and compare himself to the manna from heaven consumed by the Israelites during the Exodus, decide to take their leave of him (John 6:60, 66): "This saying is hard," they say, "who can accept it?" We find only Jesus' core followers still with him in 6:67.

9TH SUNDAY IN ORDINARY TIME

Lectionary #85

READING I   Deuteronomy 11:18, 26–28, 32

A reading from the Book of Deuteronomy

Moses told the **people**,
"Take these words of mine into your **heart** and **soul**.
Bind them at your **wrist** as a **sign**,
    and let them be a **pendant** on your **forehead**.

"I set **before** you here, **this** day, a **blessing** and a **curse**:
    a **blessing** for **obeying** the **commandments** of the L ORD,
        your God,
    which I **enjoin** on you **today**;
    a **curse** if you do **not** obey the **commandments** of the L ORD,
        your God,
    but **turn aside** from the **way** I **ordain** for you **today**,
to follow **other** gods, whom you have **not** known.
Be carefeul to observe **all** the statutes and decrees
    that I set before you **today**."

Proclaim this reading in a strong, bold tone of voice.
Emphasize in particular the phrase "heart and soul."

Pause briefly after the word "blessing" and again after the word "curse."

Emphasize the word "all" in this line.

READING I   The name "Deuteronomy" comes from Greek and means "second law." Of the five books of Moses (Genesis, Exodus, Leviticus, Numbers, and Deuteronomy), Deuteronomy stands somewhat apart from the other four. The book purports to be, for the most part, words Moses spoke to Israel at the end of its 40 years in the wilderness as the people stand ready to cross the Jordan River and enter the land of Canaan. Deuteronomy's literary style and theology have a great deal in common with the historical books of Joshua, Judges, 1 and 2 Samuel, and 1 and 2 Kings. For

this reason, many biblical scholars call these latter books the "deuteronomistic history."

The second book of Kings contains an account of the discovery of a scroll in the temple during the reign of King Josiah of Judah. Many biblical scholars have associated the book of Deuteronomy with the discovery of this scroll, particularly because Josiah's subsequent program of religious reform (see 2 Kings 23) generally squares with the theological outlook of Deuteronomy. The persistent theme of this outlook, reflected in today's reading (Deuteronomy 11:26–28), is that Israel's good fortune depends both on

its worship of God and God alone, and its refusal to tolerate the worship of other gods by anyone at all within the borders of the land.

Deuteronomy 11:18 describes a kind of legal observance that goes well beyond just following rules. The commands of God are to be taken to "heart and soul," symbolized in the vivid image of the law bound to wrist and forehead. Transforming the people from the inside out, the work of observing the law has the power to make Israel into the holy nation God desires it to be.

READING II   Romans 3:21–25, 28

A reading from the Letter of Saint Paul to the Romans

Brothers and **sisters**,
Now the **righteousness** of God has been **manifested**
　　apart from the law,
　　though testified to **by** the law and the prophets,
　　the **righteousness** of **God** through **faith** in **Jesus Christ**
　　for **all** who believe.
For there is **no** distinction;
　　all have **sinned** and are **deprived** of the **glory** of **God**.
They are **justified freely** by his **grace**
　　through the **redemption** in **Christ Jesus**,
　　whom God set forth as an **expiation**,
　　through **faith**, by his **blood**.
For we consider that a person is **justified** by **faith**
　　apart from **works** of the **law**.

Not only does this reading contain more than one long and complex sentence, but it also has some pretty challenging content. Read it slowly, letting the commas mark brief pauses in your delivery.

Read this verse slowly, emphasizing each word in bold.

READING II   Paul writes his letter to the Romans in the hope that this important Church will pray and speak up for him during his coming trip to Jerusalem (which worries him), and then provide him with assistance on a mission he is planning to Spain (Romans 15:22–23). Although he knows a few Roman Christians (see Romans 16:1–15), Paul's letter to them is a letter of introduction. But it is also an elaborate first installment of what its author hopes will be a relationship of mutual spiritual benefit (Romans 1:10–15). For both of these reasons, Paul explains himself at considerable length.

The Church at Rome was probably composed of both Jews and Gentiles. As a Jew, Paul was used to seeing the world as divided into Jews and Gentiles—that is, Jews and "everyone else"—much as ancient Greeks understood the world to be divided between Greeks and barbarians (that is, Greeks and "everyone else"). But Paul is also a Jew who calls himself an "apostle to the Gentiles" (Romans 11:12; Galatians 2:8). Paul did not reject his own Jewishness, but neither did he believe, as some in the early Church did, that being, becoming, or living as a Jew was a condition of membership in the Church.

The great theme of Romans is how God has united both Jews and Gentiles in a common plan of redemption through Jesus Christ.

In today's reading, Paul says, "For we consider that a person is justified by faith apart from works of the law" (Romans 3:28). Just as sin binds both Gentiles and Jews (Romans 3:23), so also is a right relationship with God possible for both groups through Jesus Christ. Paul's point is not that Jewish law must be rejected (see Romans 3:31), only that justification by faith in Christ apart from the law offers justification to Jews and Gentiles alike. Neither is preferred. Neither

GOSPEL   Matthew 7:21–27

A reading from the holy Gospel according to Matthew

Jesus said to his disciples:
"Not everyone who says to me, '**Lord**, **Lord**,'
    will **enter** the kingdom of heaven,
    but only the one who does the **will** of my Father in heaven.
Many will say to me on that day,
    'Lord, Lord, did we not **prophesy** in your **name**?
Did we not **drive** out **demons** in your **name**?
Did we not do **mighty deeds** in your **name**?'
Then I will declare to them solemnly,
    '**I never** knew you. **Depart** from me, you evildoers.'

"**Everyone** who **listens** to these words of mine and **acts** on them
    will be like a **wise** man who built his house on **rock**.
The **rain** fell, the **floods** came,
    and the **winds** blew and buffeted the house.
But it did **not** collapse; it had been set **solidly** on rock.
And **everyone** who **listens** to these words of mine
    but does **not** act on them
    will be like a **fool** who built his house on **sand**.
The **rain** fell, the **floods** came,
    and the **winds** blew and buffeted the house.
And it **collapsed** and was **completely** ruined."

When you proclaim this verse, raise the pitch of your voice to indicate these three questions clearly.

Declare Jesus' rebuke in this verse with a strong tone of voice.
Emphasize the word "Everyone" in this line.

Pause before and after the phrase "But it did not collapse," looking up as you proclaim it and stressing the word "not."

---

is excluded. Romans 3:29 makes this clear: "Does God belong to Jews alone? Does he not belong to Gentiles, too? Yes, also to Gentiles" (Romans 3:29).

GOSPEL   "Not everyone who says to me, 'Lord, Lord,' will enter the kingdom of heaven, but only the one who does the will of my Father in heaven" (Matthew 7:21). Jesus says this near the end of the Sermon on the Mount (Matthew 5:3— 7:27), of which today's reading is the final part. As is perhaps true of other sayings of Jesus hinting or openly declaring that some

people will not enter the kingdom of heaven, you may find this one both challenging to proclaim and difficult for the assembly to hear.

In the Sermon on the Mount, Jesus makes himself very plain that being his disciple requires more than lip service. It demands action and the observance of a heightened degree of moral and ethical behavior based on the law Jesus says he has come not to abolish, but to fulfill (5:17–19). Jesus' interpretation of the law is quite rigorous. According to Jesus, "You shall not kill" also forbids anger and insults (5:21–26). "An eye for an eye and a tooth for a tooth" in

truth means that a disciple must offer no resistance to wrongs against his or her person or property (5:38–42). There are many other examples in the Sermon on the Mount of the high bar Jesus sets for his followers.

The example of the houses built on sand and rock vividly illustrates the point that one either follows instructions or invites destruction. As a builder is responsible for the foundation of a house, so also is the disciple responsible for living a life that merits entry into the kingdom.

10TH SUNDAY IN ORDINARY TIME

Lectionary 88

READING I   Hosea 6:3–6

A reading from the Book of the Prophet Hosea

In their **affliction**, people will say:
"Let us **know**, let us **strive** to know the **Lord**;
   as certain as the **dawn** is his coming,
   and his judgment shines forth like the **light** of **day**!
He will come to us like the **rain**,
   like **spring rain** that **waters** the **earth**."

What can I do with you, **Ephraim**?
   What can I do with you, **Judah**?
Your **piety** is like a **morning cloud**,
   like the **dew** that early **passes away**.
For this reason I **smote** them through the **prophets**,
   I **slew** them by the **words** of my **mouth**;
for it is **love** that I desire, **not sacrifice**,
   and **knowledge** of God rather than **holocausts**.

The emotional register of this first verse is different than the others. The first verse contains the joyful and encouraging words of the prophet, while the others give voice to God's own anguish at the behavior of the people. Use an exuberant, cheerful tone to proclaim the first verse, but a subdued tone for the remaining verses.

Ephraim = Eh-FRY-im

Judah = JU-dah

Emphasize the words "love," "sacrifice," "knowledge," and "holocausts" for the sake of contrast.

READING I   In Hosea 6:3, the prophet says that God, "will come to us like the rain, like spring rain that waters the earth." The association of God with rain and thunderstorms runs deep in the Old Testament. Psalm 29, one of the oldest of the psalms, celebrates God's authority over the rains and describes God's voice as thunder and lightning: "The voice of the LORD cracks the cedars; the LORD splinters the cedars of Lebanon." When Hosea likens God's advent to the spring rains, he refers to this traditional association between God and the rains.

But there is an important difference. There are two main periods of rain in Israel. First come the winter rains, which can be quite heavy. Then in spring comes more rain, normally much lighter than the rains of winter. These rains turn valleys, hills, and plains green and dot them with wildflowers. God arrives, according to Hosea 6:3, not with the violence of a thunderstorm, but with the spring rains' gentle touch.

In 6:4, there is an abrupt change of speaker. The voice of the prophet gives way to God's voice, which likens the fidelity of both Israel ("Ephraim") and Judah to dew evaporating in first rays of morning. That God smote and slew people for their lack of piety probably means that Hosea interprets the violence of the mid-eighth century BC to have arrived as punishment for the worship of gods other than God (Yahweh) in Israel and Judah. According to Hosea, the people have no love or knowledge of God if they practice, or even tolerate, the worship of other gods.

READING II   Paul's major project in Romans is to show how God

READING II   Romans 4:18–25

A reading from the Letter of Saint Paul to the Romans

Brothers and **sisters**:
Abraham **believed**, hoping against hope,
    that he would become the "**father** of **many nations**,"
    according to what was said, "Thus shall your descendants be."
He did not **weaken** in faith when he considered his own body
    as already dead—for he was almost a hundred years old—
    and the dead womb of Sarah.
He did not **doubt** God's promise in **unbelief**;
    rather, he was **strengthened** by **faith** and gave **glory** to God
    and was **fully convinced** that what he had promised
    he was also able to do.
That is why it was *credited* to him as *righteousness*.
But it was not for him alone that it was written
    that *it was **credited** to him*;
    it was **also** for **us**, to whom it will be **credited**,
    who **believe** in the one who raised **Jesus** our **Lord** from the dead,
    who was **handed** over for our **transgressions**
    and was **raised** for our **justification**.

Use a strong, bold tone of voice to proclaim this reading. Paul is trying to prove a case, to persuade his audience of the basis in faith, not in works of law, of Abraham's justification.
Abraham = AY-brah-ham

Sarah = SAH-rah

Look up and make eye contact with the assembly when you proclaim the words "it was also for us."

---

has offered redemption to Jews and Gentiles alike through Jesus Christ. That God offered the same means to both Jews and Gentiles to establish a right relationship with God through Jesus was a hard case to argue. On the one hand, Paul had to show that God's grace offered in Jesus erased any meaningful distinction between the relationships with God possible for Jews and Gentiles. On the other, he could not—nor did he want to—reject or disavow Jewish law, even though the observance of this law was the chief thing distinguishing Jews from Gentiles. How could Paul show that God

redeemed Jews and Gentiles identically, but also affirm the law that separated them?

In both Galatians and Romans, circumcision is a particular legal obligation of Jews that Paul refers to even when he is really talking about Jewish law in general. Paul has already said that circumcision, and through it the law, is valuable (Romans 3:1). In today's reading, Paul attempts to show that Abraham, commonly considered by Jews to be the first Israelite, is also the patriarch of the Gentiles. The central question, as Paul sees it, is this: when was Abraham justified? Paul points out that

Abraham's justification occurred not when he was circumcised (Genesis 17:10–27), but earlier, when Abraham, though childless, still trusted in God's promise that his descendants would one day be as numerous as the stars of the sky (Genesis 15:1–6). Thus Paul claims that Abraham was justified by faith and not by law.

Now if all this about justification, law, and faith had mattered only in Abraham's case, Paul would not have bothered to explain it at such length. What is true for Abraham, Paul concludes, is true for the Roman Church as well: "But it was not for

GOSPEL   Matthew 9:9–13

A reading from the holy Gospel according to Matthew

As **Jesus** passed on from there,
  he saw a man named **Matthew** sitting at the customs post.
He said to him, "**Follow me.**"
And he **got up** and **followed** him.
While he was at table in his house,
  many **tax collectors** and **sinners** came
  and sat with **Jesus** and his **disciples**.
The Pharisees **saw** this and **said** to his disciples,
  "**Why** does your teacher eat with **tax collectors** and **sinners**?"
He **heard** this and said,
  "Those who are **well** do not **need** a **physician**, but the **sick** do.
Go and learn the **meaning** of the **words**,
  'I desire **mercy**, not **sacrifice**.'
I did not come to call the **righteous** but **sinners**."

In this reading Jesus calls a disciple with a mere two words and answers his opponents' questions. Proclaim Jesus' words in a bold tone of voice.

Pause before and after Jesus' quotation of scripture. Also stress the words "righteous" and "sinners" to highlight the contrast.

---

him [Abraham] alone that it was written that 'it was credited to him'; it was also for us, to whom it will be credited, who believe in the one who raised Jesus our Lord from the dead" (Romans 4:23–25).

GOSPEL   In Roman-occupied Palestine, the local rulers of Judea and its surrounding regions, including Galilee, were obliged to pay tribute to Rome. These rulers employed a small army of men to collect this tribute as well as additional funds for their own personal treasuries. These tax

collectors were therefore widely regarded as parasites and thieves, men hated for enriching their masters and themselves at the expense of even their poorest neighbors.

Seen in this light, the Pharisees' question to Jesus' disciples makes a bit more sense. Why indeed does Jesus willingly sit down to eat with such people?

Citing Hosea 6:6 (see commentary I), Jesus responds, first, by taking a jab at the Pharisees. He likens them to their ancient forbears who preferred outward ritual display (sacrifice) to the interior cultivation and expression of love for God and fellow human

beings (mercy). Next, comparing his ministry to a doctor's practice, Jesus explains, "I did not come to call the righteous but sinners" (Matthew 9:13).

While Matthew's Jesus offers forgiveness even to people showing no sign of repentance (Matthew 9:2–8; see also Mark 2:1–12; Luke 5:17–26), the terms of discipleship laid out in the Sermon on the Mount also call for a high degree of moral and ethical rigor (Matthew 5:3—7:27). While Matthew's Jesus indeed forgives and calls sinners, he also calls them *away* from their sin if they would become his disciples.

11TH SUNDAY IN ORDINARY TIME

Lectionary #91

READING I   Exodus 19:2–6a

A reading from the Book of Exodus

Sinai = SYE-nye

In those days, the **Israelites** came to the desert of **Sinai**
    and pitched camp.
While **Israel** was encamped here in front of the **mountain**,
    Moses went up the **mountain** to **God**.
Then the **LORD** called to him and said,

Proclaim God's words to Moses in a forceful and strong tone of voice.

    "Thus shall you say to the house of Jacob;
    tell the Israelites:
    You have **seen** for **yourselves** how I treated the **Egyptians**
    and how I **bore** you up on **eagle** wings
    and **brought** you here to **myself**.

Emphasize the word "if" in this line. This promise is not open-ended, but conditional on Israel's observance of the terms of the covenant.

Therefore, if you **hearken** to my **voice** and **keep** my **covenant**,
    you shall be my **special possession**,
    dearer to me than **all other** people,
    though **all** the earth is **mine**.
You shall be to me a **kingdom** of **priests**, a **holy nation**."

READING I In today's reading, God cites Israel's recent experience in support of a proposed covenant agreement: "You have seen for yourselves how I treated the Egyptians and how I bore you up on eagle wings and brought you here to myself. Therefore, if you hearken to my voice and keep my covenant, you shall be my special possession, dearer to me than all other people" (Exodus 19:4–5). If Israel decides to enter into a covenantal agreement with God, it will not be on the basis of blind faith. Events have *proven* God is trustworthy.

The proper consecration and ordination of men to serve Israel as priests is an important concern of future chapters of Exodus (see Exodus 28—29). The duties of priests, particularly in regard to sacrifice, are spelled out in great detail in the book of Leviticus. But what we have in today's reading is a description of the whole people of Israel as "a kingdom of priests, a holy nation" (Exodus 19:6). The whole people, not any one part or portion, must be set aside for service to God (see also Exodus 20:8–9; 31:15; Leviticus 20:26; Deuteronomy 7:6; 14:2, 21).

In the first letter of Peter, the author exhorts his Christian addressees: "let yourselves be built into a spiritual house to be a holy priesthood to offer spiritual sacrifices acceptable to God through Jesus Christ" (1 Peter 2:4; see also 2:9). The use of the language of priesthood to describe the character and behavior of the universal Church recalls God's description of Israel in today's reading (Exodus 19:6).

READING II An important and persuasive proof of God's love, as

READING II Romans 5:6–11

A reading from the Letter of Saint Paul to the Romans

Brothers and **sisters**:
Christ, while we were **still helpless**,
     yet **died** at the appointed **time** for the **ungodly**.
Indeed, only with **difficulty** does one die for a **just** person,
     though perhaps for a **good** person
     one might even find **courage** to **die**.
But God **proves** his **love** for us
     in that while we were still **sinners** Christ **died** for us.
How much more then, since we are now **justified** by his **blood**,
     will we be **saved** through him from the **wrath**.
Indeed, if, while we were **enemies**,
     we were **reconciled** to **God** through the **death** of his **Son**,
     how much more, once **reconciled**,
     will we be **saved** by his **life**.
Not only that,
     but we **also** boast of **God** through our **Lord Jesus Christ**,
     through whom we have now received reconciliation.

Look up at the assembly as you proclaim the phrase "in that while we were still sinners Christ died for us."

Slow down as you stress each word of the phrase "How much more."

Paul explains to the Roman Christians in today's reading, is that "that while we were still sinners Christ died for us" (Romans 5:8). But even more certain than this fact, Paul argues, is the salvation of Christians "from the wrath" (Romans 5:9). The subject of God's wrath arises repeatedly in Romans. Sometimes, as in today's reading, Paul writes of God's wrath as something future, making use of Old Testament traditions about "the Day of the Lord" (Romans 2:5, 8, 5:9; see commentary I, Ash Wednesday, February 6). But sometimes he writes of it as something even now beginning to be revealed (Romans

1:18). In any case, those with faith in Christ are saved from this wrath.

Paul begins Romans 5 by discussing a relationship of peace that, through Christ, has at last become possible for all human beings to share with God (Romans 5:1). The theme of peace resurfaces in today's reading when Paul discusses reconciliation. Note that Paul does not say "we reconciled with God" or "we reconciled ourselves to God," but that "we *were* reconciled" (Romans 5:11). The new relationship has already come, arriving purely as God's gift to the world.

Paul's reference to boasting in 5:11 may require a little explanation: "we also boast of God through our Lord Jesus Christ, through whom we have now received reconciliation." In Romans 5, Paul writes that "we boast in hope of the glory of God" and "we even boast of our afflictions" (Romans 5:2–3). Paul is not advising Christians to brag about themselves, but about what God has done for them. This is even true for "afflictions," because these toughen Christians, leading them on toward the resurrection, a hope that "does not disappoint" (Romans 5:5).

GOSPEL Matthew 9:36—10:8

A reading from the holy Gospel according to Matthew

At the **sight** of the **crowds**, Jesus' **heart** was **moved**
    with **pity** for them
    because they were **troubled** and **abandoned**,
    like **sheep** without a **shepherd**.
Then he said to his **disciples**,
    "The **harvest** is **abundant** but the **laborers** are **few**;
    so ask the **master** of the **harvest**
    to send out **laborers** for his **harvest**."

Then he summoned his **twelve disciples**
    and gave them **authority** over unclean spirits
    to **drive** them **out** and to **cure** every **disease** and every **illness**.
The **names** of the twelve **apostles** are **these**:
    first, **Simon** called **Peter**, and his brother **Andrew**;
    James, the son of **Zebedee**, and his brother **John**;
    Philip and **Bartholomew**, **Thomas** and **Matthew**
        the tax collector;
    James, the son of **Alphaeus**, and **Thaddeus**;
    Simon from **Cana**, and **Judas Iscariot** who **betrayed** him.

Jesus sent out **these** twelve after **instructing** them **thus**,
    "Do **not** go into **pagan** territory or enter a **Samaritan town**.
Go rather to the **lost sheep** of the **house** of Israel.
As you go, make **this** proclamation:
    'The **kingdom** of **heaven** is at **hand**.'
Cure the sick, **raise** the dead, **cleanse** lepers, **drive out** demons.
Without **cost** you have **received**; without **cost** you are to **give**."

Pause briefly between the name and description of each disciple. Read the list slowly.
Zebedee = ZEH-beh-dee
Bartholomew = bar-THOL-uh-myoo
Alphaeus = AL-fye-us
Thaddeus = THAH-dee-us
Cana = KAY-nuh
Judas = JOO-dus
Iscariot = Is-CAR-i-ot

Proclaim Jesus' words of commission to his disciples in a firm, strong tone of voice.

Look up and make eye contact with the assembly as you proclaim the phrase "The kingdom of heaven is at hand."

GOSPEL In today's reading, Jesus commissions his disciples, giving them authority and powers of healing, and commands them to proclaim a message like that of both John and himself: "The kingdom of heaven is at hand" (Matthew 10:7).

This must be a very important message to Matthew if he reports that John the Baptist, Jesus, and his disciples all proclaimed it. What does it mean?

While it is clear that the kingdom of heaven means God's rule, authority, or power exercised in human affairs, it is quite hard to say much beyond this about what Jesus precisely meant by the term. Matthew's Jesus usually speaks of the "kingdom of heaven" while in Mark, Luke, and John Jesus talks about the coming "kingdom of God" (see, for example, Matthew 4:17; Mark 1:14–15; Luke 4:43; John 3:1–5). Matthew's wording obviously differs from the others, but his meaning is the same.

Sometimes Matthew's Jesus speaks of the kingdom of heaven as something one enters (Matthew 5:20; 7:21; 18:3; 19:23–24; 21:31; 23:13). Sometimes he speaks of the kingdom in terms of its future arrival (Matthew 5:3, 10; 6:10; 8:11–12; 12:28; 16:28; 20:21; 26:29). And sometimes Matthew's Jesus speaks of the kingdom as a present spiritual reality (Matthew 21:31). The oppressed, the Gentiles, and outright sinners find welcome there (Matthew 5:3, 10; 8:11–12; 21:31). And as in today's reading, a common sign of the kingdom's proclamation is the healing of people from disease (Matthew 4:23; 9:35; 12:28).

12TH SUNDAY IN ORDINARY TIME

Lectionary #94

READING I   Jeremiah 20:10–13

A reading from the Book of the Prophet Jeremiah

Jeremiah said:
"I hear the **whisperings** of **many**:
  '**Terror** on every side!
  Denounce! let us **denounce** him!'
All those who were my friends
  are on the **watch** for **any misstep** of mine.
'Perhaps he will be **trapped**, then we can **prevail**,
  and take our **vengeance** on him.'
But the LORD is **with** me, like a **mighty champion**:
  my **persecutors** will **stumble**, they will **not** triumph.
In their **failure** they will be put to **utter shame**,
  to lasting, unforgettable **confusion**.
O LORD of **hosts**, you who **test** the **just**,
  who probe **mind** and **heart**,
let me **witness** the **vengeance** you take on them,
  for to you I have **entrusted** my cause.
Sing to the LORD,
  praise the LORD,
for he has **rescued** the **life** of the **poor**
  from the **power** of the **wicked**!"

In this reading, we find words of conspiracy the prophet supposes are being whispered about him. Deliver them in a hostile and threatening tone of voice.

Pause briefly here. Then proclaim the last lines of the reading in a joyful tone of voice.

READING I In today's reading from Jeremiah, the prophet laments to God that his enemies are closing in on him. This is not a case of paranoia, for Jeremiah made numerous enemies during his career, from false prophets, to wealthy and powerful citizens of Jerusalem, to members of the king's court. Jeremiah preached that Judah would be destroyed and its people led away captive if the poor did not receive justice and God were not rightly honored. This would be a difficult word to proclaim and to hear in any time and place.

The selection we are given in our Lectionary does not capture how truly upset Jeremiah is in this reading. Consider the verses immediately following it: "Cursed be the day on which I was born! May the day my mother gave me birth never be blessed! Cursed be the man who brought the news to my father, saying, 'A child, a son, has been born to you!' filling him with great joy" (Jeremiah 20:14–15).

If this seems like hopelessness and despair, it is not. Jeremiah still has a very firm trust that God will fight on his behalf "like a mighty champion" (Jeremiah 20:11).

READING II This reading reveals some important pieces of how Paul understood God's work of reconciliation and justification (Romans 5:1–11; see commentary II, Eleventh Sunday in Ordinary Time, June 15). Sin is not simply human wrongdoing. And neither is death just part of the human condition. Sin and death are *powers*. Paul can speak of death as a "ruler" in Romans 5:14, just as he can speak of sin "reigning" in Romans 5:21 and 6:12. The justification and reconciliation God offers in part comprise the gift of grace, which redeems

READING II   Romans 5:12–15

A reading from the Letter of Saint Paul to the Romans

Brothers and **sisters**:
Through **one man sin** entered the world,
  and through **sin**, **death**,
  and thus **death** came to **all men**, inasmuch as **all sinned**—
  for up to the time of the **law**, **sin** was in the **world**,
  though **sin** is not **accounted** when there is **no law**.
But **death** reigned from **Adam** to **Moses**,
  even over those who did **not sin**
  after the **pattern** of the **trespass** of **Adam**,
  who is the **type** of the **one** who was to **come**.

But the **gift** is **not** like the **transgression**.
For if by the **transgression** of the **one** the **many** died,
  how much more did the **grace** of **God**
  and the **gracious gift** of the one man **Jesus Christ**
  overflow for the **many**.

In this verse, which has a complex sentence structure, let the commas mark brief pauses in your delivery.
Emphasize the words "one" and "all" in this line.

In this verse, emphasize both "not" and every word of the phrase "how much more."

---

people from the powers of sin and death and places them under the authority, care, and protection of a new ruler, Jesus Christ.

This is not to say that Paul thinks people have no responsibility for their sins, or that they are mere pawns in a spiritual chess game. But it is to say that Paul thinks the odds against human beings are stacked firmly in favor of sin and death where there is no faith in Jesus Christ. To accept the full effect of the gift on offer, one need only "confess with your mouth that Jesus is Lord and believe in your heart that God raised

him from the dead" in order to cooperate in one's own rescue (Romans 10:9).

In this reading Paul refers to Adam as "a type of the one to come" (Romans 5:14). Paul lays out his meaning in an extended comparison of Adam and Christ in Romans 5:12–21. He makes a similar comparison, although much more simply, in 1 Corinthians 15:44–49. Adam and Christ are two figures whose deeds and natures have had great consequences for human beings. On this basis Adam is a "type" of Christ. But beyond that, the effects of "the gift" of grace offered through Christ cannot really be compared to

the effects of Adam's "transgression," since the effects of grace are so much more powerful than the effects of sin and death.

GOSPEL Today's reading forms part of the instruction Jesus gives to his disciples after he has given them powers of healing and exorcism, and commissioned them to proclaim the approaching kingdom of heaven (Matthew 10:1–42).

The kind of ministry Jesus commissions his disciples to do is sometimes called

Jesus is teaching his disciples in today's reading. Deliver his words with a lively and authoritative tone of voice, like a confident teacher might use with students.

In this reading, Jesus makes a series of contrasts. Keep an eye out for them as you prepare, emphasizing the key words that will clearly bring out the contrasts before the assembly.

Gehenna = geh-HEN-uh

Raise the pitch of your voice to indicate Jesus' rhetorical question.

GOSPEL   Matthew 10:26–33

A reading from the holy Gospel according to Matthew

Jesus said to the **Twelve**:
"Fear **no one**.
Nothing is concealed that will **not** be revealed,
    nor **secret** that will not be **known**.
What I say to you in the **darkness**, **speak** in the **light**;
    what you hear **whispered**, **proclaim** on the housetops.
And do **not** be **afraid** of those who **kill** the **body**
        but **cannot** kill the soul;
    rather, be **afraid** of the one who can **destroy**
        both **soul** and **body** in **Gehenna**.
Are not two sparrows sold for a small coin?
Yet **not one** of them falls to the ground
        without your Father's **knowledge**.
Even all the **hairs** of your **head** are **counted**.
So do **not** be afraid; you are worth **more** than many sparrows.
Everyone who acknowledges **me** before others
    I will acknowledge before my **heavenly Father**.
But whoever **denies** me before others,
    I will deny before my **heavenly Father**."

"itinerant," which basically means a ministry "on the move." The disciples probably did not stay long in any one place and traveled light (Matthew 10:9–11). This form of ministry was particularly suited to the rural culture of Galilee, where most people lived in small fishing villages and farm towns often separated by considerable distance.

How to deal with opposition and harassment is one of the major themes of Matthew 10 and the context for today's Gospel selection. Jesus treats it as certain that his disciples will suffer because of the

ministry he has commissioned them to perform: "Behold, I am sending you like sheep in the midst of wolves; so be shrewd as serpents and simple as doves. But beware of people, for they will hand you over to courts and scourge you in their synagogues and you will be led before governors and kings for my sake as a witness before them and the pagans" (Matthew 10:16–18).

The certainty that they will be persecuted for their ministry makes the instruction to speak publicly and fearlessly all the more bold and extraordinary: "What I say to you in the darkness, speak in the light; what

you hear whispered, proclaim on the housetops" (Matthew 10:27). By speaking the truth, by practicing their healing ministries, Jesus sends his disciples out to court arrest, torture, and perhaps death. The power and joy of discipleship in Jesus Christ are revealed in this reading: one may risk losing everything for the sake of the truth, but suffer no fear, confident in God's care and protection (Matthew 10:28–31).

SAINT PETER AND SAINT PAUL, APOSTLES: VIGIL

Lectionary #590

READING I   Acts 3:1–10

A reading from the Acts of the Apostles

Peter and John were going up to the **temple** area
    for the three o'clock hour of **prayer**.
And a man **crippled** from **birth** was **carried**
    and placed at the gate of the temple called "the **Beautiful Gate**"
    every day to **beg** for alms from the people who entered
        the temple.
When he saw **Peter** and **John** about to go into the temple,
    he asked for **alms**.
But **Peter** looked **intently** at him, as did **John**,
    and said, "**Look** at us."
He paid attention to them, expecting to **receive** something
        from them.
Peter said, "I have neither **silver** nor **gold**,
    but what I **do** have I **give** you:
    in the **name** of **Jesus Christ** the **Nazorean**, **rise** and **walk**."
Then **Peter** took him by the right hand and **raised** him up,
    and **immediately** his **feet** and **ankles** grew **strong**.
He **leaped** up, **stood**, and **walked** around,
    and went into the temple with them,
        walking and **jumping** and **praising God**.

Proclaim Peter's words in a strong, confident tone of voice.

Nazorean = Nah-zoh-RAY-an

READING I In his first public proclamation of the Gospel after the birth of the Church at Pentecost, Peter quoted the prophet Joel and prophesied that wonders and signs would come to pass "in the last days" (Acts 2:16–21). Peter's healing of the man crippled from birth, after the gift of the Spirit at Pentecost itself, is the first of such signs recorded in Acts. Peter makes this point himself in the controversy that follows his act of mercy (Acts 4:30). More signs

by Peter will follow (see Acts 5:1–11, 14–16; 9:32–34, 36–41).

Although he has no money (see Acts 2:43–45; 4:32–35), Peter gives the crippled man what he has, the gift of healing by the powerful name of "Jesus Christ the Nazorean" (see Acts 2:22; 4:10; 6:14; 22:8; 26:9; see also Matthew 2:23; 26:71; John 18:5–7; 19:19). Elsewhere in Acts, we read of the power of Jesus' name. Paul, for example, drives "an oracular spirit" out of a slave girl "in the name of Jesus Christ" (Acts 16:18). And in the comical episode of the

seven sons of Sceva (Acts 19:13–17), people unworthy of using Jesus' name as Paul does are publicly humiliated.

It is appropriate, in the light of this reading and feast, to note that in Acts Peter and especially Paul are the most important leaders of the early Church. One way to see this is to consider the sheer number of miracles performed by both men: Peter in Acts 3:1–10; 5:1–11, 14–16; 9:32–34, 36–41; and Paul in Acts 13:8–11; 14:8–10; 16:16–18; 19:11–12; 20:7–12; 28:7–9.

When **all** the **people** saw the man **walking** and **praising** God,
    they **recognized** him as the one who used to sit **begging**
    at the **Beautiful** Gate of the **temple**,
    and they were filled with **amazement** and **astonishment**
    at what had happened to him.

READING II   Galatians 1:11–20

A reading from the Letter of Saint Paul to the Galatians

I want you to know, **brothers** and **sisters**,
    that the gospel preached by me is **not** of human origin.
For I did **not** receive it from a **human being**, nor was I **taught** it,
    but it came through a **revelation** of **Jesus Christ**.

For you **heard** of my former way of life in **Judaism**,
    how I **persecuted** the church of God beyond measure
    and tried to **destroy** it, and **progressed** in Judaism
    beyond **many** of my contemporaries among my race,
    since I was even more a **zealot** for my **ancestral traditions**.
But when **God**, who from my **mother's womb** had **set** me **apart**
    and **called** me through his **grace**,
    was **pleased** to **reveal** his **Son** to me,
    so that I might **proclaim** him to the **Gentiles**,
    I did **not** immediately consult **flesh** and **blood**,
    nor did I go up to **Jerusalem**
    to those who were apostles **before** me;
    rather, I went into **Arabia** and then returned to **Damascus**.

Because Paul's main point in this section is that no human being or authority whatsoever gave him the Gospel and his apostolate, emphasize *all* of the negatives in this reading.

Pause before you deliver this line.

**Arabia = Ah-RAY-bee-ah
Damascus = Dah-MAS-cus**

READING II Today's reading contains some of the richest details about Paul's life contained in any of his letters. The entire biographical section spans Galatians 1:11—2:14.

When a writer, seemingly out of the blue, writes, "before God, I am not lying!" it is natural for a reader to have some questions. Who said anything about lying? But Paul believed he had ample reason to make this emphatic statement in his letter to the

Churches of Galatia. The Galatians, he contends, have challenged not only the Gospel he preaches, but even his right to call himself an apostle. If the charges are true, then Paul is not an apostle, his Gospel is false or incomplete, and he has intentionally misrepresented himself. Paul's emphatic statement that he tells the truth is therefore an act of self-defense: he writes to answer charges made against him.

Paul relates the personal details in this reading to support a point he makes in 1:11: "the gospel preached by me is not of human origin. For I did not receive it from a human being, nor was I taught it, but it came through a revelation of Jesus Christ." In Acts 9, Paul says that God set him apart from birth for the Gospel (that is, the revelation of Jesus). He takes care to note that when he received this revelation he talked with no one, and only came to Jerusalem after three years,

Cephas = Kay-FAS

Then after three years I went up to **Jerusalem**
   to confer with **Cephas** and remained with him for fifteen days.
But I did not see **any other** of the apostles,
   only **James** the **brother** of the **Lord**.
—As to what I am writing to you, **behold**,
   before God, **I** am **not lying**.

GOSPEL John 21:15–19

A reading from the holy Gospel according to John

Jesus **revealed** himself to his disciples and,
   when they had finished breakfast, said to **Simon Peter**,
     "**Simon**, son of **John**, do you **love** me more than these?"

Raise the pitch of your voice at the end of each of Jesus' questions.

He answered him, "Yes, Lord, you **know** that I **love** you."
Jesus said to him, "**Feed** my **lambs**."
He then said to him a second time,
     "**Simon**, son of **John**, do you **love** me?"
He answered him, "Yes, Lord, you **know** that I **love** you."
He said to him, "**Tend** my **sheep**."
He said to him the third time,
     "**Simon**, son of **John**, do you **love** me?"
Peter was **distressed** that Jesus had said to him a third time,
     "Do you **love** me?" and he said to him,

The text tells us that Jesus' third question makes Peter feel "distressed." Use an upset, unhappy tone of voice when you proclaim Peter's third reply.

     "Lord, you know **everything**; you **know** that I **love** you."
Jesus said to him, "**Feed** my **sheep**.

---

but then spoke only with Kephas (another name for Peter) and James, the brother of Jesus (Galatians 1:15–19). In 1:22, Paul will claim that, following his departure from Jerusalem, "I was unknown personally to the Churches of Judea that are in Christ." Why does Paul emphasize he had no contact with anyone, particularly the Churches of Judea, after he received his revelation?

It is likely that after Paul left them, the Galatians received Christian missionaries, either from Judea or with strong ties to its

Churches, who said that Paul was not in fellowship with them. The claim that God, not any human being, revealed Christ to him is Paul's answer to such charges. Paul disputes his opponents by first agreeing with them: he admits he relies on no human authority to do what he does, for he is "an apostle not from human beings nor through a human being but through Jesus Christ and God the Father" (Galatians 1:1). God, not any human being, made Paul an apostle.

GOSPEL   After Jesus' arrest, Peter denied his Lord three times as Jesus predicted (John 13:36–38; 18:15–18, 25–27; see also Matthew 26:31–35, 69–75; Mark 14:27–31, 66–72; Luke 22:31–34, 54–62). In today's reading, Jesus commissions Peter for pastoral ministry with three replies to Peter's threefold testimony of love. This episode helps explain to readers why Peter, who sinned so greatly during Jesus' Passion, was restored to his place among the disciples and later became so prominent in the

Amen, **amen**, I say to you, when you were **younger**,
   you used to **dress** yourself and **go** where you wanted;
   but when you **grow old**, you will **stretch** out your **hands**,
   and someone **else** will **dress** you
   and **lead** you where you do **not** want to go."
He said this signifying by what kind of **death** he would **glorify** God.
And when he had said this, he said to him, "**Follow me**."

Church. We have additional examples in the New Testament that Jesus appeared to Peter privately after his Resurrection (Luke 24:34; 1 Corinthians 15:5). Peter's authority in the early Church was likely based in part on the widespread belief that Jesus appeared to him in private.

The tradition of the early Church at the turn of the second century is that Peter died a martyr's death (1 Clement 5). Note how Jesus' cryptic reference to Peter's death immediately follows his commission to pastoral ministry. In a similar way, Jesus connected the commission of his disciples to the world's hatred of them (John 17:14). In the early Church, and even in some regions in our own day, the acceptance of pastoral ministry could be a dangerous proposition.

SAINT PETER AND SAINT PAUL, APOSTLES: DAY

Lectionary #591

READING I   Acts 12:1–11

A reading from the Acts of the Apostles

Herod = HAY-rud

In those days, **King Herod** laid hands upon some members
      of the church to **harm** them.
He had **James**, the brother of **John**, **killed** by the **sword**,
      and when he **saw** that this was **pleasing** to the **Jews**
      he proceeded to **arrest** Peter **also**.
—It was the **feast** of Unleavened Bread.—
He had him **taken** into **custody** and put in **prison**
      under the **guard** of four squads of four soldiers each.
He intended to bring him before the people after **Passover**.
Peter thus was being kept in **prison**,
      but **prayer** by the **church** was **fervently** being made
      to **God** on his behalf.

On the very night before Herod was to bring him to **trial**,
      Peter, **secured** by double chains,
      was **sleeping** between two soldiers,
      while outside the door guards kept **watch** on the **prison**.
Suddenly the **angel** of the **Lord** stood **by** him
      and a **light** shone in the **cell**.
He tapped **Peter** on the **side** and **awakened** him, saying,
      "**Get up quickly**."
The chains **fell** from his **wrists**.

All of the angel's words are commands.
Proclaim them in a strong, authoritative
tone of voice.

READING I According to Acts, the period of persecution that followed Stephen's murder eventually gives way to a period of peace (7:54—8:4; 9:31). But in 12:1, persecution of the Church begins anew. For the first time in Acts, civil authority oppresses the Church, with Herod Agrippa I (ruler of Judea from 41–44 AD) executing James, the brother of John. James and his brother John were two of Jesus' earliest disciples (Matthew 4:21–22; Mark 1:19–20; Luke 5:10), witnesses of the Transfiguration (Matthew 17:1; Mark 9:2; Luke 9:28) and present during Jesus' agony in Gethsemane (Matthew 26:37; Mark 14:33). They may even have rivaled Peter for authority among the disciples (Matthew 20:20–28; Mark 10:35–45). This must have been a devastating loss to the Church.

"Now I know for certain that [the] Lord sent his angel and rescued me." So Peter speaks upon finding himself freed from prison by an angel's help. This sudden dawn of awareness that God has accomplished something marvelous for him recalls an earlier incident in which Peter at last came to understand the meaning his vision of clean and unclean food (Acts 10:9–16). In response to the centurion Cornelius' testimony that "a man in dazzling robes" told him to send for Peter, Peter comprehends the meaning of a vision he previously received: "In truth, I see that God shows no partiality. Rather, in every nation whoever fears him and acts uprightly is acceptable to him" (Acts 10:30, 34). In both

The angel **said** to him, "Put on your **belt** and your **sandals**."
He **did** so.
Then he said to him, "Put on your **cloak** and **follow me**."
So he **followed** him out,
    not **realizing** that what was **happening** through the angel
       was **real**;
    he **thought** he was **seeing** a **vision**.
They passed the first guard, then the second,
    and came to the iron gate leading out to the city,
    which **opened** for them **by itself**.
They emerged and made their way down an alley,
    and **suddenly** the angel **left** him.
Then Peter recovered his senses and said,
"Now I know for certain that
    the Lord sent his angel
    and rescued me from the hand of Herod
    and from all that the Jewish people had been expecting."

Acts 10 and today's reading, Peter, without at first understanding, obediently follows God's direction. Only in retrospect does he realize the magnitude of what God has done.

READING II Although Paul almost certainly did not write the two New Testament letters to Timothy, the person who did knew Paul's work and cared deeply about his legacy. In today's reading, Paul sits in jail, expecting execution. The author, writing in Paul's voice, describes his situation quite vividly: "I am already being poured out like a libation, and the time of my departure is at hand." He immediately follows up this sacrificial image with an image of himself as an athlete: "I have competed well; I have finished the race" (2 Timothy 4:6–7). Poured libations of wine were sacrifices commonly offered in the course of athletic competitions in antiquity. Ever confident of God's strong support (2 Timothy 4:17–18), Paul compares his career and the twilight of his life to different aspects of an ancient athletic match.

The Roman historian Tacitus writes that Nero falsely accused the Christians of Rome with starting a destructive fire in the city, ordering many of them tortured and killed. It is probable that both Paul and Peter were martyred during this persecution around 64 AD.

READING II   2 Timothy 4:6–8, 17–18

A reading from the second Letter of Saint Paul to Timothy

Proclaim Paul's words in a clear, confident tone.

I, **Paul**, am **already** being poured out like a **libation**,
    and the **time** of my **departure** is at **hand**.
I have **competed** well; I have **finished** the **race**;
    I have **kept** the **faith**.
From now on the **crown** of **righteousness** awaits me,
    which the **Lord**, the **just judge**,
    will **award** to me on that day, and not **only** to **me**,
    but to **all** who have **longed** for his **appearance**.

Emphasize this line in particular, looking up at the assembly as you proclaim it.

The **Lord** stood by me and gave me **strength**,
    so that through **me** the **proclamation** might be **completed**
    and **all** the **Gentiles** might **hear** it.
And I was **rescued** from the **lion's** mouth.
The **Lord** will **rescue** me from **every** evil threat
    and will bring me **safe** to his **heavenly kingdom**.
To him be **glory** forever and ever. **Amen.**

Clement of Rome, writing to Corinthian Christians in the late first century, says that Paul reached the limit of the West (see Romans 15:19–22) and bore witness in front of rulers before he died. Some biblical scholars think Clement means that Paul eventually reached Spain as Romans shows he hoped to do (Romans 15:24, 28). Others, however, assume Clement simply means that Paul wound up in Rome and testified in the seat of imperial power before he died.

Luke hints at Paul's martyrdom in Acts 20:21–24 and leaves Paul in Rome without ever mentioning Spain (Acts 28:11–31).

GOSPEL   Matthew and Mark place Peter's confession in the region of the northern city of Caesarea Philippi (Matthew 16:13; Mark 8:27). Luke gives no specific location, noting only that Peter made his confession out of earshot of the crowds when Jesus and his disciples were alone together (Luke 9:18). All three evangelists record that Jesus demands secrecy after Peter confesses (Matthew 16:20; Mark 8:30; Luke 9:21).

The specific content of Peter's confession differs slightly among the three evangelists (Matthew 16:13–16; Mark 8:27–30; Luke 9:18–21). But a feature common to all three accounts is the answer to Jesus' question, "But who do you say that I am?" The English word "messiah" translates Matthew's Greek word *christos,* which means "anointed one." The meaning of this term varied widely at different times and among different groups

Caesarea = Seh-sah-REE-ah
Philippi = FIL-lih-pye

Make sure to raise the pitch of your voice
at the end of both of Jesus' questions.

When you ask these questions, make eye
contact with the assembly as much as
possible.

GOSPEL   Matthew 16:13–19

A reading from the holy Gospel according to Matthew

When Jesus went into the region of **Caesarea Philippi**
    he asked his **disciples**,
      "**Who** do people say that the **Son of Man** is?"
They replied, "**Some** say **John** the **Baptist**, others **Elijah**,
    still others **Jeremiah** or one of the **prophets**."
He said to them, "But who do **you** say that **I** am?"
Simon Peter said in reply,
    "**You** are the **Christ**, the **Son** of the **living God**."
Jesus said to him in reply, "**Blessed** are **you**, **Simon** son of **Jonah**.
For **flesh** and **blood** has **not revealed** this to you,
      but my **heavenly Father**.
And so I **say** to you, **you are Peter**,
    and upon this **rock** I will **build** my **Church**,
    and the **gates** of the **netherworld** shall **not prevail** against it.
I will give you the **keys** to the **Kingdom** of **heaven**.
Whatever you **bind** on **earth** shall be **bound** in **heaven**;
    and whatever you **loose** on **earth** shall be **loosed** in **heaven**."

of Jews. Jews knew it from scripture as a common title of kings (Psalm 18:51: "You have given great victories to your king, and shown kindness to your anointed, to David and his posterity forever"). Many Jews in the first century hoped for a messiah— a king, prophet, priest, angel, or some combination of all four—in expectation of God's direct intervention in the world at the end of days. In the light of the advent, life, ministry, Passion, Crucifixion, and Resurrection of Jesus, the disciples came to share in Peter's confession and proclaim it to the world. Indeed, the custom of referring to

Christ as though it were Jesus' last name, which we find already in the earliest Christian writings (Paul's letters), likely grew out of a Christian confession similar to Peter's: "Jesus of Nazareth is the Christ" or "Jesus is the Christ."

Alone among the evangelists, Matthew records Jesus' testimony that he will build his Church on the "rock" that is Peter. Matthew 16:17–19 has long been important to Catholic belief in the primacy of Peter among the apostles and of Rome, the Petrine See, among the world's dioceses.

14TH SUNDAY IN ORDINARY TIME

Lectionary #100

READING I Zechariah 9:9–10

A reading from the Book of the prophet Zechariah

Thus says the LORD:
Rejoice **heartily**, O daughter **Zion**,
    shout for **joy**, O daughter **Jerusalem**!
See, your **king** shall **come** to you;
    a just **savior** is he,
meek, and riding on an **ass**,
    on **a colt**, the **foal** of an ass.
He shall **banish** the **chariot** from **Ephraim**,
    and the **horse** from **Jerusalem**;
the **warrior's** bow shall be **banished**,
    and he shall proclaim **peace** to the **nations**.
His **dominion** shall be from **sea** to **sea**,
    and from the **River** to the **ends** of the **earth**.

Zion = ZI-yon

Ephraim = Eh-FRY-im

bow = boh

READING I Today's reading is part of a longer prophecy heralding the rise of a royal messiah, perhaps a king of David's lineage. Although kings of David's royal line no longer ruled in the fifth and fourth centuries BC when Zechariah 9—14 was likely composed, the desire and hope for the restoration of the house of David remained strong.

If you read Zechariah 9:9–17, you will see that the human king of today's reading, who will establish his realm "from sea to sea" enjoys the military support of God, Israel's heavenly king. The depiction of Israel's God, Yahweh, marching to battle and waging war with Israel against its enemies is a traditional element of the religion of ancient Israel. One of the oldest poems of the Bible, Judges 5, contains an account of Israel's battle against one of the peoples of Canaan in which God also marches forth to war (Judges 5:4–5), enlisting even the stars to fight from heaven on Israel's side (Judges 5:20). In the days of the monarchy, when a king of Israel or Judah celebrated his reign and military successes at festivals, God, the heavenly king, also was honored for having favored and supported the earthly king (see, for example, Psalm 118). This idea of God the divine king and warrior supporting his earthly counterpart is the likely original religious context of these verses.

In their description of Jesus' triumphal entry into Jerusalem, all four evangelists portray a scene borrowing heavily from Zechariah 9:9 (Matthew 21:1–9; Mark 11:1–10; Luke 19:29–40; John 12:12–16). Matthew and John both quote the verse directly (Matthew 21:5; John 12:15). The testimony of the evangelists is that the prophet Zechariah's messianic hopes have been fulfilled in Jesus of Nazareth.

READING II Romans 8:9, 11–13

A reading from the Letter of Saint Paul to the Romans

Brothers and **sisters**:
You are **not** in the **flesh**;
on the **contrary**, **you** are in the **spirit**,
if only the **Spirit** of **God** dwells in **you**.
Whoever does **not** have the **Spirit** of **Christ**
does **not belong** to him.
If the **Spirit** of the one who **raised Jesus** from the **dead**
dwells in you,
the one who **raised Christ** from the **dead**
will give **life** to your **mortal bodies** also,
through his **Spirit** that **dwells** in you.
Consequently, **brothers** and **sisters**,
we are **not** debtors to the **flesh**,
to live **according** to the **flesh**.
For if you live **according** to the **flesh**, you will **die**,
but if by the **Spirit** you put to **death** the **deeds** of the **body**,
you will **live**.

This reading opposes flesh to spirit and does so in a fairly complicated way. Proclaim it slowly.

Pay close attention to the contrast between flesh and spirit, life and death, as you prepare this reading.

READING II You will quickly see in these few verses that Paul understands "spirit" and "flesh" to be opposites. But what Paul means by "flesh" in these verses is perhaps not immediately obvious. While Paul sometimes uses "flesh" *(sarx)* to mean the stuff of human and animal bodies (see 1 Corinthians 15:39), this is not his meaning in today's reading.

In Romans 8:7–8, Paul writes, "the concern of the flesh is hostility toward God; it does not submit to the law of God, nor can it; and those who are in the flesh cannot please God." By "in the flesh," Paul cannot

mean "in a human body." If he did, then he would mean that neither he, nor the Roman Christians, nor anyone else living on earth could ever please God. What Paul actually means by flesh we might define as a state of mind and heart in open defiance of God.

Paul conceives of the individual bodies of men and women, as well as the body of the Church, as arenas of theological combat where the powers of death and flesh war with life and spirit. But Paul does not see people individually, or the Church together, as passive onlookers to this struggle. In his letter to the Churches of Galatia, Paul lists

vices, which he calls "works of the flesh," and virtues, which he calls "fruit of the Spirit" (Galatians 5:19–26). To be "in the spirit" and to stay there is not simply a matter of belief in the Gospel, but also a matter of practice and sustained exertion.

GOSPEL In Matthew 18, Jesus' disciples gather to ask him, "Who is the greatest in the kingdom of heaven?" Jesus does not exactly answer their question. Instead, he makes his reply by inviting a child into their midst, saying, "Amen, I say

Emphasize in particular the words "All" and "wishes."

Pause before you proclaim verse 30, looking up and making eye contact with the assembly as you do so.

GOSPEL   Matthew 11:25–30

A reading from the holy Gospel according to Matthew

At that time Jesus exclaimed:
"I give **praise** to you, **Father**, **Lord** of **heaven** and **earth**,
    for although you have **hidden** these things
    from the **wise** and the **learned**
    you have **revealed** them to **little ones**.
Yes, **Father**, such has been your **gracious will**.
All things have been handed over to me by my **Father**.
No one knows the **Son** except the **Father**,
    and no one knows the **Father** except the **Son**
    and **anyone** to whom the **Son wishes** to **reveal** him.

"**Come** to me, **all** you who **labor** and are **burdened**,
    and I will give you **rest**.
Take my **yoke** upon you and **learn** from me,
    for I am **meek** and **humble** of heart;
    and you will find **rest** for yourselves.
For my **yoke** is **easy**, and my **burden light**."

to you, unless you turn and become like children, you will not enter the kingdom of heaven." See how Jesus turns a question with more than a whiff of grandiosity into a word about the importance of humility. In today's reading, Jesus says something in a similar vein, thanking his Father for concealing things from "the wise and the learned" but revealing them to "the childlike" (Matthew 11:25).

One of the characteristics of the kingdom of heaven Matthew's Jesus proclaims is its total reversal of human fortunes and expectations. In the list of blessings with

which Jesus begins his Sermon on the Mount, the kingdom of heaven belongs not to happy people or those held in high esteem, but to the "poor in spirit" and people persecuted for the sake of righteousness (Matthew 5:3, 10). The elders of the people and their chief priests will see "tax collectors and prostitutes" preceding them into the kingdom (Matthew 21:23–32). Likewise, Jesus proclaims that the kingdom ("these things" in 11:25) is not grasped, as one might expect, by "the wise and the learned," but by "the childlike." These are only a few of the surprises of Matthew's kingdom of heaven.

15TH SUNDAY IN ORDINARY TIME

Lectionary #103

READING I — Isaiah 55:10–11

A reading from the Book of the Prophet Isaiah

This reading is a single sentence. Read it slowly, letting the punctuation indicate brief pauses.

Thus says the LORD:
Just as from the **heavens**
    the **rain** and **snow** come down
and do not **return** there
    till they have **watered** the earth,
    making it **fertile** and **fruitful**,
giving **seed** to the one who **sows**
    and **bread** to the one who **eats**,

Pause briefly before you deliver this verse, emphasizing each of its first five words and reading them slowly.

Emphasize the word "not" in this line.

so shall **my word** be
    that goes **forth** from my **mouth**;
my word shall **not** return to me **void**,
    but shall **do** my will,
    achieving the **end** for which I **sent** it.

READING I The tone of Isaiah 55, like much of Isaiah 40—66, is quite joyful. The occasion for joy is the predicted return of captives from Babylon, citizens of Jerusalem and Judah taken hostage decades earlier when the Babylonians invaded Judah and destroyed Jerusalem. The captives have not yet been allowed to return, but things are looking up. The expected return is reason not only for the captives' eagerness and joy, but also for the delight and celebration of nature itself: "Yes, in joy you shall depart, in peace you shall be brought back; Mountains and hills shall break out in song before you, and all the trees of the countryside shall clap their hands" (Isaiah 55:12).

In today's reading, the prophet quotes God's comparison of rain and snow, which do not dissipate until they have nourished the earth, to divine words commanding the release of the captives. The comparison emphasizes the certainty of return, for rain and snow *always* turn brown hills green. The people's hope, therefore, is no mere possibility or likelihood, but a hope that "does not disappoint" (Romans 5:5).

From the wide-angle perspective of world history, the return of many of the captives from Babylon was of very small significance, the tiny drama of a tiny people, before which the story of their liberator, Cyrus of Persia (see Isaiah: 44:28; 45:1, 13), was of epic importance. The author of today's verses did not see things this way. History is not Cyrus' story, but God's. Cyrus conquers only because God has commanded it and chosen to send the people home.

Proclaim this reading in a cheerful, confident tone of voice.

READING II   Romans 8:18–23

A reading from the Letter of Saint Paul to the Romans

Brothers and **sisters**:
I consider that the **sufferings** of this present time are as **nothing**
    compared with the **glory** to be **revealed** for us.
For **creation** awaits with **eager expectation**
    the **revelation** of the **children** of **God**;
    for **creation** was made subject to **futility**,
    not of its **own** accord but because of the one who **subjected** it,
    in hope that **creation itself**
    would be **set free** from **slavery** to **corruption**
    and **share** in the **glorious freedom** of the **children** of **God**.
We know that **all creation** is **groaning** in labor pains
        even until **now**;
    and not only **that**, but **we ourselves**,
    who have the **firstfruits** of the **Spirit**,
    we also groan within **ourselves**
    as we wait for **adoption**, the **redemption** of our **bodies**.

Look up and make eye contact with the assembly when you read Paul's description of himself and his audience amid the groaning creation.

GOSPEL   Matthew 13:1–23

A reading from the holy Gospel according to Matthew

On that day, **Jesus** went out of the house and sat down by the **sea**.
Such large crowds gathered around him
    that he **got** into a **boat** and sat down,
    and the whole crowd stood along the **shore**.

READING II In confessing that Jesus Christ rose from the dead, many early Christians also affirmed that something fundamental in the fabric of the universe had changed. The new life of Christ was something previously unavailable, but in which they, through the Holy Spirit, could now share. They also affirmed that Christ would one day return to elevate them, bodily and spiritually, to a higher level of life even more like his own. The Church shares the new life of Christ in a partial sense, awaiting the full realization of something it has only begun to experience.

Paul writes of "the firstfruits of the Spirit" as something the Church possesses now. Indeed, it is because Paul and the Roman Christians have these "firstfruits" that they "groan within" as they await "adoption, the redemption of our bodies" (Romans 8:23). The interior groans of Christians join the groaning chorus of creation, which Paul has earlier described as "groaning in labor pains" (Romans 8:22) in eager expectation of "the revelation of the children of God" (Romans 8:19).

What are we to make of all this groaning? Paul's meaning, informed by philosophical language and concepts, is that all God's creation feels the beginning of its eventual, complete renewal. But the renewal has only just begun. Only the "fristfruits" of the Spirit have arrived, which is just enough for creation to sense that its present "slavery to corruption" will soon give way before the "glorious freedom of the children of God" (Romans 8:21). Paul believes that Christians occupy a central role in the drama of creation's renewal.

Pause briefly before each occurrence of the word "some."

And he **spoke** to them at length in **parables**, saying:
"A **sower** went out to **sow**.
And as he **sowed**, some seed fell on the **path**,
and **birds** came and **ate** it up.
Some fell on **rocky ground**, where it had **little soil**.
It sprang up **at once** because the **soil** was not **deep**,
and when the **sun** rose it was **scorched**,
and it **withered** for lack of **roots**.
Some seed fell among **thorns**, and the **thorns** grew up
and **choked** it.
But some seed fell on **rich** soil, and produced **fruit**,
a **hundred** or **sixty** or **thirtyfold**.
Whoever has **ears** ought to **hear**."

Pause here briefly. Matthew is shifting from Jesus' public ministry to a private session with his disciples.

The disciples approached him and said,
"**Why** do you speak to them in **parables**?"
He said to them in reply,
"Because **knowledge** of the **mysteries** of the **kingdom**
of **heaven**
has been **granted** to **you**, but to **them** it has **not** been granted.
To **anyone** who has, **more** will be **given** and he will grow **rich**;
from **anyone** who has **not**, even what he **has** will be
taken away.
"**This** is why I speak to them in parables, because
they **look** but do **not see** and **hear** but do **not listen**
or **understand**.
Isaiah's **prophecy** is **fulfilled** in them, which says:
*You shall indeed **hear** but **not understand**,*
*you shall indeed **look** but **never see**.*
*Gross is the **heart** of **this people**,*
*they will **hardly hear** with their **ears**,*
*they have **closed** their **eyes**,*

Slow down as you proclaim the passage from Isaiah 6:9–10, taking care to emphasize its key terms.

GOSPEL | The parable of the sower is the occasion in Matthew, Mark, and Luke when Jesus explains his reasons for speaking in parables and offers his disciples a guided tour of the dark and hidden parts of this story (Matthew 13:3–23; Mark 4:3–25; Luke 8:5–18).

One of the features distinguishing Matthew's version of this parable is the importance Jesus places on both hearing and understanding God's word. In Mark's Gospel, "those sown on rich soil are the ones who hear the word and *accept it* and bear fruit thirty and sixty and a hundredfold" (Mark 4:20). Luke records that Jesus interpreted the seed falling in good soil to be "the ones who, when they have heard the word, *embrace it* with a generous and good heart, and bear fruit through perseverance" (Luke 8:15). But in Matthew's Gospel, "the seed sown on rich soil is the one who hears the word and *understands it*, who indeed bears fruit and yields a hundred or sixty or thirtyfold" (Matthew 13:23).

If indeed bearing fruit as a disciple of Jesus is partly a matter of understanding even Jesus' most cryptic utterances, then we should note that Jesus probably does not mean an understanding that requires wisdom or even much intelligence. Remember Jesus' prayer to his Father in Matthew 11:25: "I give praise to you, Father, Lord of heaven and earth, for although you have hidden these things from the wise and the learned you have revealed them to the childlike." Jesus refers here to the disciples he has just

*lest they **see** with their **eyes***
*and **hear** with their **ears***
*and **understand** with their **hearts** and be **converted**,*
*and I **heal** them.*

"But **blessed** are **your** eyes, because they **see**,
and **your** ears, because they **hear**.
Amen, I say to **you**, **many prophets** and **righteous people**
longed to see what **you** see but did **not** see it,
and to **hear** what **you** hear but did **not** hear it.

"**Hear** then the **parable** of the **sower**.
The seed sown on the **path** is the one
who **hears** the **word** of the **kingdom** without
understanding it,
and the **evil one** comes and **steals** away
what was **sown** in his **heart**.
The seed sown on **rocky ground**
is the one who **hears** the **word** and receives it **at once** with **joy**.
But he has no **root** and lasts **only** for a **time**.
When some **tribulation** or **persecution** comes because
of the **word**,
he **immediately** falls away.
The seed sown among **thorns** is the one who **hears** the word,
but then **worldly anxiety** and the **lure** of **riches choke** the word
and it bears **no fruit**.
But the seed sown on **rich soil**
is the one who **hears** the **word** and **understands** it,
who indeed bears **fruit** and yields a **hundred** or **sixty**
or **thirtyfold**."

[Shorter: Matthew 13:1–9]

Pause here briefly. Matthew moves from Jesus' explanation of why Jesus speaks in parables to the explanation of the parable he tells earlier.

commissioned for ministry (see Matthew 10—11). These are not wise or even especially sharp men. The critical fact distinguishing them from others is that Jesus selected and called them, and they came.

The principle underlying Jesus' reason for speaking in parables to the crowds while reserving explanations for his disciples may seem unfair: "anyone who has, more will be given and he will grow rich; from anyone who has not, even what he has will be taken away" (Matthew 13:12). Yet understanding Jesus is not only a matter of human wit, something simply left up to the ability and willingness of each believer. It is also a matter of God's grace.

16TH SUNDAY IN ORDINARY TIME

Lectionary #106

READING I   Wisdom 12:13, 16–19

A reading from the Book of Wisdom

Proclaim this reading slowly, in a strong and dignified tone of voice appropriate for praise speech.

lenient = LEE-nee-ent

Let the punctuation indicate brief pauses in your delivery, and emphasize the word "all" in particular, which is repeated throughout today's reading.
temerity = teh-MAIR-uh-tee
clemency = KLEM-en-see

There is **no** god besides **you** who have the **care** of **all**,
    that you need show you have not unjustly condemned.
For your **might** is the source of **justice**;
    your **mastery** over **all** things makes you **lenient** to **all**.
For you **show** your **might** when the **perfection** of your **power**
    is **disbelieved**;
    and in those who **know** you, you **rebuke** temerity.
But though you are **master** of **might**, you **judge** with **clemency**,
    and with much **lenience** you **govern** us;
    for **power**, whenever you will, **attends** you.
And you **taught** your **people**, by these **deeds**,
    that those who are **just** must be **kind**;
and you **gave** your **children** good ground for **hope**
    that you would permit **repentance** for their **sins**.

READING I   The major theme of Wisdom 11—19 is the role of holy wisdom in the Israelites' Exodus from Egypt. (On holy wisdom in the Old Testament, see commentary VI, Easter Vigil, March 22.) Today's reading digresses somewhat from this theme, concerned as it is with the specific topic of God's mercy (Wisdom 11:15—12:22). The larger issue concerning these verses is the nature of God's mercy and justice to all peoples, particularly the Canaanites, whom the Israelites subdued when they conquered their land.

The author of the book of Wisdom calls the Canaanites "an accursed race from the beginning," referring to Noah's curse on Ham (Wisdom 21:11; Genesis 9:18–27). These words should, at the very least, raise our eyebrows and invite our skepticism. But the author also knows that despite God's preferential love of Israel, God also loves Israel's ancient enemies: "For you love all things that are and loathe nothing that you have made; for what you hated, you would not have fashioned" (Wisdom 11:24). The love of the Creator for *all* creation is a fact greater than ordinary human rivalries and prejudices.

In today's reading, the author writes that when God repeatedly showed the Canaanites mercy, Israel was provided an example of merciful behavior to imitate: "And you taught your people, by these deeds, that those who are just must be kind; And you gave your sons good ground for hope that you would permit repentance for their sins" (Wisdom 12:19).

Look up and make eye contact with the assembly as much as possible as you proclaim this reading. Paul's point that prayer arises from the stirring of the Holy Spirit—and not the unaided human mind and heart—is a very important one.

READING II   Romans 8:26–27

A reading from the Letter of Saint Paul to the Romans

Brothers and **sisters**:
The **Spirit** comes to the **aid** of our **weakness**;
    for we do **not** know how to **pray** as we **ought**,
    but the **Spirit himself intercedes** with inexpressible **groanings**.
And the one who **searches hearts**
    knows what is the intention of the **Spirit**,
    because he **intercedes** for the **holy ones**
    according to God's **will**.

GOSPEL   Matthew 13:24–43

A reading from the holy Gospel according to Matthew

Jesus proposed another **parable** to the crowds, saying:
"The **kingdom** of **heaven** may be likened to a **man**
    who sowed **good seed** in his **field**.
While everyone was **asleep** his **enemy** came
    and sowed **weeds** all through the **wheat**, and then went off.
When the crop **grew** and **bore fruit**, the **weeds** appeared as well.
The **slaves** of the **householder** came to him and said,
    '**Master**, did you **not** sow **good seed** in your **field**?
Where have the **weeds** come from?'
He answered, 'An **enemy** has done this.'
His slaves said to him, 'Do you want us to **go** and **pull** them **up**?'

Be sure to indicate clearly the slaves' questions by raising the pitch of your voice.

READING II | In his letter to the Christians in Rome, Paul lays out much of his Gospel to a community he has never met. One of the subjects he deals with in depth is the way in which God's grace is more than sufficient to handle the powers of sin and death. The way Paul writes about death can be a little confusing. On the one hand, it is clear that death is an enemy of human beings, "the last enemy to be destroyed" as he describes it in relation to

the second coming of Christ (1 Corinthians 15:26). On the other hand, the rite of baptism enables the person being baptized to participate in Christ's own death. And this participation in death is a good thing, Paul says, "For a dead person has been absolved from sin" (Romans 6:7). Although death is humankind's enemy, "baptism into death," meaning Christ's death, is the only way to pass from the authority of sin and death to the safety of Christ's authority, where Christians "live in newness of life" (Romans 6:4).

The move from the authority of sin and death to the authority of Christ, in Paul's view, introduces the newly baptized person to a life surrounded and filled by the Spirit. In today's reading, which comprises a meager two verses of the sumptuous eighth chapter of Romans, Paul writes that the Spirit both guides prayer and intercedes "for the holy ones according to God's will" (Romans 8:27). Lest one think "the holy ones"

He replied, 'No, if you **pull up** the **weeds**
 you might uproot the **wheat** along with them.
Let them **grow together** until **harvest**;
 then at **harvest** time I will **say** to the **harvesters**,
 "First **collect** the **weeds** and tie them in bundles for **burning**;
 but gather the **wheat** into my **barn**." ' "

Pause in your delivery between each parable.

He proposed another parable to them.
"The **kingdom** of **heaven** is like a **mustard seed**
 that a person took and sowed in a field.
It is the **smallest** of all the seeds,
 yet when **full-grown** it is the **largest** of plants.
It becomes a large bush,
 and the '**birds** of the **sky** come and **dwell** in its **branches**.' "

He spoke to them another parable.
"The **kingdom** of **heaven** is like **yeast**
 that a woman took and mixed with three measures
 of wheat flour
 until the whole batch was **leavened**."

Deliver these verses slowly and with emphasis.

All these things Jesus spoke to the crowds in parables.
He spoke to them **only** in parables,
 to **fulfill** what had been said through the **prophet**:
 I will **open** *my* **mouth** *in* **parables**,
 I will **announce** *what has lain* **hidden** *from the* **foundation**
 of the **world**.

Then, dismissing the crowds, he went into the house.
His disciples approached him and said,
 "**Explain** to us the parable of the **weeds** in the **field**."
He said in reply, "He who sows **good seed** is the **Son** of **Man**,
 the **field** is the **world**, the good seed the **children**
 of the **kingdom**.

represent some special class of Christians, recall that this is a common term of address Paul uses for the Christians with whom he is in fellowship (see Romans 1:7; 1 Corinthians 1:2; 2 Corinthians 1:1; Philippians 1:1). For Paul, the prayer of the Christian does not arise from the individual alone, but from the Spirit enlivening the whole community of "holy ones."

GOSPEL There is no way to define with precision the meaning of the word "parable" as the evangelists use it. For example, in Luke 4:23 Jesus states something our Bible calls a "proverb," although the Greek word is *parabolē*, which is usually translated as "parable." The translation makes sense, for what Jesus then says ("Physician, cure yourself") has more in common with an ordinary proverb or popular saying than with the parables we find in today's reading, which are laden with hidden meaning.

Matthew offers us three parables comparing the kingdom of heaven to things that grow seemingly of their own accord. Jesus' examples are drawn from the rustic world of farming and peasant life in which he and his Galilean audience were raised. In all three cases, the growth is set in motion by human beings, but comes to maturity by other means

The **weeds** are the **children** of the **evil one**,
  and the **enemy** who **sows** them is the **devil**.
The **harvest** is the **end** of the **age**, and the **harvesters** are **angels**.
Just as **weeds** are **collected** and **burned up** with **fire**,
  so will it **be** at the **end** of the **age**.
The **Son** of **Man** will send his **angels**,
  and they will collect out of his **kingdom**
  all who cause others to **sin** and all **evildoers**.
They will **throw** them into the **fiery furnace**,
  where there will be **wailing** and **grinding** of **teeth**.
Then the **righteous** will **shine** like the **sun**
  in the **kingdom** of their **Father**.
Whoever has **ears** ought to **hear**."

[Shorter: Matthew 13:24–30]

not immediately apparent. The woman leavens her dough, but it rises on its own. Likewise, the kingdom of heaven may be anticipated, proclaimed, and prepared for, but its full advent is not the result of human effort but rather an act of God.

Matthew reports that Jesus told the crowds nothing except in parables, but explained the parable of the wheat field to his disciples in private (Matthew 13:36). Mark makes the general statement that "without parables he [Jesus] did not speak to them [the crowd], but to his own disciples he explained everything in private" (Mark 4:34). This testifies to the special qualifications of the disciples to interpret Jesus' words and explain them to others, but also highlights how great is their responsibility for upholding that teaching and remaining faithful to what they have been permitted to understand.

17TH SUNDAY IN ORDINARY TIME

Lectionary #109

READING I   1 Kings 3:5, 7–12

A reading from the first Book of Kings

Solomon = SAH-loh-min

Look up at the assembly as you deliver God's words to Solomon.

The LORD appeared to **Solomon** in a **dream** at night.
God said, "**Ask** something of me and I will **give** it to you."
Solomon answered:
"O **LORD**, my **God**, you have made me, your servant, **king**
    to succeed my father **David**;
    but I am a mere **youth**, not **knowing** at **all** how to **act**.
I **serve** you in the **midst** of the **people** whom you have **chosen**,
    a people so **vast** that it **cannot** be numbered or **counted**.
Give your **servant**, therefore, an understanding **heart**
    to **judge** your **people** and to **distinguish right** from **wrong**.

Make sure to raise the pitch of your voice to indicate Solomon's question.

For **who** is able to **govern** this vast people of **yours**?"

The LORD was **pleased** that Solomon made this request.
So God said to him:
    "**Because** you have asked for this—
    not for a **long life** for **yourself**,
    nor for **riches**,
    nor for the **life** of your **enemies**,
    but for **understanding** so that you may know what is **right**—
    I do as you **requested**.
I give you a heart so **wise** and **understanding**

Emphasize the words "never" and "anyone."

    that there has **never** been **anyone** like you up to now,
    and after you there will come **no one** to **equal** you."

READING I One among David's many sons, Solomon was born after his father conquered Jerusalem and had made it his capital (2 Samuel 5:13–16). He was younger than those of his brothers born in David's former stronghold of Hebron (2 Samuel 3:1–5). While Solomon was still a boy, one of these older brothers, Absalom, a dashing, handsome, and popular prince (2 Samuel 14:25; 15:1–6), tried to seize David's throne in a doomed coup (2 Samuel 17:14). But Absalom died in the attempt (2 Samuel 18:9–18). In David's old age, Adonijah, another

son, schemed to acquire the throne for himself. But due to the intervention of Nathan (David's most favored prophet) and Bathsheba (Solomon's mother), Adonijah's desire was thwarted and Solomon was proclaimed king (1 Kings 1:5–53). Even then, Solomon had to devote the early part of his reign to settling accounts with his opponents (1 Kings 2:12–34). Solomon's path to the throne of Israel, which 1 Kings 3:1 describes as "firmly in his grasp," was neither easy nor certain.

"Ask something of me and I will give it to you," God says to Solomon (1 Kings 3:5).

In reply, Solomon requests "an understanding heart to judge your people and to distinguish right from wrong" (1 Kings 3:9). The Hebrew word our Bible translates as "heart" is *lev*. The word's literal meaning is "heart," although the heart in ancient Israel was often considered the seat of thought. Thus a translation of *lev* by "mind" works well in this case. Solomon is asking God for sound reason, wisdom, fairness, and discernment. Like Abraham's faith, Solomon's wisdom (see 1 Kings 3:16–28; 5:9–14; 10:23–24) became legendary (see Matthew 12:42; Luke 11:31).

Deliver this reading in a cheerful tone of voice.

Emphasize the reading's opening lines especially, making eye contact with the assembly when you proclaim them.

READING II   Romans 8:28–30

A reading from the Letter of Saint Paul to the Romans

Brothers and sisters:
We know that **all** things work for **good** for those who **love God**,
    who are **called** according to his **purpose**.
For those he **foreknew** he also **predestined**
    to be **conformed** to the **image** of his **Son**,
    so that he might be the **firstborn**
    among **many** brothers and sisters.
And those he **predestined** he also **called**;
    and those he **called** he also **justified**;
    and those he **justified** he also **glorified**.

Matthew stacks several short, quite vivid parables of Jesus one on top of the other. Read them slowly! Pause after you deliver each one, giving the assembly time to consider each before you move on.

Emphasize in particular the word "Again" both times it appears.

GOSPEL   Matthew 13:44–52

A reading from the holy Gospel according to Matthew

Jesus said to his disciples:
"The **kingdom** of **heaven** is like a **treasure** buried in a **field**,
    which a person **finds** and **hides** again,
    and out of **joy** goes and sells **all** that he has and **buys** that field.
Again, the **kingdom** of **heaven** is like a **merchant**
    searching for **fine pearls**.
When he finds a **pearl** of great **price**,
    he goes and sells **all** that he has and **buys** it.
Again, the **kingdom** of **heaven** is like a **net** thrown into the **sea**,
    which collects **fish** of **every kind**.

READING II   In his letter to the Church at Philippi, Paul expresses anger at opponents of his mission, people he contends "conduct themselves as enemies of the cross of Christ" and occupy their thoughts with "earthly things" (Philippians 3:18–19). "But our citizenship is in heaven," Paul says, contrasting the Philippians and himself with these opponents. And Christ will come for his heavenly citizens: "He will change our lowly body to conform with his glorified body by the power that enables him also to bring all things into subjection to himself" (Philippians 3:21).

Today's reading from Romans also concerns the conformity of the Christian to Christ. Here Paul writes that those whom God has selected are "conformed to the *image*" of Christ (Romans 8:29). While this language is somewhat different than "conformed to the body of his glory" (Philippians 3:21), the conviction of both passages is quite similar: being Christian involves the fundamental transformation of the whole person from conformity to earthly things to conformity to heavenly things. The Christian, in Paul's view, is practically a new species (2 Corinthians 5:15–17).

But one significant difference between Philippians 3:20–21 and today's reading is *when* Paul says this conformity to Christ takes place. In today's reading, Paul writes that those whom God has predestined, called, and justified, "he also glorified" (Romans 8:30). In Philippians, conformity to "the body of his glory" lies in the future (Philippians 3:20–21). In Romans 8, unlike Philippians 3, Paul's main focus is on the transforming power of the life-giving Holy Spirit at work in the community *now*.

When it is **full** they haul it ashore
   and sit down to put what is **good** into **buckets**.
What is **bad** they **throw away**.
Thus it will be at the **end** of the **age**.
The **angels** will go out and **separate** the **wicked** from
     the **righteous**
   and throw them into the **fiery furnace**,
    where there will be **wailing** and **grinding** of **teeth**.

"Do you **understand** all these things?"
They answered, "**Yes**."
And he replied,
"Then **every** scribe who has been **instructed**
    in the **kingdom** of **heaven**
   is like the **head** of a **household**
   who brings from his **storeroom** both the **new** and the **old**."

[Shorter: Matthew 13:44–46]

GOSPEL For the third Sunday in a row, the Lectionary offers us parables of Jesus according to Matthew. Given what Matthew says in 13:36, we should probably assume that the evangelist means us to understand that today's parables come from a private discussion between Jesus and his disciples.

As on last Sunday, Jesus compares the kingdom of heaven to certain imaginative scenarios. But whereas the parables from last Sunday compared the kingdom of heaven to things growing of their own accord, the first three parables of today's Gospel compare the discovery of the kingdom of heaven to people's *discovery* of precious things and receipt of great abundance.

The man's behavior in the first parable—burying treasure in a field, then selling all he owns to buy the field—hardly seems sensible. But then Jesus' teachings of how to prepare for the advent of the kingdom of heaven rarely seem "sensible" in a conventional sense. Jesus' advice to the rich young man hardly sounds like sensible behavior for a rich man: "go, sell what you have and give to [the] poor, and you will have treasure in heaven. Then come, follow me" (Matthew 19:21; see also Mark 10:21; Luke 18:22). And what is sensible about Jesus' word to his disciples about the way of the cross? "Whoever wishes to come after me must deny himself, take up his cross, and follow me" (Matthew 16:24; see Mark 8:34; Luke 9:23).

Such responses to the kingdom of heaven may seem extreme to some. But those who discover these treasures, like the people in today's parables, may find that such responses make good sense in the light of the quality of what has been found.

18TH SUNDAY IN ORDINARY TIME

Lectionary #112

READING I   Isaiah 55:1–3

A reading from the Book of the Prophet Isaiah

Thus says the LORD:
All you who are **thirsty**,
   come to the **water**!
You who have no **money**,
   come, receive **grain** and **eat**;
Come, **without** paying and **without** cost,
   drink **wine** and **milk**!
Why spend your **money** for what is not **bread**;
   your **wages** for what **fails** to **satisfy**?
Heed me, and you shall **eat well**,
   you shall **delight** in rich fare.
Come to me **heedfully**,
   listen, that you may have **life**.
I will **renew** with you the **everlasting covenant**,
   the **benefits** assured to **David**.

Make sure to raise the pitch of your voice to indicate this question.

READING I   In Isaiah 40—55, which most biblical scholars believe was mostly composed toward the end of the Babylonian captivity, God repeatedly refers to the provision of water in the wilderness. God's gift of water to thirsty Israel in these chapters evokes the water God provided during the Exodus (see Isaiah 48:21; Exodus 17:1–7; Numbers 20:1–13). In Isaiah 43, God recalls the parting of the waters during the Exodus, but says that the new waters welling up in the wilderness and the return of the captives from Babylon are feats far superior to that great deed of

old (Isaiah 43:16–20). "I will pour out water upon the thirsty ground," God speaks by the voice of the prophet, "and streams upon the dry land; I will pour out my spirit upon your offspring, and my blessing upon your descendants" (Isaiah 44:3).

The expectation of the captives' return also raises the hope that the kingdom of Judah will be reestablished. In line with this hope, the prophet in today's reading reports God's promise: "I will renew with you the everlasting covenant, the benefits assured to David" (Isaiah 55:3). God's covenant with David was, in a manner of speaking, a polit-

ical covenant, for according to its terms God assured David an endless dynasty. In 2 Samuel 7, the prophet Nathan receives a vision in which God instructs him to tell David, "Your house and your kingdom shall endure forever before me; your throne shall stand firm forever" (2 Samuel 7:16).

The destruction of the independent kingdom of Judah and the exile of many of its citizens appeared to end this covenant. But the hope of return in turn raises the hope that the covenant still stands, that the kingdom of Judah will rise from the rubble of its destruction.

READING II   Romans 8:35, 37–39

A reading from the Letter of Saint Paul to the Romans

Brothers and **sisters**:
What will **separate** us from the **love** of **Christ**?
Will **anguish**, or **distress**, or **persecution**, or **famine**,
   or **nakedness**, or **peril**, or the **sword**?
No, in **all** these things we conquer **overwhelmingly**
   through **him** who **loved** us.
For **I** am **convinced** that neither **death**, nor **life**,
   nor **angels**, nor **principalities**,
   nor **present** things, nor **future** things,
   nor **powers**, nor **height**, nor **depth**,
   nor any other **creature** will be able to **separate** us
   from the **love** of **God** in **Christ Jesus** our **Lord**.

This reading is a sweeping rhetorical flourish. Read it slowly in a cheerful and confident tone of voice.

Pause briefly between each of these listed terms.

Smile broadly and make eye contact with the assembly when you proclaim the phrase "in all these things we conquer overwhelmingly."

GOSPEL   Matthew 14:13–21

A reading from the holy Gospel according to Matthew

When **Jesus** heard of the **death** of **John** the **Baptist**,
   he **withdrew** in a **boat** to a **deserted** place by himself.
The crowds heard of this and followed him on foot
   from their towns.
When he disembarked and saw the **vast crowd**,
   his heart was moved with **pity** for them,
      and he **cured** their **sick**.

In this reading, Jesus knows what he intends to do while the disciples are somewhat confused. Proclaim Jesus' words in a strong, clear tone of voice, but use a worried or flustered tone for the uncomprehending disciples.

READING II | This is the fifth consecutive Sunday the second reading has been drawn from the eighth chapter of Paul's letter to the Romans. In this letter Paul strives to show that Jews and Gentiles, whom he believes have long stood in different relationships to God, at last have access to the same means of redemption through faith in Jesus Christ. Oppressed by, though also participating in, the powers of sin and death, people accepting the free gift of grace through faith receive the means to escape these powers, fleeing them to the safety of God's protection (Romans 1—5). By Baptism, believers make their escape. By this sacrament they participate in Christ's death and Resurrection, dying to the powers of sin and death, but rising in new life supplied by the Spirit, who fills, surrounds, and sustains the Church.

Paul, like most ancient people, accepted that the world was literally filled with supernatural beings. He saw it as a challenging and sometimes dangerous place not least because of the spiritual and supernatural powers at work in it. In today's reading, "angels" and "principalities" probably refer to such beings, for these terms were commonly used in this way in antiquity.

Paul's point in these confident and stirring verses is that nothing earthly or spiritual can snatch Christians away from their Lord. No power is that strong.

GOSPEL | The feeding of the 5,000 is the only one of the miracles Jesus performed in Galilee that is recorded in all four Gospels (Matthew 14:15–21; Mark 6:35–44; Luke 9:12–17; John 6:1–13). Matthew and Mark record an additional feeding of

Slow down to emphasize the action of this verse.

When it was evening, the disciples approached him and said,
    "This is a **deserted** place and it is already **late**;
    dismiss the crowds so that they can **go** to the **villages**
    and buy **food** for themselves."
Jesus said to them, "There is **no need** for them to go away;
    give them some **food yourselves**."
But they said to him,
    "Five loaves and two fish are **all** we **have** here."
Then he said, "**Bring** them here to **me**,"
    and he **ordered** the crowds to **sit down** on the grass.
Taking the **five loaves** and the **two fish**, and looking up to **heaven**,
    he said the **blessing**, **broke** the loaves,
    and **gave** them to the **disciples**,
    who in turn gave them to the **crowds**.
They all **ate** and were **satisfied**,
    and they picked up the **fragments** left over—
    twelve wicker baskets full.
Those who **ate** were about **five thousand men**,
    not counting **women** and **children**.

4,000 (Matthew 15:32–38; Mark 8:1–9). In Matthew's Gospel, the feedings warn the disciples against the Pharisees' teachings (Matthew 16:5–12). Mark uses the feedings to display the disciples' ongoing ignorance of Jesus' true identity and greatness (Mark 8:14–21).

    This miracle foreshadows Jesus' institution of the Eucharist at the Last Supper (Matthew 26:26–29; Mark 14:22–25; Luke 22:19–20; see also 1 Corinthians 11:23–26). Jesus' main action in Matthew's account of

the feeding of the 5,000 is blessing, breaking, and distribution of the loaves: "he said the blessing, broke the loaves, and gave them to the disciples" (Matthew 14:19). At the Last Supper, "Jesus took bread, said the blessing, broke it, and giving it to his disciples said, 'Take and eat; this is my body'" (Matthew 26:26). A sequence of blessing, breaking, and distribution forms the core of both scenes. In the first case, Jesus miraculously feeds people who are hungry in a literal sense. In the second case, Jesus institutes the sacrament of the Eucharist feeding people in a spiritual sense.

    Matthew's Jesus adds a unique layer of meaning to the miraculous feedings he performs. Having asked his disciples to recall the many basketsful left over from the few loaves, Jesus then asks the following in 16:11: "How do you not comprehend that I was not speaking to you about bread? Beware of the leaven of the Pharisees and Sadducees!" Thus, Matthew records that concealed within this public demonstration of Jesus' power is a private warning to the disciples to resist the influence of opposing teachings.

19TH SUNDAY IN ORDINARY TIME

Lectionary 115

READING I   1 Kings 19:9a, 11–13a

Horeb = HO-reb

Elijah = Eh-LYE-jah

A reading from the first Book of Kings

At the mountain of God, **Horeb**,
   Elijah came to a cave where he took shelter.
Then the LORD said to him,
   "Go outside and stand on the mountain before the LORD;
   the LORD will be passing by."
A strong and heavy wind was **rending** the mountains
   and **crushing** rocks before the LORD—
   but the LORD was **not** in the **wind**.
After the wind there was an **earthquake**—
   but the LORD was **not** in the **earthquake**.
After the earthquake there was **fire**—
   but the LORD was **not** in the **fire**.
After the fire there was a **tiny whispering sound**.
When he **heard** this,
   Elijah hid his face in his cloak
   and went and stood at the entrance of the cave.

READING I   In today's reading, Elijah is on the run for his life from Ahab and Jezebel, having deeply angered the queen for publicly embarrassing her, Baal (her god), and killing hundreds of Baal's prophets (1 Kings 18:20–46). Concerning the killing of the prophets, the furious Jezebel sends word to Elijah: "May the gods do thus and so to me if by this time tomorrow I have not done with your life what was done to each of them."

Afraid, alone, and on the verge of despair, Elijah flees southward to Judah, where he begs God to take his life. Instead, an angel appears to make sure he eats something and informs him that he will be going on a journey. In a reverse reenactment of Israel's 40 years of desert wandering, Elijah leaves Judah and walks 40 days and nights to Horeb, also known as Sinai (Deuteronomy 5:2), the mountain where Moses received the law (1 Kings 19:1–8).

On the mountain, a voice asks Elijah, "Why are you here, Elijah?" He replies, "I have been most zealous for the LORD, the God of hosts, but the Israelites have forsaken your covenant, torn down your altars, and put your prophets to the sword. I alone am left, and they seek to take my life" (1 Kings 19:9–10).

The voice does not console Elijah, nor gives any hint that its owner has even heard him. It simply directs him to go stand on the mountain, for "the LORD will be passing by" (1 Kings 19:11). But unlike in the days of Israel's wandering, God is not present in smoke, fire, and quaking earth (Exodus 19:18). Although Elijah witnesses wind, earthquake, and fire, the text quite clearly says that the Lord is not "in" any of these things.

At last, Elijah hears "a tiny whispering sound" (1 Kings 19:12). Moving to the mouth

READING II   Romans 9:1–5

A reading from the Letter of Saint Paul to the Romans

Brothers and **sisters**:
I speak the **truth** in Christ, I do **not** lie;
    my **conscience** joins with the **Holy Spirit**
        in bearing me **witness**
    that I have great **sorrow** and constant **anguish** in my heart.
For I could **wish** that I **myself** were **accursed**
        and **cut off** from **Christ**
    for the **sake** of my **own people**,
    my **kindred** according to the **flesh**.
They are **Israelites**;
    theirs the **adoption**, the **glory**, the **covenants**,
    the **giving** of the **law**, the **worship**, and the **promises**;
    theirs the **patriarchs**, and from them,
    according to the **flesh**, is the **Christ**,
    who is over **all**, **God blessed forever**. **Amen**

Israelites = IS-ree-ah-lites

Read the list of the possessions of Israel slowly and clearly, pausing briefly between each item so they do not all run together.

Conclude this reading in the solemn and dignified tone of voice normally used in public prayer.

GOSPEL   Matthew 14:22–33

A reading from the holy Gospel according to Matthew

After he had fed the people, Jesus made the disciples
    get into a boat
    and **precede** him to the other side,
    while he dismissed the crowds.
After doing so, he went up on the mountain by himself to **pray**.

Matthew tells us that when the disciples see Jesus walking on the sea, they are "terrified" and cry out. Therefore, proclaim their frightened exclamation in a fearful tone of voice and slightly louder than you deliver anything else in the reading.

of the cave, Elijah hears the question of 19:9 repeated: "Elijah, why are you here?" Elijah repeats his lament. And how does the voice respond? It gives him further instructions (1 Kings 19:15–18).

It almost seems like a cruel joke. But it is not. God has indeed passed by, although not as in the days of Moses. Instead of smoke and fire, God is present to Elijah in the voice of prophecy. And although Elijah has not asked to hear this voice, he obeys it.

READING II In today's reading, Paul laments the rejection of his

Gospel by so many of his fellow Jews. He speaks of his heart's "great sorrow and constant anguish," wishing himself "accursed and separated from Christ" for the sake of his Jewish kinsmen (Romans 9:2–3). He honors their election by God and their history. Though a self-proclaimed apostle and minister to Gentiles (Romans 11:13; 15:16; Galatians 1:16; 2:2, 8–9), Paul remains fully, utterly Jewish.

Although Paul admits the wrong of having persecuted the Church (Galatians 1:13; 1 Corinthians 15:9; Philippians 3:6), he also speaks with pride of his achievement as

a pious Jew. In Galatians, he says, "I . . . progressed in Judaism beyond many of my contemporaries among my race, since I was even more a zealot for my ancestral traditions" (Galatians 1:14). In Philippians, he recalls that in earlier days "in righteousness based on the law I was blameless" (Philippians 3:6). Paul rejected neither Judaism nor his Jewishness. But because he had come to believe that the Gospel he proclaimed about Jesus Christ was the end, goal, and consummation of Judaism, he was deeply troubled that more Jews had not accepted the Gospel.

Proclaim Jesus' words of greeting on the sea in a strong, reassuring tone of voice.

Deliver the first of Peter's lines in a confident and eager tone of voice. But then, as he begins to sink, deliver his plea to Jesus in the same tone you used with the disciples' previous exclamation.

Make sure to raise the pitch of your voice to make it clear that Jesus is asking Peter a question.

When it was evening he was there **alone**.
Meanwhile the boat, already a few miles offshore,
   was being **tossed about** by the waves,
      for the wind was against it.
During the fourth watch of the night,
   he came toward them **walking** on the **sea**.
When the disciples **saw** him walking on the sea
   they were **terrified**.
"It is a **ghost**," they said, and they cried out in **fear**.
At once Jesus spoke to them, "Take **courage**, it is **I**;
   do **not** be **afraid**."
Peter said to him in reply,
   "**Lord**, if it is **you**, **command** me to **come** to you on the **water**."
He said, "**Come**."
Peter got out of the boat and began to **walk** on the **water**
   toward **Jesus**.
But when he **saw** how strong the **wind** was
   he became **frightened**;
   and, beginning to sink, he cried out, "**Lord**, **save me**!"
Immediately Jesus stretched out his hand and **caught** Peter,
   and said to him, "O **you** of **little faith**, **why** did you **doubt**?"
After they got into the boat, the **wind** died down.
Those who were in the boat did him **homage**, saying,
   "**Truly**, **you** are the **Son** of **God**."

GOSPEL One of the unique features of Matthew's version of the story of Jesus walking on the water is Peter's decision to leave the boat and walk out to meet him (see also Mark 6:45–56; John 6:15–21). All goes well until fear gets the better of him. As Peter begins to sink, he begs Jesus to save him. "O you of little faith," Jesus says as he rescues his disciple, "why did you doubt?"

In Matthew 14—18, Jesus has a great deal to say about faith and the lack of faith. To a Canaanite woman who, despite Jesus' initial rebuffs, persists in seeking healing for daughter, Jesus says, "O woman, great is your faith! Let it be done for you as you wish" (Matthew 15:28). Twice Jesus chides the disciples for having little faith (Matthew 16:8; 17:20). On one of these occasions, Jesus cites the disciples' lack of faith as the reason they were unable to heal a boy possessed by a demon (Matthew 17:14–20). "Why could we not drive it out?" the disciples ask? "Because of your little faith," Jesus replies. "Amen, I say to you, if you have faith the size of a mustard seed, you will say to this mountain, 'Move from here to there,' and it will move. Nothing will be impossible for you."

Back in the boat, Jesus' disciples worship him (the Greek word *proskuneō* means "to bow down in worship") and testify, "Truly, you are the Son of God." This is a much different description of the disciples' reaction than Mark records. According to Mark, the disciples' surprise is evidence of their failure to comprehend the multiplication of the loaves (Mark 6:30–44) and their hardness of heart (Mark 6:52).

ASSUMPTION OF THE BLESSED VIRGIN MARY: VIGIL

Lectionary #621

READING I   1 Chronicles 15:3–4, 15–16; 16:1–2

A reading from the first book of Chronicles

David assembled **all Israel** in **Jerusalem** to bring the **ark**
of the **LORD**
to the place that he had **prepared** for it.
David also called together the sons of **Aaron** and the **Levites**.

The **Levites** bore the ark of **God** on their **shoulders** with **poles**,
as **Moses** had ordained according to the **word** of the **LORD**.

David commanded the **chiefs** of the **Levites**
to appoint their **kinsmen** as **chanters**,
to play on musical instruments, **harps**, **lyres**, and **cymbals**,
to make a loud sound of **rejoicing**.

They brought in the **ark** of **God** and set it within the **tent**
which **David** had **pitched** for it.
Then they offered up **burnt offerings** and **peace offerings** to God.
When **David** had **finished** offering up the burnt offerings
and peace offerings,
he **blessed** the people in the **name** of the **LORD**.

Aaron = AY-run
Levites = LEE-vites

Look up and make eye contact with the assembly as you proclaim the last words of this reading.

READING I   The books of 1 and 2 Chronicles do not often appear in the Lectionary. The main sources used by the author of the books of Chronicles were 1 and 2 Samuel and 1 and 2 Kings. A reader will frequently come across many stories and narrated events in Chronicles also found in the four latter books. Chronicles was written well after these books, perhaps a full century or more after the first of the captives taken to Babylon in 587 BC and their descendants had been permitted by Persia (present-day Iran) to return to their homes in Judah and Jerusalem. During much of what biblical historians call "the Persian period" (539–323 BC), Jerusalem and the territory of the former kingdom of Judah lay mired in poverty and partial ruin. The author of Chronicles appears to have addressed the trauma the exile caused by reasserting the people's ancestral connection to the land and the continued vitality of the former institutions of temple and monarchy.

In 1 Chronicles 15 and 2 Samuel 6, David brings the ark to Jerusalem. What the author of 2 Samuel describes as a largely military maneuver, the author of 1 Chronicles records as mainly a liturgical procession. To be sure, the permanent removal of the ark to Jerusalem was an event of both military and religious significance. Perhaps more than anything, this event provides evidence of David's political shrewdness. The presence of the ark made Jerusalem, David's new capital (see 2 Samuel 5:6–10; 1 Chronicles 11:3–8), the most important city for Israelites of all tribes who considered the ark the greatest source of religious authority in the land. And it asserted that David and his descendants, who ruled the city, were the ark's sole, legitimate guardians.

A reading from the first letter of Saint Paul to the Corinthians

Brothers and **sisters**:
When that which is **mortal** clothes itself with **immortality**,
　　then the word that is written shall come about:

　　　Death is **swallowed** *up in* **victory**.
　　　Where, O **death**, *is your* **victory**?
　　　Where, O **death**, *is your* **sting**?

The **sting** of death is **sin**,
　　and the **power** of sin is the **law**.
But thanks be to God who gives us the **victory**
　　through our Lord **Jesus Christ**.

Pause and look up at the assembly before you proclaim these questions. Be sure to raise your voice at the end of each short sentence to clearly indicate the questions. And be sure to emphasize the word "where." Paul's answer to these questions, of course, is *nowhere!*

READING II The core of the Gospel, as Paul tells it, is a report. "For I handed on to you as of first importance," Paul writes to the Church at Corinth, "what I also received: that Christ died for our sins in accordance with the scriptures; that he was buried; that he was raised on the third day in accordance with the scriptures" (1 Corinthians 15:4–3).

But Paul's Gospel also contains reports of appearances of Christ after he rose (1 Corinthians 15:5–8). In answer to the question "how do you know Christ was raised," Paul could count off people who had seen him: Kephas, the 12 apostles, 500 brothers (that is, fellow believers) at once, James, all the apostles, and finally Paul himself. On the strength of eyewitness testimony, therefore, Paul can tell the Corinthians that Christ was truly raised from the dead.

But if Christ's Crucifixion, death, Resurrection, and appearances are, as Paul says, matters "of first importance," then why does he inform the Corinthians, whom he has already evangelized, of this fact? Surely they already know the Gospel!

But in fact, Paul says, the Corinthians do not understand the Gospel—at least not fully. One cannot both believe in Christ's Resurrection and deny that there is also a general Resurrection of the dead. But some in Corinth apparently do not think that there will be such a general Resurrection (1 Corinthians 15:11–19). First Corinthians 15 is Paul's argument that there will be a Resurrection of the dead, and a bodily Resurrection at that. Today's reading comes from Paul's triumphant summation of this subject in 1 Corinthians 15. The victory and

Imagine a woman raising her voice above the noise of a crowd and Jesus responding to her in kind. Proclaim the woman's blessing and Jesus' reply in a tone much louder than you proclaim Luke's narration (just don't yell).

Pause briefly between the woman's blessing and Luke's narration of Jesus reply.

GOSPEL   Luke 11:27–28

A reading from the holy gospel according to Luke

While **Jesus** was speaking,
    a woman from the crowd called out and said to him,
    "**Blessed** is the **womb** that **carried** you
    and the **breasts** at which you **nursed**."
He replied,
    "**Rather**, **blessed** are those
    who **hear** the **word** of **God** and **observe** it."

---

sting of death need never touch those whose fates have been joined, by faith and sacrament, to that of the triumphant Christ.

GOSPEL Today's reading is a snapshot in words of a moment of Jesus' ministry. One sees, amid a boisterous crowd's waves of conversation, the woman's blessing and Jesus' quick reply each rising for a split-second above the din before vanishing back into the clamor.

Quite early in its history, the Church adopted the language of family to express the intimacy its members shared in Christ.

In the earliest Christian writing of all, 1 Thessalonians, Paul addresses the Christians of that city as "brothers loved by God" (1 Thessalonians 1:4). In Luke's Gospel, we read that Jesus' mother and brothers once tried to meet with him, but that Jesus, when he learned they had come and were waiting outside, replied, "My mother and my brothers are those who hear the word of God and act on it" (Luke 8:19–21; see also Matthew 12:46–50; Mark 3:31–35). Luke also records even stronger words of Jesus on this subject in 14:26. It is therefore important to note that included among the core group of disciples

remaining in Jerusalem between Jesus' ascension and Pentecost were Jesus' mother and brothers (Acts 1:14).

The idea underlying Jesus' reply in today's reading is basically the same as what we find in his reply in Luke 8:21. The woman calls out a blessing upon Jesus' mother. Jesus does not reject her blessing, but he redirects it toward "those who hear the word of God and observe it" (Luke 11:28).

ASSUMPTION OF THE BLESSED VIRGIN MARY: DAY

Lectionary #622

READING I   Revelation 11:19a; 12:1–6a, 10ab

A reading from the Book of Revelation

Proclaim this report of John's vision slowly, in a clear and confident tone.

God's **temple** in heaven was **opened**,
    and the **ark** of his **covenant** could be **seen** in the temple.

A great **sign** appeared in the **sky**, a woman **clothed** with the **sun**,
    with the **moon** beneath her feet,
    and on her head a crown of **twelve stars**.
She was with **child** and **wailed aloud** in **pain** as she **labored**
        to give **birth**.
Then **another sign** appeared in the **sky**;
    it was a **huge red dragon**, with **seven heads** and **ten horns**,
    and on its heads were **seven diadems**.
Its tail **swept away** a third of the **stars** in the **sky**
    and **hurled** them down to the **earth**.
Then the **dragon** stood before the **woman** about to **give birth**,
    to **devour** her **child** when she **gave birth**.
She **gave birth** to a **son**, a **male** child,
    destined to rule **all** the nations with an **iron rod**.
Her **child** was caught up to **God** and his **throne**.
The **woman** herself **fled** into the **desert**
    where she had a place **prepared** by **God**.

READING I   In Revelation, it is claimed that the book is the work of someone calling himself John and contains a record of visions John received on the isle of Patmos (in the eastern Aegean sea). John says that the vision came to him while he was "caught up in spirit on the Lord's day," which presumably means that he was deep in prayer, or in a sort of spiritual ecstasy, on a Sunday (Revelation 1:10). His instructions are to write what he sees and to send copies to the local Churches in seven cities of Asia Minor (present-day Turkey) (Revelation 1:9–11, 19). The visions depict, in highly symbolic form, a struggle between God and Satan for control of heaven and earth. The very first verse of Revelation tells the reader that the book has been written to show "what must happen soon" (Revelation 1:1).

In today's reading, we read that "God's temple in heaven was opened, and the ark of his covenant could be seen in the temple" (Revelation 11:19). This heavenly temple is a divine counterpart to the earthly temple. That there was such a temple in heaven is a religious notion we also find both in Hebrews (see Hebrews 9) and in the non-canonical Jewish writing, 1 Enoch (see 1 Enoch 14 especially).

The woman of Revelation 12 has often been seen in Catholicism as a symbol of both Mary and the Church. There is nothing in the text of Revelation to demand this

When you proclaim this verse, do so in a somewhat louder voice than the previous verses, and slightly lower the pitch of your voice if you can.

Then I heard a loud voice in **heaven** say:
  "Now have **salvation** and **power** come,
  and the **Kingdom** of **our God**
  and the **authority** of **his Anointed One**."

READING II   1 Corinthians 15:20—27

A reading from the first Letter of Saint Paul to the Corinthians

Look up and make eye contact with the assembly when you proclaim these words.

Brothers and **sisters**:
Christ has been **raised** from the **dead**,
  the **firstfruits** of those who have **fallen asleep**.
For since **death** came through **man**,
  the **resurrection** of the **dead** came **also** through **man**.
For just as in **Adam all die**,
  so too in **Christ** shall **all** be brought to **life**,
  but **each one** in proper order:
  Christ the **firstfruits**;
  then, at his **coming**, those who **belong** to Christ;
  then comes the **end**,
  when he hands over the **Kingdom** to his **God** and **Father**,
  when he has destroyed **every sovereignty**
  and **every authority** and **power**.
For he must **reign** until he has put all his **enemies** under his **feet**.
The last **enemy** to be destroyed is **death**,
  for "he subjected **everything** under his **feet**."

---

interpretation, nor is there anything prohibiting this interpretation. Her precise identity, therefore, remains a mystery. The 12 stars on her crown likely represent the 12 constellations of the zodiac. With such a symbol of heavenly order set in a symbol of royal authority, her crown, the woman stands with God and the forces of cosmic order arrayed against Satan's destructive power.

READING II   The main issue Paul addresses in 1 Corinthians is disunity in the local Church. Paul sees the

Corinthians' disunity expressed in many different ways, from problems of Church leadership and spiritual pride (1 Corinthians 1—4), to the acceptance of multiple and contradictory teachings about the Resurrection of the dead (1 Corinthians 15). The solution to all this disunity, Paul urges, is unity: "I urge you, brothers, in the name of our Lord Jesus Christ, that all of you agree in what you say, and that there be no divisions among you, but that you be united in the same mind and in the same purpose" (1 Corinthians 1:10).

Today's reading is Paul's description of how the end of days will unfold, with special attention placed on Christ's role. Paul offers this description in support of an argument: if one accepts the Good News that Jesus Christ was crucified, buried, and raised, Paul reasons, then one must also accept that there will be a general Resurrection of the dead (1 Corinthians 15:12–19). This is what Paul means when he calls the resurrected Christ "the firstfruits of those who have fallen asleep" (1 Corinthians 15:20). In terms of the Resurrection, Christ is unique

GOSPEL   Luke 1:39–56

A reading from the holy Gospel according to Luke

Mary set out
  and traveled to the hill country in haste
  to a town of **Judah**,
  where she entered the house of **Zechariah**
  and greeted **Elizabeth**.
When **Elizabeth** heard Mary's **greeting**,
  the infant **leaped** in her womb,
  and **Elizabeth**, **filled** with the **Holy Spirit**,
  cried out in a loud voice and said,
  "**Blessed** are **you** among **women**,
  and **blessed** is the **fruit** of your **womb**.
And **how** does this happen to **me**,
  that the **mother** of **my Lord** should come to **me**?
For at the **moment** the sound of your **greeting** reached my **ears**,
  the **infant** in my **womb leaped** for **joy**.
Blessed are **you** who **believed**
  that what was **spoken** to you by the **Lord**
  would be **fulfilled**."

And **Mary** said:
  "My **soul** proclaims the **greatness** of the **Lord**;
    my spirit **rejoices** in **God** my **Savior**
    for he has **looked** upon his **lowly servant**.
  From this day **all** generations will call me **blessed**:
    the **Almighty** has done **great things** for **me**,
    and **holy** is his **Name**.
  He has **mercy** on those who **fear** him
    in **every** generation.

Judah = JOO-duh
Zechariah = Zeh-car-RI-yah

Emphasize the word "blessed" both times
it occurs.

---

not because he was raised, but because he was raised first.

At the same time he is trying to explain his doctrine of the Resurrection of the dead, Paul also works in a point about unity. Despite his power, Christ does *not* claim authority for himself, but rather "hands over the kingdom to his God and Father, when he has destroyed every sovereignty and every authority and power" (1 Corinthians 15:24). Even during the end of days, Christ serves

the cause of unity in heaven. Should not Christ's followers act as true disciples, pursuing the same ends in the Church on earth?

GOSPEL It is hard to overstate the importance of the Holy Spirit to the Gospel of Luke. It is even harder in the case of Acts. The Spirit is the great driving force behind the people and events in each work. This is particularly apparent when we explore Luke's concept of being "filled with the holy spirit," a phrase Luke uses of Elizabeth in today's reading (Luke 1:41).

Perhaps the crowning spirit-filled event of Luke and Acts is the birth of the Church at Pentecost, where Luke records that the disciples "were all filled with the Holy Spirit and began to speak in different tongues, as the Spirit enabled them to proclaim" (Acts 2:4). As Peter explains to some confused witnesses to the events of Pentecost, the disciples' spiritual Baptism confirms Old Testament prophecy, which was itself granted through the same Spirit (Acts 2:14–36). In this way, Luke asserts the continuity

Abraham = AY-bra-ham

Pause briefly between the end of Mary's prayer (also known as the Magnificat) and these last lines of narration.

He has **shown** the **strength** of his **arm**,
  and has **scattered** the **proud** in their **conceit**.
He has cast down the **mighty** from their **thrones**,
  and has **lifted** up the **lowly**.
He has **filled** the **hungry** with good things,
  and the **rich** he has sent away **empty**.
He has come to the **help** of his **servant Israel**
  for he has **remembered** his promise of **mercy**,
  the **promise** he made to our **fathers**,
  to **Abraham** and his **children for ever**."

Mary remained with her about three months
  and then returned to her home.

of the Church with the religion and traditions of Israel.

In the light of the Spirit's establishment of continuity between the prophets of Israel and the birth of the Church, it is important to note those occasions in Luke and Acts when people prophesy in direct response to being filled with the Spirit. John's father, Zechariah, proclaims the blessing of Luke 1:68–79 in response to being filled with the Spirit, as does Peter in Acts 4:8, the whole Church in Acts 4:31, Stephen in Acts 7:55, and Paul in

Acts 13:9. To these we may add Elizabeth in today's reading. Luke's description of her as being filled with the Holy Spirit does not mean that she is simply overjoyed, or suddenly possessed of extraordinary conviction, but that she is speaking the word of God under the same power and authority as did the prophets of Israel.

20TH SUNDAY IN ORDINARY TIME

Lectionary #118

READING I   Isaiah 56:1, 6–7

A reading from the Book of the Prophet Isaiah

Thus says the LORD:
Observe what is **right**, **do** what is **just**;
    for my **salvation** is about to **come**,
    my **justice**, about to be **revealed**.

The **foreigners** who join themselves to the LORD,
    ministering to him,
loving the name of the LORD,
    and **becoming** his **servants**—
all who keep the **sabbath** free from **profanation**
    and **hold** to my **covenant**,
them I will **bring** to my **holy mountain**
    and make **joyful** in my **house** of **prayer**;
their burnt **offerings** and **sacrifices**
    will be **acceptable** on my **altar**,
for my **house** shall be **called**
    a **house** of **prayer** for **all peoples**.

Emphasize in particular the words "Observe" and "do."

Look up and make eye contact with the assembly before you proclaim the reading's final phrase, emphasizing the word "all."

READING I   Today's Lectionary offering omits Isaiah 52:2–5. These verses are quite important, for they establish the context for God's invitation to foreigners to participate in the worship life of Israel in 56:6–7.

In Isaiah 56:3, we read: "Let not the foreigner say, when he would join himself to the LORD, 'The LORD will surely exclude me from his people'; Nor let the eunuch say, 'See, I am a dry tree.' " On the contrary, God says, "To the eunuchs who observe my sabbaths and choose what pleases me and hold fast to my covenant, I will give, in my house and within my walls, a monument and a name better than sons and daughters; an eternal, imperishable name will I give them."

Why are these two groups of people mentioned together, and why does the prophet anticipate their laments? The likely reason is found in Deuteronomy 23:1–8, where eunuchs and certain foreigners are together refused entry to "the community of the Lord." In the worship context, these prohibitions amount to the rejection of these people from the liturgical life of the Jerusalem temple. God's words of acceptance and inclu-sion in Isaiah 56:1–8 expand the boundaries of the worshipping community of Israel and foreshadow the future "catholic" (universal) mission of the Church.

READING II   Jesus' ministry was conducted almost entirely among Jews in rural Palestine. But by the final decades of the first century, the Church, the successor to Jesus' ministry, was enjoying its greatest expansion among Gentiles in the cities of the Mediterranean world.

Gentiles = JIN-tiles

Raise the pitch of your voice at the end of the sentence to indicate this question clearly.

Look up and make eye contact with the assembly as you proclaim this line.

READING II Romans 11:13–15, 29–32

A reading from the Letter of Saint Paul to the Romans

Brothers and **sisters:**
I am **speaking** to you **Gentiles.**
Inasmuch as I am the **apostle** to the **Gentiles,**
   I **glory** in my **ministry** in order to make my race **jealous**
      and thus **save** some of them.
For if their **rejection** is the **reconciliation** of the **world,**
   what will their **acceptance** be but **life** from the **dead?**

For the **gifts** and the **call** of **God** are **irrevocable.**
Just as you once **disobeyed** God
      but have now **received mercy** because of **their** disobedience,
   so they have now **disobeyed** in order that,
   by **virtue** of the **mercy** shown to **you,**
      they too may now **receive mercy.**
For God delivered **all** to **disobedience,**
   that he might have **mercy** upon **all.**

According to Acts, the Church's decision to include Gentiles was ordained by the Spirit (Acts 10), while its move away from Jews is depicted as the response by two of its most prolific missionaries, Paul and Barnabas, to continued Jewish hostility (Acts 13:46–47).

The failure of the Church to convert Jews in large numbers was sometimes a difficult fact for its early members to explain, both to themselves and to outsiders. Luke's description in Acts of the mutual decision of Paul and Barnabas is one attempt at such an explanation. In today's reading from Romans, Paul himself offers another.

Recall that the main theme of Romans is that God has offered both Jews and Gentiles a common path to salvation through the cross of Jesus Christ. Where once Gentiles and Jews did not have the same theological status before God, there is now no distinction between them: just as all people have sinned, so also have all been mercifully offered a right relationship with God through belief in the Good News about Christ's Resurrection.

In today's reading, Paul explains to the Gentile Christians at Rome that the widespread refusal of Jews to believe his Gospel

does not mean God has abandoned the Jews. The election of the Gentiles does not cancel out the election of the Jews: "For the gifts and the call of God are irrevocable."

GOSPEL In Matthew 10:5–15, Jesus commissions his disciples for ministry, saying, "Do not go into pagan territory or enter a Samaritan town. Go rather to the lost sheep of the house of Israel" (Matthew 10:6). In today's reading, Jesus justifies his initial reluctance to help the Canaanite woman by saying, "I was sent

Tyre = Tire
Sidon = SEYE-don
Canaanite = CAY-nah-nite

Proclaim the woman's entreaties in a worried, desperate tone of voice.

Proclaim the words of the disciples in an annoyed tone of voice.

Proclaim Jesus' reply in a tone of wonder and surprise.

GOSPEL   Matthew 15:21–28

A reading from the holy Gospel according to Matthew

At that time, **Jesus** withdrew to the region of **Tyre** and **Sidon**.
And behold, a **Canaanite** woman of that district came
     and called out,
   "Have **pity** on me, **Lord, Son** of **David**!
My **daughter** is tormented by a **demon**."
But Jesus did not say a **word** in answer to her.
Jesus' disciples came and asked him,
   "**Send** her away, for she keeps **calling out** after us."
He said in reply,
   "I was sent **only** to the **lost sheep** of the **house** of **Israel**."
But the **woman** came and **did** Jesus **homage**, saying,
   "**Lord, help** me."
He said in **reply**,
   "It is not **right** to take the **food** of the **children**
   and **throw** it to the **dogs**."
She said, "**Please**, Lord, for **even** the **dogs** eat the **scraps**
   that **fall** from the **table** of their **masters**."
Then **Jesus** said to her in reply,
   "O **woman, great** is your **faith**!
Let it be **done** for you as you **wish**."
And the woman's daughter was **healed** from that hour.

---

only to the lost sheep of the house of Israel" (Matthew 15:24). On the basis of these two statements, one might reasonably conclude that Matthew's Jesus had no interest in ministering to Gentiles.

And yet Matthew also contains examples, like today's incident with the Canaanite woman (see also Mark 7:24–30), in which Jesus meets Gentiles, marvels at their faith, and does what they ask. In Matthew 8:5–13 (see also Luke 7:1–10), a centurion, a Roman army officer, asks Jesus to heal his servant. Jesus agrees to come with him. But the centurion says Jesus' visit is unnecessary, for he trusts that Jesus can as easily heal the servant from a distance as he can up close. "Truly I tell you," Jesus replies, "in no one in Israel have I found such faith" (Matthew 8:10). We also find Matthew's Jesus in the region of the Gadarenes, who, like the people in the vicinity of Tyre and Sidon, were predominantly Gentiles (Matthew 8:28–34; see also Mark 5:1–21 and Luke 8:26–40).

Notice the woman says nothing about her faith while she verbally jousts with Jesus. Instead, it is Jesus who recognizes and points out her faith. He sees that the strength of her refusal to be pushed aside is matched only by the strength of her trust in his ability to do what she asks.

Lectionary #121

Shebna = SHEV-nah

Eliakim = Eh-lee-ah-KEEM
Hilkiah = Hil-kee-YAH

Judah = JOO-duh

READING I   Isaiah 22:19–23

A reading from the Book of the Prophet Isaiah

Thus says the LORD to **Shebna**, **master** of the **palace**:
"I will **thrust** you from your **office**
    and **pull** you **down** from your **station**.
On that day I will summon **my servant**
    Eliakim, son of **Hilkiah**;
I will **clothe him** with **your robe**,
    and **gird him** with **your sash**,
    and **give** over to **him your authority**.
He shall be a **father** to the **inhabitants** of **Jerusalem**,
    and to the **house** of **Judah**.
I will place the **key** of the **House** of **David**
    on **Eliakim's** shoulder;
    when he **opens**, no one shall **shut**
    when he **shuts**, no one shall **open**.
I will **fix** him like a **peg** in a **sure spot**,
    to be a place of **honor** for his **family**."

READING I   Shebna and Eliakim are perhaps not very well known figures from the Bible, but they were quite powerful government officials in the late eighth-century royal court of King Hezekiah of Judah. They were key players during a perilous time in Judah's history, around 701 BC, when the Assyrian army advanced to the walls of Jerusalem. In 2 Kings 18, Hezekiah dispatches "Eliakim, son of Hilkiah, the master of the palace; Shebnah the scribe; and the herald Joah, son of Asaph," to speak with an Assyrian negotiator (2 Kings 18:18).

These three men were charged with the dangerous duty of leaving the relative safety of the walled city and entrusting themselves to the Assyrian invaders. They were allowed to return safely, bearing the negotiator's threats, which was perhaps not even necessary since the Assyrians were so close that soldiers atop Jerusalem's walls were within earshot of the conversation and the Assyrian negotiator insisted on speaking Hebrew (see 2 Kings 18:26).

In today's reading, we meet Shebna under much less heroic conditions. Shebna appears to have been found guilty by the prophet of some wrongdoing or abuse of his authority. The precise circumstances are hard to make out, though the judgment of the prophet is not: "you disgrace to your master's house!"

This reading presupposes that not the king only, but also his officials, serve at God's pleasure. Isaiah does not present the removal of Shebna and the elevation of Eliakim as the decision of the king, but as God's decision. What power Eliakim has comes from God.

READING II — Romans 11:33–36

A reading from the Letter of Saint Paul to the Romans

Oh, the **depth** of the **riches** and **wisdom** and **knowledge** of **God**!
How **inscrutable** are his **judgments** and how **unsearchable**
    his **ways**!
    For **who** has known the **mind** of the **Lord**
        or **who** has been his **counselor**?
    Or **who** has given the **Lord anything**
        that he may be **repaid**?
For **from** him and **through** him and **for** him are **all** things.
To **him** be **glory forever**. **Amen**.

Proclaim Paul's exclamation in a tone of awe and wonder.

Be sure to raise the pitch of your voice to indicate this question.

GOSPEL — Matthew 16:13–20

A reading from the holy Gospel according to Matthew

Jesus went into the region of **Caesarea Philippi** and
    he asked his **disciples**,
    "**Who** do people say that the **Son** of **Man** is?"
They replied, "Some say **John** the **Baptist**, others **Elijah**,
    still others **Jeremiah** or one of the **prophets**."
He said to them, "But who do **you** say that **I** am?"
Simon Peter said in reply,
    "**You** are the **Christ**, the **Son** of the living **God**."

Caesarea = Seh-sah-REE-yah
Philippi = FIL-lih-pie

Make sure to raise the pitch of your voice at the end of Jesus' sentences to indicate these questions. As you proclaim Jesus' question, look up and make eye contact with the assembly, emphasizing the word "you."

Elijah = Eh-LI-jah
Jeremiah = Jeh-reh-MI-yah

READING II Romans 9—11 constitute the core of Paul's letter to the Church at Rome. In these chapters, Paul continues to argue his letter's main point, that Jews and Gentiles, through the cross of Jesus Christ, stand as equals before God and are united in a single plan of redemption. Paul interprets a dizzying number and variety of scriptural passages to show that scripture bears witness to God's fidelity to Israel has not wavered. The fact of God's mercy to the Gentiles does not mean that God's covenant with Israel has been scrapped.

Today's reading comes from the climactic final verses of Romans 9—11. On its own, the main point of the reading is that people can do little more than marvel at the evidence of God's thought and plans, for a full understanding of God lies well outside humans' grasp. In the context of Romans 9—11, these verses express Paul's wonder and praise of a God who has chosen to redeem all the world, not just one nation here, or one people there.

The reading is built around a scriptural quotation in Romans 11:34. It comes from Isaiah 40:13. Isaiah 40 heralds the approaching end of Israel's exile in Babylon and praises the God of all creation for bringing it about in such an extraordinary way. For Paul, no less extraordinary is the way God has rescued the world from the powers of sin and death through the cross and Resurrection of Jesus Christ, thus ending the exile of the Gentiles by at last including them in the unbroken promises made long ago to Israel.

GOSPEL The Gospels of Mark and Luke both report that Peter

Simon = SI-mon
Jonah = JO-nah

Jesus said to him in reply,
"**Blessed** are **you**, **Simon** son of **Jonah**.
For **flesh** and **blood** has not **revealed** this to you,
  but my **heavenly Father**.
And so I **say** to you, **you** are **Peter**,
  and upon this **rock** I will **build** my **church**,
  and the **gates** of the **netherworld** shall **not prevail** against it.
I will **give** you the **keys** to the **kingdom** of **heaven**.
Whatever you **bind** on **earth** shall be **bound** in **heaven**;
  and whatever you **loose** on **earth** shall be **loosed** in **heaven**."
Then he **strictly** ordered his **disciples**
  to tell **no one** that he was the **Christ**.

made a confession about Jesus quite similar to what we find in today's reading: "You are the Messiah, the Son of the living God" (Matthew 16:16). Luke gives no location, though Mark and Matthew place it in Caesarea Philippi, a city well north and west of Jesus' and the disciples' homes in Galilee (Mark 8:27–30; Luke 9:18–21).

The Greek word that our Bible translates as "messiah" is *christos*. It means "anointed one." The name "Jesus Christ" (in Greek, *Iēsous Christos*), and sometimes "Christ Jesus," is probably a shortened form of the statement "Jesus of Nazareth is the

Christ" or "The Christ is Jesus of Nazareth." In the early decades of the Gospel's proclamation, Christians shortened this testimonial statement so that the name "Christ," together with "Jesus," in the minds of many people came to be thought of as the Lord's proper name.

As we shall see next week, Peter remains somewhat foggy on the idea that his Messiah must die and rise from the dead. And we can hardly blame him for not understanding this. Would God allow his "anointed one" to die a humiliating and painful death on the cross? Would a messiah as powerful

as Jesus has already shown himself to be permit such a thing?

In Matthew, unlike Mark or Luke, a blessing and a promise to Peter follow his confession that Jesus is the Messiah (Matthew 16:17–19). This is an extremely important text to Catholic understandings of the position of Peter among the 12 apostles, as well as the authority of the Pope, the bishop of Rome, among all the world's bishops. Later Church tradition evolved into the belief that Peter was the first to hold the office of the bishop of Rome.

22ND SUNDAY IN ORDINARY TIME

Lectionary #124

READING I   Jeremiah 20:7–9

A reading from the Book of the Prophet Jeremiah

Proclaim this reading in an exasperated tone of voice. Jeremiah is faithful to his prophetic calling, but he often finds it almost too much to bear.

You **duped** me, O LORD, and I **let myself** be **duped**;
    you were **too strong** for me, and you **triumphed**.
All the **day** I am an **object** of **laughter**;
    everyone mocks me.

Whenever I **speak**, I must **cry out**,
    violence and **outrage** is my **message**;
the **word** of the LORD has brought me
    derision and **reproach** all the day.

Proclaim this line with emphasis.

I say to myself, I will **not** mention him,
    I will speak in his name **no more**.
But then it becomes like **fire** burning in my **heart**,
    imprisoned in my **bones**;
I grow **weary** holding it **in**, I **cannot** endure it.

READING I Babylon arose to challenge Egypt for power over the eastern Mediterranean in the second half of the seventh century BC. Jerusalem sat squarely between the two rivaling kingdoms, much as had been its position when Egypt and Assyria were contending against one another. In 721 BC, the Assyrians wiped out the northern kingdom of Israel. Now, in the final years of the seventh century BC, Babylon began to put enormous pressure on Judah. It was in this historical situation that Jeremiah prophesied during the latter part of his career.

What Jeremiah prophesied was often pretty unpopular among the wealthy and Judah's political and religious authorities. He prophesied that Judah's people, particularly its leaders, had sealed everyone's doom by their idolatry and injustice to the poor and powerless. Babylon will come for them all.

Today, the prophet laments that he must proclaim what he, like practically everyone who listens to him, hates to hear: "Whenever I speak, I must cry out, violence and outrage is my message; The word of the LORD has brought me derision and reproach all the day" (Jeremiah 20:8). Who can bear to hear

someone say that one's family, friends, livelihood, home—all one has ever known—will perish in "violence and outrage"?

So why did Jeremiah not simply keep his mouth shut? The prophet's answer is that *whether* he speaks, as well as *what* he says, is simply not up to him. Indeed, he might have better luck at not breathing than to stop the oracles of God: "I say to myself, I will not mention him, I will speak in his name no more. But then it becomes like fire burning in my heart, imprisoned in my bones; I grow weary holding it in, I cannot endure it" (Jeremiah 20:9).

READING II   Romans 12:1–2

A reading from the Letter of Saint Paul to the Romans

I **urge** you, **brothers** and **sisters**, by the **mercies** of **God**,
   to offer your **bodies** as a **living sacrifice**,
   holy and **pleasing** to **God**, your **spiritual worship**.
Do **not conform** yourselves to this **age**
   but be **transformed** by the **renewal** of your **mind**,
   that you may **discern** what is the **will** of **God**,
   what is **good** and **pleasing** and **perfect**.

Give special emphasis to Paul's advice here.

Slow down to emphasize the final part of this reading, emphasizing each of the qualities of proper objects of discernment.

GOSPEL   Matthew 16:21–27

A reading from the holy Gospel according to Matthew

Jesus began to show his **disciples**
   that he **must** go to **Jerusalem** and **suffer greatly**
   from the **elders**, the chief **priests**, and the **scribes**,
   and be **killed** and on the **third day** be **raised**.
Then **Peter** took **Jesus** aside and began to **rebuke** him,
   "**God forbid**, Lord! **No** such thing shall **ever** happen to you."
He turned and said to Peter,
   "**Get behind** me, **Satan**! You are an **obstacle** to me.
You are thinking **not** as **God** does, but as **human beings** do."

Deliver Peter's words to Jesus in a strong but slightly worried tone of voice.

Proclaim Jesus' reply to Peter in a bold, even harsh tone of voice. Although Peter is Jesus' intimate friend and disciple, Jesus is quite angry that Peter denies, for whatever reason, the destiny of the Son of Man.

READING II In Romans 1—11, Paul explains how God has redeemed Jews and Gentiles from the hostile powers of sin and death. By believing the Good News about Jesus' death and Resurrection, Christians are placed into a right relationship with God. By incorporation into the body of the Church through Baptism, the Christian exchanges enslavement to sin and death for a new life brimming over with the Holy Spirit under God's protective care. In Romans 12—15, Paul explains what are some of the practical demands placed on

people who have submitted to and undergone this total transformation of themselves.

The first practical consequence of the new life is so obvious that it is easy to overlook, although one can hardly imagine the Catholic Church without it: the Christian is no longer an isolated individual, but a member of a community, the Church. We see this in the very first verse of Romans 12: "I urge you therefore, brothers, by the mercies of God, to offer your bodies as a living sacrifice, holy and pleasing to God" (Romans

12:1). Note how Paul moves from the plural "bodies" (in Greek, *sōmata*) to the singular "sacrifice" *(thusiān)*. The bodies of the Roman Christians together comprise a single sacrifice to God.

The unity of the Church is on Paul's mind in Romans 12—15. In 12:4–5, Paul uses the image of the body to show how a basic unity underlies the variety within the Church: "For as in one body we have many parts, and all the parts do not have the same function, so we, though many, are one body in Christ and individually parts of one another."

Then **Jesus** said to his disciples,
  "Whoever wishes to come after me must **deny himself**,
  take up his **cross**, and **follow me**.
For whoever **wishes** to **save** his life will **lose** it,
  but whoever **loses** his **life** for **my sake** will **find** it.
What **profit** would there be for one to gain the **whole world**
  and **forfeit** his **life**?
Or what can one **give** in **exchange** for his **life**?
For the **Son** of **Man** will **come** with his **angels**
    in his Father's **glory**,
  and then he will repay **all** according to his **conduct**."

GOSPEL It is intriguing that in a mere eight verses Jesus both blesses Peter (Matthew 16:17) and insults him in anger (Matthew 16:23). The turn from blessing to insult comes in today's reading, with Jesus' first prediction of his Passion and Peter's rebuke of him for speaking so. Despite the insight and understanding that led him to confess Jesus as the Messiah, Peter has not yet understood that the Messiah "must go to Jerusalem and suffer greatly from the elders, the chief priests, and the scribes, and be killed and on the third day be raised" (Matthew 16:21).

Repeatedly in Matthew's Gospel Jesus predicts his Passion (16:21; 17:22–23; 20:18–19; 26:2). In the second, third, and fourth predictions, Jesus does not mention himself by name, but instead refers to himself as "the Son of Man." The meaning of this title is somewhat obscure. In the book of the prophet Ezekiel, it is roughly equal to "mortal," a term by which God addresses the prophet. But in Daniel 7:13, the "One like a son of man" appears to describe a mysterious divine figure given great authority by God. In the Gospels, the evangelists confess the belief of the early Church that Jesus is both

the Messiah *and* the divine Son of Man, whose authority, although a secret in the time of his earthly ministry, will be made quite plain upon his return in glory (see Matthew 26:64; Mark 14:62; Luke 22:69).

Jesus follows his outburst at Peter with stern words to all his disciples: "Whoever wishes to come after me must deny himself, take up his cross, and follow me." Not only does Jesus, by referring to the cross, allude to the way he himself will die, but he also holds up the way of the cross as the way of true discipleship.

23RD SUNDAY IN ORDINARY TIME

Lectionary #127

READING I   Ezekiel 33:7–9

Use a clear, strong tone of voice when you proclaim this reading.

A reading from the Book of the prophet Ezekiel

Thus says the LORD:
You, son of man, I have appointed **watchman**
    for the **house** of **Israel**;
    when you hear me say **anything**, you shall **warn** them for me.
If I tell the wicked, "**O wicked one**, you shall **surely die**,"
    and **you** do **not speak** out to dissuade the wicked from his way,
    the **wicked** shall **die** for **his** guilt,
    but I will hold **you** responsible for his **death**.
But if you **warn** the **wicked**,
    trying to **turn** him from his way,
    and he **refuses** to turn from his way,
    he shall **die** for **his** guilt,
    but **you** shall save **yourself**.

Emphasize the personal pronouns in this verse.

READING I   Ezekiel was a prophet and a priest of the Jerusalem temple. He was taken captive by the Babylonians in 597 or 596 BC at the same time as King Jehoiachin of Judah. In exile, Ezekiel lived among other Judean captives (see Ezekiel 3:15) and presumably died there. The earliest date he offers for any of his oracles is the fifth year after King Jehoiachin was deported (593 BC). His entire prophetic career occurred in captivity.

Despite the many dates Ezekiel provides us, it is not clear when he received the oracle of which today's reading is a small piece. God's commission of Ezekiel as "watchman for the house of Israel" (see also Ezekiel 3:17–19) recalls Jeremiah 6:17, in which God recites the many ways in which Judah has been urged to repent and escape destruction: "When I raised up watchmen for them: 'Hearken to the sound of the trumpet!' they said, 'We will not hearken.'" Jeremiah, however, was prophesying from Jerusalem before the exile. Ezekiel prophesies several decades later, once Babylon's victory and Judah's loss are accomplished facts. Despite all that has happened, God still raises up "watchmen" for the people.

Today's reading is also powerful testimony to the responsibility of the prophet to proclaim God's word. As we saw a week ago in the case of Jeremiah (commentary I, Twenty-second Sunday in Ordinary Time, August 31), the choice to proclaim God's word or be silent is not the prophet's choice to make. In today's reading, the consequences of silence are spelled out in clear, dreadful detail.

While Ezekiel has little good to say about the exile community and not much in

Proclaim this reading in a gentle tone of voice.

READING II   Romans 13:8–10

A reading from the Letter of Saint Paul to the Romans

Brothers and **sisters:**
Owe **nothing** to anyone, except to **love** one another;
    for the one who **loves** another has **fulfilled** the law.
The commandments, "You shall **not commit adultery;**
    you shall **not kill;** you shall **not steal;** you shall **not covet,**"
    and whatever other commandment there may be,
    are **summed up** in this saying, namely,
    "You shall **love** your **neighbor** as **yourself.**"
Love does **no evil** to the **neighbor;**
    hence, **love** is the **fulfillment** of the **law.**

Look up and make eye contact with the assembly as you proclaim this line.

GOSPEL   Matthew 18:15–20

A reading from the holy Gospel according to Matthew

Jesus said to his **disciples:**
"If your **brother** sins **against** you,
    go and tell him his **fault** between you and him **alone.**
If he **listens** to you, you have **won over** your brother.
If he does **not** listen,
    take **one** or **two** others along **with you,**
    so that '**every fact** may be **established**
    on the **testimony** of **two** or **three witnesses.**'
If he **refuses** to listen to them, tell the **church.**

---

the way of good news to pass on to them, in Ezekiel 33:10 God orders the prophet to answer the exiles' sadness after the final fall of Jerusalem (587 BC) with words to fight off despair: "As I live, says the Lord GOD, I swear I take no pleasure in the death of the wicked man, but rather in the wicked man's conversion, that he may live. Turn, turn from your evil ways! Why should you die, O house of Israel?"

READING II "You shall love your neighbor as yourself," Paul quotes from Leviticus 19:18, saying that this com-

mand sums up *all* commandments and naming the fifth, sixth, seventh, ninth, and tenth commandments specifically (see Exodus 20:2–17; Deuteronomy 5:6–21; CCC, #2052–2557). He concludes in Romans 13:10 that "love is the fulfillment of the law." This is not love as emotion or feeling, however passionate. It is love as foundation and structure, the stone and girders of the Roman Church.

In its New Testament context, Leviticus 19:18 expresses the fundamental character of what it means to be a disciple of Jesus Christ and a thriving member of the community of the Church. We find this command

repeated in multiple verses of the New Testament (Matthew 19:19; 22:39; Mark 12:31; Luke 10:27; Galatians 5:14; James 2:8). In Matthew 22:34-40, a "scholar of the law" asks Jesus, "Teacher, which commandment in the law is the greatest?" Jesus responds that loving God with all one's heart, soul, and mind is the first and greatest commandment. And the second commandment, Jesus says, is like the first: "You shall love your neighbor as yourself. The whole law and the prophets depend on these two commandments" (see also Mark 12:28–34). In Luke's

Gentile = JIN-tile

Pause and look up as you deliver the
final verse.

If he refuses to listen **even** to the **church**,
    then **treat** him as you would a **Gentile** or a **tax collector**.
Amen, I say to you,
    whatever you **bind** on **earth** shall be **bound** in **heaven**,
    and whatever you **loose** on **earth** shall be **loosed** in **heaven**.
Again, **amen**, I say to you,
    if **two** of you **agree** on **earth**
    about **anything** for which they are to **pray**,
    it shall be **granted** to them by my **heavenly Father**.
For where **two** or **three** are **gathered** together in **my name**,
    there am **I** in the **midst** of them."

Gospel, Jesus' answer leads the man to pose a further question: "And who is my neighbor?" To his question Jesus responds with the parable of the Good Samaritan, defining a neighbor as someone showing mercy to another, considering nothing except meeting the person's need (Luke 10:25–37).

GOSPEL Today's Gospel contains instruction for the resolution of conflict. These are not general conflicts, however, but conflicts between and among Christians. The first clue that we are talking about conflict resolution in the Church is Matthew's use of the term "brother" *(adelphos),* a common term of address in the early Church, to designate the offender (Matthew 18:15). Note also that the Church is the final authority in the dispute: Jesus says nothing about appealing to civil authorities.

We know, however, that early Christians did sometimes take one another to court. In 1 Corinthians 6:5–6, Paul confronts the Church at Corinth on this issue: "Can it be that there is not one among you wise enough to be able to settle a case between brothers?

But rather brother goes to court against brother, and that before unbelievers?"

It is *only* after publicly establishing the facts and providing the offender multiple opportunities to set right his wrong, that the person sinned against may finally turn his or her back and have nothing more to do with the person. A personal grievance or resentment kept to oneself does not fit the bill at all. To treat someone as "a Gentile or a tax collector," is, in Matthew's eyes, to shun the person. And this is a sad and *final* resort.

EXALTATION OF THE HOLY CROSS

Lectionary #638

READING I   Numbers 21:4b–9

A reading from the Book of Numbers

With their patience **worn out** by the journey,
the people **complained** against **God** and **Moses**,
"**Why** have you brought us up from **Egypt** to **die** in this **desert**,
where there is **no food** or **water**?
We are **disgusted** with this **wretched food!**"

In **punishment** the LORD sent among the people **saraph serpents**,
which **bit** the people so that **many** of them **died**.
Then the people came to Moses and said,
"We have **sinned** in **complaining** against the LORD and **you**.
Pray the LORD to take the **serpents** from us."
So Moses **prayed** for the **people**, and the LORD said to **Moses**,
"Make a **saraph** and mount it on a **pole**,
and if **any** who have been **bitten look** at it, they will **live**."
Moses accordingly made a **bronze serpent** and **mounted** it
on a **pole**,
and whenever **anyone** who had been **bitten** by a **serpent**
looked at the **bronze serpent**, he lived.

Proclaim the Israelites' complaint in an irritated or exasperated tone of voice.

Proclaim the Israelites' confession of sin in a somber, subdued tone of voice.

saraph = SAH-raf

READING I — In 2 Kings 18:1–8, we read a summary of the reign of King Hezekiah of Judah. He is one of the few kings of Judah about whom the author has an almost completely positive assessment: "Loyal to the LORD, Hezekiah never turned away from him, but observed the commandments which the LORD had given Moses" (2 Kings 18:6).

The reason for this praise has to do largely with Hezekiah's attempts to eradicate the worship of gods other than the God of Israel. This is how the author of 2 Kings 18 describes the king's zeal: "It was he who removed the high places, shattered the pillars, and cut down the sacred poles. He smashed the bronze serpent called Nehushtan which Moses had made, because up to that time the Israelites were burning incense to it" (2 Kings 18:4).

In today's reading, we read of the creation of this bronze serpent and learn that it was originally an icon or image that God ordered Moses to make in order to protect Israel from the ill effects of snakebites as it wandered in the desert.

It is most likely that this particular bronze serpent had long been worshipped in Judah as a divine being with powers to relieve illness. But if we take both today's reading and 2 Kings 18:4 at face value, then between the creation of the serpent and its destruction a significant problem developed: the icon the Creator ordered Moses to make had in time become an idol, receiving the honor and worship due the Creator.

READING II — Many scholars of the history and literature of the early Church have called Philippians 2:6–11 a hymn. We have no way of knowing if these words were written for singing or chanting,

A reading from the Letter of Saint Paul to the Philippians

Brothers and **sisters**:
Christ Jesus, though he was in the **form** of **God**,
    did not regard **equality** with God
        something to be **grasped**.
Rather, he **emptied** himself,
    taking the **form** of a **slave**,
    coming in **human likeness**;
    and found **human** in **appearance**,
    he **humbled** himself,
    becoming **obedient** to the point of **death**,
        even death on a **cross**.
Because of this, God **greatly exalted** him
    and **bestowed** on him **the name**
    which is **above** every name,
    that at the **name** of Jesus
    every knee should **bend**,
    of those **in heaven** and **on earth** and **under** the **earth**,
    and **every tongue confess** that
    Jesus Christ is **Lord**,
    to the **glory** of **God** the **Father**.

Emphasize in particular the words "form," "not," and "equality."

Look up and make eye contact with the assembly as you proclaim the words "even death on a cross."

Pause between the words "cross" and "Because." See how the perspective shifts from the deeds of Christ to the act of God the Father, from slavery and the degradation of the cross to lordship and the exaltation of heaven.

or if they were freely adapted by Paul from some other source as some scholars suggest. But there is really no reason to think that Paul could not have written these soaring words himself, wishing only to elegantly present to the Church at Philippi a superior example of self-sacrificial love.

The theme of Christ's emptying of himself to the point of dying on a cross for others fits with the main theme of this letter, which is the need for the Philippians to place the needs of others, and of the whole Church, above individual needs: "complete my joy by being of the same mind, with the same love, united in heart, thinking one thing. Do nothing out of selfishness or out of vainglory; rather, humbly regard others as more important than yourselves, each looking out not for his own interests, but [also] everyone for those of others" (Philippians 2:2).

Paul offers not only Christ as an example of self-sacrifice, but also Epaphroditus, a man Paul calls "my brother and co-worker and fellow soldier, your messenger and minister in my need" (Philippians 2:25). Paul says this of Epaphroditus: "for the sake of the work of Christ he came close to death, risking his life to make up for those services to me that you could not perform." Like Christ, Epaphroditus put his life on the line for the Philippians.

And Paul also offers himself as an example of self-sacrifice. He is, after all, writing from prison where he has landed due to his missionary work (Philippians 1:12–14). Like Christ and Epaphroditus, Paul is willing to lay down his life for the sake of the proclamation of the Gospel (Philippians 1:20–25). The Church at Philippi thus has no shortage of role models to help them pattern their own attempts at "standing firm in one spirit, with one mind struggling together for the faith of the Gospel" (Philippians 1:27).

GOSPEL   John 3:13–17

A reading from the holy Gospel according to John

Jesus said to **Nicodemus:**
"**No one** has **gone up** to **heaven**
   except **the one** who has **come down** from **heaven**,
      the **Son** of **Man**.
And just as **Moses** lifted up the **serpent** in the **desert**,
   so must the **Son** of **Man** be **lifted up**,
   so that **everyone** who believes in him may have **eternal life**."

For **God** so **loved** the **world** that he gave his **only Son**,
   so that **he** who **believes** in him might not **perish**
   but might have **eternal life**.
For **God** did not send his **Son** into the world to **condemn**
   the **world**,
   but that the **world** might be **saved** through him."

Emphasize this interesting comparison John makes between Moses and Jesus, the Son of Man.

Emphasize in particular the words "not," "condemn," and "saved."

GOSPEL "And just as Moses lifted up the serpent in the desert, so must the Son of Man be lifted up, so that everyone who believes in him may have eternal life" (John 3:14). The lifting up of the Son of Man in this verse refers to Jesus' Crucifixion. In a literal, physical sense, the cross will lift Jesus up toward the sky. But in a spiritual or figurative sense, the cross is also the greatest of Jesus' displays of his divinity.

In John 8, Jesus talks with both Pharisees (8:13) and Jews (8:22) who are all completely perplexed by the things Jesus is saying. Their questions show how deep is their confusion (8:22, 25, 33, 48, 53, 57). Thus, when Jesus refers to the lifting up of the Son of Man in 8:28, the crowds give no indication that they understand him. And while many initially believe in him (8:30), this situation does not continue for long. A literal translation of the Greek of 8:28 reads, "And Jesus said to them: 'Whenever you lift up the Son of Man, you will know that I am, and from myself I do nothing, but rather I speak these things just as the Father taught me.' " "You will know that I am" calls attention to Jesus' divinity, demonstrating that Jesus' identity is one and the same as God's (see Exodus 3:14). The "lifting up" of the Son of Man on the cross, therefore, reveals that Jesus and his Father are one (John 5:18; 10:30). But there is no hint that Jesus' audience understands this.

In John's view, which the evangelist probably came to only after decades of bitter experience, those outside the Church simply cannot understand who Jesus is. To them, the lifting up of Jesus on the cross is the end of his story, the execution of a troublemaker. But to those inside the Church, Jesus' lifting up reveals that he is God.

25TH SUNDAY IN ORDINARY TIME

Lectionary #133

READING I   Isaiah 55:6–9

A reading from the Book of the prophet Isaiah

Proclaim this reading in a strong and authoritative tone of voice.

> **Seek** the LORD while he may be **found**,
>   call him while he is **near**.
> Let the **scoundrel** forsake his way,
>   and the **wicked** his thoughts;
> let him **turn** to the LORD for **mercy**;
>   to our God, who is **generous** in **forgiving**.

Emphasize in particular the words "mercy" and "generous" in this verse.

> For **my** thoughts are not **your** thoughts,
>   nor are **your** ways **my** ways, says the LORD.

Make eye contact with the assembly as you proclaim this verse, emphasizing the words "my" and "your" throughout.

> As **high** as the **heavens** are above the **earth**,
>   so **high** are **my ways** above **your ways**
>   and **my thoughts** above **your thoughts**.

READING I   Today's reading comes from a portion of Isaiah (chapters 40 through 55) most biblical scholars date toward the end of Judah's exile in Babylon (mid- to late sixth century BC), when the rise of Cyrus of Persia in defiance and challenge of Babylon gave many Israelites — and indeed many Babylonians — hope for better lives under a somewhat gentler Persian hand.

The prophet's interpretation of the rise of Cyrus and the weakness of Babylon is that God has achieved both for the sake of Israel. The prophet sees the fate of his people, although seemingly insignificant players in the geopolitics of the day, as the main reason that global events are unfolding as they are. This global perspective pervades Isaiah 40—55. We get a taste of it today: "As high as the heavens are above the earth, so high are my ways above your ways and my thoughts above your thoughts" (Isaiah 55:9). This is not merely the God of Israel, but the God of all creation testifying that the world's future and destiny beyond human understanding.

And yet God's thought surpasses human understanding even on a much smaller level. When God ordered Samuel to anoint one of the sons of Jesse as king, Samuel was initially perplexed that not one of the strapping lads Jesse presented to Samuel satisfied the Lord. God responded to Samuel's confusion: "Do not judge from his appearance or from his lofty stature, because I have rejected him. Not as man sees does God see, because man sees the appearance but the LORD looks into the heart" (1 Samuel 16:7). While David may not have seemed to

A reading from the Letter of Saint Paul to the Philippians

Brothers and **sisters**:
Christ will be **magnified** in my **body**, whether by **life** or by **death**.
For to me **life** is **Christ**, and **death** is **gain**.
If I go on **living** in the **flesh**,
    that means **fruitful labor** for me.
And I do **not** know which I shall **choose**.
I am **caught** between the **two**.
I long to **depart** this life and be with **Christ**,
    for that is **far better**.
Yet that I **remain** in the **flesh**
    is **more necessary** for **your** benefit.

Only, **conduct** yourselves in a way **worthy** of the **gospel** of **Christ**.

Proclaim this reading in a clear, bold tone of voice. Although Paul is in prison, he nevertheless tries to bolster the Philippians' spirits.

Proclaim this verse very slowly.

---

be royal material in his father's eyes, God saw things differently. Today's reading and 1 Samuel 16:7 remind us that on both the grand scale of war and politics, as well as on the small scale of an individual human heart, God's thoughts are beyond our own.

READING II   Paul writes his letter to the Philippians from prison. We cannot be sure where Paul was when he wrote this letter, although Ephesus (present-day Turkey) or Rome is the most likely location. In today's reading (1:20–24), Paul reflects

on his own possible death. He had good reason to do so. Ancient jails were not penal institutions where a person served a sentence for a crime. They were little more than holding tanks pending judgment and the imposition of sentence. Death was a common sentence, even for seemingly small crimes. Paul is not just being dramatic when he weighs his desire "to depart this life and be with Christ" against his continued life in the Christian mission, which he tells the

Philippians "is more necessary for your benefit" (Philippians 1:23–24). Paul's life was hanging in the balance and he knew it.

Paul wants to know one thing above all about the Philippians: "that you are standing firm in one spirit, with one mind struggling together for the faith of the Gospel" (Philippians 1:27).

"One spirit" and "one mind" are the terms Paul uses here to express his wish for unity in the Church at Philippi. He returns to the theme of unity throughout the letter. In 2:2, he urges the Philippians to "complete

GOSPEL   Matthew 20:1–16a

A reading from the holy Gospel according to Matthew

Jesus told his **disciples** this parable:
"The **kingdom** of **heaven** is like a **landowner**
    who went out at **dawn** to hire **laborers** for his **vineyard**.
After agreeing with them for the usual daily wage,
    he **sent** them into his vineyard.
Going out about nine o'clock,
    the landowner saw **others** standing **idle** in the **marketplace**,
    and he said to them, '**You too** go into my vineyard,
    and I will **give** you what is **just**.'
So they went off.
And he **went out again** around **noon**,
    and around **three o'clock**, and did **likewise**.
Going out about **five o'clock**,
    the landowner found **others** standing around, and said to them,
    '**Why** do you stand here **idle** all day?'
They answered, 'Because **no one** has **hired** us.'
He said to them, '**You too** go into my vineyard.'
When it was **evening** the owner of the **vineyard**
        said to his **foreman**,
    'Summon the **laborers** and give them their **pay**,
    beginning with the **last** and ending with the **first**.'
When those who had started about five o'clock came,
    each received the **usual daily wage**.

---

my joy by being of the same mind, with the same love, united in heart, thinking one thing." Later in the letter, he will urge two feuding women, Euodia and Syntyche, "to come to a mutual understanding in the Lord" (Philippians 4:2). The women are quite important to Paul's mission, as he himself says: "they have struggled at my side in promoting the Gospel" (Philippians 4:3).

GOSPEL "Thus, the last will be first, and the first will be last" (Matthew 20:16). We find this phrase multiple times in the Gospels of Matthew, Mark, and Luke (Matthew 19:30; 20:8, 16; Mark 9:35; 10:31; Luke 13:30). In today's Gospel, the statement supports the landowner's freedom to pay all of his day laborers the same wage, no matter how long they have worked or how much they grumble. But the freedom of landowners to pay whatever wages they wish is hardly the point of this parable.

The parable of the laborers in the vineyard is a parable of the kingdom of heaven, describing both the means of entry into the kingdom and the equality its inhabitants enjoy there. The landowner, who presumably represents God, calls workers to prepare the earth for the kingdom, which has yet to bud, bloom, and bear fruit. His payment of the same wage signifies that entry into the kingdom of heaven is wage enough for anyone, no matter how long it has been since he or she answered the master's call.

Proclaim the workers' grievance in an irritated or annoyed tone of voice.

Proclaim the landowner's words in an authoritative tone of voice.

So when the first came, they thought that they would
    receive **more**,
      but **each** of them also got the **usual wage**.
And on **receiving** it they **grumbled** against the landowner, saying,
   'These **last** ones worked **only one hour**,
   and you have made **them** equal to **us**,
   who **bore** the day's **burden** and the **heat**.'
He said to one of them in reply,
   '**My friend**, I am **not** cheating you.
Did you not **agree** with me for the **usual daily wage**?
Take what is **yours** and **go**.
What if I **wish** to give this **last one** the same as **you**?
Or am I **not free** to do as I **wish** with my own **money**?
Are you **envious** because I am **generous**?'
Thus, the **last** will be **first**, and the **first** will be **last**."

Note that the laborers who have worked the longest do not complain that they are owed more money, but that the landowner has made these latecomers "equal to us, who bore the day's burden and the heat" (Matthew 16:12). Much like the elder brother in Luke's story of the prodigal son (15:11–32), the laborers who have worked the longest are upset. Why should people who have been idle most of the day be treated so well? But just as the decent, hardworking elder brother in Luke's story cannot restrict the love and mercy his father shows to his depraved and drunken sibling, so also is it not up to any of the workers to restrict the generosity of the landowner.

The idea that the kingdom of heaven in the age to come will be characterized by a reversal of human fortunes is deeply embedded in many New Testament texts. See, for example, Matthew's beatitudes, where those mourning will be comforted, and those persecuted will inherit the kingdom of heaven (Matthew 5:1–12; see also Luke 6:17–26). See also Paul's explanation of why God called the members of the Church at Corinth instead of noble, wise, or important people: "God chose the foolish of the world to shame the wise, and God chose the weak of the world to shame the strong, and God chose the lowly and despised of the world, those who count for nothing, to reduce to nothing those who are something, so that no human being might boast before God" (1 Corinthians 1:27–29).

26TH SUNDAY IN ORDINARY TIME

Lectionary #136

READING I   Ezekiel 18:25–28

Deliver this verse in an angry or offended tone of voice. This is the prophet's description of the exiled community's challenge to God.

A reading from the Book of the prophet Ezekiel

Thus says the LORD:
You say, "The LORD'S way is not **fair!**"
Hear now, **house** of Israel:
    Is it my way that is unfair, or rather, are not your ways unfair?
When someone **virtuous** turns away from **virtue**
        to commit **iniquity**, and **dies**,
    it is **because** of the iniquity he committed that he must **die**.
But if he **turns** from the **wickedness** he has **committed**,
    and **does** what is **right** and **just**,
    he shall **preserve** his life;
    since he has **turned away** from all the **sins**
        that he has **committed**,
    he shall **surely** live, he shall **not** die.

READING II   Philippians 2:1–11

Let the punctuation indicate brief pauses in this long and somewhat complicated reading.

A reading from the Letter of Saint Paul to the Philippians

Brothers and **sisters:**
If there is **any encouragement** in **Christ**,
    any **solace** in **love**,
    any **participation** in the **Spirit**,
    any **compassion** and **mercy**,

READING I   In chapter 18 of Ezekiel, God, speaking through the prophet, begins by disputing a proverb: "what is the meaning of this proverb that you recite in the land of Israel: 'Fathers have eaten green grapes, thus their children's teeth are on edge' " (Ezekiel 18:2). The precise origin and meaning of this proverb is somewhat obscure. But in Ezekiel 18, the proverb pretty obviously implies that the new generation of Israelites suffers for the sins of past generations. Speaking for God, Ezekiel disputes this notion: "As I live, says

the Lord GOD: I swear that there shall no longer be anyone among you who will repeat this proverb in Israel. For all lives are mine; the life of the father is like the life of the son, both are mine; only the one who sins shall die" (Ezekiel 8:2–3).

The underlying principle of this chapter, including today's reading, is that each person is responsible for turning either toward or away from God. Responsibility for sins one has chosen to commit cannot be laid at the feet of others. This idea is nicely captured by the Hebrew word *shuv*, which may be employed in a literal way to mean

"turning" or "returning," as in "turning left" or "returning home," but also in a figurative way to mean "turning" away from, or "returning" to, God, sin, virtue, vice, and so on.

The choice to turn "away from virtue to commit iniquity" is the choice of death, whereby a person deprives oneself of God, the proper origin and destiny of each human life. "But if a wicked man, turning from the wickedness he has committed, does what is right and just, he shall preserve his life" (Ezekiel 18:24).

Emphasize in particular the word "nothing" in this line.

complete my **joy** by being of the **same mind**,
  with the **same love**,
united in heart, thinking **one thing**.
Do **nothing** out of **selfishness** or out of **vainglory**;
  rather, **humbly** regard **others** as **more important**
    than **yourselves**,
  each looking out not for his **own** interests,
  but also for **those** of others.

Have in you the **same attitude**
  that is **also** in **Christ Jesus**,
    Who, though he was in the **form** of God,
      did not regard **equality** with God
        something to be **grasped**.
  Rather, he **emptied** himself,
    taking the **form** of a **slave**,
    coming in **human likeness**;
    and found **human** in **appearance**,
    he **humbled** himself,
    becoming **obedient** to the point of **death**,
    even death on a **cross**.
  Because of this, God **greatly** exalted him
    and **bestowed** on him the **name**
    which is **above** every name,
    that at the **name** of **Jesus**
    every knee should **bend**,
    of those **in heaven** and **on earth** and **under** the **earth**,
    and **every** tongue **confess** that
    Jesus Christ is **Lord**,
    to the **glory** of **God** the **Father**.

[Shorter: Philippians 2:1–5]

Look up and make eye contact with the assembly as you proclaim the words "even death on a cross."

Pause before the word "Because."

READING II Unity within the Church is one of the most prominent themes of Paul's letter to the Christians of Philippi (in present-day Greece). In addition to today's reading ("complete my joy by being of the same mind, with the same love, united in heart, thinking one thing"), we find the theme of unity explicitly in 1:27, 3:15, and 4:2–3.

Note that in 2:1–4 the means to achieving unity within the Church is the placement of the interests and needs of others above one's own. Paul then likens the desired self-sacrifice of the community to the example of Christ: "Have among yourselves the same attitude," he says, "that is also yours in Christ Jesus" (Philippians 2:5).

In Philippians 2:6–8, Paul holds up Jesus Christ as the supreme example of self-sacrifice. Although divine, Jesus himself did not pursue divinity, but rather "emptied himself," humbling himself by becoming human and undergoing the suffering and death of the cross. In this respect, Jesus is different than many rulers of Paul's day. It was common for Greek rulers, and later for Roman emperors, to tolerate their subjects'

worship of them as gods, to encourage their subjects to do so, or even to demand it.

But with Jesus it is precisely the opposite—he did not *overreach*, but rather *under-reached*, accepting a status well beneath what he might have enjoyed. And because Jesus acted as he did, "God greatly exalted him and bestowed on him the name that is above every name" (Philippians 2:9). Christ's example, therefore, is one of rewarded self-sacrifice. If each of the Philippians submits his or her own needs, interests, and desires to the well-being of the Church, Paul implies, they too can expect

GOSPEL   Matthew 21:28–32

A reading from the holy Gospel according to Matthew

Jesus said to the chief **priests** and **elders** of the **people:**
"**What** is your **opinion**?
A man had **two sons**.
He came to the **first** and said,
    '**Son**, go out and **work** in the **vineyard** today.'
He said in reply, '**I** will **not**,'
    but **afterwards** changed his **mind** and **went**.
The man came to the **other** son and gave the **same** order.
He said in reply, '**Yes**, sir,' but did **not** go.
Which of the two did his father's **will**?"
They answered, "**The first**."
Jesus said to them, "**Amen**, I say to you,
    tax collectors and **prostitutes**
    are entering the **kingdom** of **God before** you.
When John came to you in the **way** of **righteousness**,
    you did **not** believe him;
    but **tax collectors** and **prostitutes** did.
Yet **even** when you **saw** that,
    you did not later **change** your **minds** and **believe** him."

---

vineyard = VIN-yerd

Deliver the reply of the first son in an indignant or even hostile tone of voice, and deliver the reply of the second son in a calm and obedient tone.

Raise the pitch of your voice at the end of this question to indicate that Jesus is seeking an answer from his disciples.

---

exaltation. Indeed, Christ "will change our lowly body to conform with his glorified body by the power that enables him also to bring all things into subjection to himself" (Philippians 3:21).

GOSPEL   On his first day in Jerusalem, Jesus enters the city in a royal procession celebrated by throngs of people (Matthew 21:1–11). He also violently upsets the commerce of the temple and cures blind and lame people while children praise him at the top of their lungs: "Hosanna

to the Son of David!" And so on Jesus' second day in the city, when the chief priests and elders of the people ask him, "By what authority are you doing these things? And who gave you this authority?" we can perhaps understand why these men, who functioned something like city councilmen, took such an interest in Jesus (Matthew 21:23). He has their whole city in an uproar.

Today's reading continues the debate that begins with the chief priests' and elders' question of 21:23. To their request that he disclose the source of his authority to act as he has, Jesus responds with a

question of his own: "Where was John's baptism from? Was it of heavenly or of human origin?" Unwilling to give Jesus a straight answer, the priests and elders in turn get no answer from Jesus at all (Matthew 21:23–27). In today's reading, Jesus follows the exchange of 21:23–27 with yet another question. Its obvious implication is that the son who falsely says he will do his father's will represents the priests and elders, while the repentant son represents "the tax collectors and prostitutes" who are preceding the priests and elders into the kingdom of God.

27TH SUNDAY IN ORDINARY TIME

Lectionary #139

vineyard = VIN-yerd

READING I   Isaiah 5:1–7

A reading from the Book of the Prophet Isaiah

Let me now **sing** of my **friend**,
  my friend's **song** concerning his **vineyard**.
My friend had a **vineyard**
  on a fertile hillside;
he **spaded** it, **cleared** it of stones,
  and **planted** the choicest vines;
within it he built a **watchtower**,
  and hewed out a **wine press**.
Then he looked for the **crop** of **grapes**,
  but what it yielded was **wild** grapes.

Now, inhabitants of **Jerusalem** and people of **Judah**,
  judge between me and my **vineyard**:
What more was there to do for my **vineyard**
  that I had not done?
Why, when I looked for the crop of **grapes**,
  did it bring forth **wild** grapes?
Now, I will let you **know**
  what I mean to do with my vineyard:
take away its hedge, give it to **grazing**,
  break through its wall, let it be **trampled**!

Judah = JOO-duh
Pause briefly before and after the word "Now." Then look up and make eye contact with the assembly, inviting its members to make the judgment the prophet asks the "inhabitants of Jerusalem and men of Judah" to make.

Be sure to raise the pitch of your voice at the end of these sentences to indicate that they are questions.

READING I | **Today's reading, according to the text, is a "song" (in Hebrew, *shirah*). In 5:1–2, the prophet sings of his friend's attempts to cultivate a vineyard. Despite his best efforts, however, the vineyard does not produce the good fruit he desires. In 5:3–4, the prophet summons his audience to judgment: "inhabitants of Jerusalem and men of Judah, judge between me and my vineyard." Assuming the voice of his friend, the prophet asks what more could have been done to bring forth the good fruit**

he desired. The implied answer is that the friend did everything that could be done, but that the land would not cooperate. Therefore, the friend decides to let the vineyard be destroyed, even going so far as to "command the clouds not to send rain upon it" (5:5–6). At last, in 5:7, the prophet provides the key to understanding the deeper meaning of the song of the vineyard: "The vineyard of the LORD of hosts is the house of Israel, and the men of Judah are his cherished plant; He looked for judgment, but see, bloodshed! for justice, but hark, the outcry!"

It would be reasonable to interpret this song as prophesying God's abandonment of Judah if the book of Isaiah left matters here. But we have also Isaiah 27:2–6 to examine. This is also a vineyard song, perhaps even an interpretation of today's reading in the light of the end of the Babylonian captivity and the return of some of the exiles to Judah. And in this song God's care and protection of the vineyard (Israel) is assured. We have also the song of Isaiah 42:10: "Sing to the LORD a new song, his praise from the end of

Yes, I will make it a **ruin**:
    it shall not be **pruned** or **hoed**,
    but overgrown with **thorns** and **briers**;
I will **command** the **clouds**
    not to send rain upon it.
The **vineyard** of the LORD of hosts is the **house** of **Israel**,
    and the **people** of **Judah** are his **cherished plant**;
he looked for **judgment**, but see, **bloodshed**!
    for **justice**, but hark, the **outcry**!

READING II   Philippians 4:6–9

A reading from the Letter of Saint Paul to the Philippians

Brothers and **sisters**:
Have **no** anxiety at all, but in **everything**,
    by **prayer** and **petition**, with **thanksgiving**,
    make your requests known to **God**.
Then the **peace** of God that surpasses all understanding
    will **guard** your **hearts** and **minds** in Christ Jesus.

Finally, **brothers** and **sisters**,
    whatever is **true**, whatever is **honorable**,
    whatever is **just**, whatever is **pure**,
    whatever is **lovely**, whatever is **gracious**,
    if there is any **excellence**
    and if there is anything worthy of **praise**,
    think about these things.
Keep on doing what you have **learned** and **received**
    and **heard** and **seen** in me.
Then the **God** of **peace** will be **with** you.

Emphasize in particular the words "everything" and "all."

Proclaim this verse slowly, pausing briefly at the commas and stressing the "virtuous" adjectives and nouns.

the earth." This latter song celebrates God's redemption of Israel after its captivity in Babylon, an experience of covenant renewal that the prophet elsewhere likens to nothing less than a new Exodus (Isaiah 43).

READING II   "Keep on doing what you have learned and received and heard and seen in me," writes Paul at the close of his letter to the Philippians. Paul commonly urges the Churches to which

he writes to imitate him. In 1 Corinthians 11:1, for example, Paul tells the Corinthians to be "imitators of me, as I am of Christ." In 1 Thessalonians 1:6, Paul praises the Thessalonians in the following terms: "And you became imitators of us and of the Lord, receiving the word in great affliction, with joy from the holy Spirit, so that you became a model for all the believers in Macedonia and in Achaia." The Thessalonians not only have a model in Paul, but also have themselves become models for others. To these texts we could add many more.

Why does Paul place such an emphasis upon imitation? One of the reasons has to do with the way ancient people understood education and the formation of character. From a child's first attempt at sounding out the letters of the alphabet, to an adolescent's completion of advanced courses of study in rhetoric, students were instructed to reproduce and imitate written texts supplied to them by their teachers. In philosophical curricula, imitation was no less important. Paul's frequent instruction that

GOSPEL Matthew 21:33–43

A reading from the holy Gospel according to Matthew

Jesus said to the chief **priests** and the **elders** of the people:
"Hear **another** parable.
There was a landowner who planted a **vineyard,**
  put a **hedge** around it, dug a **wine press** in it, and built a **tower.**
Then he **leased** it to **tenants** and went on a journey.
When vintage time drew near,
  he sent his **servants** to the **tenants** to obtain his produce.
But the tenants **seized** the servants and **one** they **beat,**
  another they **killed,** and a **third** they **stoned.**
Again he sent **other** servants, more **numerous** than the first ones,
  but they **treated** them in the **same way.**
Finally, he sent his **son** to them, thinking,
  'They will **respect** my **son.'**
But when the **tenants** saw the **son,** they said to one another,
  '**This** is the **heir.**
Come, let us **kill** him and acquire his **inheritance.'**
They **seized** him, **threw** him out of the vineyard, and **killed** him.
What will the owner of the vineyard do to those tenants
    when he comes?"
They answered him,
  "He will **put** those **wretched men** to a **wretched death**
  and lease his vineyard to **other** tenants
  who will give him the **produce** at the **proper times.**"

Pause briefly and look up as you proclaim the words "They will respect my son."

For the tenants' words, use a tone of voice to suggest cunning or devious excitement.

Pause after you proclaim the parable's final words and before you proclaim the question Jesus puts to his audience.

Pause briefly before and after the reply of the chief priests and elders.

people imitate him emerges from the cultural context of ancient education.

In Philippians, imitating Paul means serving the Gospel's advancement by the cultivation of humility and self-sacrifice (see Philippians 2:1–4). Just as Paul sets aside his personal dislikes for the greater good of the Christian mission—enduring prison for the Gospel's sake—so also must the Philippians set aside their differences and maintain a unified Church.

GOSPEL In the setting of the local Church for which Matthew wrote, this parable may have been used to support the belief that the Church had replaced Israel as God's chosen people, and that the promises once made to Israel now belonged to the Church (see also Mark 12:1–12; Luke 20:9–19). The owner of the vineyard pretty clearly represents God, while his vineyard represents the covenant with Israel. The "tenants" represent the Jews, while the succession of "servants"

represents the prophets, which Jesus elsewhere accuses Israel of abusing and killing (Matthew 5:12; 23:29, 31, 37). The "son," of course, represents Jesus, to whose murder the vineyard owner responds by killing the tenants and leasing it to "other tenants." These "other tenants" have usually been taken to mean the largely Gentile Church.

But one should hasten to add that the "supersession" (that is, "replacement") of Israel by the Church is *not* authentic Catholic

Jesus said to them, "Did you never read in the **Scriptures**:
> The **stone** that the builders **rejected**
>> has become the **cornerstone**;
> by the **Lord** has this been done,
>> and it is **wonderful** in our eyes?

Therefore, I say to you,
> the **kingdom** of *God* will be taken *away* from you
> and given to a people that will ***produce*** its *fruit*."

teaching. The election of Israel stands (CCC, #839), although the Catholic Church teaches that Jesus fulfills Israel's vocation (CCC, #539). But this fulfillment does not entail God's rejection of the Jews as the landlord in today's reading rejects and seeks vengeance on his wicked tenants.

In the proclamation of this parable, it is important to bear in mind that the tone and theme of this parable in its original historical context was almost certainly supplied, at least in part, by the early experience of the Church, whose members *did* encounter opposition and hostility from *some* Jews (Matthew 10:17; 23:34; 2 Corinthians 11:24; Galatians 1:13, 22; 5:11; 6:12; Philippians 3:6). But it is also important to bear in mind the words of the apostle Paul, a man who faced some of this opposition and hostility himself: "I ask, then, has God rejected his people? Of course not! For I too am an Israelite, a descendant of Abraham, of the tribe of Benjamin. God has not rejected his people whom he foreknew" (Romans 11:1–2).

28TH SUNDAY IN ORDINARY TIME

Lectionary #142

READING I   Isaiah 25:6–10a

Proclaim this reading in a clear, joyful tone of voice, and slowly enough so that the assembly can join in the feast of the prophet's sumptuous imagery.

Emphasize each occurrence of the word "all."

A reading from the Book of the Prophet Isaiah

On this **mountain** the LORD of **hosts**
    will provide for **all** peoples
a feast of **rich food** and **choice wines**,
    juicy, rich food and **pure**, choice wines.
On this mountain he will **destroy**
    the **veil** that veils **all** peoples,
the web that is **woven** over **all** nations;
    he will **destroy death** forever.
The Lord GOD will **wipe away**
    the tears from **every** face;
the **reproach** of his people he will **remove**
    from the **whole earth**; for the LORD has **spoken**.
    On that day it will be said:

Emphasize the words "our" and "we." Be sure to look up and make eye contact with the assembly as you proclaim the words "Behold our God, to whom we looked to save us!"

"**Behold** our **God**, to whom we looked to **save** us!
    This is the LORD for whom we **looked**;
    let us **rejoice** and be **glad** that he has **saved** us!"
For the hand of the LORD will rest on this **mountain**.

READING I   Biblical scholars sometimes call Isaiah 24—27 the "Isaianic Apocalypse." These chapters have been so called because some of their features resemble later Jewish and Christian apocalyptic literature, such as Daniel 7—12 and the book of Revelation, which prophesy the course of future events and God's role in their unfolding. The composition of Isaiah 24—27 has often been dated to between the mid-sixth and mid-fifth centuries BC, during the slow rebuilding of Jerusalem and return of captives from Babylon. But it is actually quite hard to date this material with any certainty.

Early Christians found in the text of today's reading portrayals of the end time they believed was fast approaching. In his defense of the doctrine of the Resurrection of the dead in 1 Corinthians 15, the apostle Paul probably does not quote the Greek text of Isaiah 25:8 directly, but he conserves its vocabulary and the striking image of death's "swallowing up." And in the book of Revelation, John of Patmos twice quotes the second half of Isaiah 25:8: "The Lord GOD will wipe away the tears from all faces; The reproach of his people he will remove from the whole earth" (see Revelation 7:17; 21:4). Paul's description of the destruction of death and John's prophecy of the comfort of the saints in the New Jerusalem rely on their interpretations of Isaiah 25:8 as prophecy of the end of all things and the arrival of the kingdom.

READING II   In Philippians 4:10–19, Paul thanks the Philippians for their financial support of himself and his mission. No less than in the present day, talk

READING II Philippians 4:12–14, 19–20

A reading from the Letter of Saint Paul to the Philippians

Brothers and sisters:
I know how to live in **humble** circumstances;
 I know also how to live with **abundance**.
In **every** circumstance and in **all** things
 I have learned the **secret** of being **well fed** and of **going hungry**,
 of living in **abundance** and of being in **need**.
I can do **all** things in **him** who **strengthens** me.
Still, it was **kind** of you to **share** in my **distress**.

My God will **fully** supply **whatever** you need,
 in accord with his **glorious** riches in **Christ Jesus**.
To our **God** and **Father**, **glory** forever and ever. **Amen**.

Look up and make eye contact with the assembly as you proclaim these words.

This reading concludes with Paul's closing words of blessing. Proclaim them slowly and with all dignity appropriate for words of public prayer.

GOSPEL Matthew 22:1–14

A reading from the holy Gospel according to Matthew

Jesus again in reply spoke to the chief **priests** and **elders**
 of the people
 in parables, saying,
"The **kingdom** of **heaven** may be likened to a **king**
 who gave a **wedding feast** for his **son**.
He dispatched his **servants**
 to summon the **invited** guests to the feast,
 but they **refused** to come.

about money in antiquity called for tact, manners, and taste. But Paul expresses both his thanks and his ongoing financial uncertainty without groveling, begging, or demanding anything. Indeed, he entirely avoids direct talk of money, but speaks instead of "living in abundance" and "being in need." Such language, which also contains a theological or spiritual dimension, helps to justify Paul's receipt of the Philippians' money in the fist place: the money is not for his sake, but for the Gospel's (Philippians 4:12).

Paul's relations with the Church at Philippi were warm and long-standing. In 2 Corinthians, Paul reports that he accepted financial support from "the brothers who came from Macedonia" during the evangelization of Corinth. Philippi was almost certainly one of the Churches Paul claims in passionate overstatement that he "plundered" when he was working to found the Church at Corinth (2 Corinthians 11:7–8). In Philippians, Paul mentions that the Church at Philippi also repeatedly gave assistance

to his mission in Thessalonica (Philippians 4:16). From the start of Paul's European ministry (see Acts 16), the Philippians have been in Paul's corner, sometimes as his only support: "You Philippians indeed know that at the beginning of the Gospel, when I left Macedonia, not a single church shared with me in an account of giving and receiving, except you alone" (Philippians 4:15).

GOSPEL Like the parable of the bad tenants (Matthew 21:33–43; see Gospel commentary, Twenty-seventh

Proclaim the words of the king in a bold and authoritative tone of voice.

A second time he sent other **servants**, saying,
  'Tell those **invited**: "Behold, I have **prepared** my banquet,
  my **calves** and **fattened cattle** are **killed**,
  and **everything** is ready; **come** to the **feast**."'
Some **ignored** the invitation and **went away**,
  one to his **farm**, another to his **business**.
The rest **laid hold** of his servants,
  mistreated them, and **killed** them.
The king was **enraged** and sent his troops,
  destroyed those murderers, and **burned** their city.
Then he said to his servants, 'The **feast** is **ready**,
  but those who were **invited** were not **worthy** to come.
Go out, therefore, into the main roads
  and **invite** to the feast **whomever** you find.'
The servants went out into the streets
  and gathered **all** they found, **bad** and **good** alike,
  and the hall was **filled** with guests.
But when the **king** came in to meet the **guests**,
  he saw a man there **not dressed** in a **wedding garment**.
The king said to him, 'My friend, how is it
  that you came in here **without** a wedding garment?'
But he was reduced to **silence**.
Then the king said to his attendants, '**Bind** his **hands** and **feet**,
  and **cast** him into the darkness outside,
  where there will be **wailing** and **grinding** of teeth.'
Many are **invited**, but **few** are **chosen**."

[Shorter: Matthew 22:1–10]

Pause after you proclaim the words "grinding of teeth." Then look up at the assembly as you continue.

Sunday in Ordinary Time, October 5), this Gospel selection is a parable of the kingdom, and like Matthew 21:33–43, the core of this parable is a description of the shameful behavior of certain people and their punishment. Also like Matthew 21:33–43, this parable may have been taken in its original context to refer to the exclusion of Jews from the kingdom of heaven and their replacement by Gentiles.

The king likely represents God the father, the son Jesus, while the banquet, it

is clear from verse 2, represents the kingdom of heaven. Like the servants beaten by the tenants in Matthew 21:35–36, the servants mistreated and killed by the invited guests in Matthew 22:3–6 almost certainly represent the prophets (see Matthew 5:12; 23:39–49). The invited guests, who refuse or ignore the summons, or attack those bearing the invitations, represent the Jews who reject Jesus. Those gathered from the streets represent the Gentiles.

The conversion of the Gentiles does not mean that has God rejected anyone, but rather included everyone: the invitation to

the banquet of the kingdom is still being extended to the entire world. This parable was probably formed as the early Church was undergoing, or had recently undergone, its painful separation from the synagogue. The destruction of the city in Matthew 22:7 may even refer to the destruction of Jerusalem in 70 AD.

29TH SUNDAY IN ORDINARY TIME

Lectionary #145

READING I   Isaiah 45:1, 4–6

A reading from the Book of the Prophet Isaiah

Cyrus = SI-rus

Thus says the LORD to his **anointed**, Cyrus,
  whose right hand I **grasp**,
subduing **nations** before him,
  and making **kings** run in his service,
opening **doors** before him
  and leaving the **gates** unbarred:
For the sake of **Jacob**, my **servant**,
  of **Israel**, my **chosen** one,
I have called you by your **name**,
  giving you a **title**, though you **knew** me **not**.
I am the LORD and there is no other,
  there is **no God** besides **me**.
It is I who **arm** you, though you **know** me **not**,
  so that toward the **rising** and the **setting** of the sun
  people may know that there is **none** besides me.
I am the LORD, there is **no other**.

Emphasize the repeated phrase "I am the LORD." The repetition drives home the point that God, not Cyrus, is the real actor.

READING I Cyrus was a king and general from Persia (present-day Iran). In 538 BC, Persian armies defeated Babylon, the kingdom which was then holding many captives it had originally stolen from Judah 50 and 60 years earlier. Much of Isaiah 40—55, including today's reading, dates from the period when Cyrus was establishing his empire in the Middle East. To the authors of Isaiah 40—55, and not a few Babylonians, the rise of Cyrus promised some measure of liberation.

The Hebrew word for "anointed one" is *moshiach,* from which the English word "messiah" comes. A Greek translation of "anointed one" is *christos,* or "Christ." Except for Cyrus, there is no Gentile ruler in the Old Testament who is called "the Lord's anointed." This fact lets us know how fully the authors of today's reading had embraced Cyrus' cause as their own. The exiles' speculation about Cyrus' divinely ordained mission had much to do with the development of later Jewish hopes in the advent of a messiah to restore sovereignty to Israel.

The most important theological claim of this reading is that God directs Cyrus to act on Israel's behalf: "For the sake of Jacob, my servant, of Israel my chosen one, I have called you by your name, giving you a title, though you knew me not" (Isaiah 45:6). What others, even Cyrus himself, do not realize, the prophet says, is that God is using Cyrus to restore the captives of Judah to their home.

Roughly three years after the defeat of Babylon, in 536 BC, Cyrus decreed that the captives of Judah could return to Judah. Over the next century they trickled home,

READING II   1 Thessalonians 1:1–5b

A reading from the first Letter of Saint Paul to the Thessalonians

Paul, **Silvanus**, and **Timothy** to the church of the **Thessalonians**
   in **God** the **Father** and the **Lord Jesus Christ**:
grace to you and peace.
We give **thanks** to **God always** for **all** of you,
   remembering you in our **prayers**,
   unceasingly calling to mind your **work** of **faith** and **labor**
      of **love**
and **endurance** in hope of our Lord Jesus Christ,
before our **God** and **Father**,
knowing, **brothers** and **sisters** loved by God,
how you were **chosen**.
For our gospel did **not** come to you in word **alone**,
   but also in **power** and in the **Holy Spirit**
      and with **much conviction**.

Silvanus = Sil-VAH-nus
Thessalonians = Theh-sah-LOH-nee-yans

Pause after Paul's greeting before continuing with his thanksgiving.

Take great care to emphasize this verse. Deliver it while making eye contact with the assembly.

---

although many Israelites chose to remain in the regions to which they had been taken.

READING II   First Thessalonians opens with Paul identifying himself and his co-senders, and greeting their intended recipients: "grace to you and peace." As Paul's openings go, 1 Thessalonians is quite short. Romans, in contrast, spans seven verses (Romans 1:1–7).

   After his opening address and greeting, Paul's letters usually have a "thanksgiving," a short passage where he gives thanks to

God for his recipients. In 1 Thessalonians, Paul gives thanks for the Thessalonians' "work of faith and labor of love and endurance in hope of our Lord Jesus Christ, before our God and Father" (1 Thessalonians 1:3). We see the trio of faith, love, and hope more than once in Paul's letters. We not only find it in 1 Corinthians 13:13 (well known from weddings), but again in 1 Thessalonians: "let us be sober, putting on the breastplate of faith and love and the helmet that is hope for salvation" (1 Thessalonians 5:8).

   While Paul holds love above faith and hope in 1 Corinthians 13, in 1 Thessalonians

he places the greatest stress on hope. Hope, as Paul uses the term, is not simply optimism or a general belief that the future will turn out well. It is the confident expectation of Resurrection, an idea Paul expresses by the image of hope as a "helmet that is the hope of salvation." The Thessalonians have had their hope shaken, worrying about the fate of some of their community who died before Christ had returned. Paul does his best to allay their fears and to bolster their hope once again in the life of the world to come (1 Thessalonians 4:13–18).

Pharisees = FAIR-ih-sees

Herodians = Heh-ROH-dee-yans

In today's Gospel, Matthew presents the Pharisees' disciples and the Herodians as a little less than sincere. Deliver their flattering words in an insincere, saccharine tone of voice, but be careful not to overdo it.

Caesar = SEE-zer

In this verse, we find the only answer Jesus' opponents offer him in this reading. In reply to Jesus' question about whose image the coin bears, the opponents say "Caesar's." Use a dumbfounded tone of voice here, different from the syrupy tone of the original question. Jesus is outwitting them and they are realizing it too late.

GOSPEL   Matthew 22:15–21

A reading from the holy Gospel according to Matthew

The **Pharisees** went off
  and plotted how they might **entrap Jesus** in speech.
They sent their **disciples** to him, with the **Herodians**, saying,
  "Teacher, we **know** that you are a **truthful** man
  and that you teach the way of God in **accordance**
    with the **truth**.
And you are **not** concerned with **anyone's** opinion,
  for you do **not** regard a person's **status**.
Tell us, then, what is your **opinion**:
  Is it **lawful** to pay the census **tax** to **Caesar** or **not**?"
Knowing their **malice**, Jesus said,
  "Why are you testing me, you **hypocrites**?
Show me the coin that **pays** the census tax."
Then they handed him the Roman coin.
He said to them, "Whose **image** is this and whose **inscription**?"
They replied, "**Caesar's**."
At that he said to them,
  "Then **repay** to Caesar what belongs to **Caesar**
  and to **God** what belongs to **God**."

GOSPEL   Victims of Roman crucifixion often had the reasons for their executions written down and attached to their crosses. Both Mark and John use common legal terms to describe the placard attached to Jesus' cross: Mark calls it a "cause" or "charge" (in Greek, *aitia*), while John borrows the originally Latin term of *titulus* (in Greek, *titlos*). In this context, both words describe the written public notice of the legal basis for an execution. "This is Jesus, the King of the Jews," is evidence of the crime of *sedition*, the

undermining or sabotage of political authority (Matthew 27:37; see also Mark 15:24; Luke 23:38; John 19:18–22). Caesar, not Jesus, was king. To claim otherwise set Jesus up as a rival to Caesar and undermined the authority of Rome.

In today's reading, we encounter an early attempt by Jewish leaders in Jerusalem to catch Jesus on a charge of sedition. Their question is simple enough: "Is it lawful to pay the census tax to Caesar or not?" Contained in this question is an issue of Jewish religious observance: is it within the bounds of observant Judaism to pay a tax to

pagan authorities and, in this particular case, to handle money bearing the emperor's image? If Jesus says "yes," then he risks being in violation of Jewish law. If he says "no," then he courts the charge of sedition, a violation of Roman rule.

Rebuking the Pharisees and Herodians for their hypocritical flattery, Jesus does not fall into their trap. Instead, he forces them to decide for themselves whether they will handle the emperor's image and pay the tax. But contained within this answer is an even deeper question: what on earth does *not* belong to God?

30TH SUNDAY IN ORDINARY TIME

Lectionary #148

READING I   Exodus 22:20–26

A reading from the Book of Exodus

Thus says the LORD:
"You shall not **molest** or **oppress** an alien,
  for you were once **aliens** yourselves in the land of **Egypt**.
You shall **not wrong** any **widow** or **orphan**.
If **ever** you wrong them and they **cry out** to me,
  I will **surely** hear their cry.
My **wrath** will **flare up**, and I will **kill** you with the **sword**;
  then your own **wives** will be **widows**,
    and your **children orphans**.

"If you **lend money** to one of your poor neighbors
    among my people,
  you shall **not** act like an **extortioner** toward him
  by **demanding interest** from him.
If you take your neighbor's **cloak** as a **pledge**,
  you shall **return** it to him before **sunset**;
    for this **cloak** of his is the **only** covering he has for his **body**.
What else has he to **sleep** in?
If he **cries out** to me, I will **hear** him; for I am **compassionate**."

Look up and make eye contact with the assembly as you proclaim this line.

Look up again as you proclaim this line.

READING I Jews typically call the first five books of the Bible (Genesis, Exodus, Leviticus, Numbers, and Deuteronomy) the *Torah*. The Hebrew word *torah* means "instruction" or "law," and this name, when applied to these books, generally refers to the legal writing within them, as well as their uniquely authoritative status. Our reading today comes from one of the legal sections of the book of Exodus, where several of Israel's covenant obligations are laid out.

God's protection of the poor is the frequent testimony of the psalms (see Psalm 140:13). The psalms also testify to the justice God brings upon those who harm the poor (see Psalm 10:17–18).

In today's reading, we read that the administration of God's protection of Israel's resident aliens, widows, orphans, and poor has been entrusted to the people itself. The people must vigilantly protect them and punish whoever harms them. If it would remain faithful to God, Israel cannot tolerate the oppression of its most vulnerable.

In its explanation of the seventh commandment ("Thou shalt not steal"), the *Catechism of the Catholic Church* teaches: "Love for the poor is incompatible with immoderate love of riches or their selfish use (CCC, #2445). After quoting the New Testament's letter of James at length (James 5:1–6), the Catechism then quotes the great preacher and scholar, John Chrysostom: "Not to enable the poor to share in our goods is to steal from them and deprive them of life. The goods we possess are not ours, but theirs" (CCC, #2445–2446).

Paul gives thanks for the Thessalonians' faith in this reading, giving them credit for what they have done. You may also use this reading to give thanks for the faith of your own assembly by emphasizing the words "you" and "your" in this reading, looking up frequently and making eye contact with the assembly as you do so.

Macedonia = mas-uh-DOH-nee-uh
Achaia = uh-Kee-uh

READING II   1 Thessalonians 1:5c–10

A reading from the first Letter of Saint Paul to the Thessalonians

Brothers and **sisters**:
You **know** what sort of **people** we were among you for your sake.
And you became **imitators** of **us** and of the **Lord**,
    receiving the word in **great affliction**,
        with **joy** from the **Holy Spirit**,
    so that you became a **model** for **all** the **believers**
    in **Macedonia** and in **Achaia**.
For from you the **word** of the **Lord** has sounded **forth**
    not only in **Macedonia** and in **Achaia**,
    but in **every** place your **faith** in **God** has gone forth,
    so that we have **no need** to say **anything**.
For they themselves **openly** declare about us
    what sort of **reception** we had among you,
    and how you turned to **God** from **idols**
    to serve the **living** and **true God**
    and to await his **Son** from **heaven**,
    whom he **raised** from the **dead**,
    Jesus, who **delivers** us from the coming **wrath**.

READING II   The Thessalonians, Paul writes, "turned to God from idols to serve the living and true God" (1 Thessalonians 1:9). This conversion was probably not easy. What Paul calls "idols" were the only gods the Thessalonians knew. To turn from them meant turning from upbringing, family, friends, ancestry, and culture. Paul mentions that the Thessalonians' conversions happened "in great affliction" (1 Thessalonians 1:6). The Greek word our Bibles translate as "affliction" is *thlipsis*. The word can mean either "affliction" or "persecution." Paul may be referring either

to some actual harassment the Thessalonians suffered when they converted, or to inner turmoil each person felt as they did so. Perhaps the converts experienced *thlipsis* in both senses. But in any case, their "affliction" must have been less powerful than the "joy from the holy Spirit" with which they also received the word.

Whom the Thessalonians have become are "imitators" of Paul and his missionary team and Jesus Christ, as well as a "model" for believers throughout Achaia

and Macedonia (northwestern and southwestern Greece, including Corinth and Philippi). The report of the Thessalonians' embrace of the Gospel appears to have given Paul's ministry a boost throughout Greece, where people "openly declare about us what sort of reception we had among you" (1 Thessalonians 1:8–9).

What the Thessalonians have been saved from is "the coming wrath" (1 Thessalonians 1:10). This wrath is the period of judgment Paul elsewhere calls by a traditional Jewish label: "the day of the Lord" (1 Thessalonians 5:2, 4; see also Amos 5:18–20).

GOSPEL   Matthew 22:34–40

Pharisees = FAIR-ih-sees
Sadducees = SAH-doo-sees

Read Jesus' answer to this question slowly, being careful to emphasize its key terms.

A reading from the holy Gospel according to Matthew

When the **Pharisees** heard that **Jesus** had silenced the **Sadducees**,
    they gathered together, and one of them,
    a scholar of the law, tested him by asking,
    "**Teacher**, which **comandment** in the **law** is the **greatest**?"

He said to him,
"You shall **love** the **Lord**, your **God**,
    with all your **heart**,
    with all your **soul**,
    and with all your **mind**.
This is the **greatest** and the **first** commandment.
The **second** is like it:
    You shall **love** your **neighbor** as **yourself**.
The **whole law** and the **prophets**
        depend on these two commandments."

GOSPEL   The specific laws Jesus mentions in today's reading are found in Deuteronomy 6:5 and Leviticus 19:18. Matthew, Mark, and Luke each have a version of this exchange (see Mark 12:34–38 and Luke 10:25–37). In Galatians, Paul gives an even shorter version of the principle, observing, "For the whole law is fulfilled in one statement, namely, 'You shall love your neighbor as yourself' " (Galatians 5:14; see also Romans 13:9).

In Luke's Gospel, the exchange takes place between Jesus and a "scholar of the law." Unlike both Mark and Matthew, the exchange sets up the parable of the Good Samaritan, in which Jesus radically redefines what it means to be a neighbor to someone: the relationship of neighbor to neighbor is not one of loving and compassionate service without thought of religion, ethnicity, and so on.

In Paul's letter to the Churches of Galatia, the command to love one's neighbor as oneself works differently. Paul quotes it to show that Christian freedom from Jewish law does not mean "anything goes."

We cannot say on the basis of today's reading that Matthew claims Jesus cast aside Jewish law except in two instances, for Matthew's Gospel contains a high and approving view of the law. The evangelist records, for example, that Jesus called his followers to an even stricter level of legal observance than that of the Pharisees (see Matthew 5:17–20). Matthew's Jesus understood the love of God and neighbor to be the law's foundation, not its entire content.

COMMEMORATION OF ALL THE FAITHFUL DEPARTED

Lectionary #668

READING I   Wisdom 3:1–9

A reading from the Book of Wisdom

The **souls** of the **just** are in the **hand** of **God**,
  and no **torment** shall **touch** them.
They **seemed**, in the **view** of the **foolish**, to be **dead**;
  and their passing away was thought an **affliction**
  and their going forth from us, **utter destruction**.
But **they** are **in peace**.
For if in the **sight** of others, indeed they be **punished**,
  yet is their **hope** full of **immortality**;
chastised a **little**, they shall be **greatly** blessed,
  because **God tried them**
  and found them **worthy** of **himself**.
As **gold** in the **furnace**, he **proved** them,
  and as **sacrificial offerings** he took them to **himself**.
In the time of their **visitation** they shall **shine**,
  and shall **dart about** as **sparks** through **stubble**;
they shall **judge nations** and **rule** over **peoples**,
  and the **LORD** shall be their **King forever**.
Those who **trust** in him shall understand **truth**,
  and the **faithful** shall **abide** with him in **love**:
because **grace** and **mercy** are with his **holy** ones,
  and his **care** is with his **elect**.

Note the parallel poetic structure of this passage, how the author says something and then restates or amplifies it using different language. As you prepare this reading, pay attention to this feature (which biblical scholars call "parallelism").

Pause and look up, making eye contact with the assembly before you proclaim the words "But they are in peace."

The readings given here are suggestions. Any readings from the Lectionary for the Commemoration of All the Faithful Departed (#668) or the Masses for the Dead (#1011–1016) may be used.

READING I The book of Wisdom is a Jewish text, originally written in Greek and probably composed during the first century AD in the great community of the Jewish Diaspora (literally, "scattering") in Alexandria, Egypt. The book begins with an exhortation to good and virtuous living (Wisdom 1:1–15). Immediately following this comes a description of the foolish reasoning of wicked people. The thoughts of the wicked are at first filled with despair of any life beyond this one (2:1–5), then visions of pleasure (2:6–9), and finally sinister conspiracies of abuse and murder (2:10–20). The author contends that their enjoyment of the flowers of spring (2:6) leads naturally to violent crime because their pursuit of pleasure is founded not on the love of creation and its Creator, but on their despair of any life beyond this one.

The root failure of the wicked, according to our author, is a failure to reason properly on the subject of the immortality of the soul. Their despair, pleasure seeking, and sin all flow from this basic mistake. The righteous, in contrast, know "hope full of immortality" (Wisdom 3:4). Like the use of "hope" (in Greek, *elpis*) as a kind of shorthand for the Resurrection by the apostle

READING II   Romans 5:5–11

A reading from the Letter of Saint Paul to the Romans

Brothers and **sisters**:
Hope does **not** disappoint,
 because the **love** of **God** has been **poured out** into our **hearts**
 through the **Holy Spirit** that has been **given** to us.
For **Christ**, while we were **still helpless**,
 died at the appointed time for the **ungodly**.
Indeed, **only** with **difficulty** does one **die** for a **just** person,
 though perhaps for a **good** person
 one might even find **courage** to **die**.
But **God proves** his **love** for **us**
 in that while **we** were **still sinners Christ died** for **us**.
How much more then, since we are now **justified** by his **blood**,
 will we be **saved** through him from the **wrath**.
Indeed, **if**, while we were **enemies**,
 we were **reconciled** to **God** through the **death** of his **Son**,
 how much more, once **reconciled**,
 will we be **saved** by his **life**.
Not only that,
 but we **also** boast of **God** through our **Lord Jesus** Christ,
 through whom we have now received **reconciliation**.

Or:

Pause briefly before you proclaim this
verse, slowing down for emphasis.

Paul and many other early Christian writers, the author of Wisdom relates "hope" to the immortality of the soul.

According to our author, God designed not only the souls of the righteous, but also the whole of creation for immortality. God "fashioned all things that they might have being; and the creatures of the world are wholesome, and there is not a destructive drug among them nor any domain of the nether world on earth, For justice is undying" (Wisdom 1:14–15).

READING II Today's reading begins with Romans 5:5, though it makes more sense if we look back and begin with Romans 5:1. There, Paul identifies peace as the good result of finding a right relationship with God through faith in Jesus Christ. In 5:2, Paul appears to suggest that the accomplished fact of this right relationship permits boasting "in hope of the glory of God." "Hope of the glory of God" refers to the Resurrection, the life of the world to come,

which belongs to Christians by virtue of their faith in Jesus and their Baptism. This boast, it is important to note, is a boast about what God has done, not about anything the Christians of Rome have accomplished.

Paul also boasts about "afflictions, knowing that affliction produces endurance, and endurance, proven character, and proven character, hope" (Romans 5:3–4). Thus a boast about afflictions is simply a roundabout way of boasting about hope, a way of crediting the entire Christian life to the God

READING II   Romans 6:3–9

A reading from the Letter of Saint Paul to the Romans

Brothers and **sisters:**
Are you **unaware** that **we** who were **baptized** into **Christ Jesus**
    were **baptized** into his **death?**
We were **indeed buried** with him through **baptism** into **death,**
    so that, just as **Christ** was **raised** from the **dead**
    by the **glory** of the **Father,**
    we too might live in **newness** of **life.**

For if **we** have grown into **union** with him through a **death**
        like his,
    we shall **also** be **united** with him in the **resurrection.**
We know that our **old self** was **crucified** with him,
    so that our **sinful body** might be **done away** with,
    that we might **no longer** be in **slavery** to **sin.**
For a **dead person** has been **absolved** from sin.
If, then, we have **died** with **Christ,**
    we believe that we shall **also live** with him.
We know that **Christ,** raised from the **dead,** dies no more;
    death no longer has **power** over him.

Pause briefly between stanzas.

who destines all humanity, both Jew and Gentile, for eternity with himself through faith in Jesus Christ.

In common English usage, a hope is a wish, a desire, a possibility, something one wants very much, but which still might not happen. This does not describe Paul's hope in the glory of God. Paul's hope "does not disappoint," for God's love, which confirms and sustains his hope, has been proven by the reconciliation that Christ's death achieved between God and the world.

GOSPEL   The subject of Jesus' protective care of his disciples comes up multiple times in John. In John's description of Jesus' final evening on earth, Jesus petitions his Father on behalf of his disciples: "When I was with them I protected them in your name that you gave me, and I guarded them, and none of them was lost except the son of destruction, in order that the scripture might be fulfilled" (John 17:12). ("The son of destruction" refers, of course, to Judas Iscariot.) These words recall something Jesus said in his description of himself as the good shepherd: "My sheep hear my voice; I know them, and they follow me. I give them eternal life, and they shall never perish. No one can take them out of my hand" (John 10:27–28). And these words in turn echo what Jesus says to the Galilean crowds in today's reading: "this is the will of the one who sent me, that I should not lose anything of what he gave me, but that I should raise it [on] the last day" (John 6:38–39).

The last time the subject of Jesus protection of his disciples arises in John's Gospel is during Jesus' arrest in the garden.

GOSPEL John 6:37–40

A reading from the holy Gospel according to John

Jesus said to the **crowds**:
"**Everything** that the **Father** gives me will **come** to **me**,
    and I will **not reject anyone** who **comes** to me,
        because I **came down** from **heaven** not to do my **own** will
        but the **will** of the **one who sent me**.
And **this** is the **will** of the **one who sent me**,
    that I should not lose **anything** of what he **gave** me,
    but that I should **raise** it on the last day.
For **this** is the **will** of my **Father**,
    that **everyone** who **sees** the **Son** and **believes** in him
    may have **eternal life**,
    and I shall **raise** him on the **last day**."

Look up and make eye contact as you proclaim this verse.

Pause after you proclaim this line, and then look up and make eye contact with the assembly as you continue.

Identifying himself to the soldiers who have come to take him away, Jesus says, "if you are looking for me, let these men go." John continues: "This was to fulfill what he had said, 'I have not lost any of those you gave me' " (John 18:8–9). In John's Gospel, we often read that Jesus, by saying or doing something, fulfills scripture (see John 12:38; 13:18; 15:25). But here Jesus fulfills his own words, which strongly suggests that John believes Jesus' speech is of the same nature and quality as scripture (see also John 18:32).

DEDICATION OF THE LATERAN BASILICA IN ROME

Lectionary #671

READING I   Ezekiel 47:1–2, 8–9, 12

A reading from the Book of the Prophet Ezekiel

Proclaim this reading slowly in a strong tone of voice.

The angel **brought** me
    back to the entrance of the **temple,**
    and I saw **water** flowing out
    from beneath the **threshold** of the **temple** toward the **east,**
    for the **façade** of the temple was **toward** the east;
    the water **flowed down** from the **southern** side of the **temple,**
    south of the **altar.**
He led me outside by the **north** gate,
    and around to the outer gate facing the **east,**
    where I saw **water trickling** from the southern side.
He said to me,
    "This water **flows** into the **eastern** district down
        upon the **Arabah,**
    and empties into the **sea,** the **salt waters,** which it makes **fresh.**
Wherever the **river** flows,
    every sort of living creature that can **multiply** shall live,
    and there shall be **abundant fish,**
    for **wherever** this water comes, the **sea** shall be **made fresh.**

READING I When Babylon destroyed Jerusalem in 587 BC, it also destroyed the temple and carted away its riches (see 2 Kings 24–25; Jeremiah 52; 2 Chronicles 36:15–20). Today's reading from the book of the prophet Ezekiel was composed while many of Jerusalem's citizens were living in exile and its temple lay in ruins. Beginning in Ezekiel 40, the prophet describes his vision of a new temple. Today's reading is part of this vision.

Ezekiel 47:1–12 is somewhat unusual in relation to the text immediately preceding it.

We find none of the priestly concern for sacrifices and proper use of the temple space. Instead, we read of a stream welling up from the temple that "flows into the eastern district down upon the Arabah, and empties into the sea, the salt waters, which it makes fresh" (Ezekiel 47:8). *Arabah* is the Hebrew word for the desolate desert regions southeast of Jerusalem and west of the Dead Sea. "The sea, the salt waters" refers to the Dead Sea, an inland body of water so-called for its high salt content.

Beginning from a trickle and building into a torrent, the water welling from the

new house of the Lord has the power to make dead waters alive and gives life wherever it flows.

READING II One of the many things dividing the members of the Church at Corinth was the issue of leadership. Not all members accepted the authority of the same leaders. Paul addresses this situation very early in 1 Corinthians. Urging "that there be no divisions among you, but that you be united in the same mind and in the same purpose," Paul informs the

Look up as you proclaim this verse.

Along **both banks** of the **river**, **fruit trees** of every kind
   shall **grow**;
   their **leaves** shall **not fade**, **nor** their **fruit fail**.
Every month they shall bear **fresh fruit**,
   for they shall be **watered** by the **flow** from the **sanctuary**.
Their **fruit** shall serve for **food**, and their **leaves** for **medicine**."

READING II   1 Corinthians 3:9c–11, 16–17

A reading from the first Letter of Saint Paul to the Corinthians

Brothers and **sisters**:
You are **God's building**.
According to the grace of **God** given to **me**,
   like a **wise** master builder **I** laid a **foundation**,
   and **another** is building **upon** it.

Emphasize the word "you," making eye contact with the assembly as you do so.

But **each one** must be **careful** how he **builds** upon it,
   for **no one** can lay a **foundation** other than the **one** that is **there**,
   namely, **Jesus Christ**.

Pause briefly before you proclaim this line.

Do you **not know** that **you** are the **temple** of **God**,
   and that the **Spirit** of **God dwells** in **you**?
If **anyone** destroys **God's temple**,
   God will **destroy** that **person**;
   for the **temple** of **God**, which **you are**, is **holy**.

Make sure to raise the pitch of your voice at the end of this verse to indicate that it is a question. Look up as you ask it of the assembly.

Corinthians that he has heard from "Chloe's people" (probably slaves or freedmen of the household of a Christian woman named Chloe) that Corinth indeed suffers from such divisions. "I mean," Paul explains, "that each of you is saying, 'I belong to Paul,' or 'I belong to Apollos,' or 'I belong to Kephas,' or 'I belong to Christ.' "Is Christ divided? Was Paul crucified for you? Or were you baptized in the name of Paul?"

   The answer Paul expects to this last question is a clear and resounding "No." However, the issue of authority in Corinth is a bit more complicated than this. For Paul

does believe that founding the Church at Corinth has given him a unique authority there. This does not mean that other leaders, particularly Apollos (see 1 Corinthians 3:4– 6, 22; 4:6; 16:12), have no authority at all, only that Paul's own authority is beyond question. But all issues of human authority pale in comparison to the authority of God (1 Corinthians 3:1–8).

   In today's reading, Paul attempts to explain to the Corinthians the nature of his authority. Likening them to a building, Paul compares himself to an architect who planned and executed its foundation. "Like

a skilled master builder," Paul writes, "I laid a foundation, and another is building upon it" (1 Corinthians 3:10). This unnamed "another" is almost certainly Apollos (for more on Apollos, see Acts 18:24–28). We can see this from 1 Corinthians 3:6, where Paul uses a farming image to explain his and Apollos' relationship to the Church: "I planted, Apollos watered." What puts the issue of human leadership into proper perspective, however, is that both Paul and Apollos derive their authority from God: "neither the one

GOSPEL   John 2:13–22

A reading from the holy Gospel according to John

Since the **Passover** of the **Jews** was **near**,
    Jesus went up to **Jerusalem**.
He found in the **temple area** those who sold **oxen**, **sheep**, and
        doves,
    as well as the **money changers** seated there.
He made a **whip** out of **cords**
    and **drove** them **all** out of the temple area,
        with the **sheep** and **oxen**,
    and **spilled** the **coins** of the money changers
    and **overturned** their **tables**,
    and to those who sold **doves** he said,
    "**Take** these **out** of here,
    and **stop** making my **Father's house** a **marketplace**."
His disciples **recalled** the words of **Scripture**,
    Zeal for your **house** *will* **consume** *me*.
At this the Jews **answered** and **said** to him,
    "What **sign** can you **show** us for **doing** this?"
Jesus **answered** and **said** to them,
    "**Destroy** this **temple** and in **three days** I will **raise** it up."
The **Jews** said,
    "This **temple** has been under construction for **forty-six years**,
    and **you** will raise it up in **three days**?"
But he was **speaking** about the **temple** of his **Body**.
Therefore, when he was **raised** from the **dead**,
    his **disciples** remembered that he had **said** this,
    and they came to **believe** the **Scripture**
    and the **word Jesus** had **spoken**.

Proclaim Jesus' words in a strong, bold tone of voice.

Here, the Jews think Jesus is talking nonsense. Proclaim their question in a surprised tone of voice.

who plants nor the one who waters is anything, but only God, who causes the growth" (1 Corinthians 3:7).

GOSPEL | All four evangelists record that Jesus, on his first visit to Jerusalem, raised quite a ruckus in the temple precincts. Unlike Matthew, Mark, and Luke, each of whom recalls that Jesus performed this act during the final week of his life, John puts this event near the beginning of Jesus' ministry.

Jesus' aggressive actions in the temple are in the prophetic tradition. Above all, a prophet was someone who spoke oracles of God. But some prophets also performed symbolic actions in order to proclaim a particular message. In Jeremiah 19, God commands Jeremiah to buy an earthenware jug and smash it in the presence of some priests and elders of the people. After smashing it, God instructs Jeremiah to say, "Thus will I smash this people and this city, as one smashes a clay pot so that it cannot be repaired" (Jeremiah 19:11). As with Jesus in

the temple, action accompanies word as a single prophetic oracle.

In Matthew and Mark, only false witnesses at Jesus' trial claim that he said anything about destroying and raising the temple in three days (Matthew 26:60; Mark 14:57). In today's reading, John recalls that Jesus did in fact say these words, but intended them as a prophecy of his Resurrection.

33RD SUNDAY IN ORDINARY TIME

Lectionary #157

READING I   Proverbs 31:10–13, 19–20, 30–31

Pause very briefly between each stanza.

A reading from the Book of Proverbs

When one **finds** a **worthy wife**,
   her **value** is **far** beyond **pearls**.
Her **husband**, entrusting his **heart** to her,
   has an **unfailing** prize.
She brings him **good**, and not **evil**,
   all the days of her life.
She obtains **wool** and **flax**
   and **works** with loving hands.
She puts her **hands** to the **distaff**,
   and her **fingers** ply the **spindle**.
She **reaches** out her **hands** to the **poor**,
   and **extends** her **arms** to the **needy**.
Charm is **deceptive** and **beauty fleeting**;
   the **woman** who fears the LORD is to be **praised**.
Give her a **reward** for her labors,
   and let her **works praise her** at the city gates.

READING I   The first verse of the book of Proverbs reads as follows: "The Proverbs of Solomon, the son of David, king of Israel" (Proverbs 1:1). In truth, multiple authors set down the material found in Proverbs during different periods of Israel's history, spanning the monarchies of Judah and Israel to the period after the Babylonian captivity when the kingdom of Judah was reestablished under the Persians. The attribution of Proverbs to Solomon was probably due to the king's renown as an author of proverbs. First Kings claims Solomon "uttered 3,000 proverbs."

Many of the poems, hymns, and sayings found in the book of Proverbs are examples of what one might call "folk wisdom," commonsense advice about meeting life's milestones and challenges. There are also quite sophisticated and poetic sections, such as Proverbs 8, which describes divine wisdom's creative partnership with God.

Today's reading describes a feminine ideal, what our Bible calls "a worthy wife" (Proverbs 31:10). A more literal rendering of the Hebrew, however, yields something like "woman of power" or "woman of wealth." In verse 16, we read that this woman buys land and works it herself, while in verse 24 she profits from the sale of her own labor. Her love and care for her husband and children, while obviously central to who she is and what she is about, are hardly the sole dimensions of her life.

READING II 1 Thessalonians 5:1–6

A reading from the first Letter of Saint Paul to the Thessalonians

Concerning **times** and **seasons**, **brothers** and **sisters**,
  you have **no need** for **anything** to be written to you.
For **you yourselves know very well** that the **day** of the **Lord**
    will **come**
  like a **thief** at **night**.
When people are saying, "**Peace** and **security**,"
  then sudden **disaster** comes upon them,
  like **labor** pains upon a **pregnant woman**,
  and they will **not** escape.

But **you**, **brothers** and **sisters**, are **not** in darkness,
  for that **day** to **overtake** you like a **thief**.
For **all** of you are **children** of the **light**
  and **children** of the **day**.
We are **not** of the **night** or of **darkness**.
Therefore, let us not **sleep** as the **rest** do,
  but let us stay **alert** and **sober**.

Proclaim this reading slowly, in a strong, clear voice.

Emphasize this verse, making eye contact with the assembly as you do so.

READING II | Paul's description of the Christians of Thessalonica as "children of the day" in today's reading has several layers of meaning.

First, light and darkness broadly correspond to the Church and the world outside the Church. In Ephesians 5:3–14, for example, the author describes the world's vice as darkness, while using light to characterize the Church's virtue. Paul has such a distinction in mind when he describes night as a time for drunkenness and day as a time for sobriety (1 Thessalonians 5:6–7).

Second, light and darkness also correspond to understanding and ignorance. Paul tells the Thessalonians that, as children of the day, they ought not to be surprised like a thief caught in the middle of a nighttime burglary, nor "sleep as the rest do" (1 Thessalonians 5:2, 6).

The third meaning of "children of the day" has to do with "the day of the Lord." In preparation for this day's arrival, the Thessalonians are to remain sober, not drunk. And because they know this day is coming, they are not asleep in ignorance, but alert with understanding. They are the children of this day and need not fear it as those for whom it is "coming wrath" (1 Thessalonians 1:10). For Paul, the day of the Lord is the day when God judges the world and Christ returns for his Church. Immediately before today's reading, in 1 Thessalonians 4:13–18, Paul has explained what this day will unfold for all members of the Church, both living and dead. Paul preserves the ancient Israelite belief in the Day of Yahweh (Amos 5:18–20), but comprehends it anew through Jesus Christ.

GOSPEL Matthew 25:14–30

A reading from the holy Gospel according to Matthew

Jesus told his disciples this **parable**:
"A man going on a **journey**
    called in his **servants** and entrusted his **possessions** to them.
To one he gave **five** talents; to another, **two**; to a third, **one**—
    to **each** according to his **ability**.
Then he went **away**.
Immediately the one who received **five** talents
        went and **traded** with them,
    and made **another** five.
Likewise, the one who received **two** made **another** two.
But the man who received **one** went off and dug a hole
    in the ground
    and **buried** his master's money.

"After a long time
    the **master** of those servants came **back**
    and **settled accounts** with them.
The one who had received **five** talents came forward
    bringing the additional five.
He said, '**Master**, you gave me **five** talents.
See, I have made **five more**.'
His master said to him, '**Well done**, my **good** and **faithful servant**.
Since you were **faithful** in **small** matters,
    I will give you **great** responsibilities.
Come, **share** your master's **joy**.'
Then the one who had received **two** talents also came forward
        and said,
    '**Master**, you gave me **two** talents.

Proclaim the words of the first two servants in a clear, confident tone of voice, but proclaim the words of the third in a fearful, worried tone.

GOSPEL The principle underlying the master's unequal treatment of his slaves hardly seems fair: "For to everyone who has, more will be given and he will grow rich; but from the one who has not, even what he has will be taken away" (Matthew 25:29). Where is the justice here?

   If the parable were really about money (a single talent was a very substantial sum), then one could rightly call the master's speech unjust. But Jesus' story of the master and his slaves is a parable not of the marketplace, but of the kingdom of heaven.

We know this from Matthew 25:1, where Jesus says that "the kingdom of heaven will be like" ten virgins and proceeds to tell their story. It is clear from the Greek particle *hōsper* in 25:14, meaning "like" or "as," that Jesus compares today's parable to the kingdom of heaven just as he earlier compared it to the ten virgins back in 25:1.

   Even as a parable of the kingdom, today's reading is still a little odd. The master in this parable perhaps represents Jesus, although God the Father is more likely. The slaves probably represent the disciples, who, as we learn in Matthew 10, are charged

with proclaiming the kingdom and performing acts of power and healing that herald its arrival. Their investment of their master's property probably represents their labors on behalf of the kingdom, which two perform to differing degrees of confidence and diligence. The terrified one who does nothing productive with his master's property represents those either inside or outside the band of disciples, and later the Church, who refuse to work for the kingdom's advancement.

The master is well pleased with his servants at first, but very angry later on. Proclaim the master's words of approval in a happy, congratulatory tone of voice. But proclaim the master's words of rebuke in a strident, firm tone of voice.

See, I have made **two** more.'
His master said to him, '**Well done**, my **good** and **faithful servant**.
Since you were **faithful** in **small** matters,
  I will give you **great** responsibilities.
Come, share your master's **joy**.'
Then the one who had received the **one** talent came forward
    and said,
  '**Master**, I knew you were a **demanding** person,
  harvesting where you did **not plant**
  and **gathering** where you did **not scatter**;
  so out of **fear** I went off and **buried** your talent in the **ground**.
Here it is **back**.'
His master said to him in reply, '**You wicked**, lazy servant!
So you **knew** that I **harvest** where I did **not plant**
  and **gather** where I did **not scatter**?
Should you not then have put my **money** in the **bank**
  so that I could have got it back with **interest** on my **return**?
Now then! **Take** the talent from him and **give** it to the one
    with ten.
For to **everyone** who **has**,
  more will be **given** and he will grow **rich**;
  but from the one who has **not**,
  even what he has will be **taken away**.
And throw this **useless servant** into the **darkness** outside,
  where there will be **wailing** and **grinding** of **teeth**.'"

[Shorter: Matthew 25:14–15, 19–21]

OUR LORD JESUS CHRIST THE KING

Lectionary #160

READING I   Ezekiel 34:11–12, 15–17

A reading from the Book of the Prophet Ezekiel

Thus says the **Lord G**OD:
I **myself** will **look after** and **tend** my **sheep**.
As a **shepherd** tends his **flock**
   when he finds himself among his **scattered sheep**,
   so will **I** tend **my** sheep.
I will **rescue** them from **every place** where they were **scattered**
   when it was **cloudy** and **dark**.
I **myself** will **pasture** my **sheep**;
   I **myself** will give them **rest**, says the **Lord G**OD.
The **lost** I will **seek out**,
   the **strayed** I will **bring back**,
   the **injured** I will **bind up**,
   the **sick** I will **heal**,
   but the **sleek** and the **strong** I will **destroy**,
   shepherding them **rightly**.

As for **you**, **my sheep**, says the **Lord G**OD,
   I will **judge** between **one** sheep and **another**,
   between **rams** and **goats**.

Proclaim this reading in a strong, bold tone of voice.

Emphasize the word "every" in this line.

When you proclaim these verses, emphasize the pronoun "I." The prophet is saying that God, and not Israel's former shepherds, will minister to the people.

READING I In Ezekiel 34:1–10, the prophet reports that God instructed him to speak an oracle against the "shepherds of Israel." God does not mince words. God attacks the leading citizens of Judah—princes, priests, and wealthy elites—for corruption and negligence: "Woe to the shepherds of Israel who have been pasturing themselves! Should not shepherds, rather, pasture sheep? You have fed off their milk, worn their wool, and slaughtered the fatlings, but the sheep you have not pastured. You did not strengthen the weak nor heal the sick nor bind up the injured. You did not bring back the strayed nor seek the lost, but you lorded it over them harshly and brutally" (Ezekiel 34:2–4). The prophet even lays responsibility for the exile and captivity of Judah in Babylon at the feet of Israel's leaders (Ezekiel 34:5–6).

Due to the utter failure of the shepherds of Israel to serve their people, God threatens them with destruction (Ezekiel 34:7–10). Only then does God speak the gentle words of comfort we find in today's reading: "I myself will look after and tend my sheep" (Ezekiel 34:11). God alone will shepherd Israel because God is merciful, but also because

Israel's human shepherds cast aside their responsibilities.

READING II The Church at Corinth was divided in a number of different ways. Wealthy members enjoyed a sumptuous Eucharistic banquet, while poor members starved (1 Corinthians 11:17–34). Some members thought nothing of eating meat offered in sacrifice to idols despite the scandal this caused to others (1 Corinthians 8—10). According to Paul, the Church thought

READING II   1 Corinthians 15:20–26, 28

A reading from the first Letter of Saint Paul to the Corinthians

Brothers and sisters:
Christ has been raised from the dead,
   the firstfruits of those who have fallen asleep.
For since death came through man,
   the resurrection of the dead came also through man.
For just as in Adam all die,
   so too in Christ shall all be brought to life,
   but each one in proper order:
   Christ the firstfruits;
   then, at his coming, those who belong to Christ;
   then comes the end,
   when he hands over the kingdom to his God and Father,
   when he has destroyed every sovereignty
   and every authority and power.
For he must reign until he has put all his enemies under his feet.
The last enemy to be destroyed is death.
When everything is subjected to him,
   then the Son himself will also be subjected
   to the one who subjected everything to him,
   so that God may be all in all.

Emphasize those words setting up the contrast between Adam and Christ.

Look up at the assembly as you proclaim the reading's final line.

itself very spiritual, although it tolerated lawsuits between members (1 Corinthians 6), a member's decision to sleep with his stepmother (1 Corinthians 5), and rivalry over valid leadership and authority (1 Corinthians 1—4). With so many divisions, it is not surprising that Paul asks the Corinthians at the beginning of his letter, "Is Christ divided?" The Corinthians, Paul's question suggests, act as if Christ has not only been divided, but cut into bits.

   The immediate context for today's reading is a doctrinal division in the Church at Corinth on the question of the Resurrection

of the dead. Although the Corinthians originally accepted Paul's Gospel that Christ died, rose from the dead, and appeared to witnesses, some have not "done the math" and concluded that Christ's Resurrection means that there will also be a general Resurrection (1 Corinthians 15:1–19).

   The pairing of Adam and Christ, found also in Romans 5:12–21, is important to Paul's point. The Corinthians, he explains, bear both the earthly image of Adam and the heavenly image of Christ (1 Corinthians 15:39–49). The death Adam introduced by his sin in Eden has been more than overcome by the new life

Christ offers. If the Corinthians indeed bear Christ's image, then Christ is but "the first fruits of those who have died" (1 Corinthians 15:20). The Resurrection of Christ is no singular event, but rather only the first of what one must hope will be billions more.

GOSPEL   Care for the poor and those most vulnerable to misfortune is one of the more insistent refrains of the New Testament. As the letter of James makes clear in 2:14–16, Christian faith means little without works of mercy: "What good is

GOSPEL   Matthew 25:31–46

A reading from the holy Gospel according to Matthew

Jesus said to his **disciples**:
"When the **Son** of **Man** comes in his **glory**,
    and all the **angels** with him,
    he will **sit** upon his **glorious throne**,
    and **all** the nations will be **assembled** before **him**.
And he will **separate** them **one** from **another**,
    as a **shepherd** separates the **sheep** from the **goats**.
He will place the **sheep** on his **right** and the **goats** on his **left**.
Then the **king** will say to those on his **right**,
    '**Come**, you who are **blessed** by my **Father**.
Inherit the **kingdom prepared** for you
        from the **foundation** of the **world**.
For I was **hungry** and you gave me **food**,
    I was **thirsty** and you gave me **drink**,
    a **stranger** and you **welcomed** me,
    naked and you **clothed** me,
    ill and you **cared** for me,
    in **prison** and you **visited** me.'
Then the **righteous** will **answer** him and **say**,
    '**Lord**, **when** did we **see** you **hungry** and **feed** you,
    or **thirsty** and give you **drink**?
When did we see you a **stranger** and **welcome** you,
    or **naked** and **clothe** you?
When did we see you **ill** or in **prison**, and **visit** you?'
And the **king** will say to them in **reply**,
    '**Amen**, I say to you, **whatever** you **did**
    for **one** of the **least brothers** of **mine**, you did for **me**.'

Proclaim the king's address to the people at his right hand in a gentle tone of voice.

Clearly proclaim these questions *as* questions, raising the pitch of your voice at the end of each sentence.

it, my brothers, if someone says he has faith but does not have works? Can that faith save him? If a brother or sister has nothing to wear and has no food for the day, and one of you says to them, 'Go in peace, keep warm, and eat well,' but you do not give them the necessities of the body, what good is it?"

We learn from today's Gospel to look for Christ in the hungry, the thirsty, the stranger, the naked, the ill, and those in prison—and we could probably expand this list considerably. Jesus says nothing about first deciding whether they are deserving or not, nothing about their goodness, nothing

about their morality. We are to seek Christ in them all. What good news this is for those of us on both the giving and receiving ends.

Such works of mercy are indeed signs of Christian charity and even common human decency. But they are more than this. As we learn from today's Gospel, performing these works of mercy are *conditions* for entry into the kingdom of heaven (CCC, #544). Each one of us is faced with a choice: to exclude ourselves from Christ's presence by choosing the selfish isolation of "eternal fire" (CCC, #1033), or to unite ourselves to Christ by giving freely of ourselves.

Proclaim the king's address to the people at his left hand in a firm tone of voice.

Then he will say to those on his **left**,
   '**Depart** from me, you **accursed**,
   into the **eternal fire** prepared for the **devil** and his **angels**.
For I was **hungry** and you gave me **no** food,
   I was **thirsty** and you gave me **no** drink,
   a **stranger** and you gave me **no** welcome,
   naked and you gave me **no** clothing,
   ill and in **prison**, and you did **not** care for me.'
Then they will **answer** and **say**,
   'Lord, **when** did we **see** you **hungry** or **thirsty**
   or a **stranger** or **naked** or **ill** or in **prison**,
   and not **minister** to your **needs**?'
He will answer them, '**Amen**, I say to you,
   what you did **not** do for **one** of these **least** ones,
   you did **not** do for me.'
And **these** will go off to **eternal punishment**,
   but the **righteous** to **eternal life**."

Lector and Gospel Reader's Workshop: A Resource for Bringing God's Word to Life

978-1-56854-594-3
Order Code: LTPDVD **$49.95**

AUDREY SOMMERS ■ This interactive workshop is a complete program—everything you need to be an effective lector and Gospel reader is found here. From supporting materials on the CD-ROM that can be printed and handed out to useful tips discussed and presented on the DVD, *Lector and Gospel Reader's Workshop: A Resource for Bringing God's Word to Life* will help lectors and Gospel readers convey the beauty and richness of God's word to all.

The DVD combines the liturgical and spiritual aspects of being an effective lector with public speaking techniques. The CD-ROM contains support materials such as information on how to plan your workshop, word emphasis exercises, breathing techniques, handouts for home study, scriptural tongue twisters, and much more!

AWARDS:

*The 27th Annual Telly Awards;
Winner of the Silver Telly, the highest honor.*

*Herald Award from the Metropolitan Christian Council,
Detroit–Windsor Chapter*

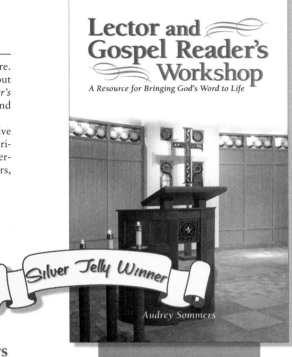

The Liturgical Ministry Series: Guide for Lectors

Saddlestitched, 6 x 9, 80 pages
978-1-56854-607-0
Order code: ELLEC

1–9 copies **$4.95**
10 or more copies **$3.95**

VIRGINIA MEAGHER AND PAUL TURNER ■ Effective for training those new to the ministry and for rejuvenating the work of veterans, *Guide for Lectors* is an important resource for all lectors. It gives lectors the background and tools they need to study, pray, and proclaim scripture well, offers sound advice for dealing with the practical everyday challenges of parish liturgies, and nurtures spiritual growth in the minister. The book can be used by individuals or groups.

Inside you'll find

- pastoral, inviting format and style
- basic theological foundation of the ministry
- liturgical catechesis about the minister's role during the Mass
- brief history of the ministry
- encouragement for deepening the spirituality of the minister
- generous quotations from the documents of the Church
- detailed, practical instruction for carrying out the ministry
- suggestions for further formation
- frequently asked questions
- advice for responding to unusual or difficult circumstances
- resource list
- glossary
- questions for reflection or discussion
- prayers

At bookstores or 800-933-1800
www.LTP.org

Pronunciation Guide to the Sunday Lectionary

Paperback, 3 x 8½, 46 pages
978-1-56854-297-3
Order Code: PRONUN **$2**

SUSAN E. MYERS ■ This handy, inexpensive pocket guide is useful for proclaimers of the Word in the Sunday assembly. It includes the words and names used in the readings for Sunday Mass and feast days, helping lectors to proclaim the Word with ease and confidence.

A Simple Guide to the Daily Mass Readings 2008

Saddlestich, 4 x 7½, 48 pages
978-1-56854-630-8
Order Code: SG08 **$3**

Want to know what the daily readings will be for your birthday, or are you preparing for a specific day and want an easy reference to the readings list? This small booklet provides a simple reference to the readings for Mass for every day of Year A, from December 3, 2007, the First Sunday of Advent, to December 31, 2008. Whether you want to know the readings to pray with every day or to plan liturgies for schools or parishes, or whether you use a Bible or a Lectionary to read from, this guide is for you.

Liturgy planners and team members, teachers, catechists, catechumens and candidates, ministers of care to the sick and homebound, and many others will find this an invaluable resource.

Signing the Scriptures: A Starting Point for Interpreting the Sunday Readings for the Deaf

YEAR A
Paperback, 8⅜ x 10⅞, 192 pages
978-1-56854-560-8
Order Code: SIGNA **$20**

YEAR B
Paperback, 8⅜ x 10⅞, 200 pages
978-1-56854-592-9
Order Code: SIGNB **$20**

YEAR C
Paperback, 8⅜ x 10⅞, 208 pages
978-1-56854-513-4
Order Code: SIGNC **$20**

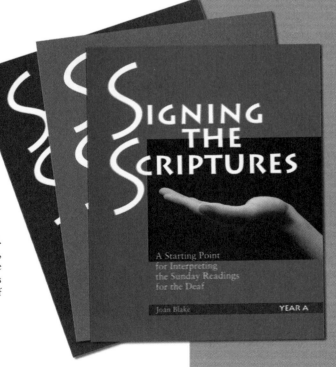

JOAN BLAKE ■ Interpreting for the deaf is an art as well as a skill. Signing the scriptures for the liturgy is a particular challenge, requiring both a sense of the poetic and an understanding of the meaning of a sacred text to a believing community. This title offers the interpreter a place to begin to develop his or her own way of interpreting the readings for the Mass.

At bookstores or 800-933-1800
www.LTP.org LTP